FAMILY PROCESS

FAMILY PROCESS

EDITED BY

NATHAN W. ACKERMAN

BASIC BOOKS, INC., PUBLISHERS

NEW YORK   LONDON

© 1970 by Basic Books, Inc.
Library of Congress Catalog Card Number: 75–135562
SBN: 465–02357–6
Manufactured in the United States of America

75 76   10 9 8 7 6 5 4 3

In memory of
Don D. Jackson

The Authors

NATHAN W. ACKERMAN, M.D.
Director of Professional Program
The Family Institute
New York, N.Y.

EDGAR H. AUERSWALD, M.D.
Director, Applied Behavior Sciences
Jewish Family Service of New York
New York, N.Y.

JOHN ELDERKIN BELL, ED.D.
Director, Mental Research Institute
Palo Alto, California

NORMAN W. BELL, PH.D.
Head of Family Studies
Clarke Institute
Toronto, Canada

DONALD S. BOOMER, PH.D.
Research Psychologist in the Laboratory of Psychology
National Institute of Mental Health
Bethesda, Maryland
Faculty Member, Group Therapy Training Program
Washington School of Psychiatry

FRANCES E. CHEEK, PH.D.
Chief, Experimental Sociology
Bureau of Research in Neurology and Psychiatry
New Jersey Neuro-Psychiatric Institute
Princeton, New Jersey

ANDREW E. CURRY, M.S.W.
Lecturer, Department of Psychiatry

University of California School of Medicine
Supervising Psychiatric Social Worker
Adult Inpatient Services
Langley Porter Neuropsychiatric Institute
San Francisco, California

ANTONIO J. FERREIRA, M.D.
Research Associate at the Mental Research Institute
Palo Alto, California
Research Consultant at San Jose State College
San Jose, California

KALMAN FLOMENHAFT, PH.D.
Assistant Professor, University of Maryland
School of Social Work and Community Planning
Baltimore, Maryland

ALFRED S. FRIEDMAN, PH.D.
Director of Research, Philadelphia Psychiatric Center
Project Director, "Drug and Family Therapy in Depressed Outpatients"
Philadelphia, Pennsylvania

D. WELLS GOODRICH, M.D.
Professor of Psychiatry
Albert Einstein College of Medicine at Montefiore Hospital
New York, N.Y.

REUBEN HILL, PH.D.
Professor of Sociology and Research Professor, Family Student Center
University of Minnesota
Minneapolis, Minnesota

DON D. JACKSON
Past Director, Mental Research Institute
Palo Alto, California

MORDECAI KAFFMAN, M.D.
Medical Director, Kibbutz Child and Family Clinic
Tel Aviv, Israel

SHELDON H. KARDENER, M.D.
Assistant Director, Outpatient Department
Head, Crisis and Brief Therapy Clinic
Assistant Clinical Professor of Psychiatry
UCLA Center for the Health Sciences
Los Angeles, California

DONALD G. LANGSLEY, M.D.
Professor and Chairman, Department of Psychiatry
University of California School of Medicine
Davis, California

ROBERT K. LEHR, M.A.
Research Associate
Department of Sociology
University of Missouri
Columbia, Missouri

ROBERT MACGREGOR, PH.D.
Director, Team-Family Methods Training Program
Illinois Department of Mental Health
Chicago, Illinois

PAVEL MACHOTKA, PH.D.
Assistant Professor of Psychology
University of California
Santa Cruz, California

W. W. MEISSNER, S.J.
Clinical Fellow in Psychiatry
Massachusetts Mental Health Center
Psychiatry Department, Harvard Medical School
Advanced Candidate, Boston Psychoanalytic Institute
Boston, Massachusetts

CELIA MITCHELL, M.S.W.
Director of Family Therapy Services
Family Mental Health Clinic
Jewish Family Service of New York
New York, N.Y.

FRANK S. PITTMAN, III, M.D.
Director of Psychiatric Services
Grady Memorial Hospital
Assistant Professor of Psychiatry
Emory University School of Medicine
Atlanta, Georgia

LESLIE Y. RABKIN, PH.D.
Mental Health Clinic
Jerusalem, Israel

RHONA RAPOPORT, PH.D.
Senior Social Scientist
Human Resources Centre
Tavistock Institute of Human Relations
London, England

URI RUEVENI, PH.D.
School Consultant, Northeastern Community Mental Health Center
Philadelphia, Pennsylvania

MURRAY H. SHERMAN, PH.D.
Psychologist, Family Mental Health Clinic
Jewish Family Service
Managing Editor, *Psychoanalytic Review*
Psychoanalyst, Private Practice
New York, N.Y.

SANFORD N. SHERMAN, M.S.W.
Associate Executive Director, Jewish Family Service
New York, N.Y.

ROSS V. SPECK, M.D.
Private Practice
Research Associate, Philadelphia Psychiatric Center
Philadelphia, Pennsylvania

STEPHEN P. SPITZER, PH.D.
Associate Professor
Department of Sociology
University of Minnesota
Minneapolis, Minnesota

MARVIN B. SUSSMAN, PH.D.
Professor and Chairman, Department of Sociology
Case Western Reserve University
Academic Affairs Consultant
Carolina Population Center
University of North Carolina
Chapel Hill, North Carolina

ROBERT M. SWANSON, M.A.
Research Director
Community Health and Welfare Planning Council
St. Paul, Minnesota

EDWARD A. TYLER, M.D.
Assistant Dean for Student Affairs
Indiana University Medical School
Bloomington, Indiana

WILLIAM D. WINTER, PH.D.
Professor of Psychology
San Jose State College
San Jose, California

Introduction

It is a pleasing task to serve as editor of this first *Family Process* volume. It offers a special opportunity to present a picture of the remarkable range of developments that are now emerging in the field of family study and treatment. The journal, *Family Process*, came into being nearly ten years ago to provide a forum for the systematic examination of the nature of family living, to nourish the growth of a science of the family, and to evolve a method of healing troubled families. Launching the journal was, in itself, a great adventure. We took the gamble, and it paid off. At the outset we had no idea as to what would happen. In fact, we came in for some real surprises. The whole field of family study and treatment has moved off into some astonishing and unpredicted directions. As of now, *Family Process*, just turning the corner of its first decade of life, reflects these unexpected developments: new and ingenious ways of observing and defining family interaction, and bold and varied explorations of the potentials of family therapy.

Family Process had made a good start. It is cultivating a readership, a writership, and a scholarship revolving around the issue of unsolved problems of family behavior. Of particular importance is the support and inspiration which this journal has given to the pioneers in the field of family and to the young professionals who elect to work on the thin edge of new knowledge about the human family. Already this new generation of workers demonstrates its merit with its own brand of innovative investigation. What the next ten years will bring, no one can really know. But one thing is certain; there will be more surprises, more startling and novel developments in the study of family transaction. In its second decade of life, it is hoped that *Family Process* will more than live up to its initial promise, that it will now move into a robust, effective maturity.

Within the covers of this volume, we make available selected papers published in *Family Process* from 1962 through the spring of 1970. Within this period some seventeen issues of the journal were printed, containing over 160 articles. The editing of a moderate-sized reader calls for a representative sampling of published contributions. This is hardly the same as picking the "best papers"; there is no such category. Of necessity, some excellent contributions are omitted. It goes without saying that their exclusion casts no reflection on their worth.

We have sought here to bring together a collage of competently designed papers, covering a range of relevant themes while keeping faith with the multidisciplinary foundation of the journal. The contributions are grouped in two main sections: theory and practice, and systematic research. On careful review of the seventeen published issues of *Family Process,* we concluded that any attempt to separate theory and practice would be both arbitrary and artificial. The theory of family therapy and its implementation in practice are inextricably bound. It seemed wise, therefore, to embrace those contributions in one section. Included in this group are some wide-ranging essays dealing with basic principles. These papers are exploratory and conjectural; they are important in their own right as contributions to theory building. The reader, we believe, offers a fair representation of the range and diversity of current-day approaches to family treatment. In the second section, we offer papers, more limited in scope, more concrete, and focusing on the hard data of systematic research. We should like to feel that this volume has value as a substantive orientation both to the pure and applied science of family behavior—a field which is fast moving and rapidly changing.

The meaning of this volume needs to be understood within the context of a complex pattern of interrelated trends. It grew out of the journal. The need for the journal emerged from a continuing revolution in the scientific conceptualization of the problems of behavior, particularly in the sphere of the dynamics of family relationships. All this, in turn, needs to be placed in the setting of the extraordinary change in social forms and in family systems, which are the mark of our time. In essence it is within this matrix of a world transformed that we strive to grasp the significance of the contemporary focus on the family phenomenon.

It is hardly an accident of history that this last decade—luridly identified as the "wild and explosive sixties," "the unbelievable sixties"—has ushered in a radical shift in our perspectives on human nature, interpersonal relationships, social values, individual and family breakdown, and the theory of healing. The revolutionary turmoil of our day has forced upon us the recognition of the extraordinary dependence of the operations of personality on the social environment. In a further step it has compelled us to a new conceptualization of behavior disorders and mental illness within the framework of family and community transaction.

Within a few years a tremendous pressure has emerged for the rigorous study of these problems. The establishment of family institutes is a response to this challenge. As of now, family institutes are rapidly proliferating in leading cities of the United States: New York, Philadelphia, Boston, Chicago, Los Angeles, San Francisco, and so on. The contagion of interest in the potentials of this new form of healing, the psychotherapy of the whole family, is a striking phenomenon. In fact, the "family therapy movement" may itself be conceived as a spontaneous explosion of a new vision of man and of the Family of Man.

Family Process was originally the brainchild of Don Jackson and myself, jointly sponsored by The Family Institute of New York and the Mental Research Institute of Palo Alto. The first editor, Jay Haley, achieved a near miracle in nourishing the journal to its present strength. Thanks to his courage and gift, *Family Process* is hale and hearty. We turn now with confidence to the new editor, Dr. Donald A. Bloch, who is solidly supported in his responsibility by the reconstituted Board of Editors. He has recently been joined by Lyman Wynne, Edgar Auerswald, Norman Bell, and Virginia Satir. We appreciate, too, the continued commitment of our cadre of advisory editors to the growth of the journal.

Finally, in the preparation of this volume, I wish warmly to acknowledge the help and guidance of Jay Haley, John Bell, and Judith Lieb.

Contents

PART TWO

RESEARCH

Part One

THEORY AND PRACTICE

The development of family therapy is a fascinating chapter in the evolution of the theory and practice of psychotherapy. It has some of the qualities of a "mutation." The properties of family therapy are unique in several respects. Family therapy is a natural rather than a contrived method of healing. It preserves the original continuity of the individual, family, and community. It interprets individual development and adaptation within the frame of the family group viewed as a behavior system. It conceptualizes inner and outer experience as a circular, interacting process. The prime orientation is to the here and now, defining within the present both the past and the future. Priority is placed on change and growth, rather than on the elimination of one set of symptoms which may only be replaced by another. Family therapy is oriented to the human problem, not to "technique." It espouses the principle of fluid, flexible improvisation of treatment procedures to accommodate the needs of the given family. Finally, it faces up squarely to the role of ethical issues in therapeutic intervention.

The climate, both social and professional, in which the principles of family therapy now evolve has changed and is continuing to change. The group environment of our time is undergoing radical transformation at an unprecedented rate of speed; it is unstable, difficult to know and predict. It provides inadequate and erratic support for the emotional needs of both the individual and the family. Only too often the individual and the family are captive to their environment. The individual is the emotional prisoner of the disordered patterns of his family. The family is the emotional prisoner of the turmoil and chaos of the surrounding community. When the group environment becomes characterized by eruptive, unforseeable change and is realistically threatening, the individual armors himself to carry the fight to the

3

environment. He externalizes his conflict and way of coping with it. Under these conditions the traditional one-to-one forms of therapy that require a stable environment no longer work. It becomes mandatory, then, to expand the sphere of the healing function to embrace the sources of pathogenic influence within the group environment as well as within the individual.

The professional climate today presents a radical contrast to that which we have hitherto known. Rapidly disappearing is the privacy and isolation of the traditional therapists' ivory tower. From the very beginning, the investigation of the properties of family therapy has been characterized by a spirit of openness, candor, and self-criticism unparalleled in the history of any other therapeutic modality. The use of technological aids, movies, closed circuit TV, the one-way mirror, and cotherapy fosters an unprecedented depth of honesty, both scientific and human, in the confrontation of unsolved problems. Family therapy evolves in a setting of changing ethos and ethics, and it, in turn, influences the nature and direction of this change.

The papers on therapy published in this volume vividly reflect the unrestricted exploration of multiple approaches. On first reading, it would look as if there are, in fact, many distinct methods of family treatment. In our view, however, this is a transitory manifestation of the incompleteness of our present-day knowledge of the relations of family and individual behavior, our changing conception of psychiatric disorder, and, above all, a reflection of the prominence of individual therapeutic style. This is the theory and practice of family therapy in transition. Family therapy is today several things rolled into one: it is human drama, it is research on change in the forms of family and community relationships in a time of crisis, and it is a specific approach to the healing of emotional distress. Ultimately, as these issues are clarified, the scientific foundations of this form of therapy will acquire a more unified character. The art and style of therapeutic performance, on the other hand, will continue to be infinitely varied.

The many forays into the unmapped terrain of family treatment act as a catalyst in the reevaluation of the theory and practice of all forms of psychotherapy. More specifically, the psychiatry and psychotherapy of the whole family bring a new dimension to the field of mental health.

1

Family Psychotherapy and Psychoanalysis: The Implications of Difference

NATHAN W. ACKERMAN, M.D., F.A.P.A.

I N OUR TIME WE ARE WITNESS to a spreading contagion of interest in the family approach to mental illness. There is a rising inquiry as to the possibility of understanding and treating psychiatric illness in a family way. Historically speaking, it was psychoanalysis that gave pointed emphasis to the role of family conflict in mental illness. It is of no small interest today, therefore, to observe how members of the psychoanalytic profession respond to the concept of the family as the unit of mental health and the unit of diagnosis and therapy. Here, as elsewhere, in matters pertaining to theory and practice, psychoanalysts are divided. Once again we discover the familiar split in the psychoanalytic family as between the conservatives and the liberals. In the evolution of ideas, here as elsewhere, there is value in both points of view. Toward the principles of family diagnosis and treatment, some analysts are critical and antipathetic from the start. They sense in it a threat to the established position of the psychoanalytic technique. One such analyst said to me: "The psychotherapy of the whole family makes me uneasy. It threatens my sense of mastery in the exclusive one-to-one relationship." Other psychoanalysts, skeptical to be sure, are otherwise open-minded and willing for the concept of the family as the unit of mental health to face the test of time.

5

Regardless of the dilemma of the psychoanalysts, present evidence suggests that this new dimension is here to stay. The family approach offers a new level of entry, a new quality of participant observation in the struggles of human adaptation. It holds the promise of shedding new light on the processes of illness and health, and offers new ways of assessing and influencing these conditions. It may open up, perhaps for the first time, some effective paths for the prevention of illness and the promotion of health.

IN THE PERSPECTIVE of the history of mental science, the emergence of the principles of family diagnosis and treatment is an inevitable development. It is the natural product of the coalescence of new conceptual trends in a number of fields: cultural anthropology, group dynamics, communication, the link of psychoanalysis with social science, ego psychology, and child development. The family phenomenon bridges the gap between individual personality and society. On this background, it is hardly a coincidence that some psychoanalytic associations now devote whole meetings to the themes of psychoanalysis and values, and psychoanalysis and family. It seems likely, therefore, that the evolution of family diagnosis and family treatment holds far-reaching implications for the future relations of culture change, behavior theory, and the evolving ideology of psychoanalysis and psychotherapy.

I shall present first a brief, impressionistic view of the techniques of family psychotherapy, and then attempt a comparison with psychoanalytic therapy within the frame of two contrasting theoretical models of psychotherapeutic process. In advance of this, however, I must mention two basic considerations. Just so long as we lack a unitary theory of human behavior and cannot accurately formulate the relations of emotion, body, and social process, we shall be unready to build a comprehensive theory of psychotherapy. We have no psychotherapeutic method that is total. We have no known treatment technique that can affect with equal potency all components of the illness process. The various psychotherapeutic methods presently available are, each of them, specialized, and exert partial, selective effects on certain components of the illness process, but not on all. It is the social structuring of a particular interview method which determines both the potentials of participant observation and the selective effects of a given therapy. In this sense, the psychoanalytic method provides one kind of participant experience, group psychotherapy another, and family psychotherapy still another. It is the specific point of entry of each of these methods which affects the kind of information obtained, the view of the illness process which is communicated to the therapist, and the quality of influence toward health that he may exert. Family interview and family psychotherapy hold the potential of shedding a different and added light on the illness phenomenon and provide still another level of intervention on the area of pathogenic disturbance.

RELEVANT CONCEPTS

Family psychotherapy and psychoanalytic therapy are different methods. For purposes of clarity, hereafter, the term "psychoanalytic therapy" will be reserved for the technique as originally formulated by Freud and his early disciples. The issue as to the essential differences between family therapy and psychoanalysis would be somewhat obscured if we were here to extend the term, "psychoanalytic therapy," to embrace the numerous neo-Freudian modifications of technique.

Psychoanalytic treatment focuses on the internal manifestations of disorder of the individual personality. Family treatment focuses on the behavior disorders of a system of interacting personalities, the family group. But in no sense need they be viewed as competitive or mutually exclusive; they may be complementary. The psychotherapy of the whole family may, in some instances, be the only method of intervention, or it may be the method of choice. In other instances, however, the psychotherapy of the whole family may constitute a required emotional preparation for intervention with individual psychotherapy, or, the two types of therapy may be employed in a parallel way. The relations between the two approaches will become more clear as we succeed in achieving a better understanding of the relations between the inner and outer aspects of human experience, between what goes on inside one mind, and what goes on between minds.

THE BASIS OF FAMILY TREATMENT is the therapeutic interview with a living unit, the functional family group, all those who live together as family under a single roof and any additional relatives who fulfill a significant family role, even if they reside in a separate place. In this context, the unit of illness and health and the unit of treatment influence is then the family group; not the single patient in isolation, but father, mother, children, and sometimes grandparents as well. In family therapy one views the psychic functioning of the one person in the wider context of reciprocal family role adaptations, and the psychosocial organization of the family as a whole, both in the here and now, and across three generations. In this special setting, amelioration of emotional illness requires step-by-step correlation of intrapsychic and interpersonal processes. Within this context, it is essential to view the balance of forces at three levels of integration:

1) A condition of overt illness with the emergence of organized symptoms.
2) A condition of vulnerability to mental breakdown.
3) A condition of effective health.

By contrast with this, in classical psychoanalysis, one focuses in a selective way on the intrapsychic distortions of one individual. The expectation is that as one modifies the internal balance of the components of the personality, emotional health in the individual's relations with the family group will be spontaneously restored. Sometimes this expectation is realized; sometimes it fails. Clearly, a shift toward health in family relationships is not the inevitable product of psychoanalytic treatment. In fact, it is by no means rare that following psychoanalytic treatment of one family member, there occurs a paradoxical worsening of family relationships.

IN THE PSYCHOTHERAPY of the family group, several main principles must be borne in mind. The breakdown of one member of the family, the nature of his disablement and the associated symptoms, may be viewed as a reflection of the emotional warp of the entire family. One can frequently delineate a specific correlation between the emotional pathology of the family group and the breakdown of a particular member. The individual who is first referred for psychiatric help is either the scapegoat for the pathology of the family or is a stand-in for a more critically disturbed member of the family. Often, a core of pathogenic conflict and associated defense patterns is contagiously passed down from one generation to the next. One must therefore be alert to the movement of a pathogenic disorder across three generations. As one observes a family at a given point in time, the elements of pathogenic conflict that originally contributed to the causation of a psychiatric disorder can still be traced in the contemporary conflicts of the family group, even though now they may be expressed in a modified way.

In disturbed families as a rule, there are multiple instances of psychiatric disorder. It is rarely the case that only one member of the family is emotionally disabled. The issue then arises as to the vicissitudes of interaction among the several disturbed members, and their further influence on the family as a whole, as well as their effect on the more vulnerable individuals. It is also clear that as one intervenes on the family, here and now, the focus of the most intense conflict and disturbance may shift from one part of the family to another. In this setting, it is possible to identify characteristic constellations of family conflict and characteristic patterns of family control. We shall return to this later.

THERAPEUTIC FAMILY INTERVIEW

In a typical therapeutic family interview, the family arrives in a state of distress. It is confused; it is in pain. Family as family has failed. The members know something is deeply wrong, but they cannot say what it is nor what to do about it. The therapist moves immediately into the life space of the family's current struggles. He joins in these struggles. He is taken into the fold as an older relative, perhaps as a grandparent endowed with some special wisdom concerning the problems of family living. He is observer, participant, supporter, activator, challenger, and reintegrator of family processes.

At the outset, the therapist observes the order of entry into the meeting room, and the spontaneous way in which the family members arrange their seats. Who sits next to whom? Who sits away from whom? Do they look at one another? Do they see, hear, and talk? What is the dominant emotion and mood—fear, hate, indifference, or apathy and resignation.

The therapist observes the characteristic reactions. Do the members lash out at or shrink from one another; are they alienated? He evaluates the quality of reaching out: Who wants what from whom and how? Is the assertion of these urges insatiable, or violent? Or is it over-controlled, denied, disguised? Or do the members now cease to ask and expect satisfaction from one another?

The first responsibility of the therapist is to arouse the dormant hope of these troubled people. He endeavors to make of the interview a touching experience. He seeks to touch and be touched, in effect, to make it a feeling experience for all. He tries to enhance the quality of interchange among the family members and with himself, to make it more live, more meaningful. Toward this end he makes pointed use of the subverbal aspects of communication: mood, facial expression, posture, gesture and movement. Words may be used to reveal or conceal valid emotion. The therapist neutralizes the common tendency to strip emotion from words. Watchful of each cue, he undercuts mouthings of trivia, in order to get access to the more significant emotional and bodily aspects of communication.

Parts of the family, individuals or alliances of twosomes or threesomes, combine with and separate from elements of the therapist's identity in accordance with need and the means of coping with conflict. The processes of joining with and individuating from the therapist involve elements both of transference and realism.

Currents of mistrust, hostility, defensiveness, and the associated trends toward alienation are noted by the therapist. He observes the configuration of emotional splits within the family, the warring factions and the protective alliances. Who is against whom? Who is allied with whom? He evokes explicit admission of hurts and barriers. He spurs an expanding awareness of fears, avoidances, and the resulting fragmentation in the relationship patterns. He pays particular attention to defensive trends toward displacement of certain conflicts, substitution of one conflict for another, or the prejudicial assault and scapegoating of one part of the family by another. He evaluates the relations between such scapegoating and the unconscious selection of one member of the family as a victim, pushing that member toward a form of breakdown. In a parallel sense, he observes the compensatory healing functions of the family, the way in which one member is unconsciously selected to play the role of healer of family conflict and thus reduce the destructive effects of scapegoating. As he does this, the conflicts between and within family members come into cleared perspective.

OFTEN THE SENSE OF TENSION and danger mounts in family interview process. The therapist must steer a path between Scylla and Charybdis. He must move between the extremes of rigid avoidance of the dangers of closeness, and the uncontrolled explosion of hostile conflict that tends toward panic and disorganization. Often, members of the family fear a loss of control. Through his own calm presence, the therapist offers the needed assurance against this danger. He marks out the interplay between individual defense against anxiety and family group defense of essential family functions. He engages in a process that I call "tickling the defenses," so as to undermine the pathogenic defense formations and encourage the substitution of healthier kinds of coping. He is alert particularly to the layers of insincerity in family relations, and attacks the hypocritical, righteous, self-justifying forms of defense. As the family conflicts become increasingly defined and more realistic solutions are sought, the intrapsychic symptom-producing conflicts of individual members tend toward external expression, that is, they are projected into the arena of family interaction.

A special challenge is the delineation of the core conflicts of the family and the family defenses. The therapist's aims in dealing with conflict are:

1) To help the family achieve a clearer, more correct perception of family conflict.
2) To energize dormant interpersonal conflict so as to bring them into the live processes of family interaction, where they are more accessible for solution.
3) To lift intrapsychic conflict to the level of interpersonal process, where again it may be coped with more effectively.
4) To neutralize unrational prejudice and scapegoating of one part of the family by another. The aim here is to remove an excessive load of anxiety from the victimized member by counteracting inappropriate displacements of hostility and conflict. Where possible the conflict is put back to its original source in the family group, often the parental pair. In this connection, the therapist often joins forces *pro tem* with the "family healer."
5) To activate an improved level of complementarity in family role relationships.

Family group defense against conflict, and the related impairment of family functions is distinct from individual defense against anxiety. Family defense may be specific or non-specific in varying degree. The end result of coping with conflict is the outcome of complex interplay between family defense and individual defense. The dominant forms of family defense play a potent part in the selection and in the operational efficiency of individual defenses against anxiety. A tentative group of family defenses is the following:

1) A shared search for a specific and suitable solution to conflict.
2) A shared avoidance or denial of a specific conflict.
3) Compromise formation: rational and irrational. This is exemplified in—
   a) emotional splitting of the family; fragmentation of the group
   b) riddance or isolation of conflict
      1) quarrels, alienation and reconciliation
      2) a shift in the zone and content of conflict by substitution, displacement, protection, etc.
      3) scapegoating and compensatory healing
4) Compensation: escape, diversion, drugs, alcohol, vacation and sexual escapades.
5) Shared acting out.

6) Reorganization of complementarity of family roles by means of:
   a) reversal of parental and sexual roles, reversal of parent-child roles
   b) "repeopling" of the family: removing or adding persons to the family unit
   c) tightening of the family organization: rigidification of authority, sharper division of labor, constriction and compartmentalization of roles
   d) loosening of the family organization:
      1) dilution of the family bond, distancing, alienation, reduced communication and role segregation
      2) thinning of the border between family and community, displacement of need and conflict from inside the family to outside

When these family defenses fail, the essential family functions become disabled, selectively and progressively. The family moves toward breakdown.

The responsibilities of the family therapist are multiple and complex. They require the most flexible, open, undefensive use of self. The therapist must be active, spontaneous, and make free use of his own emotions, though in a selective and suitable manner. His prime function is to foster the family's use of his own emotional participation in the direction of achieving a favorable shift in the homeostasis of family relationships. He loosens and shakes up preexisting pathogenic equilibria and makes way for a healthier realignment of these family relationships. In this role, his influence may be likened to that of a catalyst, a chemical reagent, a re-synthesizer. He seeks constantly to understand the relations between inner and outer, intrapsychic and interpersonal experience. He matches conscious against unconscious, reality against fantasy. He mobilizes those forms of interaction that maximize the opportunity for undoing distorted percepts of self and others, for dissolving confusion, and clarifying the view of the salient conflicts.

THE THERAPIST PROVIDES, where needed, acceptance, affirmation of worth, understanding, and support. By his own attitudes, he validates genuine expressions of emotion, whether a frustrated need or justified anger. He offers a selective support for the weaker members against the stronger; he gives recognition to thwarted personal needs, crystallizes unreal fears of injury and punishment, opens up new avenues of satisfaction, and provides an expanded interactional matrix for reality testing. He injects into the family something new, the right emotions and the right perceptions in place of the wrong ones. Crucial to the entire effort is the breaking down of anxiety-ridden taboos against the sharing of vital family problems.

The therapist facilitates the efforts of the family to balance sameness and difference, joining and individuation in the ongoing processes of family life. He affirms the positive foundations for shared experience and identification. He awakens respect for differences. In this way, new levels of sharing, support, intimacy, identity, and a greater degree of mutual need satisfaction become possible. The therapist activates the need for a critical examination of family goals and values, especially those which pertain to the basic functions of husband and wife, father and mother, parent and child, child and sibling, parent and grandparent. As the members rearrange their lines of joining and separation, the therapist spurs recognition of the potentials of new growth and creative experience in family living.

Now, LET US SUM UP THE NATURE of this approach to the family as the unit of health. It offers the challenge of evaluating and treating a system of interacting personalities. It requires continuous correlation of the inside of the mind and the outside, the ongoing interconnections of intrapsychic and interpersonal experience. It necessitates a continuous juxtaposing of conscious and unconscious, real and unreal, inner and outer experience, individual and group. It presents the problem of integrating within a single theoretical system all elements of causation, specific and nonspecific, inner and outer, generic and contemporary. The field of observation and the field of influence in family diagnosis and therapy is an expanded one. It involves the internal organization of personality, the dynamics of family role adaptation, and the behavior of the family as a social system. Family therapy deals explicitly both with the forces of illness and health. It intervenes on contemporary conflicts with the assumption that the past sources of pathogenesis are contained in the present conflicts, though now differently organized. It defines the disorders of individual personality within the broader frame of the social psychological distortions of the family system. It assumes that the forces of the individual and the forces of the family are interdependent and interpenetrating, that these relations are relevant to causation, course and outcome of illness and response to therapy.

BY CONTRAST, PSYCHOANALYSIS DEALS with the one isolated personality. It intervenes on pathogenic foci within the person, expecting that as the intrapsychic distortions are removed, the potentials for healthy readaptation will be spontaneously realized. As earlier indicated, however, this does not always occur. Psychoanalysis moves mainly from inside-outward, whereas family therapy approaches the relevant processes partly from outside-inward. In its orientation, psychoanalysis is biologistic, mechanistic, genetic. It tends somewhat to isolate the patient from family, and family from analyst. It focuses in a specialized way on older, entrenched forms of conflict with organized symptom formation. To some degree, it emphasizes the schism between fantasy and reality, pleasure and pain, individual and group, thus separating inner and outer experience. In order to minimize acting-out, it aspires to a halting of time and life, while the internal imbalance of the components of the personality are therapeutically realigned. It deals less with emotional health in a positive sense; it does not give us a picture of learning and creative expansive development. It does not give us a healthy image of family relations. To some extent, it obscures the core problem of homeostasis in family relationships.

This is not to raise the question of the one method of treatment being superior to the other. It is rather that they are differently oriented; each does something else. Of the two methods, psychoanalysis is more specialized; it achieves a unique access to disturbances which have their source in the unconscious mental life. By contrast, family therapy approaches conflict experience in a broader matrix of human relations and at multiple interpenetrating levels.

It is easy to exemplify the contrast in orientation of the two methods. Freud judged relatives and family mainly in terms of their nuisance value. In his view, they posed for psychoanalysis the threat of invasion and contamination. He said: "The interference of relatives in psychoanalytic therapy is a very great danger, a danger one does not know how to meet. . . . One cannot influence them to hold aloof from the whole affair."

PERHAPS NOWHERE IN THE WHOLE SPHERE of evolution of psychoanalytic thought is the question of the relations of the individual to his family group more crisply posed than in the field of child analysis.

Anna Freud pointedly indicated that the child's ego takes its cue from the social interaction processes of the family, but there she stopped, since she was not in a position to investigate these relationships. Interestingly enough, it was Anna Freud who first offered the candid assertion that both child analysis and the analysis of students of psychoanalysis violate the rules of analytic technique. Both in the relations of the child patient with his analyst, and in the relations of an analysand with his training analyst, there are face-to-face relations. The patient and analyst know one another as real persons. Direct gratification of need, support, control, even explicit guidance and advice, are a part of the analytic experience. To my mind, Anna Freud's significant disclosure that both child analysis and student analysis violate the classical rules of analytic technique raises some crucial questions concerning the theory of psychotherapy, as this affects the relations of real and unreal, individual and group.

At the extreme of the procedures of child analysis, Melanie Klein went so far as to prohibit the mother of a patient from sitting in the waiting room during the child's analytic session, lest this disturb the unfolding of the child's transference fantasies. The psychoanalytic philosophy concerning child-mother relationships epitomizes in a way the whole problem of the relations of the individual with his family group. In the more conservative forms of child analysis, when the mother is categorically excluded from the private sphere of the child's analytic experience, we have a representation of the tendency of psychoanalysis to isolate the one patient from mother and family. On one occasion, when I asked a well-known child analyst if she ever undertook the analysis of mothers of her child patients, her instantaneous exclamation was, "Oh, heavens no!"

IN RETROSPECT, ONE CANNOT HELP but wonder how far this historically-patterned isolation of the analytic patient from family is related to the limitations of therapeutic potency of psychoanalytic treatment. Concerning the therapeutic value of psychoanalysis, there is some persistent and lingering doubt. Weingarten's statistical survey of therapeutic results with psychoanalysis is not encouraging. Karl Menninger echoed a similar skepticism. He said: "True, Freud warned us against the emphasis on the therapeutic effect it does have, but in my opinion, were this its chief value, psychoanalysis would be doomed." Menninger emphasized not so much the therapeutic potency of psychoanalysis as its educational and research value.

Perhaps the problems of difference between family psychotherapy and psychoanalysis may be illuminated if we compare two theoretical models of psychotherapy:

1) The psychotherapeutic process conceptualized as a one-person phenomenon, non-social, though influenced by an external agent, the psychoanalyst.

2) The psychotherapeutic process viewed as a two-or-more-person, true social phenomenon.

In the first model, with a non-social matrix of psychotherapy, the analyst is not a real person; he is anonymous; he hides his face; he is a mirror reflecting only what is shown to him; he gives no direct emotional satisfaction; he withholds the usual social cues; the social representations of reality are excluded.

In the classical model of psychoanalytic process, conflict with the analyst is reinterpreted in terms of conflict with older parts of the self. It is referred back to childhood conflicts with family. Transference is dominant over the existing realities. The analyst personifies objective reality, but the testing of such reality is postponed, both as epitomized in the real person of the analyst and in the objective world of human relations. Insofar as the analyst has no face, no identity, shows no emotions, this cannot be a true social experience.

Classical analytic technique favors the reliving of the symbiotic, autistic, magic core of the psyche—the egocentric, entrenched conflicts which contain the distorted percepts of the original, joined infant-parent relation and corresponding fragments of body image. The patient projects irrational conflict-ridden emotions, fantasies, and magic expectations; that is, primary process comes into a position of dominance. The analyst injects the modifying, organizing, and disciplining effects of secondary process. The patient subordinates his ego and external reality. He expands his unconscious, while the analyst contributes insight, reason, reality, and conscious control. Between the two persons, we have the functions of one mind.

THE MOMENT WE SHIFT to the second conceptual model, a two or more person interaction model, we have a true social experience; an interaction between two or more minds, as compared with patient and analyst recreating the symbiosis of one mind in the infant-parent union. In the second model, we have an expanded foundation for the dynamics of personality, a biopsychosocial model. In this therapeutic setting, we must match:

1) Intrapsychic and interpersonal events.
2) Unconscious and conscious organization of experience.
3) Unreal and real; transference and reality.
4) Past and present.
5) Individual and group.

Transference in this setting may be conceived as a failure of social learning. Transference, resistance, working through, interpretation, reality testing, all become interrelated parts of a unified process. Patient and therapist influence one another in a circular fashion.

In Freud's psychoanalytic frame, symptom, defense, transference, change, and cure have one kind of meaning. In family psychotherapy, with face to face relations and true social interchange, symptom, defense, change, growth and cure hold a broader significance. Conflict, symptom, defense in this setting are more than a walled-off intrapsychic distortion, a phobia, a hysterical conversion or an obsession. In family therapeutic process, they acquire the broader definition of certain recurring, predictable, interactional patterns inappropriate to the prevailing realities of the group. While intended to assure stasis for the individual, they actually impair homeostasis. They produce progressive distortion in the balance of family role relationships. In family psychotherapeutic process, a symptom becomes a unit of interpersonal behavior reflected in a constellation of shared conflict, anxiety and defense which is unrational, inappropriate, automatized, rigid, repetitive, and has the effect of constricting and distorting the range of new growth. The resulting impairments in family role adaptation move in one of two alternative directions: either toward rigidification, narrowing and stereotyping of roles, or toward an excessively rapid, fluid and unstable shift of multiple roles, which entails a threat of loss of self. Healthy family role adaptation reflects a quality of behavior intermediate between these extremes. It involves an optimal balance between the need to cling to elements of the old way and the ability to try a new way. The degree of success in coping with conflict molds this balance. An excess of anxiety impels a sticky clinging to the old way, narrows the receptivity to new experience, and reduces ability to discover new and better levels of family role adaptation. A lessened anxiety shifts the balance in the opposite direction.

IN FAMILY THERAPEUTIC PROCESS, the realities of the group situation are an ever-present force. The therapist functions as a real person, as well as the target of projection. Though the realities of the group are fluid and changing over the course of time, the emotional impact on the family members is an immediate one. The family therapeutic experience offers a selective gratification of emotional needs. It favors motor release of emotion. It provides a matrix for the resolution of conflict at the level of action and reaction, in a continuous impact between the image of self and other. Conflict is lived out in interpersonal relations; it is externalized, experienced in action. Thus, therapy provides satisfaction of valid emotional needs, avenues for the solution of conflict, support of self-esteem, buttressing of healthy defenses against anxiety and an expanding interpersonal matrix for growth. In such a setting, the therapist injects something of himself that is new for the family members, the right emotions and perceptions to neutralize the wrong ones.

True change toward health comes with a progressive testing of new ways of thinking, feeling and doing. Gradually, a new synthesis of percept, affect, bodily expression and social action may be achieved.

2

A Theoretical Position for Family Group Therapy

JOHN ELDERKIN BELL, ED.D.

I WANT TO TAKE THIS opportunity to talk about my work and the evolution of my thoughts on family group therapy over the past eleven years. There is an immense gap between that which I believed when I first began and that to which I hold at this point. I recognize this transition in myself and know that others who start from the orientation I once held must make a big leap, a radical shift, if they are immediately to understand my present position. I cannot expect others to achieve in an hour, or a few days or months, what I have had the privilege of reaching gradually and progressively over a decade. This creates its own difficulties in our talking together about family group therapy.

There are some who are simply tempted to say, "This isn't so new. I've always had a family emphasis. This is just a way of rephrasing old ideas that others advanced a long time ago." I will not argue for the originality of the ideas which I discuss here. However, their application to the family, and particularly to therapeutic effort with disturbed families, is new. May I request you, then, to approach my remarks with the set that there is a new idea here that requires a reorientation in thinking and in practice.

Put yourself in my position when I started. I was acquainted with individual psychotherapy and had worked many years with children, college students, and adults. I was facing for the first time a family group consisting of a father, mother, a 16 year old boy, and a 13 year old girl who was the reason for the referral. I wished no escape, because I had said to myself, "Yes, I will try to work with a whole family." Now, what would I do? How would I help this family to deal with its problems?

Let me share with you some of the experiences I had with them. First of all, without knowing it, I had accepted the idea that the girl about whom the referral originated was *the* problem. I heard mother and father, particularly mother, who was one of those women, to quote Saki, who would have been "enormously improved by death," tell about the difficulties she and the family were having with this girl. The parents always spoke with firmness and often with rancor. Somewhat nonplussed by their attack, I would try to put myself in the place of the girl, to think about how it must feel to hear herself talked about in this way. I tried to see her father, mother, brother, and world through her eyes, to uncover the past so I could answer the question how she became the problem she is, and to engage her in a relationship through which I could understand and help her. I was full of good will. I had had individual patients like her before. I concluded that as a step towards the ultimate therapeutic goals I must help a transference relationship to develop, so I began to increase my concentration on her.

Theoretically this was fine. Practically it did not work. What had happened? The first sign it was not working came from the brother. He was restless; he began to protest that he could not see any point in coming, that he was not the problem, and besides he had many other things to do that he had given up to come to the conferences. Should I let him go or not? I scarcely knew then that whether I did nor not, I would be lost. Now I know that if he went I would lose the chance to have an impact on him, and that if he stayed he would block me from continuing to work with the others in the family since he would only become more intransigent. He left.

Secondly, I found the problem girl did not seem to welcome my help nearly as much as I thought she should. She seemed unconcerned about the things mother and father said about her. I thought she should have been unhappy and felt I would have been in her place. She was no more enthusiastic about coming than her brother. She seemed indifferent. Later I came to understand that she was showing that her parents were reciting an old familiar story against which she had long ago contrived effective ways to defend herself. In addition, however, elements of anxiety appeared that seemed primarily associated with her relationship to me and that seemed to be impelling her to the safe course of running away from the conferences.

Later, I began to hear a detailed elaboration of the story of her difficulties from mother, father, and her—and I began to think I was getting to the foundation of the problem. But then little happened. She was not much different; her attitudes to her parents were relatively unchanged, and least of all was there any shift in the ways the parents were acting.

What to do? Where to turn? I was often reasoning that the transference problems were so great that I had better arrange an individual therapist for each of the family members. "Yes," I would say, "that would seem simpler, and then all the therapists could come together and compare notes—which would seem to be a good sound way to keep a family point of view."

At other times an alternative would appear more attractive. I now seemed to have such a good understanding of the family situation that if I were only to tell the family what I knew about them and give them some prescriptions or psychological sermonettes, they would surely be able to solve their problems. This indeed some families would do, although if the truth were known their solutions would probably be little related to my advice or even to the fact of their having come to me, there being in any family group strong pressures to work out the problems with one another. Giving advice was foreign to my usual therapeutic approach, however, so I was reluctant to use it, even though others have advocated it for family work.

THE BASIC SET

Fortunately, the solution for the difficulties I seemed to experience, if not to create, came rather soon. I continued to see total families together and arrived at the point where I had a kind of intuitive grasp of what was needed. I had to wipe clean the blackboard of my mind and find a fresh piece of chalk to write large: "The *family* is the problem." I learned to reject the notion that the child who brought the family to treatment presented the problem with which I was to work. The child

might be *a* problem, his behavior having provided the occasion for starting the treatment, but I learned that I must not regard him as the problem for therapy, not even at the moment of beginning the therapy. *The
problem is the family.* Here was the crux of the matter. Here was the
transition in thought that I must make. This is the new idea, seemingly
so small, but actually so major. "The family is the problem!"

Translated into technical language, one is substituting a social psychological orientation for a clinical psychological orientation. One is
now thinking "group" rather than "individual." Therefrom follow the
goals for the therapy—to change the structure and functions of the
family group—and the technical steps through which the therapist introduces optimal conditions for producing group change.

CONTRAST WITH GROUP THERAPY

If I, who had turned my back on the individual therapist, seemed
now to be courting the group therapist, it was only an illusion. Let me
hasten to point out the gulf between the usual practice of group therapy
and family group therapy. Group therapy is treatment of a number of
individuals at one time in a group setting. Its orientation is the individual. The group exists as an instrument for accomplishing certain purposes with the series of individuals who compose it, but not as an end in
itself. We construct the group for the therapy and are unconcerned
about its ultimate fate as a group, expecting it to dissolve when the
therapy concludes. The group retains its identity as a group only as an
accident—not as a conscious goal of the therapist.

With the family we do not construct the group. That began as a
natural process many years ago. The group existed before the therapy,
it continues through the therapy, and, most important of all, it will
move into the future as a group. It is not only an instrument of the
therapy, it is an end in itself. We are to promote its well-being.

Beyond this, in family group therapy the group life persists throughout the whole week. Whereas in group therapy a group comes together
for the therapy hour and then disperses, with the family, the group is
together in one way or another all the time. The therapy hour is a continuation of family life. Thus change that is initiated in a therapy hour
is likely to have a direct and immediate transfer into the continuing
work of the family. Immediate support or reinforcement for changes
can be available on a 24-hour-a-day basis.

Family group therapy is an independent therapy, distinct from both the individual and group therapies we knew formerly. It differs because of the relationships among those who come for treatment, it differs in the definition of the problem they bring, it differs in the therapeutic techniques, and finally in the goals towards which it moves.

I hope that I have alerted you to listen with care, so that you may hear the distinctive in what I am trying to say. If so, we may proceed to deal with a number of issues that are tied in with the fundamental point I am making. To be absolutely sure that we start from the same premise, however, let me restate it. I am averring that family group therapy is a social psychological treatment method to provide help so that the natural family group may solve its problems and continue to function more efficiently as a group. From this base let us now take up a number of further considerations.

QUESTIONS OF TECHNIQUE

First, we shall give our attention to some practical matters. Regarding the family as the problem, what are the implications for technique? Or, how do we promote the changes that take place during the course of family group therapy?

Who is the Family

Let us examine the matter of who makes up the family with whom we work. About this we have no inflexible rules. It may be a matter of discussion with the parents or other family members. I have found that for the most part children younger than nine years of age are not mature enough verbally and intellectually to undertake the communication demanded in this group method. "Family" does not necessarily mean a biological relationship. It probably is best to think of the family in terms of the functioning group living together in one household and to bring together all those individuals who seem to be the functioning members of this immediate group. In choosing the group to treat, it is helpful to remember that each potential member who is excluded will be a force working against changes in the family; or he will be driven away from the rest of the family, since the distance between him and those in the group will be accentuated as cohesive processes bind the family into a group organized in new ways.

Relating to the Family as a Group

Having decided who will make up the family group, we now are able to operate according to a firm principle in dealing with the efforts of individuals to retreat or to manipulate the composition of the group in other ways. It sounds simple-minded to say that if we are going to work on the group problem, we must work with the group, but this is our first rule. If we really believe in the family as the problem, we will insist on having all members of the family come to all sessions. I expect attendance, and postpone meetings if someone cannot come. Incidentally, this happens very seldom after the rule of participation is established. We find mostly that all want to come, if they sense that we really mean to work on the family difficulties. It is when a family member feels that we are singling out an individual for especial attention and concern that he will show strong pressures to leave.

This same principle of working with the group governs the therapist when one family member wants to remove him to one side and establish a little private group with him. This happens so commonly that I refer to it as the most characteristic resistance in family group therapy. I am absolutely firm about my unwillingness to meet with a part of the family privately. I make it a rule that all relations between me and the family members must be in the group and known to all of them. Being alerted to the deviousness of their efforts to break this rule, I am prepared to affirm and reaffirm my position without apology as the need may arise. This is immeasurably reassuring to the group and protects its solidarity.

A further illustration of this principle may be found when the family begins to talk about relationships with others who are outside the group. Even though the therapist may recognize with the family that difficulties with these others are important, he brings the center of discussion back to the family group immediately in front of him. He points out how we cannot talk about these other relationships since the other people are not present to tell about how things look to them. He reminds the family that they are here to clarify what goes on among themselves.

In this same direction, I would not engage in activities with the family other than those required in the conferences. I would not have dinner with the family, I would not visit family members at work, school, in the home or the community. For even though I might learn from such occasions, I would be sacrificing the advantages and speed of treatment that follow a more disciplined and structured role for myself and a more consistent emphasis on the family group.

Towards this goal of keeping the boundaries around the family group as intact as possible, and towards strengthening them, I try to avoid intruding myself into the family group, except in line with a role that is defined for the family group and for me as demanded by the therapy. Essentially, this means that the therapist avoids, where possible, taking over functions that any family member performs for the family or may be expected to perform. Family members try to push the therapist into assuming family responsibilities. One of the places this is peculiarly evident is when we are working with a family group from which one of the parents is missing. In this case a mother may try, particularly, to seduce the therapist into acting as a father for the children and a husband for herself. Or, if the parent is the father, he may evidence his need for a wife and a mother for the children, by pressing the therapist towards acting out his conception of how this missing parent should function.

This pressure on the therapist also occurs when a complete family is in front of him. This is commonly seen when one of the family turns to the therapist and says: "What would you do?" If mother is asking the question, we have to ask if father would feel displaced if the therapist were to answer it. Very likely he would. Quite often such a question conveys a covert criticism of another family member, saying to him, in effect, that the question would not be needed if he were playing his appropriate part. Telling what you would do then takes on the implication that you concur with the devaluation of the other family member. But turning the question back to the group preserves family roles, strengthens or adjusts them, and works towards improvement of the interrelationships between them.

The above illustrations grow out of the application of the first principle of treatment that follows identification of the family as a problem. In essence the principle states that as a primary method of treatment the therapist relates to the identified family group so as to strengthen the boundaries surrounding the group as a group.

The Task for the Family

A second principle specifies that the task on which the family group is to work during the course of the treatment must be group oriented.

The task falls into three areas: (1) identification of the family problems; (2) analysis of the problems and of factors that create them; and (3) development and testing of solutions to the problems. More narrowly the task is to examine the interrelationships among the family members to determine how they may be handled better. The therapist and the family must keep the task focus on that which is to benefit the group. The therapist puts this task into words and promotes the set to work on group issues.

Requisite to the identification and analysis of the family problem is the expansion of the communication between the family members. An immediate task is to put into words what before has been left unexpressed or said in such circuitous ways that its meaning has not been transmitted. Part of this is accomplished by putting into words that which is spoken in the private language which all families use and which normally excludes the therapist from understanding what is being said, at least in its nuances. I refer to all the little gestures, facial expressions, and personalized uses of words whose special meaning was created during the family's private history. Important as is the therapist's understanding, it is even more important that the family members understand; this happens in new ways as they express themselves afresh, as they translate their messages from the easy shorthand of the private family tongue into the public language appropriate for talking with outsiders like the therapist. Towards the all-embracing goals of revision of the family group functioning, an immediate and instrumental task is to develop new forms and intensity of communication.

The group emphasis in communication demands that each family member have an equal chance to take part in the discussions. This does not mean that each will talk an equivalent amount but rather that he will have the chance to talk if he wishes to contribute to the analyses of the problems or the proposal of solutions. Further, he will participate in the decisions about solutions and thus identify them as his own solutions as well as those of the group as a whole.

The therapist tries to promote such equivalence and to maximize individual participation. He listens for the signs that persons wish to take a more active part. He helps to provide the chances for such participation, even when what one family member wishes to say may not be relished by the others, as during some of the stormy battles that we expect at certain stages of the treatment.

We find that the communication will increase in the family, but this is purposeful only as a means towards accomplishing the task of solving the family problems. If you say to a family "What are your problems, and how can we solve them?" the family normally finds these questions appropriate for it and has a clear idea of what is being asked, even if the means by which the questions may be answered seem not to be at hand. In exploring the scope of these questions through improving communication, the family usually begins to narrow the scope of the problems it wishes to talk about. This does not represent necessarily a solution of the other problems or a sign that there is a greater urgency about the issues selected. Most frequently one, two, or a few problems are sifted out for discussion as symbols of the full range of problems. They are concrete representations of the areas of tension, ambiguity, indecision, and breakdown of solidarity in the group. Around these concrete issues the ways in which the group members are functioning may be studied and revised towards a better structure for the group and better articulation among the group members in reaching for individual and group goals. Family group therapy taps the motivation of the family group to improve itself.

The therapist is an agent who works to start and keep alive this problem solving program. He works with the family on the means of study and of problem solving. Consistent with keeping outside the family group, he does not determine the goals for the family nor make its decisions for it. He helps them into the position where they recognize their goals and are free to make such decisions as are demanded in the movement towards attaining them. I have found that the family in treatment is more concerned with attaining goals that are represented in its present value system than in reaching out for new values. Most families with whom I have worked are discouraged about reaching the goals they know and respect; they want the experience of success in reaching some of these before seeking new values. The family in treatment is in crisis and is seeking a way out of the crisis first. Then may come a grappling with new and larger questions of value. At this state, it would be appropriate to call on the assistance of educational and religious agencies.

The group orientation of the task on which the family is working is reflected further in the way in which the therapist handles decisions. He will participate if these are decisions about the therapy conferences themselves. If, for instance, the family desired to change the time of the therapy hour, the therapist would work jointly with them in making the decision about the appropriate time. If, on the other hand, the decisions deal with the family life, such as deciding on a new time for the dinner hour, the therapist would remove himself openly from the decision. The therapist's task is the therapy; the family's task is solving the family problem. The therapist consciously maintains his distance from the group task, at a defined peripheral position.

No outsider therapist has enough information nor could secure enough to decide the course for the family, even though he might be tempted to attribute such omniscience to himself. If he desists, he will find that one family may elect decisions that seem diametrically opposite to those of the next family. For example, in one family a father decides that he must be the disciplinarian; in another, he decides that he must turn over this responsibility to the mother. It is not appropriate to expect the therapist to decide which solution is right. Each family must seek out and attain its own answers to its questions, for only in this way can the family enhance its own identity and solidarity.

The Therapist's Task

Now I wish to return to the point that the therapist's task is the therapy, for there is a third principle involved. It is a correlate of the two previously defined. If the family is to maintain its group status and to work on the group problem, the therapist must keep his distance, stay out of the family, and restrict his work to the therapy. He relates *to* the family, not within the family. He communicates how he will relate to the family from the beginning of the first session and tries to make his actions accord with the rules he imposes on himself. He orients the family to the limits he will adopt and then holds to them firmly and unambiguously. Having described the orientation and other techniques elsewhere,[1] I will not take the time to discuss them here. Let me illustrate, however, by one example the attitude and role of the therapist.

I insist on holding the conferences in an office rather than in the home. In the latter the therapist is a guest, subject to the conventions of that status. His freedom for determining the conditions of the conferences is restricted. In an office he can take direction of the situation. The setting there supports the authority of his actions. It cleanly separates the authority of the therapy from the authority in the home, where the therapist should not aspire to be an authority. As director of the

---

[1] Bell, John E., Family Group Therapy. *Public Health Monograph 64*, 1961, pp. 52.

therapy sessions, he can predetermine his role, communicate it to the family, relate to the family accordingly, and thereby facilitate the therapy in ways he chooses.[2]

THE STRUGGLE TOWARDS CHANGE

In a moment we will examine briefly how, from his distant position, the therapist makes the impact upon the family that produces change. First, however, we should note that change does not come easily. When the family seeks the help of a therapist, it is caught between a need to change and a need to preserve its current organization. All families, as all natural groups, experience this bind at various periods of their history, and most of them revise their interactions without outside assistance. When change and stability are desired at one and the same time, and there is no resolution of the ambiguity, anxiety and emotional disturbance follow. Under these circumstances it is common to take advantage of some personal "oddities" of an individual in the family, to conclude that the situation could be rectified if that individual would change, and to divert the attention from the group to him—a process that perpetuates the individual's difficulties, since the other choice, change in the group, is more painful.

When a family seeks out therapy for one of its members, it is facing a crisis. The balance by which the family group has operated has been disturbed. Under these conditions the family may seek ways to reinforce the scapegoat mechanism, to call in outside strength to support the projection of responsibility on to one family member and to give backing to the demand that this individual change. We had better be alert to this when one family member refers another. Unfortunately, individual therapy too often fits right in with this scapegoating, by concurring that the individual is sick. While the family wishes the individual to change, we must remember that it has found a means of preserving its group stability through the individual's difficulties, so there are probably strong unconscious pressures to keep the individual disturbed. These may be strong enough to defeat therapeutic progress and to preserve the behavior that the family says it wants to change. The simplest response to a crisis precipitating the family towards

[2] Recent experiences with lower class families that include delinquents suggest that with them treatment in the home may be preferable. It appears that the therapist may assume more control over the situation for therapy in the lower middle class home than he could in the home of a middle or upper class family.

change is to strengthen the pressures towards keeping the present organization.

A second way of handling the difficulty is to isolate the disturbed individual—to remove him from the group to the outside, so that a new family group may be formed without him. The family may not seek this openly but demonstrates its motivation in this direction by the readiness with which it accepts plans to reduce or break the individual's ties to the family. It is no accident that various forms of institutionalization have been devised to care for the disturbed. We tend to think of these as methods that professionals have arranged, and also as society's way of taking care of problem persons. I suspect, however, that our hospitals, clinics, foster-homes, and other such institutions are outgrowths as much as anything of family pressures.

A third way of regaining balance in the group is to change the internal social structure and to incorporate new behavior into the group interactions. We use individual therapy to accomplish this, and it often results in positive changes in the whole family of which the patient is a part. More frequently than desirable, however, it results in the family's transferring the scapegoat status to a new family member, so that the over-all organization remains comparable, although disturbance is now shown by a new individual. Family group therapy begins with the aim of changing the structure of the family group, but hopefully with a change that involves the interactions between the members, not just a rotation of the scapegoat pressures to someone new.

THE PROCESS OF FAMILY GROUP THERAPY

If family group therapy is able to accomplish reorganization, by what means does it seem to do so? Have we any explanations for the ways it works? For myself, I have set forth my thesis about how the therapist effects change in the family group in five propositions:

1. In all social groups, and particularly the family, the communication and interaction is structured within certain operational limits that produce stereotyped patterns of reactions between family members and a restriction on the permissible ranges of individual behavior. These are normal consequences of belonging to the family. They often result in mutual depreciation of the potentialities of the other, a kind of cynicism about what can be expected of him, and an unrealistic appraisal of what he might accomplish. Such limits are an obvious consequence of any group membership, are consistently evident in the family, and are necessary to establishing and maintaining the group operations of the family.

2. Most older children and their parents have available to them potential patterns of behavior beyond those they use in the family. These are revealed in the community in relation to persons outside the family. I refer to these as public patterns, as separate from familial patterns.

3. The therapist is a community figure in relation to whom the individual family member may show behavior that extends beyond what he normally reveals in the family. He may react in these ways towards the therapist without engendering the intense anxiety that would follow venturing these new behaviors alone in the family. The therapist seeks such public behavior from each of the family members. For the family this introduces change.

4. In response to the new patterns revealed, the rest of the family members must revise their stereotypes about the family member, must re-evaluate him, must respond to him with new attitudes, and new accommodations of their own behavior. Together they test out, thereby, potentialities for relationship, incorporating changes that prove useful, and rejecting those that fail.

5. Having developed new modes of interacting, supported by mutual commitment that they are better and should be continued, the family consolidates these new patterns. They work in common to inhibit or eradicate the old outworn patterns, and to strengthen the new. A whole field of research in learning could be spread out before us through study of the methods by which the family members act upon one another to reinforce the patterns they have newly achieved.

Reviewing these propositions, we may say that the treatment process depends on a therapist engaging each family member in a relationship in which the individual is encouraged to express himself distinctly and differently from his customary behavior in the family, and to do this in the presence of the family. It accomplishes no instructive purpose for the family if he does this alone with the therapist. The extended range of his behavior needs to be visible to the family.

Probably we can see how the clarity of definition of the therapist's role aids this process. It is designed to reduce the anxiety of each family member. It stimulates each to respond to the therapist and gives clues about how he expects him to act, which also contributes to a reduction of anxiety. It is designed to prevent intrusion of the therapist into roles already pre-empted by family members so that he may draw forth new public behavior from each individual. If the therapist takes on a family role he calls up the stereotyped family patterns; only as he separates himself from family functions and patterns does he challenge the family members to show their extra-familial behavior, to make it potentially of use in the family, and to stimulate thereby family reorganization.

Out of such social engineering comes a new family, carrying over that which is respected from the past, incorporating the new that is to its profit. The changes are changes in depth, but depth is defined first by group change rather than by intrapsychic change. This does not mean that the changes fail to touch individuals. Just as the group changes, so also do the individual members, through a learning experience that is so intense that the changes are deep. But the intrapsychic changes are secondary to changes in the relational processes, the truth of which those who have mastered individual therapy also recognize. This, then, is how I see family group therapy solidifying the family group, solving the interactional problems, and providing the individual family members with a secure status in the family, the primary condition for self-respect, true independence of spirit, and freedom for accomplishment.

3

Multiple Impact Psychotherapy with Families

ROBERT MACGREGOR, PH.D.

T HIS IS A REPORT OF an investigation into the way in which self-rehabilitating family processes can be mobilized with brief psychotherapeutic intervention.[1] The fact that families when threatened with evidence of mental illness in a child will travel relatively long distances to the University of Texas Medical Branch Hospitals at Galveston puts The Youth Development Project, an outpatient psychiatric clinic for adolescents, in a position to study families in crisis. The method employed requires devoting the entire time and facilities of an orthopsychiatric team to one family for half a week. Starting with a team-family conference, it proceeds through a series of different combinations of the people involved. It includes multiple therapist situations, individual interviews, and group therapy interspersed with brief staff conferences. Twelve families during 1957–1958 were seen by the team during the development of the procedures. In April, 1958 the development, demonstration, and study of the method was undertaken by a full-time team. Since that time fifty-five families with problem adolescents have been treated.

The work has been particularly useful with families whose participation in usual child guidance procedures could not be gained. In forty-eight of the cases, exclusion of the child from the community had oc-

33

curred or was imminent. In the remaining seven, the break-up of the home was imminent. Follow-up studies which are routine at six and eighteen months and include home visits to half the cases, indicate the method to have treatment results comparable to established intensive methods. Research results have contributed to the development of family diagnosis.

DEVELOPMENT OF THE METHOD

It is frequently felt in child guidance clinics that the decision to undertake treatment is "half the battle." It is a time when people are most accessible to the idea of giving up maladjusted patterns for more satisfying ones. Studies of psychotherapy have attributed results to theory, relationship, and technique, but have tended to regard the natural processes in the patient and family as seen in placebo control studies as extrascientific (1). Ours is an attempt to utilize and assist these processes. The study of relationship aspects of this therapy includes not only the effect of the doctor's personality, but also of the family-like self-regulatory mechanisms within the team.

In this research we have tried to identify and intensify therapeutically effective aspects of clinic intake procedures. "Multiple Impact Therapy" (MIT) is, in a sense, an expanded intake procedure involving the insinuation of our team into the family group in a manner that bespeaks our desire to participate in their problems.

Gerald Caplan has made considerable study of the way in which a therapeutic response to a family crisis may yield enduring improvement in the mental health of the whole family. The same author shows a regard similar to our own for the corrective forces which can be mobilized within families and for the therapeutic value of natural situations.

". . . during the crisis period we keep our intervention down to the absolute minimum . . . since we wish to modify as little as possible the impact of the hazardous life situation on the family, and also the family members' way of dealing with their problems both by their own efforts and through their mobilization of external sources of support and assistance. We are constantly being surprised by the strengths within and outside the family which are mobilized by the challenge of mounting tension. . . ."[2]

Most of what we have included in our program has been tried separately

[2] Gerald Caplan "An Approach to the Study of Family Mental Health" (mimeo), A summary of this paper appears in *Public Health Reports* 71, 1027–30, 1956. (2)

by others. Harris Peck (3) has applied group therapy to the intake process. Whitaker (4) has used multiple therapists as a part of brief therapy and found that resolution of countertransference problems is facilitated. Dyrud and Rioch (5) found the multiple therapist situation improved communication between co-therapists.

Considerable literature has been developed on interdisciplinary problems. While much of the literature is simply in favor of collaborative endeavors, many authors, Adelaide Johnson (6) among them, point to difficulties in communication between co-therapists.

Our experience has been that communication problems among staff members may be of diagnostic value in understanding the way the family under study tends to involve others in their patterns of pathological inter-relationships. We differ with Starr (7) who feels the alternatives are between individual therapy by separate therapists working in isolation with each family member, and a single therapist working with the mother and child in that order. Both avoid the staff interaction problems which we find useful. Use of staff interaction was described by Stanton and Schwartz (8) in understanding acting out and other symptom-formation during hospitalization. Ackerman (9) in the introduction to his recent work on treatment of family relations speaks firmly against adherence to the traditional limitations on communication within the clinical team.

There are also views in the literature as to whether the "child welfare focus" or focus on the adolescent-adult conflict (10) is more therapeutic. For example, Rosenthal (11) cites the difficulty arising in treatment where the parent's welfare is only of interest as it has bearing on the child. Otto Pollak (12) in retrospect observes that as their study of "family psychotherapy with a child welfare focus" progressed the matter of regarding the child or parent as the patient was less useful then the concept of treating "sick situations." The present project has committed itself from the outset to the interactional viewpoint in its treatment of such family situations.[3]

PSYCHOTHERAPEUTIC PROCEDURE

Planning: This work is typically carried on with families whose interest in psychotherapeutic work is not well developed. Considerable

---

[3] The experience of two other clinicians with the method are described in the following papers: Goolishian, H. A., "A Brief Psychotherapy Program for Disturbed Adolescents", *Amer. J. Orthopsychiat.*   Schuster, F. P. "Summary Description of Multiple Impact Psychotherapy", *Texas Reports on Biology and Medicine* 17: 3, 426–430, 1959.

emphasis is given before the case is scheduled to promoting in each family an attitude that the two day opportunity must be exploited to the fullest. It involves a thorough orientation of the referring agency, and it involves most of the families in an intake visit to the clinic. Frequently we include a representative from the community, such as the responsible probation officer or the resident physician who has supervised the adolescent during a period of observation in the hospital, in our treatment procedures. Thus the referring agency is better able to perform these intake operations in advance of our seeing the family. We reserve the first two and a half days of the week for MIT. The family including parents, troubled adolescent, selected siblings when relevant, community representative, and occasionally a relative who has become involved in the problem, is scheduled to arrive at nine-thirty a.m. Monday.

Briefing: The team assembles before the family arrives and speculates freely on the data at hand. From this we get an idea of each other's preconceptions and make some tentative plans as to what team member will see which family member individually after the initial team-family conference. The day then proceeds through a series of "impact" followed by "release" situations.

Initial Team-Family Conference: "Impact" starts in a team-family conference, where as far as the family can see, everything is to be talked out. One of the team breaks into initial pleasantries by citing the urgency of the situation to get some kind of a statement of what the family is really here for. After their usually restrained remarks he may develop an interpretation that "breaks the ice" for subsequent thinking such as "Obviously this boy has to stay childish in that setting. Only by extending childhood could he help mother justify her excessive attentions to him." The observation that typically follows is that the mother has been driven to meet her tenderness needs through nagging, intimidating and infantilizing her child. When a child is thus able to short circuit his energies, school work and contact with age mates suffers. This brings questions that permit us to demonstrate how such a relationship thrives on defective communication.

It is surprisingly easy for families to understand the underlying danger for the adolescent to show maturity under these circumstances and the taboos against permitting the matter to come into awareness. The team's acceptance of the exploitive aspects of family life has a calming influence.

In many of our cases the initial work involves such a study of the threats to the child's individuality. When the family has difficulty expressing personal matters, the team members may debate the family or team-family problems in front of them. One may, in a protective gesture toward the mother, criticize the team member for his premature observation. Another may venture that the mother can speak for herself and if necessary he may guess aloud what her argument might be. Whether or not there are changes from the plans made in the briefing session as to which therapist is about to see whom, the plan is openly discussed by the team in the presence of the family, who usually show considerable relief to find that they are, in fact, to be individually heard at this point (release). Each team member then invites a family member to his office. It seems important that private conferences other than the scheduled ones not occur between therapists. This forces discussion of changes in evaluation and strategy out into the open in the presence of the family.

Pressurized Ventilation: At this point each parent is under considerable pressure to have at least one person appreciate that whatever made him defensive in the group situation has an understandable history. His interviewer, meantime, gains a fair idea of what the person's mate has been up against through the years and may be very favorably disposed toward an interview with that spouse after lunch ("cross ventilation").

Initial Interview with the Teen-Ager: The interview with the teen-ager is briefer than that with the parents. In that interview a therapist tries to help the youth see his behavior as meaningfully related to family patterns. This may be a matter of revealing to the youngster that what appeared to be unreasonable behavior on his part may be the result of his having been unwittingly "taken in" to serve the poorly understood needs of others. We also acknowledge his influence in affecting present and future family patterns. The therapist may then express the concern: "Perhaps there's not enough of adult interest going on in your mother's life. Perhaps you have been making yourself too available for her instead of working on your own interests." This is a fairly brief interview, typically of a half an hour's length and the youngster may be sent off to the waiting room or may be asked to take some tests. His interviewer then telephones for permission to join in the session with either the mother or the father.

Overlapping Session: In the overlapping session the therapist reviews to the entering therapist what has been learned in the past forty-five minutes. The parent has the opportunity to listen to a summary of how he has "gotten through" to a team member. The summary may include some tentative interpretation given in a way which invites a corrective comment, consensus, or new material.[4] After the parent has indicated his attitude toward the summary, the overlapping therapist is usually moved to report that this makes some kind of sense in view of what he has been learning from their teen-ager. "You felt let down by his failure, but that's because you have been too dependent on him." At the end of the initial interviews the family members are informed that the team will talk about them at lunch. The family is encouraged to try to talk over their impressions of the morning's work and are asked to rejoin the team by one-thirty p.m.

Noon Team Conference: At noon we become quite naturally aware of each other's attitudes toward different members of the family. The team members by their manner of presentation are apt to recapitulate typical patterns the family members use to manipulate each other. Attention to each other's attitudes is quite necessary in view of the fact that we have not taken the time to be neutral. Strategy is then mapped out for the afternoon. For instance, we may plan a series of overlapping sessions, where one team member seizes an apparent pattern and goes from office to office, conferring with each member on his part in it.

Cross Ventilation: The afternoon starts with individual interviews. The interview with the father may now have the additional objective of discovering how he can be more of a resource for meeting his wife's needs. He already has gathered that there may be relief from the feelings of isolation in relation to the child who has alienated him. The interviewer, from his morning individual session with the wife, already has a grasp of the spouse's viewpoints and typically has a lot of curiosity about the mate's part in maintaining the unhealthy ones. During this period the youngster is tested. Simultaneous diagnostic work with siblings as well enables the parents to postpone their concern with the children and allows them to engage more fully in self study.

Multiple Therapist Situations: From here on frequent use is made of overlapping sessions often with two therapists and two family members. Use may be made of the previously mentioned chain of overlapping sessions to validate a point.

One therapist, facing the seemingly intractable resistiveness of a

---

[4] Ritchie, A. "Multiple Impact Therapy An Experiment", *Social Work* 5: 3, 16–21, 1960.

mother, called the social worker. He reviewed the mother's difficulty, considering as relevant to her son's problem the husband's accusations of her infidelity. The therapist, aided by just the relaxation provided by the third person's occasional intervention, was able to phrase a supportive interpretation of the problem. "Apparently this good looking husband of yours feels that just anyone can beat his time with his attractive wife." She, of course "had not thought of it this way."

While the social worker and mother continued their discussion the first therapist left "to check with others." In this case the son, having completed his psychological tests hurriedly, had been sullenly keeping his conversation on neutral matters with the psychologist. When informed of the observation about his parents, he reacted as though for the first time he was being treated as one who could understand adult matters. It brought to his mind a point that confirmed the interpretation, and his conversation for the remainder of the two day period was in keeping with his real problems and needs. This pattern supported by the son's example was used in the next office in helping the father revise his grossly inadequate picture of himself. It was also useful in later team-family conference for questioning the level of maturity and observation that the parents attributed to their child. The mother's need for outside sources of validation of her womanhood was to subside in the weeks ahead as real strength in her husband appeared in support of new found willingness to bet on him.

Team-Family Conference: A final team-family conference is used on the first day to take full advantage of family processes. Whereas the family members in individual or multiple-therapist situations may have maintained a resistive attitude toward team members, they now face each other as well. Team members, by openly telling of revised attitudes about the family and their situation, provide a climate for change. This is often furthered by a therapist's accepting from others, or offering as self-criticism, information on how his own involvement in the material interfered with understanding.

The more resistive parent senses that he is not getting the old familiar reciprocal response as he reaffirms a resistive attitude. The once antagonizing gesture lacks impact to the family against the background of the day's study. Anticipation of the forthcoming evening that the family will spend together is a little disturbing as they sense the old barriers to intimacy may not serve quite so well. The team has learned from experience to respect the tentativeness of attitudes toward changing balance of forces in the family at this point. They remain silent about their desire that the family discuss the day's work in the evening.

We permit ourselves considerable expression of the feelings engendered by attitudes of family members. This occurs in situations where one team member may respond protectively to the family member and, despite emphatically expressed disagreement, can maintain respect for the other team member. The group setting helps the family make use of this to become less afraid of fuller communication among themselves. It is a typical short-cut, to demonstrate, for example, to a paranoid person how really important he can be to another person—important enough to make the therapist angry—and at the same time undermine a delusional thought.

"I'm real sore at your son over there. He seems to have decided that what Dr. Mac gets out of this work is a tape recording. Well, I am here to learn something, and I hope (turning to the boy) you get something out of it too."

In this instance, the youngster's sullen, pseudo-inattentive attitude disappeared for the rest of the work.

Second Day Procedures: The second morning follows with more variability the pattern of the latter part of the first afternoon. Often the family's evening together has demonstrated to them the breakdown in communication discussed in the previous day. They may be defensive about not having "talked things over." Often the brief early second day team-family conference is omitted because of the urgent need by at least one of the family to discuss emotionally charged matters. This is typically a rush of early life material brought to awareness by the happenings of the previous day. Relief came to two mothers with insight into the way their own growing young womanhood had been supressed from awareness by fathers who were less attentive to their wives than to their daughters. As mothers these women had great difficulty sharing physical as well as interpersonal intimacy with the husband. From one of them: "In order for father to keep me as his assistant at home, he ran off my boy friends, allowed me no make-up, and to this day I can't go on the beach in a playsuit without feeling immodest." The hard work of dealing with factors which interfere with intimacy between husband and wife is tackled in the second morning in ways that differ as therapists differ.

Rehearsals and Applications: The second afternoon typically may start with each seeing individually the therapist whom he first saw but with whom he may have worked less. The therapist "hears" the work, perhaps revealing to the parent that the parent was, at times, trying to get prescriptions for handling the child or spouse instead of using the consultations to find principles that will help make constructive use of his own emotions.[5] Each may be reminded that from the beginning, as in any diagnostic and exploratory procedure, the team has had an opportunity to recommend a more extensive type of treatment but that the family's ability to utilize the present preparation for a treatment program to be continued by their own processes at home has not been rejected. At this point the therapist may express curiosity about the participant's ability to handle things himself, and about the kind of use he has been making of the MIT situation. "You came here feeling that your son was being deprived of your participation. Why not start by inviting him to prepare those reports to his probation officer with you? Who's on probation anyway?" The second afternoon's work is directed toward a final team-family conference. By that time the relevant recurring patterns tend to be sufficiently well into awareness so that their repetition yields suitable warning signals to all. Normal convergence of dynamic interpretations has been aided by a noon staff conference with supervisors of psychotherapy.

Final Family Conference: This is the time the family may take up specific questions such as whether Johnny goes back to the same school. Often the questioner has arrived at his own answer. Occasionally the adolescent is excused from the first part of the final conference as a demonstration of the team's attitude that he has already over-involved himself in parental problems. By asking for a follow-up visit in six months— our minimum requirement for research purposes—we put the family in the position to digest and utilize what they have learned. A vote of confidence is given by virtue of the fact that they will be proceeding without supervision. Occasionally after two days, the outlook for effective change is not promising, and the other half day is invoked. With one-quarter of our cases we have repeated a single day of the procedure after about two months.

RESULTS

Preliminary examination of the data indicates the worth of its detailed analysis and presentation. Follow-up data has been obtained on

---

[5] The procedure adapted from control supervision of therapists is one particularly useful when a participatory community representative, or the doctor who worked with the patient in the hospital and referred him for MIT has been coached by the team to be one of those who performs this function.

fifty-five families: Twenty-two treated cases have been seen at follow-up in their home communities. Thirty treated families, including nine of those followed at home, were re-examined or treated in the office following MIT. The office follow-up contacts differed in intensity. They included a range of services from routine six and eighteen month follow-up to monthly visits of two or more family members. Scheduled follow-up of six recent cases and six cases followed through agency report, telephone and correspondence complete the total.

PRELIMINARY RESULTS SUGGEST that a method of treatment is being developed having results comparable to established intensive methods. Our experience has been largely with families having a problem with an adolescent where the time commitment and the crisis, with the associated reluctance of the family to face further contact with community agencies, might exclude many from treatment. In forty-three of the fifty cases treated in the first two years of this program, family self-rehabilitative processes remain effectively mobilized. In three, while the rehabilitative processes have strengthened the home, the nominal patient, the adolescent, did not continue to live at home and does not appear to show benefit from improved family process. Of the families that appear successfully treated, nine families with older adolescents have seen the nominal patient leave after a period of participation in family rehabilitation subsequent to MIT. (One was killed in a traffic accident; five entered military service; three undertook educational or vocational plans away from home.) In seven families the presenting picture was unchanged or worse.

All seven unsuccessful cases have in common mothers who have been frankly exploitive in all their social relations. The egocentric nature of their goals seemed to thwart development of family self-rehabilitative processes. Success with another seven such cases, however, suggests that on further analysis of data other factors may shed light on this problem.

DURABILITY OF THE RESULTS of MIT as brief therapy is indicated by the fact that twenty-eight of the cases seen have continued toward self-rehabilitation after only the minimum procedures. Fifteen cases have required more attention which seems to be leading to the development of a longer term family-centered treatment method. It now appears that for some families a series of return visits at six week intervals is desirable in the first year. For a few, two month intervals seem suitable, with family sessions supplemented by occasional individual sessions with husband and wife. Typically the additional work has been done with families where the basic psychopathology is extremely severe. Nine of these cases are showing very promising results from the newly developed six week or bi-monthly repeat of procedures through the first year. These cases include the five most clinically disturbed (psychotic or near psychotic) and two very neurotic marital problems, in homes without adolescents, undertaken to increase understanding of the application of the method to other situations. We have found more recently with a number of cases where the tension of crisis is high and family pathology is lower that the one day or half day intake procedure resembling the first day of MIT with later half day follow-up conferences can yield comparable results.

In addition to attributes of the nominal patient, our data for each family are analyzed in terms of (1) a fourfold division of roles appropriate to aggressive, passive-aggressive, emotionally unstable and passive-aggressive functioning; (the amount of flexibility to operate in more than one such mode is noted); (2) a related division of labor conception of sibling relationships; (3) patterns in motherhood; (4) patterns in fatherhood; (5) patterns in value transmission and several catagories of response to crisis, help and community relations.

WHILE THE DIAGNOSIS of the adolescent in conventional terms has not proven useful, we have found that the families referred fall into four groups that are easily differentiated by a developmental classification of the type of arrest in development manifested by the adolescent. These are as follows:
1. Infantile maladjustment in adolescence
2. Childish maladjustment in adolescence
3. Juvenile maladjustment in adolescence
4. Pre-adolescent maladjustment in adolescence

The description of levels in terms of behavior approximates Sullivan's (13) use of these terms. The arrest or delay is described in terms of failure at developmental tasks as described for these levels by Ericson (14). These research findings will be published separately.[6]

DISCUSSION

It has been our experience that a crisis centering around the problems of a child can be utilized in such a way that what the parents are missing

[6] Serrano, A. C., McDanald, E. C., Jr., et al., "Adolescent Maladjustment and Family Dynamics," *Am. Jrn. Psy.*

in life is acutely re-experienced. This enables them to set aside some of the usual resistances in psychotherapy. The characteristic patterns of resistance are noticed and acknowledged as worthy attempts to maintain emotional equilibrium. When a team member argues for the present need for a defensive attitude of a family member, a reduction of the barriers to intra-familial communication usually occurs.

Caplan (2) drawing on Lindeman's studies of psychological reactions of people who had suffered bereavement and their approach to the mourning process, points out that the handling of a crisis is most efficient when intervention is brief. He points out that inner resources may develop when one attempts unaided to cope with a current crisis. This "grief work" functions in everyday situations as one matures and learns to give up what is obsolete. Ferenczi (15) called attention to the stabilizing function of clinging to the infantile fantasies of omnipotence. This resource recurs to the person in crisis who is faced with the loss of an old way of meeting needs. He is tempted to deny that he can lose a loved one, take "no" for an answer, or otherwise accept a limitation to his powerfulness. The crisis makes it possible to consider reality as offering a more efficient base for defining the boundaries of the self, a source of self-confidence, than the aloneness necessary to the maintenance of fantasied power. This is particularly so when reality is supplemented by a team of people convinced of the worth of all efforts the person makes toward equilibrium.

We noticed that there were no serious problems related to family members becoming dependent on the team. This is in part due to the fact that our method basically involves helping the natural love object, the spouse, to be more satisfying than, for example, the heretofore exploited child, or helping the widowed mother to seek the adult satisfactions of continuing growth in preference to encumbering her child by "living for him."

Gregory Bateson in a recent visit pointed out to us that some of the therapeutic efficiency in our approach may come from "cross monitoring"; that is, the person who is being talked about is there and probably listening. Repair of defective communication patterns within the family tends to follow from direct demonstration by the forthright way the team members speak among themselves in the presence of the family. Usually private matters are considered too important to be quiet about.

OUR ATTITUDE IS one of keen attention to the parents. We attempt to appeal to their own needs for attention which are, of course, high as in all times of illness and stress, with the attitude that they can do something constructive about themselves and their teen-ager. We communicate our belief that the direct benefits to them—the interruption of patterns that have interfered with happiness in their lives—will be what is best for their teen-ager. In the early stage of the work, having the adolescent tested and thoroughly appraised before we have specific comments to make appeals to them. It helps the parents accept our turning attention to their personal lives. The mother may find that there is a more rewarding route for relief from the feelings of unfulfillment as a woman. These may be feelings which typically come from having substituted a competitive relation with her husband for a more tender one or from having exploited her child to gratify unmet tenderness needs. That this new route may be through her participation with her husband in reducing his doubts about his own masculinity is usually sufficiently gratifying so that she can make short work of her initial attempts to blame her husband, his ancestors, and the school teachers of her youngster. She gains a renewed appreciation of her own femininity and the child need only cope with the problem appropriate to his being a product rather than the object of the marriage. Murray Bowen in his study of schizophrenia has for several years brought families into the hospital to participate in the treatment. He made an observation which epitomizes this basic family process.

"The striking observation was that when the parents were emotionally close, more invested in each other than either was in the patient, the patient improved. When either parent became more emotionally invested in the patient than in the other parent, the patient immediately and automatically regressed. When the parents were emotionally close they could do no wrong in their "management" of the patient. The patient responded well to firmness, permissiveness, punishment, "talking it out," or any other management approach. When the parents were "emotionally divorced," any and all "management approaches" were equally unsuccessful." (16)

We have been able to involve fathers in MIT who would not submit to conventional child guidance work and indeed have had little difficulty in keeping the significant members of the family participating. This may particularly recommend our procedures to outpatient clinics. Originally we felt the two day program was especially feasible for cases from remote parts of the state where fathers typically had to take time off to bring the family to Galveston. Yet it has turned out to be equally practical for cases involving local families with wage earners who are willing to commit themselves to a two and a half day treatment period. In the current series half of the families have come from our own and neighboring counties.

A particularly useful by-product of our study has been the speed with which an additional professional can become a member of the team. Turnover in clinic personnel has created a demand for something quicker than the full year of working together required by the National Association of Psychiatric Clinics for children. From regularly augmenting our team by using residents in psychiatry or psychology, and from the practice of including the probation officer or child welfare worker who may accompany the family, we have found that the added professional can become a full fledged team member in weeks. The effect of MIT on communication within the team is not unlike its effect on families.

Established clinics might well schedule two and a half days every second week. On the alternate week one or more days may be scheduled for intake or follow-up procedures with team and family.

REFERENCES

1. PARLOFF, MORRIS B., "Psychotherapy Research with Families," paper read in a symposium at American Psychological Association, Chicago, 1960.
2. CAPLAN, GERALD, "An Approach to the Study of the Family Mental Health," *Public Health Reports*, 71, 1027–1030, 1956.
3. PECK, HARRIS B., "An Application of Group Therapy to the Intake Process," *Amer. J. Ortho.*, 23, 338–349, 1953.
4. WHITAKER, CARL A., WARKENTIN, JOHN, and JOHNSON, NAN L., "A Philosophical Basis for Brief Psychotherapy," *Psychiat. Quart.*, 23, 439–443, 1949.
5. DYRUD, JARL E. and RIOCH, MARGARET J., "Multiple Therapy in the Treatment Program of a Mental Hospital," *Psychiatry*, 16, 21–26, 1953.
6. JOHNSON, ADELAIDE M., "Collaborative Psychotherapy: Team Setting," in Marcel Heiman, *Psychoanalysis and Social Work*, New York, Int. Univ Press, 1953.
7. STARR, PHILLIP H., "The Triangular Treatment Approach in Child Therapy: Complementary Psychotherapy of Mother and Child," *Amer. J. Psychother.*, 10, 40–53, 1956.
8. STANTON, A. H. and SCHWARTZ, M. S., "The Management of a Type of Institutional Participation in Mental Illness," *Psychiatry*, 12, 13–26, 1949.
9. ACKERMAN, NATHAN W., *The Psychodynamics of Family Life: Diagnosis and Treatment of Family Relationships*, New York, Basis Books, 1958.
10. LAUFER, MARIE L., "Casework with Parents," *Child Welfare*, 32, 3–7, 1953.
11. ROSENTHAL, MAURICE J., "Collaborative Therapy with Parents at Child Guidance Clinics," *Soc. Casewk.*, 35, 18–25, 1954.

12. POLLAK, OTTO, *Integrating Sociological and Psychoanalytic Concepts*, New York, Russell Sage Fnd., 1956.
13. SULLIVAN, H. S., *The Psychiatric Interview*, New York, Norton, 1954.
14. ERICKSON, E. H., *Identity and the Life Cycle*, New York, Int. Univ. Press, 1959.
15. FERENCZI, SANDOR, "Stages in the Development of the Sense of Reality," in *Sex in Psychoanalysis*, New York, Basic Books, 1950, pp. 213–239.
16. BOWEN, MURRAY, "A Family Concept of Schizophrenia," in Jackson, Don D. (Ed), *The Etiology of Schizophrenia*, New York, Basic Books, 1960.

4

Family Crisis Therapy—Results and Implications

DONALD G. LANGSLEY, M.D.
FRANK S. PITTMAN III, M.D.
PAVEL MACHOTKA, Ph.D.
KALMAN FLOMENHAFT, M.S.W., A.C.S.W.

M ENTAL ILLNESS IS traditionally considered a disease of the individual. Its causes have at various times been ascribed to devils, bad genes, chemical errors and early psychological traumata. The family of the mental patient is pitied for the occurrence of such an affliction. As a consequence the psychotic has usually been "alienated" from his family by banishment to a mental hospital, often one far away from his home, and this hospitalization of one member of a family reinforces the belief that the problem is within that individual rather than within the family. In recent years hospitals have changed their custodial function to a treatment approach. One rationale (rationalization?) for hospitalization has been protection of the nominal patient and others. It has been claimed that specific therapies can be better given to the "inpatient." Such claims have almost never been systematically tested. Comparisons between hospital and outpatient treatment for similar groups are extremely rare (8).

The Family Treatment Unit, established at Colorado Psychiatric Hospital in 1964 by Langsley and Kaplan, has been concerned with studying some of the relationships between mental patients, their families and psychiatric hospitals. Crisis therapy has been developed for families which include a member who would ordinarily be admitted immediately to a mental hospital (Colorado Psychiatric Hospital). The 186 cases treated by this approach are a random sample of all patients admitted to C.P.H. who live within an hour's travel of the hospital and who live in a family. After the first year's experience with 36 pilot cases, 150 such families were treated in this experimental fashion and compared with 150 "control" families drawn from the same population. In the control families, however, the identified patient had been admitted to the hospital. Baseline measures of individual and family adaptation, previous crisis management, and other ratings are obtained prior to treatment. They are repeated along with clinical evaluations by independent raters at six and eighteen months, and annually thereafter. At the time of this report, baseline and six month follow-up data on the first 75 experimentals and 75 controls are available.

The request for hospitalization of one member of a family is assumed to evolve from a series of events. A hazardous event such as a death, maturation of a child, a job change or a host of the other "usual problems of living," requires adjustment. Most families master these stresses without serious decompensation but when the family includes a susceptible individual or when the family has become used to dealing with problems by using psychiatric hospitals, the stage may be set for the symptoms of mental illness. This emphasis on the crisis in the family as a precipitant of the request for hospitalization does not underestimate the importance of the "patient's" psychopathology or the influence of his heredity and physiology. However, the family has been the basic social unit involved in the management of regressive behavior. The removal of an individual from his family to a hospital is more likely to complicate than aid the situation. It removes one member from a family, permits extrusion and scapegoating and avoids the family problem which may have precipitated the crisis. This action denies that the family can be helped to solve its own problems.

The techniques of family crisis therapy are detailed elsewhere and their application to specific family syndromes has been described (3, 4, 5, 6, 9, 10). The goals are to aid in the resolution of the crisis, to assist the patient to recompensate and to return to functioning at the previous level of adaptation. There is less concern with exploring the past than the present. There is more concern with what the family and its members do than uncovering the reasons for doing it. The average duration of treatment is approximately three weeks and it generally consists of about five office visits, a home visit and a few telephone calls. The treatment process begins at the time the patient and family come for help. Though the initial request was for hospitalization, the family are seen at once by a member of the clinical team and are promised immediate help. Absent family members are called in from home, school or work and significant others in the family are included. The history of events leading up to the crisis is obtained and the interactional aspects of the crisis are stressed. Efforts to avoid the family crisis by scapegoating one member and labeling him a "mental patient" are blocked. Regression is discouraged. Tension is reduced with active reassurance, support, and specific advice. Drugs are used for symptom relief in any member of the family. Tasks are assigned for resolving the crisis and returning each member to functioning. With this directive and supportive approach, symptomatic relief occurs very quickly (in hours or days). Conflicts in role assignments and performance can then be negotiated. When indicated, referral may be made for long term therapy of an individual or group within the family. From the beginning the family is made aware of the short term nature of this treatment and of the team's continuing availability for subsequent crises.

The 75 control cases are from the same population as the experimentals. They too include a member for whom immediate hospitalization was requested by the family and approved by the psychiatric resident on the admission service. The family and patient met the same criteria as the experimental group but were assigned by a random selection system to hospital treatment rather than family crisis therapy. At the time of admission these patients and families received the same baseline evaluations as the experimentals. After hospitalization, they were followed up in the same manner. Their treatment took place on the inpatient service of Colorado Psychiatric Hospital, a university psychiatric hospital with a high staff-patient ratio. The average length of stay was 26.1 days. Therapy included individual and group psychotherapy, therapeutic community and drugs. Families were seen collaboratively by psychiatric social workers. This group received psychiatric treatment which would be considered more than "adequate" when compared with that available in any mental health treatment setting. The setting, however, was a hospital and the focus was on the patient rather than the family.

What happens when patients who would have been hospitalized receive family crisis therapy instead? Can psychotic patients be treated outside the psychiatric hospital? If hospitalization is prevented, is it harmful to the patient and/or family in the long run? Does crisis therapy only delay hospitalization? The answers to these questions and a comparison of the effectiveness of family crisis treatment versus mental hospitalization are sought in the follow-up studies. Before proceeding to a report of the results obtained from the two groups, it is necessary to be sure that the groups are comparable. It would be folly to attempt to evaluate one treatment with another if the patients to whom it is administered are not comparable. The random assignment of patients from the same population to one treatment or the other (family crisis treatment or hospitalization) offers considerable likelihood that the two groups are comparable. To test that likelihood, the first 75 experimentals and controls have been compared on 15 characteristics, (see Table 1). These items include factors which describe the identified patient, his family, his illness, and the manner in which he came for treatment as well as the history of previous psychiatric hospitalizations. As can be seen from the table, there are no significant differences between the experimental or control groups on any of the 15 areas of comparison. It is, therefore, safe to assume that the groups are comparable and to proceed to measure the effects of the two types of treatment.

A clinical report of the results of family crisis therapy would focus on the individual, his family and the community from which they come. The immediate results are a lessening of tension. The pressures which are evidences of the state of crisis are reduced by rest, the expectation of help, and by the medication prescribed. A consequence of lowering the tension level is that previously paralyzed problem-solving capacities are freed up. In a natural disaster such as earthquake or flood, those affected initially experience a state of shock. The same is true of the individual in crisis but once the initial shock is diminished, the individual and his family begin to view the problem with new perspective. Energy previously used to cope with the crisis is now

TABLE 1

Comparison of 75 Experimental and 75 Control Patients

Number	Area of Comparison	Chi Square	Degrees Freedom	Probability
1.	Sex	.01	1	> .90
2.	Age	4.51	6	> .70
3.	Race	5.4	2	< .10
4.	Marital Status	1.28	4	< .90
5.	Religion	3.37	3	> .30
6.	Type of Family	6.77	4	> .20
7.	Referred by	.61	1	< .50
8.	Brought to Hospital by	1.07	3	< .80
9.	Social Class	4.34	4	> .30
10.	Type of Admission	4.43	2	> .10
11.	Day of Week Admitted	5.83	6	< .50
12.	Time of Day Admitted	6.02	3	> .10
13.	History of Prior Mental Hosp.	.18	1	< .70
14.	Suicidal Ideation or Attempt	4.11	3	< .30
15.	Diagnosis	4.75	3	< .20

available. The clinical symptoms begin to disappear. A recompensation is taking place. The "patient" and those around him are protected from the primitive emotions and destructive states associated with a regressive psychotic state. Family members return to work, school or household duties rapidly. The avoidance of hospitalization permits the family to maintain its functional integrity as the basic social unit. The family is spared the shame, guilt and economic stress of having one member hospitalized. For the community the results are an avoidance of expensive hospital treatment and a continuance of productive members in the jobs and roles held prior to the crisis.

In all 75 experimental cases hospitalization was avoided. But was it avoided or merely postponed? Comparison of six month follow-up data from the first 75 controls and experimentals reveals that the re-hospitalization rate among the controls was as high as the total hospitalization rate of the experimentals. Among the controls all were hospitalized during acute treatment, and 16 (21%) were readmitted to a mental hospital during the six month follow-up period. In 14 of the experimentals (19%) a psychiatric hospitalization occurred during the six months after family crisis therapy was terminated and 61 (81%) of the experimentals were never admitted to a psychiatric hospital during the acute treatment or the following six months. This is compelling evidence that family crisis therapy does more than postpone a necessary admission to a mental hospital. If crisis family treatment

TABLE 2

Rehospitalization of 75 Family Crisis Therapy Cases and 75 Hospital Cases (Controls)

	Cumulative No. of Patients Hospitalized		Cumulative No. of Hospital Days		Cumulative No. of Potential Hospital Days	% of Potential Hospital Days Used this Month		% of Sample not Hospitalized	
	FTU	Control	FTU	Control		FTU	Control	FTU	Control
Acute treatment period	None	75	None	1,959		None	100%	100%	None
1st post-treatment month	5	13	69	211	2,250	3.1%	9.4%	93%	83%
2nd month	8	13	151	401	4,500	3.6	8.4	89	83
3rd month	10	14	242	554	6,750	4.0	6.8	87	81
4th month	11	16	307	753	9,000	2.9	8.8	85	79
5th month	13	16	365	933	11,250	2.6	8.0	83	79
6th month	14	16	423	1,091	13,500	2.6	7.0	81	79
Average						3.1	8.1		

had merely postponed hospitalization, the rate of hospitalization *after* treatment should be higher for the experimentals than for the controls, but the contrary is true.

When a mental hospital admission was necessary during the six months after acute treatment, it was arranged by the family, by a treatment facility to which the family had been referred, or by the F.T.U. team itself. The lengths of those hospitalizations, however, were different from the hospitalization of the control group. Table 2 also indicates that the family crisis therapy cases spent only about a third as much time in the hospital during that six months as the controls. The 14 experimentals were in a mental hospital for 423 days (3.1% of the potential days) while the controls spent 1,091 days (8.1% of the potential days) in a hospital.

Having demonstrated that family crisis therapy does keep patients out of the hospital (or that when the hospital is needed, the admission is briefer), it is fair to ask how well these cases do. If hospital admission is avoided only to have the 75 experimental cases remain sick at home, what is the gain?

But measuring the outcome of psychiatric treatment is not a simple task. What should be measured? It was not expected that outpatient crisis treatment *or* brief hospital treatment would alter personality patterns. Consequently, no attempt was made to measure these. It was hoped that this treatment would help the "patient" who is in a state of acute decompensation to recompensate and adjust to his usual environment. It was also hoped that the symptoms of acute decompensation and regression would be improved. One instrument was chosen to measure social adjustment, and another was constructed to provide indices of functioning and recompensation. The Social Adjustment Inventory taps information in four areas of adaptation: Social and Family Relations, Social Productivity, Self-Management, and Anti-Social Behavior (1). The four area scores are added for the Total SAI Score. It is scaled so that lower scores indicate "better" social adjustment. This scale was administered to experimentals and controls on admission, three months after termination, and at six months. In a number of cases the three month scores were not obtained but baseline and six month scores are available for at least 62 of the 75 in each group. Group Mean Scores are presented in Table 3. All subtests and totals were tested against each other for significant differences by the t test. Only those t scores which reach the .05 level of significance are presented in the table.

Experimentals and controls are similar on the baseline scores and show no differences of significance in any subtests or total scores. On the total scores, the experimentals and controls each show significant improvement from baseline to three month post treatment, and both remain significantly improved at six months. The largest amount of improvement for both experimentals and controls is in Social Productivity. The experimentals also showed significant improvement in Social and Family Relations, while the controls did not. Self Management and Anti-Social Behavior do not change significantly.

The noteworthy finding is that experimentals are doing at least as well as the controls at three months and six months after the termination of treatment. Among both groups, slightly better performance is reported at three months than at six months though the changes from three to six months do not reach statistical significance.

Another instrument was developed by the Family Treatment Unit to measure the functioning of the identified patient (performance of work, school or household roles), his "health" and the symptoms associated with psychiatric illness (7). This was named the Personal Functioning Scale (PFS) and is given at admission and at the six months evaluation. Scores for 49 baseline and 57 six month experimentals and for 72 baseline and 63 six month controls are presented in Table 4. Again, lower scores indicate "healthier" functioning. The findings are similar to those of the SAI scores. Both groups improve from admission to six months post-treatment to an extent that is sta-

TABLE 3

Social Adjustment Inventory Group Mean Scores

	Social and Family Relations		Social Productivity		Self-Management		Anti-social Behavior		Totals	
	Exps.	Con-trols	Exps.	Con-trols	Exps.	Con-trols	Exps.	Con-trols	Exps.	Con-trols
Baseline	3.24	3.13	2.90	3.07	2.54	2.49	2.07	2.11	10.75	10.80
3 months	2.66	2.82	2.29	2.40	2.39	2.22	1.76	1.80	9.10	9.24
6 months	2.74	3.00	2.31	2.25	2.36	2.42	2.10	2.11	9.52	9.82

t scores where significant at .05 level or better

Baseline Experimentals vs 3 month Experimentals	2.73	2.25			3.28
Baseline Experimentals vs 6 month Experimentals	2.71	2.45			2.70
Baseline Controls vs 3 month Controls		2.93			3.30
Baseline Controls vs 6 month Controls		3.73			2.09

Baseline Experimentals N = 68
Baseline Controls N = 75
3 month Experimentals N = 41
3 month Controls N = 55
6 month Experimentals N = 58
6 month Controls N = 65

tistically significant. The experimentals do not differ significantly from the controls at any point in time. The largest amount of change is in the area of symptoms. Again, the family crisis therapy cases do as well as the hospitalized cases. It might be asked whether the picture changes when only those patients on whom *all* measures (on either scale) are available are included in the computations. For brevity the tables will not be presented here, but the results indicate no change whatever in the pattern for either the SAI or the PFS.

Does family crisis therapy produce a hardship on the family by saddling them with a non-functioning patient? Here the answer is clearly "no." Family Treatment Unit patients return to usual func-

TABLE 4

Personal Functioning Scale Group Means

	Functioning		Health		Symptoms		Total	
	Exps.	Con-trols	Exps.	Con-trols	Exps.	Con-trols	Exps.	Con-trols
Baseline	2.64	2.55	2.29	2.30	3.11	3.20	8.08	8.05
6 months	2.28	2.13	2.00	2.00	2.58	2.57	6.87	6.74

t scores where significant at .05 level or better

Baseline Experimentals vs 6 month Experimentals	2.07	2.55	4.35	3.89
Baseline Controls vs 6 month Controls	2.87	2.67	5.53	4.85

Baseline Experimentals   N = 49
6 month Experimentals   N = 57
Baseline Controls   N = 72
6 month Controls   N = 63

TABLE 5

Days Lost From Functioning in Usual Role Assignment

		Days Lost During Acute Treatment	Days Lost After Termination
75 Experimentals	Median	5.0	0
	Mean	8.1	16.9
75 Hospital Controls	Median	22.0	3.0
	Mean	24.3	48.2

tioning far more quickly than do hospitalized patients. Keeping patients out of the hospital results in shorter periods of disruption of usual family functioning and finding someone else to perform the patient's usual role in the family, a matter of considerable practical importance when the patient is a housekeeper or breadwinner. It may work hardships in some cases, but most families prefer to avoid mental hospitals.

Return to Functioning data is reported for both groups in Table 5. This is a tabulation of days lost from usual role performance during and after treatment. As is apparent, at least half the patients in both groups returned to functioning immediately after termination of treatment. However, the median experimental case had been back to usual functioning within five days of entering treatment, while the median control was not functioning during his twenty two-day hospitalization. The mean is more striking. The average experimental patient lost 8.1 days of functioning during treatment and 16.9 days afterwards, for an average loss of 25 days of functioning. This is influenced by the five patients who never returned to functioning during the six month period, including one man who never returned to gainful employment. Among the controls the average time lost was 24.3 days in the hospital and 48.2 days thereafter, an average loss of 72.5 days, about three times the duration of non-functioning for the FTU cases. This was influenced by two things. One was the large number of people who lost their jobs while in the hospital and had difficulty finding new ones because of the recent hospitalization, and second, the *fourteen* control patients who never returned to functioning during the six month period. Seven male hospitalized controls never returned to any sort of work or school.

Another area of comparison concerns the cost of treatment. Although this is not strictly a comparison of the results of treatment, it has been of very practical interest. How does the cost of family crisis therapy compare with that of mental hospital treatment. At Colorado Psychiatric Hospital the actual cost per patient day is approximately $50.00. This figure is comparable to the costs at other short stay intensive treatment hospitals. The average stay for the controls was 26 days or a grand total of about $1300 per hospitalization.

The cost of family crisis treatment requires certain estimates. A clinical team consisting of a psychiatrist, a clinical psychologist, a psychiatric social worker, a psychiatric public health nurse, and two clerical personnel would require an annual salary budget of perhaps $65,000 plus another $5,000 for overhead, supplies and local travel. It has been conservatively estimated that such a team could treat seven new cases per week or approximately 350 cases per year. Although the case load of the FTU clinical team has usually been less than that, the team has spent a great deal of its energy doing research and teaching. The psychologist member of the team has spent almost all of his time on research and very little on clinical activities. Consequently, seven new cases per week seems to be a reasonable estimate. This would bring the total cost per patient to approximately $200. $1300 per treated case as opposed to $200—this factor of six and a half, if borne out in practice, would be of no small consequence. These estimates do not consider time lost by the patient or other family from productive work and all of the other costs that make psychiatric hospitalization and its resultant stigma so exhorbitantly costly for society.

This report has summarized some of the results of the comparison of family crisis therapy and mental hospital admission for two groups of 75 patients each. The eighteen-month material and the 300 cases (rather than the 150 of this report) should offer an even more rigorous test of the comparison described here. The results are reported at this time, however, because they are sufficiently convincing to justify a preliminary report.

What are the implications of these findings? Having demonstrated that family crisis therapy can recompensate applicants for hospital admission and keep them functioning as well as those hospitalized, we bear a responsibility for setting these findings in place. The basic principles behind crisis therapy have been used by general practitioners and other types of health services. Any clinician can cite occasional cases from his practice where similar techniques have been used for the isolated case, and it is increasingly fashionable to see whole families together. The contribution of this project can hardly be the discovery of the usefulness of the conjoint family approach. Instead, the contribution resides in having systematically tested family crisis therapy as an alternative to mental hospitalization in similar populations. Nor has anyone yet elaborated the implications of family crisis therapy for theory, and for those who establish mental health services.

These data strongly suggest that those who investigate crises should look at the family setting in which they arise. A crisis seems far more related to the immediate settings, recent stresses and current events than to past history. Early experiences and the development of coping mechanisms (ego apparatuses) may determine whether or not a given individual responds to a current stress adaptively or poorly. But the onset of mental illness (regressive behavior) requires not only an understanding of the present ecological situation, but an *active use* of it. It suggests the need to expose the maladaptive family properties, and the value of using the family's adaptive mechanisms to reverse regression. This is probably the most important implication for theory—the need to look at interaction. Insight is not required to change acute symptoms or sudden maladaptive behavior (2). The non-specific factors stressed by Frank seem more important in crisis therapy than the uncovering of unconscious conflicts. There need be no effort in crisis therapy (family or individual) to delve into unconscious intrapsychic conflict.

It is currently popular to attack the "medical model." By the medical model most imply a "disease" orientation to psychiatric illness in which the problem resides within the affected individual and is best treated by biological specifics. This is a straw-man argument. It is obvious that behavior is influenced by important people around any given individual as well as by his past and by his physiology. Medical practice has shown increasing attention to the environment in which illness arises and the environment in which it is treated. The current state of mental health practice also attends increasingly to the family as one source of problem for the designated patient and as an important source of help in overcoming stress and subsequent decompensation.

Another area with implications for theory is the study of the "normal" crisis. The work reported here has been with very sick individuals and highly troubled families. The hazards which may have precipitated a family crisis in these groups are events which other families may have mastered easily. Crisis theory has defined the crisis as the hazardous event (stress) and the subsequent reaction to that event. A real contribution to increased understanding of crisis would arise from systematic investigation of family and individual reactions to the same kinds of stresses. The Family Treatment Unit has attempted to evolve a classification of crises, but none has really proved satisfactory. Tentative categories have included the following:

        (1) The "bolt from the blue" crisis
        (2) The caretaker crisis
        (3) The developmental crisis
        (4) The exacerbation crisis

The "bolt from the blue" views the unexpected external hazard as the important contribution; given a strong enough external shock, any family or person will capitulate. The caretaker crisis also attends to external stress—one where a caretaker responds pathologically to a situation which is not unusual for that family. The developmental crisis is more concerned with the family itself than with external events and assumes that there is a natural history of the family with tasks to be mastered at various stages of development (4). The exacerbation crisis assumes an external stress in the family which has had a long term pattern of less than ideal functioning and, therefore, focuses on both the hazard and the social field in which it occurs.

These categories have not really been satisfactory and most cases seen by the FTU fit into the "exacerbation" model. To date a typology of crises which adequately deals with the stress and the family is not available. This challenge is a worthy one.

The implications of the findings reported here for organizing mental health services are reasonably plain. Family crisis therapy ought to be available as an alternative to removing "patients" to a mental hospital. The hospitalization of any family member has been shown to have profound effects on the member himself, his family and the course of his illness. It should be possible to keep the vast majority of patients out of mental hospitals according to these findings though, of course, a small number of hospital beds will continue to be required. It is hoped that further study will clarify for which "patients" and families hospitals are unavoidable. It would seem from this clinical experience that those most likely to be hospitalized in the future are the group which have been hospitalized in the past. Other implications for practice raise questions about action versus passivity in therapy. The passivity of the psychoanalyst is used to help create a transference neurosis. Activity in therapy usually concerns itself with current problems, with rapid alteration of maladaptive behavior and with current symptoms rather than ancient problems. Family crisis therapy should not be the *only* approach to the problems of mental illness; it should be one of many.

The current American scene makes the availability of mental health services a right of all citizens rather than the privilege of the wealthy few. Relief of distress for acute decompensation within an individual and a family is best treated with an active approach which gets results reasonably quickly. Hospitalization does not relieve symptoms quickly; it encourages chronicity.

Family crisis therapy is effective in keeping acutely decompensated psychiatric patients out of a mental hospital. Some, usually those with previous hospitalizations, may be institutionalized subsequently but at a rate no higher than the rehospitalization rate of a comparable group of hospitalized controls. Those treated by family crisis therapy recompensate and return to functioning more quickly than the hospitalized controls and maintain this functioning at least as well. When subsequent hospitalizations occur they are markedly shorter. The cost of family crisis therapy is less than one-sixth the cost of hospital treatment. This approach produces less chronicity and family disruption. The remarkable success with a very small amount of professional effort raises many questions about theories of human behavior and the organization of mental health services.

REFERENCES

1. BERGER, D. G., RICE, C. E., SEWALL, L. G. and LEMKAU, P. V., "Post-Hospital Evaluation of Psychiatric Patients: The Social Adjustment Inventory Method," *A.P.A. Psychiatric Studies and Projects*, ⧓15, 1964.
2. FRANK, J., *Persuasion and Healing: A Comparative Study of Psychotherapy*, Baltimore, Johns Hopkins Press, 1961.
3. HALEY, J. and HOFFMAN, L., "Cleaning House: An Interview with Frank Pittman III, Kalman Flomenhaft, and Carol DeYoung," in *Techniques of Family Therapy*, New York, Basic Books, 1967, pp. 361–471.
4. LANGSLEY, D. G., FAIRBAIRN, R. H. and DEYOUNG, C. D., "Adolescence and Family Crises", *Canad. Psychiatric Assn. J.*
5. LANGSLEY, D. G., KAPLAN, D. M., PITTMAN, F. S., MACHOTKA, P., FLOMENHAFT, K. and DEYOUNG, C. D., *The Treatment of Families in Crisis*, New York, Grune & Stratton.
6. MACHOTKA, P., PITTMAN, F. S. and FLOMENHAFT, K., "Incest as a Family Affair," *Fam. Proc.*, 6, 98–116, 1967.
7. MACHOTKA, P., Personal Communication, 1968.
8. PASAMANICK, B., SCARPITTI, F. R. and DINITZ, S., *Schizophrenics in the Community: An Experimental Study in the Prevention of Hospitalization*, New York, Appleton-Century-Crofts, 1967.
9. PITTMAN, F. S., DEYOUNG, C. D., FLOMENHAFT, K., KAPLAN, D. M. and LANGSLEY, D. G., "Techniques of Crisis Family Therapy", in *Current Psychiat. Therapies*, 6, Masserman, J. (ed.), New York, Grune & Stratton, 1966, pp. 187–196.
10. PITTMAN, F. S., LANGSLEY, D. G., and DEYOUNG, C. D., "Work and School Phobias: A Family Approach", *Amer. J. Psychiat.*

5

Family Diagnosis and Therapy in Child Emotional Pathology

MORDECAI KAFFMAN, M.D.

I N THIS paper, we want to limit ourselves to the formulation of our theoretical and clinical model of family psychotherapy as it is being applied by us at two outpatient Israeli clinics. The detailed analysis of the data, clinical histories, comparative psychopathological findings and analysis of parental attitudes of Kibbutz and urban families, and evaluation of clinical results will be reported in subsequent articles.

It may be well to state at the start that even for our own particular method of treatment the use of the plural term family *therapies* instead of the singular represents the reality of everyday clinical practice. There are no two families to which the same therapeutic plan can be applied. Family therapy as we practice it in Israel requires substantial variability in the therapist's ways of activity according to the patient's ethnic and cultural background, social values, level of sophistication, age, etc. It also demands a high degree of plasticity regarding length, frequency and distribution of the therapeutic interviews.

Our clinical method includes the combined use of family group sessions and parallel separate sessions with individual members of the family or family subgroups. For different practical and theoretical reasons we do not adhere rigidly to the exclusive use of joint family sessions. We include a large percentage of patients of the working class who find it difficult to come as a group for obvious reasons. In addition we consider that concomitant separate sessions with the child and other family members constitute an important tool to strengthen the therapeutic rapport, to find the most meaningful level of communication with the individual child or parent, and to work out specific problems which cannot always be dealt with in full detail at the joint family group interview. However, the joint treatment sessions remains the central therapeutic tool of our clinical method. It is a precious instrument to observe, evaluate, elicit and influence normal and disturbed patterns of interaction in the "here and now" family-therapist transaction.

Family sessions are attended by both parents, the referred child and occasionally by other siblings or significant members of the family. Therapeutic interviews are usually held once a week for one to two hours. The time is divided in a flexible way and successively utilized for the joint, sub-group and individual sessions. The length of treatment has varied in our clinical work from two months to three years, the average being three months in instances selected for short-term therapy and one-and a half year in cases receiving more prolonged therapy. For follow up care, sessions are held according to clinical needs.

We should stress that no different approach or technique is utilized for short or long-term family therapy. The length of therapy is basically determined by the severity of pathology and unfortunately also by the shortage of available therapists for prolonged treatment. Quite a large number of families with severe emotional pathology, where intensive long-term therapy seemed to be obviously indicated, were accepted for brief family therapy. Despite this apparent incongruency, sustained changes in family dynamics and improvement or elimination of distressing symptoms were frequently achieved by the use of abbreviated psychotherapy (1). Even with adolescents we did not find, in the vast majority of the cases, unusual difficulties or resistance to participation in the group family treatment program.

All family members were treated and seen both at the joint and separate sessions by a single therapist instead of the usual team work approach. The place and value of the collaborative approach have been well established, but we believe that the single therapist approach is equally effective and allows for significant saving in time and effort, a cohesive view of family dynamics and, consequently, a consistent therapeutic intervention. When—as it happens in Israel—the shortage of therapists becomes a crucial issue, and when immediate reality confrontation of the members of the family with the findings of the family-therapist interaction is designed to be one of the most important effective therapeutic elements, a team work approach does not appear to be feasible or adequate.

In short, we may define our method of family therapy as a flexible therapeutic plan, which includes at least the referred child and his parents, the treatment being carried out by a single therapist throughout joint family interviews as well as separate individual and sub-group family sessions for a short or prolonged period of time.

THE CLINICAL POPULATION

The data for this study was drawn from interviews with 320 Israeli families seen by the author during the past three years (1961–64) as a Consultant Child Psychiatrist, at the Oranim Clinic of the Kibbutzim and Haifa Mental Health Clinic of Kupat Holim. Most of the families were referred because of a child-centered problem. Altogether the group constituted a largely representative sample of the distribution of the most serious psychopathology to be found among Israeli Kibbutz and non-Kibbutz child outpatients. Only occasionally, the original referral was parent or family centered. There were instances of patients previously treated by a psychotherapist who in the course of individual therapy found it necessary to tackle the integrative family problem in order to break a deadlocked therapeutic situation. Out of the 320 families, 194 were Kibbutz families from more than one hundred Kibbutzim scattered throughout the country. The remaining 126 families lived in the city of Haifa or its surroundings. Both groups were significantly different with regard to methods and practices of child-rearing, cultural characteristics and socio-economic status. A detailed description of Kibbutz child-rearing practices and its specific problems has been reported elsewhere (2, 3). Most of the Kibbutz children are brought up in children's houses which constitute functionally independent units. Each house provides quarters for a relatively small and stable group of peer-age children, including room space for day play and learning activities, dining and bedroom facilities. Kibbutz children see their parents daily according to a prearranged schedule for about three hours after work time, besides shorter eventual contacts during the day as determined by practical possibilities of parents and children. The Kibbutz metapelet (nurse) and the teacher are responsible for the physical, intellectual and emotional development and well-being of the children in their charge. They assume a decisive role as a training and socializing agent in areas such as feeding, toilet training, independence and social interaction. However, despite the crucial function of nurses and teachers regarding both the quality of tasks and amount of time spent with the child, the parents constitute, in the Kibbutz as well as in the traditional family situation, the most important and stable object of emotional attachment. Actually, all the manifold possible types of parent-child relationships, healthy and unhealthy, can be discovered in the Kibbutz family life. All the degrees and varieties of parental attitudes are present and constitute by and large the most important environmental factor in the child's interpersonal experience.

Although the Kibbutz is a rural settlement maintaining a highly mechanized, diversified and prosperous agricultural economy, its members cannot be considered as regular farmers according to usual standards. As a matter of fact, the Kibbutz members maintain a higher socio-cultural level of life than the average Israeli urban working class. A large number of Kibbutzim have set up permanent advisory committees, which include experienced educators and specially trained people, in order to screen and deal with mild to moderate child emotional disturbances. It follows that most of the Kibbutz families which have been referred to us at the Oranim Child Clinic represent an already selected sample of more severe pathology, asking for professional help usually after unsuccessful therapeutic trials. By and large, these families are referred and "conditioned" as prospective candidates for long-term psychotherapy.

The urban Haifa families constituted a more varied group regarding socio-economic status. The patient population ranged from unskilled workers with a pressing low income, large families, crowded housing facilities and poor socio-cultural standards to lower middle class and professional people. Although the indicators of social status utilized in Hollingshead's Index of Social Position (Education, Occupation and Address) (4) cannot be mechanically transferred to

Israeli society, we might state for the purpose of appraisal and comparison that roughly speaking the urban families of our clinical material include patients of Class III, IV, and V distributed evenly in these three social categories. Even the families with a higher social status in the urban sample lacked similar facilities to those established in the Kibbutz for early detection and treatment of the emotionally disabled child. Therefore, on the whole the urban group offers more neglected, although not necessarily more severe, psychopathology than the Kibbutz group.

A basic difference between the two groups is the almost complete absence of previous therapeutic trials in the urban group. We assume that this difference along with less sophisticated approach to psychological matters as compared to Kibbutz members would explain the positive attitudes, expectancies and eventually good results of short-term psychotherapy in this urban group.

DYNAMIC FAMILY DIAGNOSIS

For each one of the 320 families which had been referred to the clinics because of child-centered problems, we tried to establish a dynamic family diagnostic assessment. At present, we feel that we still have a long way to go to work out a comprehensive and acceptable family diagnostic terminology for child psychiatry needs. Unfortunately we lack an agreed upon framework and distinct criteria to include, synthesize and assess in the diagnostic label the interaction between the constitutional, maturational and learning data of the child with his past and present significant social environment. The complicated nature of each one of the constitutional and experiential components in child development and the manifold variables in the child-environment interplay, makes it very difficult to find a reasonable middle-of-the road diagnostic terminology between the current incomplete oversimplified diagnostic categories used in child psychopathology (5) and some extensive descriptive assessments suggested by different psychological schools which fail to meet practical needs.

In our clinical material, we have tried to arrive at a comprehensive family diagnostic assessment by evaluating the child's psychopathological condition, the significant social environment of the child, and the assumed interaction of child and environment. We are still unable to summarize our findings, but at the present we can conclude that the conjoint family sessions represent a very effective tool for arriving at an integrative diagnosis in child psychopathology. The family interview gives ample opportunity for diagnostic assessment of child pathology in terms of patterns of child deviational behavior, and clustering of specific clinical syndromes, according to the usual descriptive diagnostic nomenclature. Furthermore, the family interview allows a good appraisal of the presumptive significant environmental factors with particular emphasis on their impact on the child from the point of view of privation, deprivation or satisfaction of basic emotional needs.

For the time being, we have selected from the multiple possible patterns of parent-child relationship, six polar opposition variances of parental attitudes to be considered in the comprehensive diagnostic assessment:

I.	Accepting Love;	Affective Barrier-Rejection
II.	Fostering Mutual Autonomy;	Fostering Control and Dependency
III.	Good Frustration Conditioning;	Poor Frustration Conditioning
IV.	Adequate Stimulation;	Under or Overstimulation
V.	Adequate Protection;	Under or Overprotection
VI.	Consistency;	Inconsistency

In our clinical experience, this simple conceptual model of parental behavior, whose detailed description and application would be the subject of a special paper, appears to be useful enough to embrace all basic dimensions of parental attitudes. It is a dichotomized evaluation including a separate assessment of both parents.

The family interviews, together with the data previously collected by the Psychiatric Social Worker at the Intake Process (1), were considered sufficient in the majority of our cases, to lead to a reasonably founded diagnostic assessment which included evaluation of the nature and severity of the child pathology, significant parental attitudes according to the above conceptional model, and focal areas of conflict and disturbed patterns of interaction. No claim is made that proper dynamic psychiatric diagnosis cannot be established using other exploratory ways, e.g. absolutely separate interviews of the different members of the family. Our only point is that in our clinical experience, the conjoint family session, along with the parallel family, subgroups and individual interviews, constituted an expeditious, safe, and valuable procedure, which allowed the clinician to experience concretely the family dynamics and arrive at a comprehensive diagnostic assessment.

Diagnosis and treatment are interwoven even in the early interviews. In order to achieve adequate diagnostic evaluation, the clinician plays a leading active role by focusing problems, asking questions, confronting behavior and feelings of the members of the family and giving opportunity of self-expression to the child and the parents. The diagnostic procedure, which is meant to attain clarification of feelings, attitudes, definition of roles and identification of areas of conflict, has obvious concomitant therapeutic implications. The following are two summarized examples of family diagnostic interviews to illustrate our approach.

CASE I

Ruth, 9 years old, an intelligent Kibbutz child, was referred on account of a severe problem of encopresis. The soiling started at the age of 4 and became gradually worse to the extent that not less than ten times a day she would defecate in her clothes and hide the soiled underwear in different places. Both parents, especially the mother, were extremely concerned about the intense soiling which they assumed to be caused by an unrecognized physical condition. The mother complained that the child did not get enough attention and physical care at the Kibbutz children's house. She strongly criticized the Kibbutz nurses, blaming them of neglecting her daughter mainly in regard to bowel care, food needs and physical health. Both parents spent one hour every day out of the three hours of shared time of children and parents, cleaning Ruth's gluteal skin. Ruth was repeatedly examined by different physicians and underwent all the possible laboratory and radiologic tests, which did not disclose any organic findings.

Both parents very reluctantly accepted the suggestion to come together with the child for a psychiatric joint-talk. The family interview gave a vivid picture of the family interaction as well as of the separate individual psychopathology providing the necessary diagnostic clues to determine the treatment plan.

The mother took over the initiative to express her extreme concern regarding the child's soiling. Meanwhile, Ruth started drawing a pretty girl, whom she named "The Queen." She would alternately draw and participate in the talk. While the mother voiced her concern, Ruth smiled and did not appear to be particularly preoccupied with the soiling. She even agreed with me when I pointed out that she seemed to be unaffected and even pleased regarding the problem which worried her mother so much. Ruth hurried to add that she did not wish to be worried like her mother, who was constantly worried not only about the soiling, but also about everything around her. The mother brought up several recent examples to justify her concern about the physical well being of the daughter. She had tried hard but unsuccessfully to get Ruth's cooperation in improving her food habits, to visit the toilet room more frequently, to walk in an erect position to avoid backbone deformities, to keep her hair combed, etc. As the mother went on expressing her disappointment, anger and concern about the antagonistic response of Ruth to her oversolicitous attention and devotion, the girl reacted with open hostility towards her mother and accused her of tyrannical and incessant attempts to control her body and actions. Ruth had already finished the drawing. She identified herself with the queen figure, displaying her own feeling of narcissistic pleasure and omnipotent control of her parents. The active role of both the mother and the child in creating an ambivalent interlocked situation of mutual antagonistic dependency became obvious. The father adopted a passive attitude of submissive agreement with the arguments and criticism of the mother. However, he was able to point out the extreme degree of mutual aggression and oppositional response in the mother-daughter interaction. He had not yet completed his point of view when the mother interrupted with a heavy criticism on some minor attempt of his to influence Ruth's sloppiness. The father accepted the criticism and reassumed his passive attitude. This and similar incidents in the current interaction of both parents served to illustrate the almost complete surrender of the paternal role, as determined by a combination of the passive personality of the father and his active exclusion by the monopolizing-hostile control of the mother.

Ruth's reproaches concerning the excessive and oppressing maternal interference led to a counter-attack on the part of the mother, who brought evidence to show the daughter's initiative in having the mother constantly taking care of her as if she were a little child. For instance, Ruth would not do anything to clean up after soiling, or she would expect parental initiative with regard to activities and games as long as she remained in her parents' home. It was easily elicited that the mutual aggressiveness in the mother-child relationship as seen in the everyday struggle for the goal of control was not aimed at achieving real autonomy and more mature patterns of behavior in the child but actually served the purpose of ambivalent dependency at an early childish fixated level. At this point in the first joint interview each one of the family members was able to accept—not only intellectually but also emotionally—the relation between the soiling problem and the family conflict. It became clear that for some reason to be disclosed in the course of the treatment, the soiling and health concern constituted an important way of communication and feeling interchange for the entire family. The need of psychotherapy for the whole family was recognized and accepted.

This summarized version of the highlights of the family interview may suffice to illustrate the possibility of utilizing the "here and now" interaction of the family to arrive at a good comprehensive diagnostic understanding.

The soiling proved to be one of several symptomatic expressions of a marked infantile fixation with an already structured child neurotic conflict. The mother-child relationship appeared characterized by an affective barrier, hidden rejection, and neurotic need of the mother to foster control and dependency. The strong ambivalent tie between mother and daughter was enhanced by the severe neurosis of the mother, who used obsessive health concern and physical overstimulation of the child as displaced expression of aggressive behavior. The father appeared as a personality problem, the passive-aggressive type, inadequate in his double role of father and husband.

CASE II

David, 13 years old, was referred to the Child Guidance Clinic of the Kibbutzim because of long-standing uncontrollable aggressive outbursts directed against his parents, his younger brother, teachers and peers. The aggressive behavior was considered severe to such an extent that following several unsuccessful trials of individual child psychotherapy and parental case work, the psychotherapist and the teacher agreed that residential treatment remained the only workable alternative. The family was sent for a joint psychiatric diagnostic assessment as a required formal step before implementing the recommended suggestion.

The boy's aggressive outbursts were characterized by extreme loss of control incongruent with the mild precipitating event which preceded it. A minor critical observation or an unexpected friendly touch or stroke coming from a child or a grown up could be enough to make him unmanageable, destructive, involved in serious physical fighting, biting, throwing stones, with the impossibility of reaching him through words and often requiring forceful restraint. After each one of these frequent aggressive attacks, David would avoid any social contact, sometimes for several days. Then he would wander around without attending school and even without visiting his parents. In spite of an average intelligence, he did poorly in all his school work. He was unable to sit still for more than a few minutes. Because of his disruptive behavior, he was socially isolated. His truancy was rather welcomed since David's school attendance constituted a source of constant trouble in the classroom. Persistent nocturnal enuresis was also an accompanying symptom.

At the initial joint family interview, which was attended by both parents and the boy, David looked like a weak, frightened, insecure child. He was tense and eager to avoid any contact with the psychiatrist. Physically and emotionally David seemed to be the exact contrast of the dangerous figure described in the referral form. The father, a strongly built big man, was extremely upset and puzzled about the meaning and causes of David's aggressiveness. He reported that in his most recent outburst, which had followed a mild critical remark, David had run away for several hours after having broken two window panes in his parents' room and had shouted coarse insults at the parents. The father said that he had done his best all along, using all possible corrective measures he knew from his own disturbed childhood experience to improve David's behavior. Although he was against corporal punishment, and knew that the Kibbutz strongly disapproved of it, he found it impossible to avoid when David's misdeeds assumed such a serious proportion. By now, things were out of control and fear of punishment did not work anymore. The relationship between the boy and the parents could not be more strained and full of quarrelling and bitterness. The father did not hide his fear that David was on the way to becoming a delinquent.

David did not attempt to defend himself; he appeared to be quite overwhelmed by the severe accusations, bent his head, and appeared to be engaged in some scribbling. David broke his silence when I mentioned the fact that the aggressive outbursts always followed a situation in which he felt hurt or attacked. David wholeheartedly agreed, and with my encouragement and support, he was able to express his feelings, although the verbal communication remained greatly restricted because of his severe anxiety. He felt as if he was constantly scrutinized, criticized and attacked. Asked if his "attacks"—as he called them—appeared always after physical provocation or threat, David replied that they could also occur after children called him names. With some encouragement, he mentioned some of the names which aroused his anger and tension. All of them were derogatory names used by the kids to state that David was mentally retarded or crazy. When the therapist focused on the child's inability to maintain emotional equilibrium under minor physical or verbal stress experiences, the father revealed unexpected understanding and acceptance of David's difficulties, which he compared with parallel behavior characteristics and reactions of his own. The mother hastily accepted the analogy drawn by the father between his son and himself, and she criticized both of them for their common loss of control. She reported cases of out-of-control paternal reactions to David's behavior, like severe beating and threats to send him away or even to kill him. She mentioned all this with very little feeling, objectively presenting facts which were unacceptable from a logical point of view. The mother insisted she could not see any relation between David's uncontrolled reactions and the preceding events. She appeared emotionally cold, with rigid standards, critically watchful in a very nagging way over David's failure in school performance, personal care and cleanliness. She brought up several incidents to prove her thesis that David was the only one to be blamed. David became very restless and anxious. It was easy to point out and connect his increased tension with the overloaded shower of maternal criticism.

The obvious contrast between David's fearful appearance and lack of self-assertiveness, which seemed to be a primary component of the child's personality, and the hyperaggressiveness, which appeared to be of a reactive type, constituted another focal theme in the family-therapist interaction. The father felt that to some degree there was realistic justification in David's feeling of fright of being constantly under attack. He expressed his own ever present concern and fear regarding David's future social adjustment and hinted that his own father had exactly the same concern. He remembered having spanked David when he was less than three years old, as punishment for the "stealing" of a box of expensive sweets. The father was able to recognize that neither his corrective punitive approach nor his wife's constant criticism proved in any way to be useful to prevent or change David s disturbances. At this point in the family interview, the father and the son had gained enough insight to recognize the close relationship between the aggressive outbursts, the running away, the tension and physical restlessness, on the one hand, and David's chronic as well as acute panicky fears, on the other hand. The father was also able to perceive that the fears of the child were obviously determined and affected by the total family interaction. It took longer to obtain a similar insight gain on the part of the mother.

From a diagnostic point of view, the joint family interview enabled the formulation of an integrative diagnosis. The problems of the child were labeled as a combination of severe primary behavior disorders with an already internalized anxiety neurotic reaction. Acute anxiety attacks constituted a very prominent part of the clinical picture. The fear of being bodily and mentally damaged together with a poor self image and low self esteem also appeared in the course of the first family session. In the separate interview with the child, which followed the joint session, David became reticent but was cooperative in joining the psychiatrist in a shared game of drawing—transforming meaningless scribbling into a subject of his own choice. David drew over and over again pitiful figures of ugly deformed clowns and he identified himself with them in his verbal explanation of the drawing.

The father's insecurity and fears of his own loss of control were partly shifted to the child through constant checking, restriction and punitive correction of misbehavior. From a formal diagnostic standpoint, the family interview produced enough clues to categorize him as a character disorder in the sense of an emotionally unstable personality. Although essentially the father accepted the child and had a positive feeling towards him, the father-child communication was blocked as a consequence of the paternal fear of delinquent behavior which contributed to fixate the antisocial child responses. The paternal aggressive loss of control served as a model of identification for the child as well as a source of acute anxiety regarding body integrity.

In the light of the joint family interview, the mother appeared as a neurotic, compulsively rigid personality, unable to give affection in her double role of wife and mother. The marked deficit in maternal loving care and warmth seemed to play an important etiologic role in the inability of the child to use other social attachments in the Kibbutz group situation in order to correct the emotional deprivation in the family life.

Incidentally, the child was not sent to a residential center. Instead, family therapy, which included frequent contacts with the teacher and nurse, was recommended and carried out during two years on a once-a-week ambulatory basis. The outcome of David's treatment was excellent. His anxiety state, aggressive outbursts and antisocial behavior completely disappeared. He did integrate into his social age group and was able to find his way back to a normal school and work life. The relationship with both parents, particularly with the father, became a very positive one. The whole family is presently functioning at a more mature level of cohesiveness and mutual understanding.

THE THERAPEUTIC APPROACH AND ITS CONTENT

It appears to be an established truth that along with the differences and areas of disagreement discernible in each of the diverse methods of psychotherapy, one may recognize effective elements and factors which lack specificity and are common to the manifold therapeutic approaches (6). It should be properly acknowledged that very often it becomes impossible in the course of therapy to evaluate separately the relative weight and priority of both the specific and the common factors present in all psychotherapy. We still do not know in clinical practice how to measure and weigh separately significant effectiveness of each of the partial multiple components of any psychotherapeutic method. We assume that all forms of family therapy are not an exception to the general rule that common factors present in every system of psychotherapy need to be considered as contributory elements in the clinical results. Obviously all types of therapy are apt to exert a positive placebo effect since distress, anxiety, and helplessness lead the patient to invest any healing method with the so much needed protective power ascribed to the therapist. We should not forget that all degrees of improvement, sometimes permanent or sustained positive changes, may be obtained as a by-product of the positive therapeutic relationship, which leads the patient to an emotionally charged identification with the therapist's aim of more adequate, healthy and mature behavior.

In this paper, we do not consider necessary to enumerate and evaluate the generic therapeutic factors which appear as a common denominator in all psychotherapy including naturally our own clinical method of family therapy. Instead, we are interested in focusing on the more specific elements of our therapeutic approach, which aims essentially at obtaining a sound understanding of the nature of the family clash and the present sources of stress and anxiety in order to help attain improved interpersonal relations of the entire family.

We strongly believe that chances to achieve significant therapeutic gains increase considerably if the different members of the family are helped from the very beginning of the therapeutic transactional process to understand, face and recognize the essential areas of family conflict. Through the joint interaction of the family and the therapist, a clear-cut definition of the basic problems which are under discussion should be obtained at the more convenient level of communication suitable for each member of the family group. Active intervention of the therapist is required to define the conflicts and expose the close interdependence, mutual influence and contagiousness of the individual feelings, attitudes and behavior of the different members of the family. These two preliminary insight gains—the precise definition of the conflict and problems for which solution is sought and the awareness of a complementary role in the emotional integration and disintegration of the family—seem to be of fundamental importance in our clinical practice. This is valid not only for the adult members of the family but also for children over the age of five, even if the essential channel of communication is maintained through play activity with minimal verbalization on the part of the child. Actually, the same applies to adults with low socio-cultural standards, poor capacity of conceptualization and reduced aptitude of verbal communication. In our experience, these types of families require a much more intensive interference and distinct verbal activity on the part of the therapist in the family interview than is usually necessary with relatively sophisticated patients. In these cases, the clinician has to learn to restrict his vocabulary and express himself in a concrete, concise language, parallel to the patient's way of communication, so as to make possible an adequate translation of the interaction and the full understanding of the above mentioned double aim.

In our experience, there is a substantial parallel relation between the achievement of adequate recognition and understanding of the basic conflict motivating the family crisis and the degree of therapeutic success. This relation is vividly clear in instances of more or less acute family crises. Once the conflict and symptoms have been freed from their previous mysterious, threatening quality and a new realistic level of understanding of the problem has been achieved, ability to master anxiety would be considerably reinforced. In our clinical work at the Kibbutz and Haifa clinical settings, we have often witnessed the rapid resolution or improvement of distressing conflicts after a family shared a clear picture of the essential basic issue as it emerged in the therapeutic process. Among multiple clinical examples to illustrate this point, we would like to present, in the most concise way, the bare outlines of three cases of children coming from totally different socio-cultural backgrounds.

Ephraim, a Yemenite boy, 11 years old, was brought to the clinic by his distressed parents—simple, honest, unlearned, hardworking laborers—who demanded "the doctor's help and advice" because of the boy's stubborn refusal to go to school for the past six months, his aggressive behavior towards his siblings and his moderate stealing at home and in the neighbourhood. Sara, a bright 9 year old girl, was referred to the psychiatric clinic by her parents after having been involved, for about one year, in repeated stealing episodes which puzzled and concerned them very much. Further history revealed overeating, diverse fears and low school achievement despite her superior intelligence. Both parents were busy, successful, highly educated professional people. The third child, Joseph, an 11 year old Kibbutz boy, was referred to the psychiatrist by a general practitioner, who had formerly suspected a viral encephalitis which was not confirmed by continued clinical control and laboratory tests. After convalescing from a mild virus infection, Joseph refused to leave his parents' room to return to school activities, complained of severe headaches and had frequent crying spells. Having eliminated the possibility of organic illness, the child was referred for psychiatric advice together with his parents, who were devoted, average members of the Kibbutz with a high school education. They were seen three months after the beginning of the acute symptoms.

Although there were many specific features associated with each particular family, a common fact was the extreme bewilderment of the family group—parents and child—regarding the meaning of the presenting problems. Family perplexity and confusion considerably increased the level of anxiety. In all three cases, the joint family interview made it possible to identify and unmask clearly, at the very beginning of the therapeutic process, a situation of acute separation anxiety and fear of desertion fostered by current parental attitudes and activated by specific precipitating events (birth of sibling; trip of one of the parents; restriction of parent-child contact because of change in the parent's work schedule; illness, etc.). When ambiguity regarding the significance of the disturbed behavior and symptoms was replaced by a clear-cut emotional and rational recognition of the sources and sense of the distressing troubles, the anxiety elicited by uncertainty became obviously reduced. Every one of the members of the family felt his fears alleviated, now being able to face a concrete enemy after having experienced the tortures of an obscure perplexing Kafka's trial. In all three children, the referral symptoms disappeared within a month of family therapy. Clinical improvement was sustained as shown by the follow up for two years.

The group family situation can and should be used as an efficient tool to reduce individual distortion concerning reason for treatment and self role perception in the family conflict. In individual therapy, the patient seems to be able to preserve longer a distorted self-image through the one-way use of denial, displacement and projection. The lack of reciprocal confrontation often permits the maintainance of a passive role of self justification, in which case psychotherapy might constitute a shelter whose main function is to give insight on the "deep roots" of the problem without opening avenues for the active solution of the conflict.

We try, by all means, to avoid the neutral benevolent position in therapy where the patient is totally accepted—including his immature attitudes and behavior. More than once we have met patients who had already undergone individual psychotherapy and continued to keep the genuine conviction that therapy in some way means identification or sympathy with symptoms and absolution of individual responsibility for actions. A girl, 19 years old, whom I saw after two years of unsuccessful psychotherapy because of severe problems of antisocial behavior, expressed sincere surprise at the first joint family session when her own active role and responsibility were disclosed. She stated that for two years she had felt she was entitled to act as a rebel against parents and society, since she understood from the treatment that her symptoms had an adequate psychological explanation which justified them.

The initial joint family interview has considerable importance in the step-by-step family therapy sequence. The meaning, procedure and goals of family therapy need to be conveyed to the whole family from the very beginning of the therapeutic process in such a way that every one, including the child, will be able to assimilate the therapist's expectancies in all these respects. No secret is made by the therapist of his own set of expectations in the focused transaction between himself and the family members. He constantly encourages facing therapy as a *shared* exploration of the basic characteristics of family relationships so as to arrive at a *shared* evaluation and eventually to positive changes with regard to distressing areas of conflict, ways of expression of anxiety, forms of defense against anxiety and distorted image of the self in the family conflictual interplay. The therapist should also be alert to pick up and answer, in the first joint session, any individual misconception or specific fear regarding treatment. He should be prepared to deal actively with the emotional reaction displayed by the child—should it be anger, fear, withdrawal or whatever else in response to feelings and anxieties aroused by therapy. These feelings are commonly aggravated by the usual inappropriate, coercive or confusing means and explanations utilized by parents to bring the child to the clinic. Every member of the family is expected to feel and understand that the therapeutic group constitutes a safe framework within which no one enjoys special status. It is a setting where the therapist actively discourages any attempt to identify psychotherapy with a trial where blame is allocated as individuals judged in white or black colors.

Once a reasonable understanding of the essence and nature of the family conflict has been achieved by the separate family members at the beginning of treatment, the subsequent group and individual sessions serve as a gradually progressive process of reality clarification to bring further gains in the awareness of factors, reactions and situations which preserve or aggravate the conflict. Parallel to the progress in distinguishing the meaning of the emotional attitudes and symptomatic responses of the other family members, the individual patient in the family group is expected to become more sensitive in perceiving his own active role in determining or aggravating other's reactions. Gradually the parents and the child are enabled to face, uncover, and do something about the motivational aspect of each one's behavior. They are expected to achieve increased mastery in understanding what lies behind the patient's deviation of behavior, whether expressed in aggressive actions, disobedience, acute fears, psychosomatic complaints or any other symptomatic response. Confusion in role perception may be detected and interpreted more accurately and effectively in the emotionally charged family-therapist interaction. The unrealistic self-image of superlative good mothering on the grounds of sacrificing attitudes, overconcern, excessive control and constant nagging can be easily perceived and grasped, free of contamination in the family interaction, as aggression which gives place to anxiety, counter aggressive behavior and guilt feelings. The disturbed patterns of family interaction are apt to be improved through the active intervention of the therapist who uses this reality confrontation technique to help the family members find out, analyze and cope with anxiety producing situations and factors in a common attempt of seeking ways for new modes of healthier family adjustment.

The improved interpersonal conflict in family relationships may eventually have a noticeable positive impact on the individual intrapsychic conflict, although the need for further individual treatment has to be considered for the specific case. As it has been previously stated, we have learned from clinical experience that there are no two families to which the same therapeutic sequence can be applied. Flexibility on the part of the therapist in planning the respective distribution, frequency and duration of joint and individual therapy remains a major clinical fact.

In this paper, we do not attempt to review and assess the percentage of successful outcomes achieved with our specific technique. A preliminary report on the results of short-term family therapy in a group of 29 families has been presented previously (1). At this point we have treated and followed up 60 families, two thirds of them on a short-term treatment basis. A comprehensive evaluation of results of family therapy in our clinical experience will be discussed in a separate paper. Here we can only corroborate our preliminary conclusion that in more than three quarters of the cases of both groups—Kibbutz and urban families—this therapeutic method was demonstrated to be a highly effective form of treatment leading to a definite improvement as shown by more mature family functioning and total disappearance of the central symptoms and referral problems.

REFERENCES

1. KAFFMAN, M., "Short Term Family Therapy," *Fam. Proc.*, **2**, 216–234, 1963.
2. SPIRO, M. E., *Children of the Kibbutz*, Cambridge, Harvard University Press, 1958.
3. KAFFMAN, M., "Children of the Kibbutz: Clinical Observations," in Masserman, J. H. (Ed.), *Current Psychiatric Therapies*, **3**, 171–179, New York, Grune and Stratton, 1963.
4. HOLLINGSHEAD, A. B. and REDLICH, F. C., *Social Class and Mental Illness*, New York, Wiley, 1958.
5. *Diagnostic and Statistical Manual Mental Disorders*, Washington, American Psychiatric Association, 1952.
6. FRANK, J. D., *Persuasion and Healing*, Baltimore, Johns Hopkins Press, 1961.

6

Adolescent Problems: A Symptom of Family Disorder

NATHAN W. ACKERMAN, M.D.

THE ADOLESCENTS OF OUR TIME are hoisting distress signals. In many ways, both direct and indirect, they let the rest of us know that they are in trouble. Their disordered behavior today is an almost universal phenomenon. We have in the United States of America the teenage gangs and beatniks; in England, the "angry young men"; in Germany, the "Bear-Shirts"; in Russia, the "Hoodlums"; in Japan, the split of the teen-agers into "wet" and "dry." These are but a few examples of semi-organized group expressions of wide-spread adolescent conflict. Conspicuously in evidence are signs of disorientation, confusion, panic, outbursts of destructiveness and moral deterioration. The disordered behavior of the adolescent needs to be understood not only as an expression of a particular stage of growth, but beyond that, as a symptom of parallel disorder in the patterns of family, society, and culture.

In a setting of world crisis the distress of the adolescent may be viewed as a functional manifestation of the broader pattern of imbalance and turbulence in human relations. The family, as a behavior system, stands intermediate between the individual and culture. It transmits through its adolescent members the disorders that characterize the social system. In our native community we confront the special challenge of the anarchy of youth. The recurrent bursts of bizarre teen-age violence are emblazoned for us in the daily papers and other mass media. This is dramatic and frightening. But the problem embraces far more than juvenile delinquency. While some adolescents explode crudely in extremes of destructive anti-social action, others manifest their distress in a more subtle, indirect and concealed way, no less serious for its inconspicuousness. Fundamentally, what underlies the entire range of disorders is the adolescent's fierce, often failing struggle to find himself in this chaotic world. He is searching for a sense of identity, for a sense of wholeness and continuity, in a society that is itself anything but whole and anything but steady in its movement through time.

But let us not imagine that it is the adolescent only or exclusively who experiences this painful struggle. It is all of us, at all stages of life, who echo in our personal lives the disorder of the social system. The agitation of the adolescent surely does not exist in isolation. It is matched and paralleled by the emotional insecurity of his parents, the imbalance of the relations between them, and the turbulence and instability of the family life as a whole. The family, as family, does not know clearly what it stands for; its resources for solving present day problems and conflicts are deficient. Not only are families confused, disoriented, fragmented and alienated; whole communities sometimes exhibit these same trends.

Let us glance for a moment at the community response when there is an eruption of teen-age destructiveness. Generally, there is an immediate outcry, a show of fright, shock, worry, righteous indignation; then talk and more talk. Soon the excitement simmers down, until the next shocking eruption, and the process repeats itself. The recurrent bursts of savage, inhuman violence among juveniles strike a note of alarm in the community. They stir a deep-rooted anxiety among parents, teachers and community leaders. The community turns desperate. There is a loud call for action, for a program; something must be done. But the demand for action arises not only out of a sense of desperation; it expresses also a profound helplessness, a feeling of sheer impotence to do anything about it. Why? Because the finger of accusation points responsibility not to the delinquent adolescent alone, but to the whole disordered character of the human relations pattern of present-day family and community as well. Yes, there is something deeply wrong, and it is not just with our adolescents; it is with our whole way of life. Our social health is failing; and the effects of the failure cast a long shadow on our mental health.

With each outbreak of juvenile destructiveness comes a spate of suggested remedies—vocational training, work camps, recreational facilities, group activity and guidance programs, and finally, freer use of the big stick, physical punishment at home and in the schools; ultimately, stricter policing and even penalization of the parents who are presumed to be negligent. At the peak of such community agitation, there is much talk and a strong resolve to act, but as is the case with New Year's resolutions, nothing much comes of it. The conviction grows that these measures are mere sops, a feeble attempt to plug the hole in the dam. Then comes widespread disillusionment and finally, perhaps, the grudging admission that the real problem is not the adolescent alone, but rather the sources of disintegrative influence in a sick or broken family. And exactly at this point the loud talk subsides because no one yet has a program to offer for what ails the family. It is this that explains the adults' sense of helpless resignation and their temptation, shame-facedly, to turn away from the problem. In effect, then, these waves of panic and agitation are a kind of shadow boxing. People rant and rave, they lash out at the shadow, but are impotent with the real thing—the disorder of family life itself.

Trends in Juvenile Problems

Let us examine now the range of adolescent symptoms. The outstanding features are: (a) a tendency to anti-social behavior, specifically expressed in acts of violence; in close association, a vulnerability toward mob action with a propensity toward organized prejudice, bullying and scapegoating of innocent victims; (b) a revolution in sexual mores, shown in a tendency to promiscuity; (c) a wave of contagion that makes an obsession of everything "hot"—hot jazz, hot dancing, hot-rods; closely associated with a compulsive quest for an ever new kind of kick, as in the use of such drugs as benzedrine, marijuana and even cocaine; (d) a leaning toward overconformity with the peer group; (e) a quest for a safe niche, a sinecure, a steady job with a pension in industry, a "couple of little mothers" as they say in teenage jargon; a split-level home with an electrified kitchen in suburbia; (f) a tendency to withdrawal; a closely associated tendency toward a loss of hope and faith, disillusionment and despair with a gradual destruction of ideals; a conspicuous product of this trend is the static mindedness of many adolescents, the lack of adventuresomeness and loss of creative spark; (g) disorientation in the relations of the adolescent with family and community; an inability to harmonize his personal life with the goals of family and society; in consequence, a trend toward confusion or loss of personal identity; (h) as the outcome of this magnified social disorder, the intensified vulnerability of adolescents toward mental breakdown.

THE ANARCHY OF YOUTH in contemporary society is a thorny problem. Since 1948 there has been an over-all increase of juvenile delinquency of over 70%, although the child population has increased only 16%. Since 1950, this represents a rise four times as fast as the population. F.B.I. data show that a sizable percentage of the major aggressive felonies (murder, manslaughter, rape, assault, robbery, larceny and automobile theft) are committed by young people under the age of 18. In 1956, the youth in this age group accounted for 45% of all arrests for such crimes, and two-fifths of these offenders were under 15. According to the F.B.I., the number of killings committed by juveniles continues to rise. About half of these young killers are under 18, and one-third are children below 16. It is estimated that by 1965, more than a million children will appear before the courts. As J. Edgar Hoover puts it, "Gang style ferocity, once the domain of hardened adult criminals, now centers chiefly on cliques of teen-age brigands."

A psychiatrist, Dr. Wertham, expressed his alarm a different way: "This is the age of violence and it began with the dropping of the first atom bomb on Hiroshima ... younger and younger children commit more and more serious and violent acts ... the current spate of child murders is like the difference between a disease and an epidemic. One such killing would be a crime, but ten or a hundred or a thousand, that is a social phenomenon."

Three main features can be discerned in this trend: the gross numerical increase of these acts of violence, the deepening severity of these acts, and the universality of the trend, as many nations throughout the world affirm the findings of the F.B.I.

A few illustrations: Not long ago, the public was stunned by the strange tragedy of Cheryl Turner Crane, her actress mother, Lana Turner, and her broken family. The pathos of this story is still sharply etched in our memory. Shortly after this event, I saw in consultation a friend of Cheryl Turner's, a young girl of 13. She had just tried to poison her father's whiskey.

In *The New York Times* there appeared the following item: A young army man, assigned to security work, was found dead in the burned wreckage of his car. He had sprayed the interior of his car with gasoline, poured gasoline all over himself and then set fire. What possibly could have been this young man's state of mind to induce this fiendishly violent form of suicide?

Again, not long ago, we were struck with horror by the photographs of that fanatic Japanese boy who stabbed to death a leading political figure.

ANOTHER ASPECT OF THE ANARCHY of youth is the tendency to indiscriminate sexual behavior. Mostly the grown-ups in the community are loath to look squarely at this problem, not because it is sex, but rather because it is sex in such a shocking form. It is the subhuman or even inhuman quality of adolescent sexual conduct that compels us to turn our faces away. There are the recurrent reports of organized sex clubs for teen-agers, group orgies that combine violence and indiscriminate sexual indulgence. Such behavior is not in any sense confined to members of any one social class, certainly not confined to the working class or the uneducated. It also appears in our institutions of higher learning, the universities. In occasional instances a single disturbed girl in a college dormitory can wreak havoc with the student population, not only by multiple seduction of college boys, but also by disrupting the sexual standards of the female students. In such situations, the college authorities are hard put to know what to do. The dean and faculty have no desire to inflict harsh punishment, but neither can they permit a contagion of disorganized, irresponsible sex orgies. The community demands action and somebody's head must roll. Frequently enough, the reputation of innocent persons is hurt.

Closely related, emotionally speaking, is the almost hypnotic trance into which adolescents fall as they become absorbed in hot music, hot dancing, hot-rods and the crazy craving for ever new kinds of thrill and excitation, even the use of narcotic drugs. Observers have been forcibly struck by the madness that seems to take hold of these young people. It is as if they are caught in a spell. At the very peak, they become transformed into elemental beings and are oblivious to all else but the excitement of their senses. They seem to be drawn off to another world. Most of them recover, to be sure; for some, however, there is a point of no return.

Of course, it is not one-sidedly implied here that such behavior is purely regressive and emotionally sick. It is only to be expected that the adolescent should have hot blood and venture forth in the search for the rhythm of life. It is normal for them to try to capture the rhythm of life for themselves; in fact, to become one with it. In many instances, it is surely true that an active quest for Nature's rhythm brings an enormous relief of tension and actually offsets the danger of destructive outbursts. If adolescents can feel the rhythm of life down to their bone marrow, they can more easily reorient their bodily surgings to the existing world and do so in more constructive ways.

AT THE OPPOSITE EXTREME there is a tendency toward a rigid conformity with the standards and expectations of the peer group. Such behavior is mostly undramatic and inconspicuous. It is nevertheless important insofar as it reflects the severity of the pressure to conformity, even to the extent of the adolescent's experiencing a submergence or loss of his individual self. In the extreme, this is exemplified by the fashions of the zoot-suiters, the black stocking fad, the contests involving the swallowing of gold fish and the squeezing of college boys like sardines into a phone booth. Also, the habit of going steady and getting pinned, just because everyone else is doing it. This leaning towards submission to the peer group constitutes a danger precisely because of its implied renunciation of qualities of individual uniqueness and difference.

A GREAT SEGMENT of the adolescent population is turning painfully cautious and conservative. In a topsy-turvy world with a radical change proceeding at a galloping pace, adolescents paradoxically turn cautious. They want to hold the world still long enough to catch up with it. So we see them seeking routine, dependable safe jobs in industry. They become scared of adventure, withdraw from the center of strife and turmoil, pull away from politics, move to the suburbs and raise babies. They become good organization men, but they lose their sense of adventure and surrender their creative dreams.

The adolescent experiences the greatest hardship in building a satisfying sense of personal identity. He is pained by his failing effort to harmonize his personal life goals with the goals of family and community. This induces in him a terrible dilemma. It is almost a commonplace that adolescents in our day cannot say who they are, where they belong, where they are going in life. They complain of a sense of emptiness, futility, and boredom—so why try!

Then there is a tendency of the adolescent to flee from conflict into a state of isolation and withdrawal. Often some depression is linked to this withdrawal. Both of these tendencies serve the purpose of self-preservation in the face of excessive conflict and anxiety. However, these efforts boomerang insofar as they can be indulged only up to a point and at the cost of progressive weakening of the personality. One manifestation of this withdrawal is the inability to face up to the urgent life questions such as boy-girl relations and choice of career. On the part of many adolescents, there is an urge to escape from these necessary decisions, or at least to stall them.

From still another angle, there is the frequent trend toward loss of faith or resignation to the defeats of life, a disintegration of ideals, and a shift of mood toward cynicism. This is especially evident in relation to the future rewards of work and family life. It is conspicuously manifested in attitudes of disillusionment toward authority figures—parents, community and political leaders. Sometimes there is a cynical rejection of interest in the larger affairs of community, nation and world.

From all this there are serious consequences; the social disorders of the adolescents tend ultimately to sexual deviation and mental breakdown. In our time there is a tendency not only toward a rising incidence of breakdown, but also toward an increasing severity of breakdown.

So FAR I HAVE HAD TO INDULGE in some sweeping generalizations, which inevitably carry with them unavoidable risks of misunderstanding. There is the whole question of establishing the distinction of normal and abnormal adolescent behavior. Let us therefore introduce a few needed qualifications. A healthy, vibrant, sparkling adolescent is a pleasure to behold. There are still enough of them, even in our troubled world. Adolescent behavior is characterized by enormous variability. Within this range, it is entirely possible for a healthy teenager for a time to exhibit some of the above trends and yet recover his emotional balance, relatively untouched and unharmed. This is simply a phase of growth. In most instances the tendency toward such disturbance is mild, transitory, benign and reversible. It is influenced by a multiplicity of factors—social, economic, cultural, geographic, familial and personal. Of central importance, of course, is the emotional conditioning of the adolescent within a particular type of family. Nonetheless, while we recognize explicitly that most youngsters survive, the fact remains that these trends represent a distinct vulnerability for the adolescent group as a whole.

What I have described cannot be viewed simply as a phase of the normal growth, the inherent instability of adolescent personality. It is much more than this. The significant source of such disturbance is something outer rather than inner. Basically these adolescent trends are a sign and symptom of a sick kind of family living and a sick community. Significant anthropological studies have demonstrated that adolescents can mature in certain cultures without undergoing critical emotional storms and without serious explosions of destructive conduct. The trend in our particular culture is a dangerous one. It is a disposition to a type of social and emotional disorder that can have profound consequences for mental health.

Illustration of Disturbed Family and Adolescent

Let us view the above adolescent disorders as symptoms of the social psychopathology of the adolescents of our time. We must then make the further step of relating this to the social psychopathology of the family of our time. The misbehavior of the adolescent may be regarded as a symptom of chronic pathology in the whole family. The adolescent acts as a kind of carrier of the germs of conflict in his family. In many instances, he seems to act out in an unrational manner among his extra-familial relationships the conflicts and anxieties of his family, particularly disturbances existing in the relations of his two parents.

The following illustration is typical:

A man of middle years makes an appointment for psychiatric consultation for his 18-year old son. John has flunked out of three schools, cannot concentrate, steals money from his mother, gambles, and while playing truant, escapes to the low-class movie houses on 42nd Street. He is frightened of encounters with homosexual men, and yet paradoxically goes exactly to those places haunted by them. He has been accosted and propositioned by these characters many times.

The psychiatrist requests that the whole family come for an office interview. Instead, John appears only with his mother. When asked, "Where is your father and older brother?" John and his mother in a single voice instantly exclaim, "Oh, you'll never get Pop here. He's against psychiatrists; he doesn't believe in them."

John is a boy of medium height, with attractive, delicate, girlish features. He has almost a baby face. He is nattily dressed and his skin-tight trousers stand out conspicuously. Despite the obvious care invested in clothing, his posture is slouched over, his head is bowed; he observes the interview proceeding in a detached, blank way. Now and then, he bursts into a fit of child-like giggling. He is amused at the silly quarrels between his parents. He thinks his father is cute, puts on quite an act. He handles his body awkwardly. He is self-conscious about his body. He is ashamed of his well-developed breasts and his "big can." He admits his fear of looking like a girl. Therefore, he won't appear in a bathing suit. He is fearful of homosexuals, but also very curious. He is apathetic toward girls. He has only a single interest—gambling; he wants to play the Wall Street game as his father does. His father brags of his talent in gambling. He swears he can beat the Wall Street game. With a false, exhibitionistic modesty, he declares he is a "gambling degenerate."

In subsequent sessions, Pop did come and treatment was begun with the whole family on the assumption that John's disturbance echoed the family disturbance. Pop put on a show. He was a real ham. He insisted on talking for everyone else in the family. He barely gave the others a chance to open their mouths; he intruded on them time and time again. He is a bright, quick, but tense, agitated, overaggressive man. He is plagued by diffuse hypochondriacal fears, cancer, cardiac collapse, bleeding from the rectum, etc. From the word go, the father launched a critical, reproachful, intimidating tirade against his family. In the most dramatic manner, he depicted himself as a hero and a martyr to the family cause. He described vividly how he came up the hard way on the streets of the East Side. He is a devoted father who "gives and gives and gives" to his family out of his pocketbook. He talked of nothing but the dollar, how hard it is to "make a buck," and how his family robs him. They demand more and more; they're never satisfied. He has to make sacrifices to keep "doling out the dough."

Severely provocative, the father stirred his family to counterattack. Mother kept quiet, but her face was depressed, embittered, and a sly contemptuous grin played about the corners of her mouth. She was intensely hostile. It was the older son, Henry, who assumed for the mother the role of attacking the father. He did so viciously. On the other hand, the younger son, John, merely grinned. He felt unable really to talk with his father. He was frightened of him. The only way he could reach him was to love him up physically. Each evening, when his father comes home, John hugs him and kisses the top of his head, he caresses him; sometimes he playfully pokes him in the belly with his fist, or as he says lovingly, "I wring the neck my father hasn't got." Father has a very short neck.

Here is a bird's-eye glimpse of a disturbed family in action, containing one pre-delinquent adolescent boy; a family in which John's failure in school, his stealing, his tendency toward homosexuality, and his insatiable craving to gamble, are symptoms of the disturbance of his entire family group. This disturbance has its origin in certain basic unsolved problems in the relations between mother and father.

From the word go in this marriage, there was trouble. According to father, mother shunned his love, she rejected him sexually, she was cold, ungiving. Mother, on the other hand, declared that he was excessively demanding. For the first week, he did not leave her bedroom. By his own admission, father was afraid to let mother out of his sight because he was jealous of other men. He imagined that she might be unfaithful. On the other hand, mother was filled with bitter feelings against father. He left her alone night after night; he never stayed home, he went out with the boys, drinking and gambling, and looking at other women. He amused himself with dirty pictures and dirty stories. Throughout the entire twenty years of marriage, mother and father could not agree about anything. If mother said white, father said black. Father terrorized mother with his explosive tantrums. She in turn took vengeance in sly, covert ways. She emasculated him. She declared openly for years that he was undersexed. She allied both boys with her against father; she made it three against one. The father felt rejected and exiled. He then turned about to become seductive with his younger son, John. He carried on an open flirtation with him. John became the second woman for his father, substituting for mother. Mother in turn trained her older son, Henry, to be her fighting arm against father.

Disturbances in Social Norms

Now, besides the familial conflicts one must consider the wider disturbances in social norms that reverberate in the behavior of adolescents. Today, the goals of society and family life are unclear. Between the two there is little harmony. In general, human relations are agitated, turbulent, out of balance. Families as families are confused and disoriented; it is difficult to be clear as to aims, ideals and standards. People marry earlier, separate and divorce more frequently. The small nuclear family gets separated from the extended family representations. Grandparents and other relatives fade out of the picture. Mother has no built-in mother's helper, no dependable sustained support for her duties with the children. The family moves about from place to place; it fails to grow roots in the community; it is weakly buttressed by church, school, social services, etc. In effect, there is a long gap between the old and new way of life—a discontinuity from one generation to the next. The connection of the family with its past is severed;

its horizontal supports in the wider community are thin and unpredictable. It cannot see what lies ahead.

The family of our day therefore does not succeed in planning ahead.
It deals with its problems in hit-and-miss fashion; it improvises, it
often reacts in extremes. It fails frequently to achieve a real unity;
parents are confused as to the kind of a world for which they are training their children. The binding power of love and loyalty in family living is fickle and undependable. The contemporary family cannot somehow hold itself together very well. Instead, each member tends to go
his own way.

The emotional climate of the family is often pervaded by mistrust,
doubt and fear; there is less feeling of closeness, less sharing, less intimacy and affection. The symbols of authority, the patterns of cooperation, the division of labor, are confused. No one knows clearly what
to expect of anyone else in the family. There is considerable fuzziness
concerning appropriate behavior for father, mother, and child. Because
of this, it is extremely difficult to maintain the needed balance and
harmony of essential family functions and thus the stability of family
life is thrown into jeopardy.

Since father and mother do not know what to expect of one another,
neither is sure what to expect of the child. Emotional splits develop
within the group; one part of the family sets itself against another.
There is a battle between the generations, or a battle between the sexes.
Under the stress and tension of daily living, the family sacrifices one
essential family function in order to maintain another. Family life
gets rigid, it gets stereotyped; it also grows sterile and static. No longer
is the kitchen the place of cozy exchange of family feeling; instead, it
is the shiny, cold, impersonal, machine-like kitchen. Family relations
get cold and almost dehumanized.

The two parents compete; neither can take the allegiance of the
other for granted. The father tries to be strong, but fails. Mom takes
the dominant position; Pop recedes to the edge of the family. Out in
the world, Pop is a somebody; he counts for something. At home, he
is not sure he has any role to play. According to Loomis, the modern
father is something of a cross between an absentee landlord, a vagrant
and a sap. He pursues what is called the suicidal cult of masculinity.
It is not enough to be man, he must be a superman. The sexual relation
ceases to be love-making; it becomes a proving-ground for technique,
the struggle for competitive dominance. It becomes impersonal, dull,
a hollow ritual; it dies a slow withering death. Within the family, often

it is unclear who is the man and who is the woman. In fact, all the family roles tend to be confused; sometimes the children act like parents, they usurp control. The parents lean on their children for a sense of guidance which they do not derive from other sources. In this way, the natural difference between the two generations becomes obscured.

Parents seem to be afraid to love their children. It is as if loving is losing something they need for themselves. They function with an image of profit and loss in family relations. They fear to sacrifice that which they may need to spend on themselves. They feel that the demands of their children are exorbitant, they project to their children their fears and hates and unwanted qualities of their inner selves; they intimidate and scapegoat their children, and in turn are scapegoated by them. They do not give their children an appropriate sense of responsibility; often they are overprotective. They become self-conscious, stilted professional parents. They compete with their own children and sometimes try to play the role of big brothers and sisters rather than parents. Out of a sense of weakness and guilt they take recourse to manipulation and coercion. Their efforts to discipline the children are feeble and ineffective, and they resort weakly and artificially to devices of deprivation, or so-called reasoning with the child, but have no confidence that the discipline will work.

So, in our adolescents we see anarchy and violence, sexual revolt, excessive conformity, a quest for a safe, secure, unadventurous, uncreative niche in industry, or we see withdrawal, a sense of defeat and cynicism and a loss of faith, hope, and idealism; certainly a profound and bitter disillusionment in the symbols of parental authority. In this setting, the adolescents live out unrationally the elements of conflict, imbalance and destructive competition in the relations of parents and grandparents and also the conflicts between family group and the wider community.

From these considerations, one learns one simple lesson: the disturbed behavior of adolescents is not only a reflection of a personality problem, but also a symptom of a disordered family. The two components must be correlated, the adolescent disturbance and the parallel imbalance in family relationships. One needs to trace the fluid, shifting processes of identity relations of adolescent with family and family with the wider community. More precise diagnosis of these multiple interdependent, interpenetrating sets of influence would enable us to develop a more effective remedy, an appropriate merging of family life education, social service and psychotherapy.

7

Network Therapy—A Developing Concept

ROSS V. SPECK, M.D.
URI RUEVENI, PH.D.

A SOCIAL NETWORK is defined as that group of persons who maintain an ongoing significance in each other's lives by fullfilling specific human needs (5). In working with the social network of a family containing a labelled schizophrenic person, we have sought to assemble all members of the kinship system, all friends of the family and wherever possible friends of kin of the family, plus the neighbors of the nuclear "schizophrenic" family. Experience with about a dozen such social networks would indicate that the typical lower middle class or middle class white urban "schizophrenic" family has the potential to assemble about 40 persons for network meetings.

Previous papers by Speck (1, 2, 3), Speck and Olans (4), Speck and Morong (5) have reported our experiences in treating the social networks of several schizophrenic families. The treatment of four additional social networks in the first six months of 1968 has added further experience particularly in supplying new concepts and methods.

Perhaps psychiatrists have been "hung up" in dealing with single patients, dyads, the nuclear family or small groups for reasons similar to runners a few years ago who did not believe it was possible to do the four minute mile. We have been working on the hypothesis that pathology and schizophrenia involve higher social levels than the nuclear family. We subscribe to a multi-generational transmission process as outlined by Hill (6), Bowen (7), Laing (8), and others.

We believe that significant pathology is present in the kinship system of the schizophrenic, in their friends and in their neighbors. We believe that "madness" is basically a failure in communication and that "mad" modes of communication are maintained in the entire system around the labelled "schizophrenic person" and his family. We begin with the hypothesis that the social network of the schizophrenic family is the main mediator between madness in the culture and madness in the nuclear labelled family. Our goals are to increase the communication within the social network and in particular between individual members of the schizophrenic family and their kin, friends and neighbors.

We conceptualize this process, modified after Bott (9), as tightening the bonds between members of the social network of the nuclear schizophrenic family, loosening the double binds in significant dyads or triads, and tightening the network of relationships within the whole social field. Social networks are composed of persons. The relationships between these persons, in some degrees extremely loose, in others non-existent, make up the web of interconnected relationships within the social network. By simply gathering the network together in one place at one time with the purpose of forming a tighter organization of relationships, potent therapeutic potentials are set in motion. The assembly of the tribe in crisis situations with an expectation that something is about to happen probably had its origins in prehistoric man. Tribal meetings for healing purposes are well known in many widely varying cultures.

Recently, sociologists such as Sussman (10) and others have rediscovered that even in our own culture of nuclear families the extended family kinship system still plays a significant role in the adaptation of nuclear families, sometimes over a period of many years. The extended family kinship system still is overtly acknowledged throughout the entire Eastern Hemisphere as the primary supplier of emotional, physical and economical stability to the younger generations. It has been hypothesized that decreased rates of mental illness and juvenile delinquency result when a person has a large social network which is actively functioning and intervening in one's life. By convening the social network of the schizophrenic family we are reconstituting a forgotten, covert, and often hidden group of persons and relationships. The purpose is to make the entire group as intimately involved as possible in each other's lives and to supply a strong sense of tribe support, reassurance and solidarity.

The Presenting Network Problem

The A family had been treated by conventional family therapy for a few sessions in the past with little success because JoAnn, the twenty-six year old daughter and labeled "schizophrenic person" had refused to attend any of the sessions. The rest of the family lacked sufficient motivation to continue the family therapy or to sufficiently involve JoAnn in the process. Mr. A was an alcoholic and a bright, unsuccessful professional. Mrs. A worked and provided most of the financial support for the family. JoAnn was a single, unemployed, housebound young woman who had only left the home on one or two occasions at night to walk the dog during the past five years. She had never been employed. Verna, her twenty-four year old sister was in graduate school, doing well with her studies, but somewhat shy and timid. It was the family's fond hope that she would someday become a psychiatrist. John, the sixteen year old brother had dropped out of school at the age of twelve and was living a hippie-like existence in a nearby large city.

JoAnn had had several bouts of individual psychiatric therapy beginning in her early childhood and occurring sporadically over a ten year period. Mrs. A and Verna consulted us because of JoAnn's repeated suicidal threats, her refusal to work or leave the house, Mr. A's alcoholism, the strong symbiotic dependency openly admitted between Mrs. A and JoAnn, and John's incipient schizophrenic withdrawal. Verna was complaining that she would never be able to escape the family and that she would become eventually their financial support and their healer. She felt trapped and did not even feel that she would be able to leave town and pursue a career in medicine. She developed a notion that she was being groomed to be a psychiatric healer for her family. Verna put the pressure on her mother to seek help to try and change the family. The network was suggested as the most rational approach to produce change in such a rigidly malfunctioning family system. Our assessment of the situation was that Verna's motivation was insufficient to overcome the deep family resistances to any approach to treatment, including family treatment.

Goals and Rationale

We seek a therapeutic approach which will be effective in modifying the strategy of a schizophrenic patient and which will provide a broad enough matrix to enable emotional encounters on a variety of levels by the network members; which will tighten the interpersonal relationship bonds between network members and provide a therapeutic climate for change. Specifically our approach seeks to, 1. create conditions for a climate of trust and openness among all network members, 2. facilitate and increase interpersonal relationships between the network members themselves as well as between the immediate family members and the network members, 3. focus on the consequences of the patient's behavior within the network setting for the purpose of enabling the patient to begin to modify and possibly cope differently with his destructive strategies, 4. alter the relationships between tribe members in order to change the state of the network as a whole, increasing communications and human relationships, strengthening bonds between people and removing pathological double binds.

PROCEDURES

Six four-hour evening sessions were conducted. The meetings were held in the home of the "schizophrenic" family and responsibility for the arrangement of space as well as invitation of immediate family members, relatives, neighbors and friends was delegated to the family.

Along with the fact that we are dealing with crisis situations where few alternatives aside from hospitalization present themselves, our experience is that there is no particular difficulty in assembling the tribe. When crisis referral is received by one of us we indicate to the referring person, who is usually a member of the nuclear family, that our preference would be to do a tribe treatment and that the family is to get on the phone and call all of the persons who are significant in their lives. The invited persons are told that they are assembling for a tribe meeting in order to help the crisis in the nuclear family. They are also told that there will be a team of professionals present who will structure the meetings and treat the tribe. Recently we have suggested that invited members of the social network be told that they should expect to attend for a minimum of six evenings. Each meeting is held for about four hours on a successive weekly basis.

In the network sessions we are more prone to talk the "not" language of schizophrenia. We are apt to ask the assembled group what they should tell the schizophrenic family *not* to do. It is only in the later phases of the network meeting that we turn to a more secondary process type of advice-giving by the assembled network to the family.

It is possible that one of the problems in schizophrenia is a locking of a failed dialectic (11) (in other words a strong polarity of black versus white is present with no possibility of any synthesis into shades of gray). The task of the group is to get the family inside the dialectic. This structure fits into our theoretical position of remaining at a meta-level to wherever the group is at any given time. The meta-level is the level which forces the polarity to resolution and synthesis. We negate the bind and force it to go to the synthesis.

A) Pre-Session

During the pre-session, which was about a half an hour to fifty minutes before the main session began, group members began to assemble in the house. The therapists arrived early, observed the arrival of network members and installed the tape recorder. They chatted with the immediate family members as well as other network group members, primarily focussing on the latest news related to the family. Attention was paid to gossip and generally interesting comments or observations which could be utilized later on in the main session. We have found that these pre-sessions are extremely useful and colorful, providing a great deal of information which is quite helpful in conducting the six sessions.

B) Main Session

When the entire network was present, the tribe members were asked to assemble into two concentric groups which we called the "inner group" and the "outer group." This structure was used to intensify interpersonal relationships among the network members as well as to facilitate and sensitize the group members to each other and to the "schizophrenic" family. At the end of each of the main sessions, a post-meeting reaction sheet was given to each group member to write, very briefly, his feeling about how the session went that evening, the strong points, the weak points and any other additional comment he might have. Those sheets were not signed but were collected and the contents of the group reactions was copied on large sheets of paper and brought in to the next meeting to be hung on the walls and read to the group. This provided a wealth of material for the group members to interact with.

A Typical Network Meeting

The authors of this paper have been operating recently as a co-therapy team. In addition we have invited two to four other professionals to act as consultants to us. Their role is essentially a training one in network or tribe therapy, but because of the large numbers of persons assembled and the multiplicity of interpersonal events which occur at any one time, it is an advantage to have another group of professionals who can make observations and report these to the team heads so that we can "huddle" at times to plot strategy or change our approach in the operation of the network meetings. Our team members fan out through the living room area of the home, talking to various persons in the network and picking up network gossip or news. We are constantly informed about the state of the network both from the conscious and unconscious point of view by our team members who act as network information gatherers. The network members are told at the beginning that this is not similar to most conventional psychotherapies, that we are dealing with the tribe, that there are no secrets or collusions which will be treated in a confidential manner. We explain that confidences will be violated routinely and that our purpose is to make all communication in the network as overt as possible. Before a social network session begins there is a great air of tension and expectancy in the room. We routinely tape record from the moment we enter the home. Tensions in the group tend to rise and fall. It is exceedingly noisy. It is quite easy to observe when the entire tribe has assembled and at this point we begin our formal meeting. In first sessions we give a ten or fifteen minute talk on the purposes of the network assembly and the goals of the group. In subsequent network meetings we have a network news time in which we bring everyone in the network up to date on all the things which have been happening and all the things which have been said. We purposefully violate all confidences which have been revealed in one-to-one relationships. This tends to heighten the tension among network members.

The network is told that they have assembled to help the family. We then set up an inner group and an outer group with the purpose of sensitizing the entire assembled network to the expression of feeling and intimacy in the large group. We have found that by using an inner and an outer group a type of dialectic is set up in which a polarity of feelings occurs. Splitting the tribe into two concentric groups with different assigned tasks produces an increase in group tension which is desirable in the process of tightening the network. The two critical and competitive groups generate increasing tension which leads to deeper interpersonal involvement and tribe commitment. When the tension between the two groups becomes unbearable, cohesiveness of the whole tribe is facilitated. We have called this process the synthesis.

The inner group starts first and tends to get intimate and strip itself of conventional social defenses. The outer group tends to be very critical of the inner group. The inner-and-outer group technique increases the speed of total group (network) involvement. This we regard as important in the rapid polarization of affects which must occur if a six session treatment of a social network is to be successful. Once a strong polarity has occurred, the therapists work on bringing about a synthesis so that the two groups then unite into one group with strong and cohesive feelings. When this has occurred, hopefully early in the network therapy, the therapists again set up a polarity and a dialectic so that a new movement toward synthesis must occur. With each polarization there tends to be a movement deeper into the material which is dealth with. When the outer group says that the inner group is superficial, a negation dialect is set up so that it provokes the inner group to try harder. The interaction between inner group and outer group makes the outer group try harder in turn. This forces all persons to try to heal each other.

C. Post-Session

Following the main session, the tribe members remained for coffee and usually met in small groups to discuss whatever was important to them. These meetings usually took from a half an hour to an hour after the therapists left the group. Again we felt that these post-sessions provided the group members with a chance to interact on a very informal basis, feel each other out and even talk about the therapists who had just left.

RESULTS

Results of network therapy, as in any other type of psychotherapy, are extremely difficult to measure. That changes occur throughout the network, that individuals change jobs, tighten significant relationships, and become more aware of themselves and others, we have no doubt. The primary goal of our therapy with this particular network was accomplished—the loosening of the symbiosis between JoAnn and her mother. JoAnn, who did not want the network meetings and tried to terminate them, improved rapidly. Prior to the meetings, she only left the house on rare occasions. By the third meeting, JoAnn was employed by a network member. By the sixth meeting she was determined to move to her own apartment (a move which she has since made). For the first time in her life she is interesting in dating. She is currently a very valuable assistant therapist in another network being treated by the authors.

At the sixth network meeting an evaluation questionnaire was administered. The responses revealed that 17 network members felt the network therapy was either a phenomenal or good success. Seven felt it was fairly successful. No one felt that the network therapy was unsuccessful. Seventeen members wished to continue the network meetings after the therapists had finished their task. Two months later, an average of twenty persons were still attending weekly meetings in different member's homes. (These meetings were conducted by the tribe, without the attendance of any professional persons.)

At the sixth session network members felt, according to their answers on the questionnaire, that the strongest points in the network sessions were:

1. "The cooperative communal spirit and desire to help."
2. "Group can be instrumental in helping to change people."
3. "People really caring for each other."
4. "Creation of an atmosphere in which honesty is indispensable."
5. "Unique experience. I appreciated seeing the therapists are more warmly human."
6. "Increased ability to communicate."

Network members felt that JoAnn changed in the following respects:

1. "JoAnn will talk in front of many people."
2. "JoAnn works now. That's a good sign."
3. "JoAnn was encouraged to go out of her home to work."
4. "JoAnn enjoys now more being with people."
5. "JoAnn discovered she has many friends."
6. "JoAnn has been confronted with reality and has been forced to start accepting it."
7. "JoAnn is more animated, more lively."

8. "JoAnn improved socially."
9. "JoAnn finds pleasure in communicating with others, has a more hopeful outlook of life."

Network members felt that JoAnn's father:
1. "Seems more competent and relaxed."
2. "Is alive and more communicative."
3. "Like the cowardly lion of oz, has been given courage."
4. "Has become a man."
5. "Breaks down certain inhibitions."

Network members felt that JoAnn's mother:
1. "Is more satisfied—finally came to grips with the problem."
2. "Has gained much self-confidence."
3. "Sees that her situation can change."

Network members felt that the following had happened to themselves:
1. "Made us realize how many problems we all humans share."
2. "Appreciate family relationships more now."
3. "Enabled me to be less inhibited in expressing feelings."
4. "I don't have to keep everything inside now."
5. "I can see myself more clearly, my 'hangups' are clearer."
6. "I saw my own difficulties mirrored in the father. It helped me tremendously."
7. "These experiences helped me to express myself more openly."
8. "I have been encouraged to communicate."
9. "Helped me to discover a whole new set of compassionate human beings."

SUMMARY

In this paper we have discussed the concept of network therapy of the social network of a "schizophrenic family." Forty network members attended, consisting of the immediate and extended kin, neighbors and friends of the "schizophrenic family." In order to accelerate the network process a variety of sensitivity training techniques were introduced. The network therapy appeared successful in modifying the relationships in the schizophrenic family, in tightening their social network (meetings are still continuing without the attendance of professionals) and in providing a viable social structure for continuing encouragement, support, employment, and avoidance of hospitalization.

REFERENCES

1. SPECK, R., "Psychotherapy of the Social Network of a Schizophrenic Family", *Fam. Proc.*, 6, 208–14, 1967.
2. SPECK, R., "Psychotherapy of Family Social Networks." Paper presented at the Family Therapy Symposium, Medical College of Virginia, Richmond, May, 1967.
3. SPECK, R., "The Politics and Psychotherapy of Mini- and Micro-Groups." Paper presented at Congress on Dialectics of Liberation, London, July, 1967.
4. SPECK, R. and OLANS, J., "The Social Network of the Family of a Schizophrenic: Implications for Social and Preventive Psychiatry," paper presented at the annual meeting of the American Ortho. Assoc., Mar., 1967.
5. SPECK, R. and MORONG, E., "Home-centered Treatment of the Social Network of Schizophrenic Families: Two Approaches," paper presented at annual meeting of the American Psychiatric Assoc., May, 1967.
6. HILL, L., *Psychotherapeutic Intervention in Schizophrenia.* Chicago, Univiersity of Chicago Press, 1955.
7. BOWEN, M., "A Family Concept of Schizophrenia," in Don D. Jackson (Ed.) *The Etiology of Schizophrenia*, New York, Basic Books, 346–372, 1960.
8. LAING, R. and ESTERTON, A., *Sanity, Madness and the Family*, London, Tavistock Publications, Ltd., 1964.
9. BOTT, E., *Family and Social Network*, London, Tavistock Publications, Ltd., 1957.
10. SUSSMAN, M. and BURCHINAL, L., "Kin Family Network," *Marriage and Family Living*, 24, 320–332, 1962.
11. GIOSCIA, V., personal communication, 1968.

8

Family Therapy as Conducted in the Home

ALFRED S. FRIEDMAN, PH.D.

THE HOME VISIT in psychiatry and social work has not always been regarded with favor and has been out of style for many years. Even in the field of general medical practice, it has become a frequent complaint in recent years that it is difficult to get a doctor to come to the home. Now, with the new emphasis on conceptualizing emotional illness in terms of family and social roles, and with the advent of a new family therapy, there is need for reassessment of the place of the home visit. This assessment is indeed being made, and we find that there are some advantages in making the evaluation of the family in its own setting in the home.

Once we have gone out to the home for this purpose, the next question follows naturally: Why not return there regularly and conduct the family therapy on the spot, rather than admitting the primary patient to the hospital? Therapy of some sort can perhaps be conducted in any setting. A more meaningful question might be whether a family unit therapy conducted in the home is more effective than a family therapy conducted in the clinic or hospital; also whether a family therapy in any setting is as effective as individual therapy. We are, however, not in a position as yet to answer these important questions. The necessary controlled comparative studies have not been conducted. This paper will only present some of the initial experiences, and some of the problems that occur in conducting home therapy. These are presented mostly in the form of anecdotes and observations, because we are still in the first data-collecting stage of our knowledge in this field.

FIRST, IT IS NECESSARY to justify why one would ever consider going to the home to conduct therapy in the first place; to present a rationale and make a few speculations about possible advantages of this approach, as follows:

1. There may often be an advantage in maintaining the responsibility for the patient and his illness within the family, and not permitting the family to deny or "exorcise" what it considers to be the sick or "bad" part of itself by sending the patient to the hospital. It is very tempting for the family to push the whole responsibility for this difficult problem onto the doctor, and then perhaps to suffer guilt later for this action. In addition, this hope of escaping the responsibility usually turns out to be only illusory.

2. Many patients are brought unwillingly to the mental hospital by their families by means of subterfuge, threat or force. This does great damage to the relationship and results in a further estrangement of the patient even when it is recommended and clearly indicated. With a withdrawn, housebound patient, the most practical procedure for the situation may be to initiate the family therapy on the spot in the home.

3. Temporary resistances sufficient to break office or clinic therapy may be overcome by this home treatment arrangement, and family members may stay in treatment longer. In a sense, the family becomes a captive patient in the home therapy approach, just as the individual patient becomes when he is hospitalized.

4. The transfer value of a psychotherapy conducted "in vivo" in the real milieu of the family and home, is greater than that of psychotherapy done in the socially isolated context of office or hospital. In conventional therapy the patient has to transfer what he has learned in his therapy, secondarily, over to the relationships with the members of his family.

5. The process of therapy is altered when it moves into the home setting, as a function of the heightened reality context in which the therapy occurs; of the possible participant-observer role of the therapist; the more active involvement of the family members, and the opportunity for immediate analysis of their actual ongoing behavior in the here and now laboratory of family therapy.

THE DIRECT OBSERVATION of the family in the natural background of their own home can bring into quicker focus the significant dynamics in the life of the family, and can be of great service in guiding the treatment. It sometimes serves dramatically to remove the facade of adjustment which the family has been presenting to the therapist, and to the community outside, and makes it possible to deal directly with the family's real problems.

This family myth of adjustment serves the purpose of covering up the basic defect in the parents' marital relationship—as, for example, the fact that they have not been living together as husband and wife for years, or that there has been a significant reversal of their sex role functions in the family. The parents desperately cling to the facade and denial, so that it constitutes a massive resistance in the early stages of family therapy.

The therapist, as a participant-observer, has the opportunity to experience directly the emotional climate of the home, and to see through the facade to the underlying unverbalized family problems. If the therapist contacts the family experience in an actively empathic way, his insight will be more profound and his influence on the family will be greater. The family may respond to him as to an active, guiding and warm parent or grandparent figure. This kind of therapeutic relationship may lead only to a dependency transference cure. It is obviously not an attempt at a psychoanalysis of every family member. But it will be more likely to result in some change from the family's almost impossible stalemated condition. One might contrast the quality of this transference with the transference that develops in the more traditional neutral, aloof role, in which the therapist is more likely to be perceived in the Victorian image of an unobtainable and prohibiting father authority figure.

SOME UNIQUE FEATURES OF HOME THERAPY

I shall now relate a few sample incidents that can occur during family therapy in the home. These incidents obviously would not be as likely to occur in a different therapy setting, and would not be available to add to the therapists' understanding of the family behavior and symptomatology, or for him to make use of in the therapy. All of the following examples are derived from families with an adolescent schizophrenic member and who have been part of a family treatment project, sponsored by Philadelphia Psychiatric Hospital, during the past two years.

A withdrawn schizophrenic girl stayed locked in her bedroom upstairs during the first two sessions in the home and would not come down to join the therapy. The family, after discussing her resistance, became so involved that they marched upstairs in a body to batter down her door and bring her into the therapy. In the therapist's discussion of this incident, there was—first of all—the opportunity for the family to see how they were permitting the patient to maneuver and control them by the use of her illness. In the next session, the therapist started to go up the steps by himself to talk to the patient through the bedroom door. At this point, the mother instinctively ran to the staircase to block the therapist's way. This behavior was very revealing and dramatic, in that the mother had just a few minutes before been proclaiming that the patient needed treatment, and complaining that the patient made no effort to leave the home and make any social contacts. There was opportunity to discuss this incident in connection with the mother's beginning realization that—in part at least—she did not want the patient to get well and that she herself actually would be threatened if the patient were to assert herself and become more successful and outgoing in her behavior.

This same girl patient, at a later phase in therapy, began to dress up and to show some sexual interest in one of the therapists. This time, when she again stayed up in her bedroom during part of one family session, her behavior was discussed with her in terms of her wanting to have the therapist come upstairs and be alone with her. It was also noticed that the patient's new sexual interest and excitability was projected onto the patient's female dog. The dog, during this phase of therapy, would become excited when the therapist walked into the room, would wiggle her body and jump up on his lap.

The mother in this family often complained that the girl would never put on a dress or be properly attired. This was indeed true, but it was later shown that the mother had resisted several requests by the girl over a period of a year to buy her a dress. The girl actually did not have a single dress that could possibly fit her, since she had become very obese during her years at home. The mother had to be challenged by the therapist to produce the girl's dresses before she would accept the fact that this was true. The male therapist found it necessary to assume an active mother role toward the girl, and to discuss the details of her grooming and appearance over several sessions. In this procedure, he presented a model to the family of what a mother-daughter relationship should be like.

Still later, the family dog and family cat both were revealed to have the same phobia that the primary patient had. They rarely went out of the house voluntarily, and they trembled in fear when they were taken near the door. This phobia had started with the mother and had affected all the family members to the extent that it had become a family symptom.

THERE WERE SEVERAL EXAMPLES observed of how family pet animals were made into important transference figures and were humanized to some extent by particular members of the family. In one family, it was observed that whenever the father became particularly anxious or tense during a session, he would reach over for the female family dog and begin to stroke her rather intensely. It was later revealed in the therapy that the tragedy of this father's life was that he had lost a daughter to whom he was most attached when she died at five years of age. He was able to talk about how he had transferred this feeling and attachment to the dog after the girl's death. The therapy team could now understand why it was that this father had originally seriously suggested including the dog as a member of the family and rating the dog on the *Leary Interpersonal Check List*, when these had been originally filled out by the family. The relevant point here is that observation of behavior in relation to family pets can add to the understanding of the family libidinal relationships and to other family dynamics.

In another family, the father was being pressed by the therapist to assert himself more as the male and authority figure in the family. He became quite anxious at this point, and walked over to the cage where the family kept its large tropical bird. He let the bird loose so that it flew around the room, creating such havoc that it completely broke up the therapy session for 15 minutes. Here was resistance to therapy so obvious and dramatic, that hopefully it could be interpreted to even the most naive patient.

In the same family as above, the housebound male schizophrenic patient had the delusional idea that he would die and go straight to Hell if he left the house. He revealed this delusion only at the point that the therapists had gained his confidence sufficiently for him to consider going out for a ride with them in the car. The family priest was also brought into the session to give additional reassurance to the boy against this fear.

MATERIAL RELATING TO FEEDING and eating habits appears to come into family therapy more often when it is conducted in the home. An older male sibling who was characteristically in and out of the sessions and on the fringe of the therapy during the initial phase, would go into the kitchen and take something to eat, so that he could hear what was going on in the family session in the living room, but without being held accountable. In another family, a member would go into the kitchen for just a few minutes to get something to eat or drink whenever he became anxious during the session, and then would be able to return. A mother in one of the families followed the pattern of going to the kitchen and doing some work during part of the session whenever her schizophrenic daughter launched a verbal attack on her. She not only controlled her own aggressive feelings toward the daughter this way, but by this one maneuver, was able to show that she was a good mother in that she was fulfilling her family role in preparing the family meal, and was able to resist the therapy at the same time.

ISSUES OF CLEANLINESS, dress, and bathroom and bedroom behavior also come into the therapy with a greater impact of concrete reality when it is conducted in the home. In general, it appears that the families do not as readily ignore or hide their real ways of living and relating to each other when they are seen in their own homes, as they do when they come to the office.

AS A FINAL EXAMPLE, I shall cite an instance of direct authoritative intervention by the therapy team which the therapists would not have adopted had they been seeing the family in their office. This particular family had participated very actively in a series of "therapeutic" sessions around the kitchen table, in which they indulged in intense mutual recriminations, pointed out each others' faults and projected their problems onto each other. Neither the mother, father, or 25-year-old schizophrenic son showed any sign of improvement or change in their attitudes, but appeared to enjoy the hostile sessions in a sado-masochistic manner. They even held extra "therapy" sessions of this type on their own. The therapists saw that part of the problem in this family was the striking reversal of the usual sex roles in the parents. The mother was extremely dominant and assertive and was, in effect, the head of the household, the leader in the small family business and the man in the family. She was contemptuous of her husband who was an anxious, immature, passive individual. He, the father, wanted to make his son into the little girl he had lost, and the mother just wanted to keep this grown son as a little boy. (She said her mother taught her that the way to get along with men was to treat them as little children; to bully them and to give them a lot of affection so as to fool them and make them believe you are getting down to their level.) The marital sexual relationship had broken down. One of the typical recurring patterns of marital interaction was that she would defy her husband's sexual interest in her, would lock herself in her room, and he would pound on the door and shout in impotent rage that he would get her yet and force her to submit sexually. Such behavior was enacted openly in the presence of the son, and reenacted and discussed in the family therapy sessions.

When the father was challenged by the therapists to put the joint checking account in his own name and to run the business himself, he stated that his wife would kill him if he did this. Mother denied that she would actually kill him, but said she would fight him tooth and nail every step of the way.

Discussion and direct interpretation had proved ineffective. The therapy team considered this family hopeless for the family therapy approach and had about arrived at a decision to terminate after a trial of six months. At this point, no loss could result from an experiment to determine whether any temporary changes could be made in the family relationships. As a final desperate measure, it was decided to try controlling and directing the family authoritatively by giving specific instructions and stating that the therapy would cease if these were not followed.

The instructions were given primarily to mother, as she was considered the one most likely able to change. She was told that she would have to make a major change in her life. She would have to stay out of the business completely, become the wife in the family, obey father in all respects whether she likes it or not, whether he is right or not, have sexual relations with him, and apologize for anything that upset father and try to make him as comfortable as possible. Mother looked quite bleak at this point and tried to protest as usual. But on the insistence of the therapy team and with their reassurance that she was selected for special reasons to be the one to change, she finally agreed. Father was delighted.

The rather amazing thing then happened. In the session of the week following the ultimatium, the family atmosphere was dramatically improved. Mother had followed the instructions almost to the letter. She claimed that she was sincere in her new role, although father could hardly believe this, and that she had actually always wanted to be this womanly way. Both mother and father seemed quite happy, but the son appeared rather uncomfortable with the rapprochement between his parents. He complained mildly that he wasn't getting enough attention from mother.

In the three months that have followed, this striking improvement has been maintained. There has been some minor backsliding and bickering, but never again to the intense destructive degree that had occurred continuously before.

The therapy team had resorted to still another active intervention and manipulation with this family, on an earlier occasion: The schizophrenic son was about to marry a girl in the neighborhood who had recently given birth to a baby, out of wedlock, by another man. The patient had had very little contact with his intended bride. He was fanatically religious and maintained that it was his religious duty to get married. The therapists could see no possible good result of this marriage. The parents made only very weak, ineffectual efforts to stop it. The therapists called in the minister to advise against the marriage, but to no avail. With the marriage date only two weeks off, the decision was made to persuade the intended bride to participate in the family therapy sessions. She did so, and after she observed the patient and the family interaction through two sessions, the marriage plans were mutually cancelled.

SPECIAL PROBLEMS OF HOME THERAPY

The approach of going to the home to conduct family therapy has its own disadvantages and complications, of course, and we are just beginning to learn what some of them are.

One of the first questions that arises is whether the entrance of the therapy team into the home is seen as an invasion of their privacy by the family, whether they feel that they are being spied on, and that their intimate secrets will be exposed. These reactions undoubtedly occur initially, but the therapist does not remain a stranger for long, and he may soon come to be seen as an understanding and helping person. He can, by his own attitude, demonstrate that many of the so-called intimate secrets and confidential matters can be discussed openly with the family, and that the other family members can be trusted to share them. It is in fact, by now, a commonplace observation in work with families, that what one member thought was his secret problem and which he felt had isolated him from the rest of the family, turns out actually not to be a secret at all, but to be common family knowledge.

Secondly, there are certain implications for the power and authority relationships between the therapist and the family that are raised by the therapist going to the home. Not only certain family members, but the therapists as well can be threatened by this situation. Some therapists may interpret the fact that they go to the family rather than having the family come to them, as a reduction of their professional prestige. While the therapist does not have to feel this way about it, it is true that the usual custom is such that, except in an emergency, the patient seeks out the doctor rather than vice versa. If the therapist interprets his going to the family as a narcissistic devaluation, both he and the family are likely to fall into a trap. Some therapists have expressed initial anxiety related to being a visitor sitting in a strange living room rather than being the host in their own office, and have even likened it to feeling like a sitting duck out on a patrol on the front lines of the enemy. But after all, the father of the schizophrenic patient, if he has to go for the first time into the strange forbidding atmosphere of the consulting room, may feel a threat to his status and authority position in his family. It can work either way.

Sometimes the issue of the authority position in the home therapy is played out over the initial seating behavior in the living room, and over the choice of seat which the family offers to the therapist. Some therapists, of course, may not wait to be offered a seat, but may move into the big armchair that is usually father's, and take over the authority role in the situation. When a therapist enters a family situation, he automatically becomes a new important figure of influence in the family, and this will inevitably result in some disturbance of and realignment of the balance of forces that existed between family members at that time. He does not completely avoid this course of events in the therapy, either by trying to sit on the sidelines or to assume a passive role. The entrance of any intruder over a period of time into their midst, particularly one who concentrates on breaking down the barriers, may constitute a threat to the family, and particularly to the parent most responsible for isolating the family from the rest of the community. This will most often be the mother, but it may also be the father. There is, in addition, a specific threat that the father of the family experiences, both in regard to his marital heterosexual role and his role as the supposed leader of the family, when one or two more powerful males than he move into the family situation as therapists. But in a family type of therapy, at least, the therapist is available to discuss this imagined threat with the father and to help him deal with it. If his wife were going to the therapist's private office, the father might experience the same heterosexual threat and have less direct recourse to deal with it.

There are, of course, in addition to the few briefly touched on in this paper, many other problems and issues raised by conducting psychotherapy in the home. Some of them we already perceive, but only vaguely and incompletely as yet. Much careful observation and analysis will be required to delineate them clearly. Additional new issues will undoubtedly appear as the story of family living and family pathology unfolds through the medium of family home therapy. Whether these issues turn out to be advantages or complications in the process of therapy, they will have presented a unique opportunity to learn about family problems and about schizophrenia.

9

The Study
of the Family

DON D. JACKSON, M.D.

FOR THE PAST six years, we at the Mental Research Institute in Palo Alto have been studying family interaction to see whether and how such interaction relates to psychopathology or deviant behavior in one or more family members. The "normal" as well as the "disturbed" family is studied in order to infer conditions conducive to mental health. Our approach has been interaction-oriented because we believe that individual personality, character and deviance are shaped by the individual's relations with his fellows. As the sociologist Shibutani has stated:

> Many of the things men do take a certain form not so much from instincts as from necessity of adjusting to their fellows.... What characterizes the interactionist approach is the contention that human nature and the social order are products of communication.... The direction taken by a person's conduct is seen as something that is constructed in the reciprocal give and take of interdependent men who are adjusting to one another. Further, a man's personality—those distinctive be-

havioral patterns that characterize a given individual—is regarded as developing and being reaffirmed from day to day in his interaction with his associates (14).

Thus, symptoms, defenses, character structure and personality can be seen as terms describing the individual's *typical interactions which occur in response to a particular interpersonal context*. Since the family is the most influential learning context, surely a more detailed study of family process would yield valuable clues to the etiology of such typical modes of interaction.

PROBLEMS OF FAMILY STUDY

Operating from this interactionist view, we began (as did many other family study centers) by studying families which had a schizophrenic member, to see whether or not these families had processes in common.[1] Various projects have since gone on to study families with delinquent, neurotic, or psychosomatically ill members.

Although our original approach—assessment of the family's influence on the individual patient—yielded many useful concepts, hunches, and observations, it also had inherent difficulties and potential fallacies. To study family process *per se* is difficult enough; to try to uncover the origins of pathology inevitably becomes part science and part crystal ball.

Problems of Theory

When searching for one-to-one relationships between an identifiable family process and a characteristic individual response, it must be kept in mind that:

I. The same behavior in two people can spring from quite different interactional causes. Thus, according to the principle of equifinality, different causes may produce similar results; e.g., two different sets of family reactions may each produce a child who steals.

II. Behavior is multi-determined. A child is exposed to a vast number of learning contexts, all of which help to mold behavior.

III. Stress resulting from outside pressures on the family can exacer-

---

[1] Before the formation of the Mental Research Institute in March 1959 I had worked five years with Gregory Bateson on his "Communication in Schizophrenia" project. Jack and Jeanne Bloch, Virginia Patterson and I studied the families of neurotic and autistic children at the Langley Porter Neuropsychiatric Institute from 1953–1956.

bate family processes destructive to a child's development. As a matter of fact, stress may so alter family processes that even after the circumstances producing it have ceased, there may be a "snowball" effect.

IV. Certain variables might be present which help to soften the effect of a destructive family process. A child might, by happy circumstance, escape the family often enough to form a protective relationship with a school teacher, for example. Another child might not come upon such an opportunity.

V. There is a possible importance of so-called constitutional factors, even though such factors are not independently assessable by present methods except in cases of severe mental deficiency.

Most important of all, however, is to remain alert to the fundamental precariousness of using the symptom as a starting point from which to investigate family interaction. Families of schizophrenics, delinquents, and neurotics may be more alike than different, both in their formal structure and in their response to society's discovery that they contain a deviant member. (The Bateson group, when first studying families of schizophrenics, recognized all these problems. We labeled each index case *schizophrenia p* in order to signify: "This is a way of describing the *people* we are observing, and not of describing all schizophrenics.")

When the symptom is used as the starting point, the problem is further compounded by the fact that the psychiatric nosology, or system, for labeling deviance is not only individual-oriented but often idiosyncratic and not clearly related to observed behavior. Psychiatrists are often more interested in pinning the patient with a label than in studying how he got into the spot of being pinned. Psychiatric terms frequently include labels for different kinds of individual behavior, in widely varying interpersonal contexts; for example, the word "delinquent" covers children who steal, rape, beat up others, truant, etc. When labels that are used for individuals are extended to describe a *dyad*, they are unhelpful because they are undifferentiating. For example, the label "sadomasochistic," when applied to a couple, describes little; from our observations, almost all troubled marital pairs can be described this way.

All these impediments to family theory and research can be seen to be variations of two related conceptual issues:[2] individual versus in-

---

[2] To the proponents of a new theory falls the sometimes pedantic and arid, but more often illuminating, task of boring down to basic premises, to conceptual models and meta-

teractional process, and linear versus circular causality. From our resolution of these issues will emerge general criteria of family theory by which the rest of this presentation will be guided.

Individual versus Interactional Process

We have just noted that to focus on a family because of the psychiatric symptom[3] of a family member introduces an inappropriate individual bias, making the analysis of interactional processes more difficult. But even if the object of study is ostensibly the family unit, any examination of the characteristics of the various individual family members remains in the domain of individual theory. When we say that the patient is disturbed but one or both of his parents cause this, or that various family members manifest perceptual, emotional, or cognitive disturbances, or that a family member other than the identified patient is "really" sick—in all these ways we may quantitatively increase the number of individuals under study, but the theory remains individual in orientation. It is only when we attend to *transactions between* individuals as primary data that a qualitative shift in conceptual framework can be achieved. Yet our grasp of such data seems ephemeral; despite our best intentions, clear observations of interactional process fade into the old, individual vocabulary, there to be lost, indistinguishable and heuristically useless. To put the problem another way, we need measures which do not simply sum up individuals into a family unit; we need to measure the characteristics of the supra-individual family unit, characteristics for which we presently have almost no terminology. We can only use this rule of thumb: the whole is more than the sum of its parts, and it is that whole in which we are interested.

Linear versus Circular Causality

Much of the work done in the behavioral (and many other) sciences can be said, essentially, to be devoted to finding *causes* for given observed effects. These causes are supposed to be lineally related to their

theoretical considerations, which those who have a broad framework of agreement, theoretically, need not constantly remind each other of. When alternative premises, methodologies, and data are proposed, the old and the new must be laid out side by side for comparison, and the newcomer has the duty to state with maximum possible clarity just what he does and does not assume.

[3] Or absence thereof, which amounts to the same thing.

effects, i.e., event B happens (or happened) because event A is happening (or previously happened). Since longitudinal studies are, unfortunately, the exception, and cross-sectional or time-sample studies predominate our researches, this assumption has never been adequately tested. Still, despite an embarrassing simultaneity of observation, the "cause" and "effect" are treated as if they occurred in linear series and in the appropriate order. One important concept ignored by this theory is that of *feedback*, which proposes that information about event B impinges on event A, which then affects B, etc., in a circle of events which modify each other. Since psychological "events" seldom occur only once, but rather persist and overlap with maddening complexity, this circular model is often more appropriate than one which artificially abstracts such events from the intricate time sequence in which they occur.

When applied to the family, the notion of linear causality is particularly inappropriate and leads directly to several of the problems outlined earlier, (especially equifinality, multi-determination of behavior and even the process whereby the patient is labeled). Faced with the undeniable fact that family members act constantly on each other, modifying each other's behavior in the most complex ways, a conceptual model which would have us delineate event A from event B, much less put them in causal order, is of little help. Furthermore, such goals are sterile because they must ultimately lead to unanswerable questions such as whether the parents of the schizophrenic are the way they are because they have an organically ill child, or the patient is schizophrenic because of his parents' behavior. The study of *present process* in the family, then, seems both more accurate and more fruitful.

(The "double-bind" theory (3) has been subject to considerable misunderstanding on this issue and provides us with a good example. It was not immediately clear in the original paper that there was no "binder" and no "victim" in the relationship described as a double bind, but rather two binder-victims. This is obvious when one realizes that there is no possible response to a double bind *except* an equally or more paradoxical message, so if neither can escape the relationship, it can be expected to go on and on until it matters little how it all got started. Thus, both for theory and for therapy, we do much better to study the present operation of this pathological interaction than to seek the ultimate villain.)

It follows that the first step must be to study family interaction *per se;* to study interaction patterns in families of *all* kinds, whether or not the family has a labeled symptom-bearer. The goal is to classify families in terms of how they characteristically interact, in other words, to try to build a typology of families. While this is being done it might also be possible to note any one-to-one relationships between certain kinds of family interaction and certain types of individual behavior. Such a task is, of course, Herculean, since one can look at family interaction in a variety of ways and draw from many different theoretical formulations. Our approach has been exploratory and crude. But while polyadic systems are unquestionably more complex than our present research strategies can assess, there is the curious fact that attention to such systems—because of their lawfulness—*simplifies* the observation of human behavior.

FAMILY RULES

Briefly stated, the major assertion of the theory to be outlined here is that *the family is a rule-governed system:* that its members behave among themselves in an organized, repetitive manner and that this patterning of behaviors can be abstracted as a governing principle of family life.

Theoretical Background

Both common sense and clinical observations argue for the organized nature of family interaction. If there were not some circumscription of the infinity of possible behaviors in which its members might conceivably engage, not only the daily chores but the very survival of the family unit would be in question. And, indeed, we can observe more or less strict divisions of labor and of power which comprise the cultural and the idiosyncratic "styles" of family life. (The latter may, for instance, bewilder the small child when he begins visiting friends' families and discovers they have a way of doing things which is alien to his privately held definition of family operations.)

We need not rely only on the practical argument that family life *must be* organized (and therefore, have "rules" of organization), nor on the commonly shared observation that family behavior *is* organized (and that we can and do infer the "rules" governing this organization). The theory of communication and interpersonal relations, even in its present infancy, permits logical deduction of the hypothesis of family rules. To accomplish this derivation, it is necessary to review a few pertinent aspects of communications theory.

In 1951, Bateson (1, see also 10) noted that communications[4] can be said to have two distinct aspects or functions, *report* and *command*. Most obviously, every communication bit conveys information of a factual nature which, presumably, can be evaluated in terms of truth and falsity, and can be dealt with logically as the "object" of communication; this is the communication *report;* e.g., "the streets are icy," "Darwinian evolution does not necessarily invalidate the concept of a Supreme Being," or a shake of the head.

But, in addition to this report, and of immeasurably more interest to our theory of interpersonal relations, the same communication bit also conveys a *command* which indicates *how this information is to be taken.* Although this theory holds for a wider variety of communicational phenomena, we will limit ourselves to human communication, where we will see that the command aspect can be paraphrased "this is how I define the relationship in which this report takes place, i.e., this is how *you* are to see *me* in relation to you." None of the examples above was in the imperative mood grammatically, yet each effectively defines the nature of the relationship in which it occurs. Even the (superficially) impersonal statement about Darwinian evolution is not the sort of opinion one renders to the barber or even to one's wife without defining the relationship in a highly specific manner.[5]

This definition may not be accepted; it may be rejected, countered, modified, or ignored. It may also be redundant—confirming a long-standing or stereotyped relationship agreement such as teacher-student. But the offering of a "command" and the response by the other are distinguishable issues. Their interaction will be taken up shortly. Here, we can summarize the general report-command theory of communication into terms suitable for the specific aspects of human communication: *Every message (communication bit) has both a content (report) and a relationship (command) aspect; the former conveys information about facts, opinions, feelings, experiences, etc., and the*

---

[4] By communication is meant *behavior* in the widest sense: words and their non-verbal accompaniments, posture, facial expressions, even silence. All convey messages to another person, and all are subsumed in our term "communication."

[5] The relationship of the report to the command aspect of communication can be seen to be one of logical levels. One classifies the other, but is also classified by the other. For the sake of exposition, we will leave this reciprocity implicit and speak of command as a "higher" level than report.

latter defines the nature of the relationship between the communicants.
It is the relationship level of communication which will be our primary
focus in this paper.

In every communication, then, the participants offer to each other
definitions of their relationship, or, more forcefully stated, each seeks
to determine the nature of the relationship. Each, in turn, responds
with his definition of the relationship—which may affirm, deny, or
modify that of the *vis-à-vis*. This process, at the relationship level of
interaction (communication), warrants close attention.[6]

One of the simplest examples is the behavior of strangers in public
places (in an airplane, in a bar, waiting in line). They may exchange
trivial comments which lead to, say, a "small talk" relationship being
agreed upon; or one may seek such a relationship and the other may
quell it; or they may mutually define theirs as a "stranger" relationship
—a special relationship with its unique rules, rights, and expectations.
Note especially that the *context* exchange in these circumstances (offering a cigarette, comments about the weather, chuckling "to oneself")
is of little consequence; it may be false or virtually non-existent
(feigned deafness, pretended concentration, simple ignoring). But the
relationship struggle and resolution are definitive even in the unlikely
case where they simultaneously decide to ignore each other.

If we now narrow our focus even more, from human communication
in general to ongoing (perdurable) relationships only, we see that
what is relatively simple and unimportant between strangers is both
vital and complex in an ongoing relationship. An *ongoing relationship*
may be said to exist when, for some reason, the relationship is (a) "important" to both parties and (b) assumed to be of long term duration,
as is true of some business relationships, between friends and lovers,
and especially in marital and familial relationships. When these conditions impinge on a relationship, the determination of the nature of that
relationship cannot *not* be accomplished, nor can it be a haphazard
process. The give and take of relationship definitions must stabilize or
lead to a so-called runaway which would endanger the maintenance
of this ongoing relationship, i.e. divorce, desertion, or disaster would
ensue, and there would be no relationship to study.[7]

---

[6] In our view, the definition of the self, the relationship, and the other are an indivisi-
ble whole. We especially do not isolate or abstract the individual from the individual-in-
this-relationship-with-this-other. This bias is implicit throughout the present work, and
any tendency to read otherwise in the following will only lead to confusion.

[7] However, relationships do not necessarily terminate in actuality when they terminate

Thus, the population of families which is ours to study—those which remain family units—have stabilized the process of determining the nature of their relationship, "agreeing" on a mutually acceptable definition or at least on the limits for dispute. These relationship agreements, which are here called *rules*, prescribe and limit the individuals' behaviors over a wide variety of *content* areas, organizing their interaction into a reasonably stable system.

By way of illustration, we might speculate how rules must develop and operate in a new relationship: Boy meets girl on their first date. Take any aspect of the many behaviors involved; say, he arrives a little late. Suppose further that she delays her entrance (consciously or not) by exactly the amount of time he kept her waiting. He gets the message that she will not tolerate his keeping her waiting. At the same time, though, he cannot be sure whether this is just her mood tonight, or coincidence, or characteristic of her. If they are exceptional persons, they might discuss this "interchange," which would be a step toward resolution or change. But, whether they verbalize it or not, real change would require several repetitions of the corrected behavior. That is, if he were really unavoidably detained the first time, he would have to be on time the next several times to "prove" this. So suppose they still have this question, undiscussed, and unresolved. In the course of the evening, he decides they should go to a movie, and while she agrees, she picks the movie. He could decide he must treat her as an equal and start practicing equality; she responds by treating him equally, that is, she does not overdo it and push him around. Within a few dates, they would have something which could last a lifetime—although of course we cannot prove this. Mate selection must be in large part the matching of certain expected behaviors (and self-definitions) in certain crucial areas.

At this point we must, proleptically, digress to lay to rest questions of "consciousness", "intention", "purposefulness," or any of a variety of other terms implying that extremely troublesome issue: Is the behavior motivated or not? (And if so, how?) To propose that every individual moves to determine the nature of his relationship with another would seem to imply a theory of the individual which is based upon an Adlerian motivation to power. This is emphatically not so. *No* theoretical assumptions about the individual have been or need be invoked, only

---

in legality. Many divorced persons, for instance, remain intensely involved with each other and have even been known to participate in "marital" therapy.

assumptions on the nature of communication *qua* communication. Only the premise of a report-command duality of communication is necessary to our theoretical model. Similarly, although we find it convenient to say family members "agree" on relationship rules, we do not intend or need to assume that this is a conscious process. Most relationship rules are probably out of our awareness, but the issue is moot and irrelevant in this context.

The Rule as Redundancy in Relationships

If a man from Mars were to hover outside some living room window any given night, he might discover four people sitting around a small table, passing pasteboard rectangles to one another and muttering such phrases as "one no-trump." After watching for awhile and noting redundancies in the players' behavior, our intelligent Martian could discern that what these people were doing was highly rule-governed. He might discover, for example, that spades are higher than clubs, that play goes from left to right, etc. He might or might not immediately discover certain other rules of bridge, depending on whether special circumstances arose while he happened to be watching. For instance, it is assumed that no one will cheat. If one partner gives the other a significant glance, his opponents scowl angrily as a warning that this behavior is on the road to out-and-out cheating. Or, a really clever extraterrestrial observer might realize that the players *could* gain advantage by cheating, and that since they consistently refrained from this behavior, it must be against the rules. However, groups who have played together for some time will follow rules that are not overtly evident and which could only be inferred by an outsider after long, patient observation and recording of redundancies. Even if he spoke English and queried the players, it might not occur to them to mention certain rules that they abide by but are not consciously aware of observing. For example, A may "know" that when B says "one no-trump," he usually has minimal points and therefore A needs a strong hand to raise B.

When the game is family relationships, behavioral scientists are alien observers. The rules of play are not known completely even to the participants. What confronts the observer is a plethora of behaviors (communications) from which rules can be inferred which "explain" the patterning of the behavior. Just as a relatively few rules permit games as complex as chess or bridge, so a few family rules can cover the major aspects of ongoing interpersonal relationships. (The comparative difficulties of deducing many possible behaviors from a few given rules and of inducing the rules from a wide variety of behaviors should, however, be obvious.)

In other words, a redundancy principle operates in family life. The family will interact in repetitious sequences in all areas of its life, though some areas may highlight these repetitions (or patterns) more quickly and systematically that do other areas.

The rule approach to the study of family interaction is similar to that of the biologist studying genes and to Bateson's approach to the study of the learning process. As Maruyama (13) describes the former, biologists were long puzzled by the fact that the amount of information stored in genes is much smaller than the amount of information needed to account for the structure of the adult individual. However, this puzzle is solved if one assumes that the genes carry a set of *rules* to generate information for the whole system. Similarly, Bateson (2) described "deutero-learning" or "learning to learn," which concisely governs the wider range of *what* is learned. Although the family-as-a-unit indulges in uncountable numbers of different specific behaviors, the whole system can be run by a relatively small set of rules governing relationships. If one can reliably infer the general rules from which a family operates, then all its complex behavior may turn out to be not only patterned but also understandable—and, as a result, perhaps predictable.

Again, we must emphasize the rule is an inference, an abstraction—more precisely, a *metaphor* coined by the observer to cover the redundancy he observes. We say a rule is a "format of regularity imposed upon a complicated process by the investigator," (8) thereby preserving the distinction between theoretical term and object of Nature which is also maintained by many of our more sophisticated colleagues in the natural sciences. A rule is, but for our paucity of expression, a formula for a relationship—No one shall control anyone else, Father shall overtly run the show but Mother's covert authority shall be respected, Husband shall be the wooer and Wife the helpless female. Such formulations are inferences, just as is the concept of gravity; they explain the data in the sense that they incorporate the relevant visible evidence *and* relate it to a larger heuristic framework.

A Lexicon of Rules

I have come to refer to family relationship rules in general as *norms*. This usage not only corresponds roughly with similar (non-family) notions in the literature (7, 12, 15), but it also connotes some of the important characteristics of the concept:

(I) That the norms are usually phenomenologically unique for each family observed. We thus keep our focus firmly centered on the family unit, with individual and broader social or cultural considerations remaining secondary, even though we assume that a given set of norms or relationship rules is more common in one culture than another.

(II) That the norm is a setting or baseline on which family behavior is measured and around which it varies to a greater or lesser degree.

Norm thus implies both the focus and the mechanics of our theory. This might be represented schematically as in Figure 1, which can be seen to resemble a graph for a mechanical regulating device such as the household furnace thermostat, in which case the "range of behavior" would be the temperature scale and the "norm" the desired temperature setting.

One type of norm, described elsewhere, (9), is the marital *quid pro quo*. This term (literally "something for something") is a metaphorical statement of the marital relationship bargain; that is, how the couple has agreed to define themselves within this relationship.

Inseparable from our definition of norm would have to be a definition of *homeostatic mechanisms*, the means by which norms are delimited and enforced. The scowl the Martian observed on a bridge player when his competitor might have cheated indicated that the rules of the game had been or were about to be violated, or to put it another way, indicated that the class of behaviors in which the offending player has just indulged is to be excluded in their future dealing.[8]

Homeostatic mechanisms are therefore an extension, in an ongoing relationship, of the give and take of relationship definitions by which the original rules were worked out. It can be safely assumed, however, that the homeostatic mechanisms probably operate to restrict behavior to a much narrower range when the interactional system has stabilized into a family system than when the relationship was first being worked out. Couples, such as described earlier, who may engage in wondrously varied behavioral ploys during courtship, undoubtedly achieve con-

[8] Most of us, as bridge players, would readily perceive that our opponents meant to exclude not only the specific cheating tactic just attempted but *any* cheating behavior at all. Further, few of us would interpret the specific behavior (e.g. the exchange of significant glances) to be excluded in subsequent *non-bridge* situations. But the classification of behavior is not always so self-evident. The problems of mutually understood generalizations from specific behaviors will be dealt with in detail in a later article

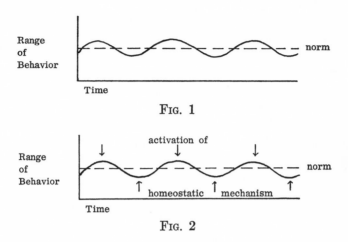

FIG. 1

FIG. 2

siderable economy after a while in terms of what is open to dispute, and how it is to be disputed. Consequently they seem both to have mutually excluded wide areas of behavior from their interactional repertoire (and never quibble further about them), *and* to have learned to cue each other homeostatically with a privately understood "code," so that little gestures may mean a lot. Such economy, of course, is inversely related to the effort required of the researching observer.

In terms of the schema just presented for norms (Figure 1 above), homeostatic mechanisms can be seen as behaviors which delimit the fluctuations of other behaviors along the particular range where the norm is relevant.[9] Again, the analogy with the household thermostat is useful: when the temperature deviates from a pre-set norm, this deviation is registered and counteracted by the homeostatic mechanism of the thermostat system. (See Figure 2.) Thus, if the norm of the family is that there be no disagreement, when trouble begins to brew, we might observe general uneasiness, a sudden tangentialization or change of topic, or even symptomatic behavior on the part of an identified patient, who may act out, talk crazy, or even become physically ill when family members begin to argue. The family is distracted and brought into coalition (frequently against the patient) and the norm holds until the next time.

It is significant in the development of family theory that it was the observation of homeostatic mechanisms in the families of psychiatric

---

[9] Again, homeostatic behaviors obviously belong to a higher level, logically, than the behaviors to which they refer. We might speculate that this higher range of behaviors also has norms and if so, that paradoxes might arise.

patients (11) that led to the hypothesis of the family as a homeostatic, and eventually specifically as a rule-governed, system. For norms become quickly apparent if one can observe the reaction to their abrogation and infer therefrom the rule which was broken. Tiresome long term observation of the beaten path, with careful noting of possible routes which were *not* taken, can eventually yield a fair guess about the rules of the game. But the observable counteraction of a single deviation is like a marker to our goal. Therefore, though it is still difficult to assess exactly the norms of the system the schizophrenic patient and his family maintain when the patient is "ill," one need only witness the immediate and frequently violent reaction to his recovery to be convinced that there are powerful family mechanisms for maintaining these norms.

Norms and Values

Norms as herein defined and discussed are not to be confused with the important sociological concept of *values*. Certainly both constructs represent guideposts which organize behavior, and both are enforced by observable sanctions. So one might be tempted to put the two in the same class and distinguish them on some minor ground, e.g., values are generally presumed to exist *a priori* and to result in ("cause") certain behavior patterns, while norms are inferred *from* behavior and are not seen to be causative; or, one might propose that values are overt and acknowledgeable while norms are covert, the two being analogous perhaps to laws, customs, respectively.

These apparent comparabilities are, however, superficial and misleading. *A norm describes interpersonal relations;* that is, they are interpersonal both in unit and subject matter. Values, on the other hand, are *non-personal* in subject matter and *individual* in unit. One person can value something or "have" a certain value, and several family members (individually) can value something, but a family *as a whole* cannot. Even if all family members concur in a certain value the result is a summation of individuals—and therefore remains in the domain of individual theory.

Where, then, do values fit into our scheme of family rules? Certainly not in terms of specific injunctions for or against certain individual behaviors, or in the meaning of these behaviors for the individual (in terms of dissonance, guilt, etc.). Behavior which may be guided by a presumed value is not distinguishable from any other kind of behavior in our interactional framework. But values, or more precisely, the invocation of values, can have interpersonal ramifications: values can be cited to demand, enforce, or justify a particular kind of behavior in a relationship. If the family norm proscribes disagreement, when a family discussion begins to get out of order, almost any member can invoke the shared *value* of democratic functioning (taking turns, etc.), and thus re-establish family order. In short, *values in this theory of the family are one kind of homeostatic mechanism.* Because values represent an extra-familial coalition (with religion, society, culture, etc.), they exert leverage on relationships within the family. Thus, from our perspective, inside the family looking out, so to speak, values are used as interpersonal tactics which affirm or enforce a norm.[10]

Mother and infant, for example, have a strictly complementary relationship (that is, one based on differences which fit together), in which the norm is that the infant is totally dependent on the mother for all gratification. As the child grows older, he may engage in behaviors which abrogate this norm, especially masturbation. Whatever else masturbation may mean to either individual, in this ongoing relationship, it is an indication of self-sufficient pleasure on the part of the child (10) and as such threatens the norm of their relationship, i.e., that the mother controls all the child's needs and pleasures. If the mother is unwilling to accept this change in the norm, she may punish the child, and/or she may invoke strong moral injunctions against the "deviant" behavior. In this case, her value judgment against his masturbation represents a forceful coalition of mother and society, a coalition which may in fact succeed and perpetuate the complementary norm to absurdity.

As is readily apparent, values usually have recognizable origins in the culture, subculture, ethnic background, or social group, but there are idiosyncratic values as well. Some may be ignored, some espoused with special fervor, as these values tend to fit into the enforcement of the family norms. Thus, while the psychoanalyst often sees values as rationalizations of intrapsychic phenomena, and the sociologist and anthropologist discuss them as idealized constructs somehow "possessed" by the individual, or on which many individuals concur, this

---

[10] This is not, of course, the same as saying that this is *all* a value is—the student of value orientations cuts the pie quite another way and validly so—but this is all a value can be within the theory here outlined if consistency is to be maintained.

family theory focuses on the communicative function of value-guided behavior and concludes that such behavior is tactical, within the family, where it serves as a homeostatic mechanism.

This use of the term "value" corresponds with that of others who have previously used "norm" as it is defined here. Thibaut and Kelley, in "The Social Psychology of Groups" (15), describe a norm as a behavioral rule that is accepted, at least to some degree, by both members of a (non-family) dyad. They state that the observer, after noting a regularity in behavior or regular routine shifts in the activities of the pair, can help explain this regularity by inferring that the behavior is organized around norms. They also note that if the regularity is disrupted, the "injured" person will often attempt to restore it by exercising his personal power to enforce the norm, or *by appealing to a supporting value.*

Garfinkle (7) discusses what he calls "constitutive rules"—rules which one is not aware of until they are broken or abrogated. "Constitutive rules" correspond, in some ways, to my use of the word "norm." For example, supermarket shoppers were disconcerted to observe a graduate student buy a package of cigarettes and then proceed to open the pack and count the cigarettes. This deliberately staged behavior called into question the norms of the relationship between shopper and producer which might be paraphrased as: "If I (shopper) buy a pack of cigarettes, I can count on you (producer) to put 20 cigarettes in the pack." Thus the shopper is spared the impossible task of verifying the size, weight, and number of everything he purchases; in other words, a certain level of trust is established. If some shopper discovered only 10 cigarettes in a package, he might or might not realize the exact nature of his trust in the producer, but he would probably write him a letter invoking values, even laws. (The effect on other shoppers produced by the psychology student's behavior is an indication that people react against discovering their own norms. It is similar to becoming aware of one's breathing—what once worked silently and smoothly is now a problem.)

Rules versus Roles

Probably the most generally accepted notion in family study is that of *roles*, which has wide currency among an unusually varied group of investigators—psychoanalysts, sociologists, learning theorists, to name a few. A family role is a model abstracted from the legal, chronological,

or sexual status of a family member (mother, husband, son, sister, etc.);
this model describes certain expected, permitted, and forbidden behaviors for the person in that role. Several kinds of analysis follow
from the family role concept: study of the process of learning the role
behaviors, of the inevitable multiplicity of roles with which any given
individual is labeled (spouse and parent, child and sibling, and so on),
and of course of the integration of roles into a family structure.

This last field of study would seem, perhaps, to be very similar to our
proposed theory of family rules, focusing as both do on the interlocking
behaviors of family members. This is not true, for a number of reasons.
Most important, in the role concept we again face a term which is
basically *individual* in origin and orientation and which, therefore, is
ill-suited for the discussion of family process. A role encases the individual as a separate unit of study so that the *relations between* two
or more individuals must necessarily be secondary phenomena. If we
would study relationship first, then we cannot, as will be illustrated
shortly, base this study on individual constructs.

A second point of difference is the inseparability of the role concept
from a culture-limited view of family structure. There is no clear line
between the role as descriptive or as idealistic; that is, people are classified by conformity or non-conformity to predetermined categories
which are products either of cultural stereotype or of theoretical bias.
The implication is that a healthy family has Father in the father role,
Mother in the mother role, Son in the male child role, etc. This neglects
and even obscures the aspects of interactional process which may be
significant, which may in fact be the more general phenomena of which
role-taking is only a by-product.[11]

This leads to a more basic difference between rules and roles—the
reliance on observation as opposed to *a priori* definitions. A role, with
its theoretically concommitant behaviors, exists independently of behavioral data. That is, not only the general notion of role but the specifics of the various sorts of family roles are theoretical, not phenomenological. When observational data is involved, it is in relation to the
theoretical role as a model ("inadequate performance of a role," "role

---

[11] There is a growing body of theory on idiosyncratic family roles especially in relation
to psychopathology, e.g., the notion of the identified patient as the family scapegoat (4),
as well as Berne's (5) pungent descriptions of the many roles for many persons which
comprise the interactional setting of various forms of symptomatic behavior. These certainly bring us much closer to interactional data, but there is a tendency to inject such
formulations with individual motivational schemes (such as masochism), which detract
from the originality of the descriptive approaches.

breakdown," "role reversal"). It seems apparent that analysis of such discrepancies between model and reality only emphasizes further the gap between category and data.

To illustrate that rules and roles are two fundamentally different ways of looking at family data, let us consider a specific role theory—the sex-role view of marriage—and an alternative view which has been proposed in terms of family rules. (9) The incontrovertible and inevitable fact that marriages are composed of one man and one woman only has led to the belief that sex differences between spouses are highly significant in the nature of marriage. Men and women have certain fundamental differences at birth which are presumed to be amplified by social learning of a wide variety of sex-linked behaviors and attitudes; in short, each adult should have achieved a male or female role. The convergence of the two roles, as the only immediately obvious similarity between all marriages, is commonly assumed to be the key to marriage as an institution. Thus sexual compatibility is greatly stressed as vital to the success of a marriage (though this may be only a special case of the more general necessity for *collaboration* in marriage). Conformation by each spouse to the proper role stereotype is presumed to be basic, not only to sexual compatibility, but to the mental health of the spouses and their children and the permanence of the marriage.

There are, however, other characteristics true of marriage (and of almost no other relationships) which might therefore be just as reasonably considered basic to the nature of marriage as is its sexual composition. These are seldom considered, I feel, because they refer, not to individual spouses, but to the *relationship* of marriage and thus do not fit our usual language. Consider that the marriage (not the persons involved) is (a) a voluntary relationship, (b) a permanent or at least open-ended, non-time-bound relationship, (c) an exclusive relationship which is supposed to suffice for the partners in a great many areas of human functioning, and (d) a broadly and complexly goal-oriented relationship, with vital tasks covering not only a wide cross-section of human affairs, but extending indefinitely through time. This is a unique and by no means spurious, inconsequential combination of characteristics and must certainly be considered at least as important to the nature of marital relationships as individual sexual factors.

Thus, the marital *quid pro quo* (as defined earlier) has been proposed. The *quid pro quo* theory of marriage is used as an illustration here because it represents a full reversal of the role theory of marriage: *the individual differences which are unquestionably present in a mar-*

riage are seen as results of the active process of working out this unique and difficult relationship, not as the primary cause of the relationship phenomena.

Let us review the distinction we have made between rules and roles, in terms of these two specific theories of marriage. First, sex-role constructs are inevitably individual in orientation; any deductions about relationship consequences must be greatly limited by the premises to which these individual notions are limited. Second, there are theoretical and cultural preconceptions about "proper" sex roles, such that men are supposed to work, be strong and not openly emotional, defend the home, etc., while women are to keep house, stay inside it, be soft, loving, and maternal. No allowance is made for the relationship which underlies this arrangement, or for the possibility that this is a good way of working out rules for a relationship *but not the only way.*

This brings us to point three, which is that real marriages may deviate widely from these cultural stereotypes and be highly successful, because an equally workable relationship agreement (*quid pro quo*) has been maintained. There seems to be little question that difference *per se* is necessary in marriage: the specifics of such differences are much less important than the circularity of their evolution and maintenance. Therefore, *a priori* categories of differences will only lead us astray.

Some of the problems of family theory and research have been considered, and general criteria have been suggested by which these problems might be avoided. A theory of the family has been proposed, based on the model of the family as a rule-governed, homeostatic system. A companion paper to follow will discuss clinical and experimental applications of this theory, with special emphasis on pathological family systems.

REFERENCES

1. BATESON, G., "Information and Codification: A Philosophical Approach," in Ruesch, J. and Bateson, G., *Communication: The Social Matrix of Psychiatry*, New York, Norton, 1951, pp. 168–211.
2. BATESON, G., "Social Planning and the Concept of 'Deutero-Learning'," *Science, Philosophy, and Religion*, Second symposium, New York, 1942.
3. BATESON, G., JACKSON, D. D., HALEY, J. and WEAKLAND, J., "Toward a Theory of Schizophrenia," *Behav. Sci.*, 1, 251–264, 1956.
4. BELL, N. W. and VOGEL, E. F., "The Emotionally Disturbed Child as

the Family Scapegoat," in Bell, N. W. and Vogel, E. F. (eds.) *The Family*, Glencoe, Ill., Free Press, 1960.

5. BERNE, E., *Transactional Analysis*, New York, Grove Press, 1961.

6. VON BERTALANFFY, L., "An Outline of General Systems Theory," *Brit. J. Philos. Sci.*, 1, 134–165, 1950.

7. GARFINKEL, H., "The Routine Grounds of Everyday Activities," *Soc. Prob.*, 11, 225–249, 1964.

8. HALEY, J., "Family Experiments: A New Type of Experimentation," *Fam. Proc.*, 1, 265–293, 1962, p. 279.

9. JACKSON, D. D., "Family Rules: The Marital *Quid Pro Quo*" (to be published in *Arch. Gen. Psychiat.*)

10. JACKSON, D. D., "Guilt and Control of Pleasure in Schizoid Personalities," *Brit. J. Med. Psychol.*, 31, 124–130, part 2, 1958.

11. JACKSON, D. D., "The Question of Family Homeostasis," *Psychiat. Quart. Supp.*, 31, 79–90, 1957.

12. LEARY, T., *Interpersonal Diagnosis of Personality*, New York, Ronald Press, 1957.

13. MARUYAMA, M., "The Second Cybernetics: Deviation-Amplifying Mutual Causal Processes" (unpublished manuscript, September 1962).

14. SHIBUTANI, T., *Society and Personality*, Prentice-Hall, Englewood Cliffs, New Jersey, 1961, pp. 20–23.

15. THIBAUT, J. W. and KELLEY, H. H., *The Social Psychology of Groups*, Wiley, New York, 1959.

10

Thinking About the Family—
Psychiatric Aspects

W. W. MEISSNER, S. J.

THE LAST DECADE has seen a remarkable progression in psychiatric thinking. Since the turn of the century the dominant concern has been with the management of the transference phenomenon. The basic frame of reference for this orientation was provided by psychoanalytic theory; the basic assumption within this framework was that the intrusion of any other persons into the patient-therapist relationship would contaminate the transference. Gradually the focus of concern was broadened to include significant figures related to the patient, particularly the mother. Once the focus of therapeutic interest had been extended to the realm of interpersonal relationships, it was only a matter of time for the entire family to be drawn into the picture. The last decade, however, has seen a significant development within this progression, namely the shift from a basically individual orientation to a specifically family-centered orientation (107).

The important shift from seeing family relationships in terms of the patient to seeing the patient in terms of the family structure

131

really marked the beginning of family therapy as such and launched the study of family processes into a new era of exploration (28). This was possible because the understanding of developmental processes, the conceptualization of interpersonal relationships, the understanding of individual functioning and intrapsychic dynamics, were now cast in a new framework and could be approached from a relatively new perspective. The question which this development posed for psychiatric thinking was whether the shift in perspective required a correlative shift in theoretical orientation or not. The question remains unanswered, but we shall try to explore in this study the evidential bases and theoretical formulations which bear upon it. Our ultimate objective will be the clarification of issues and problems which must be thought through in working toward an understanding of the family.

SURVEYING THE EVIDENCE

Scientific understanding, particularly in psychiatry, is so closely dependent on empirical data that accurate understanding is easily subverted if we move too far away from it. The theoretical branches of the tender young tree of psychiatry are too fragile and they will very likely break if we move too far away from the roots of empirical evidence. Therefore, before we move on to consider current attempts to understand the family process, it would seem expeditious to try to synthesize the available evidence relative to the family. The published literature is too bulky and is growing too rapidly to permit any sort of exhaustive survey, but it will be sufficient for our purpose to concentrate on the main findings.

Most of the available evidence has been gathered in the study of schizophrenic families, however our interest here is not specifically with schizophrenic processes but with the family. One of the unanswered questions is the extent to which schizophrenia can be related to specific factors in the family. It may be that schizophrenia itself is symptomatic of the exaggeration (or defect) of elements which can be found in any family. The resolution of this and other problems must come from the available evidence.

The Mother

Attention has been directed to defining personal characteristics of parents whose children manifest various pathologies. Mothers of school phobic children are described as anxious, ambivalent, hostile, immature, insecure in their maternal role, and demanding (5, 23, 26, 35, 40). Mothers of children with adjustment problems are found to be ineffective, irresponsible, weak, self-critical, competitive for authority, completely giving, completely rejecting, mothering, and hostile (12, 112, 124). Children suffering from ulcerative colitis seem to have mothers who are insecure, inadequate in their maternal role, and ambivalent (75, 98). The young addict's mother is controlling, over-powering, guilt-ridden, narcissistic, hostile, inconsistent, and seductive (58, 94). The manic-depressive's mother is dominant and ambiv-alent (47), while the so-called schizophrenogenic mother is labelled as dominant, rigidly perfectionistic, lacking in confidence, distrusting, cold, masochistic, low in self-esteem, inconsistent, rejecting and de-pendent (44, 82, 84, 90, 113, 123, 132). Both Lidz (44) and Bowen (17) have noted the lack of a consistent pattern in the mother of a schizo-phrenic child, and the same inconsistency seems to be reflected in the other types of pathology.

The impact of the mother upon the child and the general charac-teristics of the mother-child relation have been intensively explored. We can only touch here on a small fragment of research. Mal-adjustment in children has generally been found in association with maternal conflict and a tendency to maintain the children in a dependent relationship. The overprotective attitude of mothers of children suffering from school phobia sets a representative pattern: these mothers tend to establish a close emotional relationship with the child which fosters the child's dependence on the mother and which thereby seems to afford a species of emotional satisfaction to the mother (5, 24, 26, 35, 97). A similar pattern obtains in children manifesting antisocial behavior, with the added variant that these mothers seem incapable of finding a medium ground in their relation-ships to these children: giving means limitless surrender and in-dulgence, while frustration of wishes means total deprivation and hostile, repressive control (112). Strong emotional ties and a de-pendent relationship to the mother was also characteristic of young boys committing murderous assaults (31). Mothers of addicted young-sters were also found to be overprotective and incapable of granting independence to their children (94). The powerful need to infantilize in these mothers has a tremendous impact on these children, as is reflected in the intense and binding pattern of identification charac-teristic of this relationship, which may relate to the addict's frequent

homosexual conflict (58). The same pattern of symbiotic infantiliza-
tion turns up in psychosomatic involvements (40, 87, 98), and Lidz
has noticed that sometimes the disturbance of the mother-child
relation in psychosomatic cases is more severe than in schizophrenia
(81). In ulcerative colitis, as an example, the conflict between the
mother's needs to keep the child dependent and her own unconscious
destructive impulses is regarded as central (40). Finch and Hess refer
to the development of a "surrogate ego" in the child, i.e., an ego which
is functionally and permanently dependent on the mother (40).

The same type of relationship which is found so widely at levels of
lesser maladjustment is also found on the level of more severe, psychotic maladjustment. The combination of demanding conformity
and dependent fear of the mother are characteristic of the maternal
relationship of the manic-depressive (47). They have also been found
repeatedly in studies of schizophrenic children and their maternal
relationships (14, 15, 29, 44, 81, 88, 91, 92, 113). Delay (29) speaks
of "erotization of the mother-child relation," and of course, many
authors have stressed the symbiotic characteristics of the relationship
(14, 42, 44, 88, 113). Despite the frequent references to maternal rejection, Searles (123) has emphasized the positive character of the
emotional relationship between the schizophrenic and his mother.
He feels that feelings of tenderness, adoration, and attachment are
more characteristic than the negative emotions of hate and rejection.
The intense emotional relationship has led Bowen to refer to it as
an "emotional oneness" (15), but it is all the same a functional relationship in that it provides a mechanism by which the mother controls her own immaturity by caring for the immaturity of her child
(14). Any disturbance of the relationship would thereby serve as a
threat to the mother.

The Father

In more recent years, the broadening of awareness has turned attention to an examination of personal characteristics of the father.
Here too the maladjustment of the child was found to be associated
with personality disturbance, as had been the case in research on
mothers. Fathers of poorly adjusted children were often found to be
domineering, authoritarian, hypercritical, or passive, ineffectual, unable to cope with family responsibility, and engaged in a passive-
aggressive undercutting of the mother's authority (12, 31, 116, 124).

In cases of school phobia, the father's position was often weak ineffectual and passive (26, 77, 97). In contrast to the strong, influential position of the mother, the father of the drug addict provided little more than a shadowy background figure (94); a similar constellation has been observed in fathers of manic-depressives (47). It is in relation to schizophrenia that the bulk of work on characteristics of the father has been done. The father of the schizophrenic has been described as relatively uninvolved in the family life, except to punish or give financial support (34, 82, 113). He is pictured as weak, immature, passive, and totally inadequate in fulfilling his paternal role (34, 46, 81, 84, 86, 113, 132); yet he is also portrayed as cruel, sadistic, domineering, hostilely dependent on his wife, distant, aloof and brutal (44, 46, 84, 111). The variation in paternal pattern is recognized by Lidz and his coworkers who have set up five different categories of schizophrenic fathers ranging from the totally passive and submissive to the utterly domineering and tyrannical (81, 86). They have also pointed out a sex-related pattern in which fathers of schizophrenic girls tend to be narcissistic and dominant, whereas fathers of schizophrenic boys tend to be ineffectual and passive (44).

The diversity of paternal functioning, not only in schizophrenic families but also in families with other types of malfunctioning, tends to lessen support for the notion that there is any significant connection between parental characteristics and the form of pathology in the patient. The effective absence of the father has been noted in a variety of contexts (9, 22, 29, 31, 34, 35, 94, 97), and Bowen (17) has pointed out that the pattern of withdrawal on the part of the father depends upon his exclusion from the intense mother-child relation. In his attempts to intervene and strengthen his own relationship with the child, he must often oppose the mother by a more or less cruel, dominating approach. On this view, parental characteristics are to some extent determined by the interactions within the father-mother-child triad.

Overprotection-Rejection

Much has been written in support of either parental overprotection or parental rejection as operative factors in mental illness. Rejection is a common theme in the family histories of disturbed children and adolescents (31, 100), and by the same token overprotection seems to recur frequently in the histories of phobic children (5, 35, 97) and drug addicts (94). Although overprotection has been emphasized in the histories of schizophrenics (29, 45), rejecting attitudes are nonetheless prominent (44, 120). In a large schizophrenic population, Wahl (130) was able to find rejection and/or overprotection in only half of the cases. It seems likely, therefore, that the emphasis given to these factors in the genesis of mental illness has not been altogether warranted. The question is more complex, however, since it has been noted that the decline in the dependence of the mothering figure on the child in cases of adolescent maladjustment is often experienced by the adolescent as rejection (124). By the same token, Bowen (14) has reported that in his small group of research families, none of the mothers was rejecting, but that they were all perceived by the schizophrenic patient as rejecting. The critical variable was the mother's anxiety: when high, they are hovering and infantilizing; when less anxious, they give less attention to the child. The change is experienced by the child as rejection.

Related to the problem of rejection is that of parental deprivation. Childhood loss of parent through death or separation is frequent in cases of delinquency, antisocial and psychopathic behavior, and schizophrenia (51). Bowlby (18) has argued that the period of vulnerability is considerably broader than the first year of life, but the fact remains that some bereaved children develop quite adequately. Factors which seem to mitigate the destructive effect of such loss are the compatibility of parents who function with well defined parental roles prior to death, and the development of a separation tolerance in the child prior to loss (57). In other words, the damaging effects of parental deprivation are lessened where the parents have been functioning maturely and where the child is not involved in a relationship of emotional dependency—Bowen's "emotional oneness" (15).

Parental Pathology

One of the more striking findings of family research is the high degree of association between parental pathology and pathology in the child. The indications of this are varied. A follow-up study of adults who had been treated psychiatrically as children found overt personality disturbance in nearly half the parents (100). Depressive and neurotic symptoms are frequent in the parents of phobic children (26, 35), and study of a broader spectrum of psychiatric diagnoses has indicated a frequent relationship to mental illness or suicide in the parents (52). The parents of the schizophrenic are no exception. Lidz's group (44, 82) has found that almost all of these parents are disturbed to some extent and that in his families one or both parents revealed serious psychopathology. Delay's (29) catalogue of disturbed parental types regards the "psychotic character" as the most frequent and he describes this as a type of latent schizophrenia. Another classification of schizophrenic parents divides them into pseudoneurotic, somatic, pseudodelinquent, and overtly psychotic (71). In general, it seems safe to say that there is a positive relation between the degree of parental symptoms and the degree of illness in the child, or that maladjustment in the parents increases the probability of maladjustment in one or more of the children (41, 49, 67, 125). Ehrenwald (32, 33) even goes so far as to speak of "psychological contagion," applying it to the transmission of symptomatology from parent to child.

Marital Choice

The association of mental illness is high not only between parents and child, but also between spouses themselves (74). Kaufman (71) also found that the parents of schizophrenic children tended to fall in the same category of disturbance with significant frequency. If the categories (29, 71) can be regarded as related to degrees of immaturity, this would indicate a tendency for people of equivalent personal immaturity to marry. There are also some indications that the mutually supportive meshing of neurotic needs is an important factor in determining the marriage partner (121). The individual would, then, seek for a partner (consciously or unconsciously) who would give promise of maximum need-gratification. The need patterns of the two partners would consequently be complementary (ascendent-submissive, sadistic-masochistic, etc.). Such a pattern of need complementarity has been found in supposedly normal couples (133) and has also been noticed in neurotic couples (102).

Bowen (14) remarks that clinical experience suggests that people tend to choose spouses who have achieved an equivalent level of immaturity, but who have opposite defense mechanisms. In the schizophrenic families studied at NIMH this pattern seems to be verified: both marital partners were equally immature and their relationship tended to fall into an overadequate-inadequate pattern (14, 15). Consequently, there would seem to be some notable support for a hypothesis of complementarity of needs in marital partners not only with regard to type of need, but also in intensity of need as related to immaturity of development. Although some attention has been paid to the perceptions of the respective spouses of each other prior to marriage (14), we do not have much information. One might wonder whether the perceptions were governed by projections related to the inner personality needs of the respective spouses.

Parental Interaction

Considerable research effort has been directed to the exploration of patterns of interaction between the marital partners as related to kinds of pathology in the children. Some general trends can be indicated. As a general rule, where one partner assumes a more dominant, ascendent, or aggressive stance, the other partner is found to occupy a more submissive, compliant, dependent or passive position. This can be found in families where the child is phobic (5, 77), maladjusted (12, 124), and schizophrenic (29, 39, 45, 46, 86, 111). In the case of schizophrenia, as an example of more general trends, no clear-cut pattern is discernible (62, 82) but reciprocal functioning is the usual finding (54). Even so, there are some families in which the reciprocal functioning is masked or impossible to discern (82). Even in these cases, however, it is apparent that the parents are both functioning immaturely. Bowen (15) has described the pattern of reciprocal functioning as the "overadequate-inadequate reciprocity," and he adds that in the families he studied either parent could assume either position. This would suggest that such patterns of family interaction are relative to and dependent on the family situation. Consequently, their significance is not so much as patterns of family interaction but rather as indications of or reflections of the level of immature functioning attained by the marital partners.

The possibility remains open that extrafamilial influences are at work in establishing such interactional patterns within the family structure (60, 119). This is not surprising since the family is the mediating agency of cultural influences. There seems to be a trend in this country for the mother to be the more dominant figure in lower class families (76, 101). Ethnic and cultural differences have been reported (59), particularly in Opler's work on Irish and Italian schizophrenic families (104, 105, 106). He found that the Irish family is typically mother-dominated and the Italian family is typically father-dominated. These differences also seem to be reflected in the respective symptomatologies.

Conflict

The presence of conflict and disharmony in the families of disturbed children has often been noted. Conflict in the family has thus been linked to adjustment problems at home and in school, adolescent rebellion and anxiety attacks (21, 22, 38). Conflict between the parents of a schizophrenic child is a frequent finding, and it is usually severe and chronic (29, 39, 41, 86). Gerard and Siegel (46) studied the family backgrounds of 71 male schizophrenics and found open discord between the parents in 87% of the cases. Such conflict is frequent enough to permit Lidz to divide his research families into schismatic and skewed groups (42, 44, 82). Marital schism involves a chronic failure to achieve complementarity of respective roles, communication consisting in coercive efforts and defiance or in masking attempts, a chronic undercutting of the worth of the other parent to the children, and a prominent tendency to compete for the childrens' loyalty (82). This is a typical pattern, but not universal. Another prominent pattern was that of the skewed family in which one parent was extremely dependent or masochistic and the other strong and supporting. Conflict was infrequent in this type of family because of the threat it posed to the close emotional bonds which seemed necessary to the stability of each partner (82).

"Emotional Divorce"

The conflict issue relates to a somewhat more complex and refined analysis of family functioning. Bowen (14) has noted that a certain emotional distance was characteristic of all his schizophrenic families. The parents maintain this distance by a variety of techniques ranging from calm, controlled divergence to overt hostility and conflict (15, 17). He has labeled this phenomenon as the "emotional divorce." Similar patterns of emotional distance have been described in families with adolescent adjustment problems and autistic children (34, 124). As Bowen describes the emotional divorce, it is closely related to the pattern of overadequate-inadequate reciprocity. Either parent can function in either position, but any shift in these functioning positions is accompanied by intense conflict and tension. The emotional divorce is a device for avoiding such conflict and making the relationship as bearable as possible; it not only circumvents conflict but helps to avoid the anxiety involved in any shift in the delicate balance of emotional forces within the family (15). The tendency for the parents of the schizophrenic child to establish alternately close relationships to the child is another aspect of the emotional divorce. When the divorce broke down, either conflictually or otherwise, and the parents could become more invested in each other than either was in the child, the child automatically improved. When either parent became more invested in the child than in the other parent (thereby re-establishing the emotional divorce) the child regressed (14). This periodic alternation between conflictual and reciprocal patterns between the marital partners would seem to be very close to the patterns of schism and skew described by Lidz (82), except that they can be found within the same family at different stages of interaction. It is quite likely that Wynne's perceptive analysis of alignments and splits within the family structure is dealing with the same phenomenon (135). He points out that an alignment in any portion of the family is followed by the emergence of a split in some other segment, and conversely, every split has its accompanying alignment. We have already seen that in Bowen's analysis of the emotional divorce that the split between the parents is often accompanied by an emotional investment or alignment of either parent with the child, just as the investment of the parents in each other is accompanied by a split in the emotional relation to the child.

Parent-Child Interaction

An apparent facet of family interaction is the strongly dependent relation of the disturbed child to the parents, and the strong reciprocal need in the parents to infantilize the child and keep him dependent (13). There are indications, however, that the patient's need for emotional support is not restricted to the confines of the family. Strong mutual dependence together with a pattern of reciprocity has been identified as a common feature of *folie-à-deux* (110). There is also evidence that the preschizoid is able to obtain emotional support and temporary stabilization from extrafamilial figures in the environment (8). Consequently it is unlikely that the dependency relation found in so many disturbed families is indigenous to the family structure as such.

It is necessary to stress the strongly interactional aspect of these intrafamilial processes (2, 50). Mother, father and child are caught up in an intense emotional interdependency (14). The parents of a schizophrenic child see the child as seriously ill and fragile (65), but in the premorbid relationship this perception is determined more by parental feelings than by objective fact. The parents are incapable of distinguishing fact from feeling in this matter, apparently because the chronic and inaccurate assumption that the child is the cause of difficulty masks and desensitizes the intense emotional problem in the parental relationship itself (30). The psychosis becomes a living confirmation of this assumption and becomes a necessary element in the family interaction in order to perpetuate the anxiety-alleviating mechanism. One can form the impression that the child is more or less victimized in this situation, but as Wynne (135) has pointed out, any suggestion of rejection of the parent constitutes a threat to the parents' sense of worth. The anxiety thus aroused erupted in parental conflict; thus the parent-child split was accompanied by an interparental split. The child could thus precipitate the parents into renewed conflict and bitter recriminations by the mere suggestion of rejection. The parents and child in these families are caught up in a relationship of reciprocal victimizing (135). Bowen (14) has described the typical situation in these terms:

> The child makes his emotional and verbal demands on the mother by exploiting the helpless, pitiful position. Patients are adept at arousing sympathy and overhelpfulness in others. All the research families have eventually found their homes geared to the demands of the patient. The parents are as helpless in taking a stand against the patient as the patient in taking a stand against parents.

Within this complex involvement, influences are at work which contribute strongly to the child's internalized value orientation and effective dispositions. Wynne (134) has noted that an important aspect of the family interaction is the creation of a subculture within the family of myths, legends and ideology, which reinforces and supports the neurotic adjustment. It is difficult to judge the extent of transferred attitudes and values, but it seems clear that the aggressive behavior of children and adolescents who have perpetrated murderous attacks is pre-conditioned by parental expectations and approval of physical violence and antisocial aggression (31). Antisocial acting out on the part of children is unconsciously initiated, sanctioned and fostered by parents who work out their own conflicts and gratify their own antisocial impulses through the acting-out of the child (48). There is some evidence to suggest that such influences may play a part in homosexual deviations (96) and psychosomatic illness (95). More needs to be done to clarify the manner of communication of such factors, but it seems clear that suggestions, nuances, innuendoes, and a whole spectrum of nonverbal forms of communication are in play (10, 13, 48, 83).

Unconscious Communication

In disturbed families, disturbances of communication are a prominent aspect of the family interaction (38, 113), and it seems safe to say that the idea of unconscious communication, however it is to be described or accounted for, is essential to the understanding of family processes (53). The disturbance seems generally to take the form of a lack of congruence between communications on the same level or on different levels (63). Contradictory demands have been observed in the communications of parents of maladjusted children (22), drug addicts (94), and schizophrenics (65, 83, 89, 132). Schizophrenic parents will "mask" or obfuscate communications relevant to the anxiety producing situation by various forms of concealment, denial, acting as if the situation did not exist, etc. This chronic pattern of dealing with the problem produces a climate of habitual masking which is an irrational form of communication and which creates an unreal atmosphere within which the child is raised (83). Bateson (10) has formalized this pattern of communication in the schizophrenic family in terms of the "double-bind." Bowen (14) describes the same process when he points out that the parent (usually the mother) makes two demands on the child: an emotional demand that the child remain helpless, and a verbalized demand that the child become a mature person. Much of the emotional demand is communicated on an action level, outside the awareness of both parent and child. The level of verbal communication is in direct contradiction to the level of action communication. Jackson and Weakland (65) have also emphasized the importance of incongruent communication in schizophrenic families. The pattern can even be detected in the letters of mothers to their schizophrenic sons (132).

Parallel Pathology

One of the most significant findings to emerge from the shift in perspective from the individual to the family is the association of changes in other family members with the change in functioning of the patient. Both the onset of illness and the recovery of the patient can precipitate significant changes in the rest of the family. The onset of schizophrenic symptoms may be accompanied by disturbances in other family members in a kind of family decompensation (43). The psychosis may represent the severance of the symbiotic attachment to the mother, and may thereby be accompanied by the elevation of anxiety levels in the mother (14). On the other hand, the patient's improvement during therapy may occasion and be accompanied by severe disturbances in other family members (1, 7, 24, 56, 61, 64, 65, 66, 121, 126). Alcoholism, threats of divorce, and symptoms of anxiety and depression in the marital partner have been found following on therapeutic improvement of the patient (73). Improvement is not always followed by the eruption of symptoms, but may be accompanied by maturation of the marital partner (121) or by a realignment of relations leading to greater emotional separation and flexibility (24, 70). There seems to be some agreement that the improvement of the schizophrenic child makes him less vulnerable to the mother's neurotic control and conflicting demands, thereby threatening the mother's emotional needs and rousing her anxiety (10, 14). The outbreak of symptoms in peripheral family members and the correlative improvement in functioning of family members remains to be explained.

Resistance to Change

The course of therapy with disturbed families is complicated not only by eruptions of pathology in other members, but also by the tremendous resistance which the family offers to any change in the basic pattern of interaction within the family (122, 131). Many families seem to be well motivated for therapy but begin to express resistance to the therapist as soon as changes in the patient sufficiently alter the family interaction to activate anxiety in the other family members. As soon as the anxiety becomes severe enough, the parents revert to the former ways of functioning (17). The family thus forms a sort of highly inflexible system which is quite resistant to any external alteration (54, 76, 115). It has been found that even advice given to the parents is badly distorted by the emotional involvement of the parents in the child's symptoms (78). In this connection, Bowen (16) has described the difficulties in treating families with a pre- or post-adolescent behavior problem or neurosis. The parents are extremely reluctant to admit and focus on their own problem, but constantly shift back to the location of the problem in the child. This would seem to reflect the pattern of the family dynamics in which the parents had made the child's symptoms the defense against their own conflict and anxiety.

Selective Involvement

Our attention thus far has been centered on the mother-father-patient triad and the patterns of interaction characteristic of their mutual interdependence. We must not forget the other members of the family, the so-called "well siblings." Most of the work has been done on siblings in schizophrenic families with some interesting results. They have been found to be suffering from various degrees of maladjustment (27, 29), or they present a typically shallow and superficial personality picture (27). They seem to have withdrawn from the intense emotional interaction of the family and to have achieved a more detached relation to their parents (27, 29, 89, 124, 127). They are involved in the family problem but not so deeply that they cannot separate themselves from the intense dependency centered in the triad (15) nor so frequently that involvement interferes with their own capacity to function (30). In schizophrenic families, the parents are able to reach decisions about the nonschizophrenic siblings rather easily, whereas decisions related to the schizophrenic child are made with difficulty if at all (30). The role patterns between the mother and these two types of child are completely different: she is more inclined to leave the nonschizophrenic child alone, but to do so with the schizophrenic child is a source of great anxiety (88). Consequently, while the schizophrenic child is typically compliant and responsive to the demands and expectations of his parents, the nonschizophrenic sibling tends to be more independent and ignores these parental demands (88, 89). The reasons for the sometimes striking differences in the relation of siblings to the family interaction are difficult to pin down. Ehrenwald (33) seems to appeal to the balance of susceptibility and resistance in the individual, but this seems less than satisfactory. Others feel that the situation in the family at the time of the child's birth has a great deal to do in determining the child's role within the family constellation and his special relationship to the parents (89). It has been pointed out that the affected child was often a sick or unusual infant which required greater care or that the mother was sometimes under severe strain at the time of the child's birth (88). Bowen (14) believes that the selection of a particular child is determined by the mother's unconscious functioning in the prevailing reality situation. He gives an example of a close attachment to a deformed child as a situation which might come closer to fulfilling the mother's needs than would a normal child. My own experience includes a mother who had six healthy and well-adjusted children; the seventh suffered brain damage in delivery. The defective functioning of this child activated her feelings of guilt and self-doubt and at the birth of her eighth and last child, she resolved that this time there would be no defect in her mothering. This child shows every sign of emotional retardation and behavioral difficulties. A similar pattern has been observed in mothers of phobic children (35).

There is also some evidence to suggest that influences stemming from the extended family exercise an influence on the selective involvement of children. Bowen (14) cites the example of the mother who had normal relations to her first two children, but established an intense attachment to the third child who was born shortly after the death of her own mother. Subsequent investigation into the patterns of interaction in the extended family suggests that with surprisingly high frequency parental involvement with a given child is associated with the occurrence of emotionally disrupting events (deaths, serious illness, accidents, etc.), most frequently in the direct line, less frequently in the collateral line. The problem of selective involvement is one of the crucial questions in the understanding of the family. As we shall see, its solution is involved in the most essential aspects of family dynamics.

The Extended Family

Keeping our attention on the extended family for a moment, it is a frequent finding in disturbed families that one or both parents have a strong emotional attachment or disturbed relationship with their own parents (22, 26, 35, 42, 75, 79, 87, 98, 123). It seems quite clear that the experiences and residues of the interaction within the family of origin can decisively affect the course of subsequent marital adjustment and the evolution of patterns of interaction within the marital family (10a, 36, 93, 128, 129). As Lidz and his group have pointed out, the personality of each parent is a product of the interaction within his own family and the structure of their marital relationship depends on what each partner brings to it (85). But this is only part of the picture. It is important to realize that the nuclear family is not a static unit, isolated from the influence of emotional currents in other parts of the extended family. Emotionally significant events and sequences of events occurring in the respective families of origin and in their collateral branches exercise an ongoing contemporary influence which is often of major significance. The influence of the extended family does not stop at the formation of parental personalities. Both husband and wife function concurrently not only in mutual interaction, but also in a continuing engagement and involvement with their respective families of origin. Consequently current patterns of interaction within the structure of the nuclear family cannot be adequately understood without reference to the extended family.

The Schizophrenic Family

A great deal of effort has gone into the attempt to define the distinguishing characteristics of the schizophrenogenic family. Comparative studies of schizophrenic and neurotic or normal families suggest that in large measure the patterns of interaction are more or less common (15, 25, 41, 55, 76, 91, 92, 103, 113, 114, 122). Significant differences have been isolated between families with a schizophrenic child and families without. Schizophrenic families are characterized by an excessively punitive and hostile father-child relation (113), parental maladjustment with significant disharmony (41, 76), greater maternal dependence (76), and greater capacity in the parents to distort reality to suit personal needs (92). Schizophrenogenic parents, like neurotic parents, have a need to infantilize the child and perceive him as incompetent, but they do not merely overlook recognized abnormalities and contradictions (as did neurotic parents), they actually distort the meaning of behavior, accept deviant tendencies, and deny the significance of obvious abnormalities (68, 92). Bowen (15) expresses much the same observation in terms of feeling: neurotic families are better able to distinguish feeling from fact and to act on the basis of reality. Schizophrenic, or psychotic-level families, are more inclined to evaluate a situation in terms of feeling, to consider the feelings as factual, and to act on the basis of feelings rather than facts.

It should be clear from our previous discussion that these differences are not exclusive. Schizophrenic parents do raise neurotic and normal children besides one or more schizophrenic children. The mere fact, moreover, that the merely neurotic families did not raise any psychotic children does not mean that they might not have done so, given the conjunction of certain other factors. Most of the differential indicators can be discounted on this ground since they cannot be regarded as specific for schizophrenia. We are left, then, with a general impression that schizophrenogenic parents appear to be functioning at a somewhat more emotional and immature level than the parents of less disturbed children, but that the same general patterns of interaction and the same mechanisms for handling anxiety are operative in all disturbed families.

Summary

To more or less summarize the more significant aspects of this rather sketchy survey and to lay a foundation for the subsequent discussion of theory, we can set forth the following conclusions:

1) Selection of marital partner is determined in part by two principles: (a) equivalence in level of maturity, and (b) complementarity of needs.
2) Mother, father, and disturbed child form an emotionally interdependent triad, such that the functioning of each member is reactive to and dependent on the functioning of the others.
3) Within these emotionally involved relationships, incongruent communication and contradictory demands are frequent.
4) The children of emotionally immature parents are involved in and influenced by the emotional interaction within the family in varying degrees.
5) Parental maladjustment increases the probability of maladjustment in at least one child.
6) Patterns of interaction within the family are not specific to any type of pathology.

7) Specific techniques by which parents relate themselves to disturbed children cannot be consistently related to child pathology.
8) Parental dysfunction and inadequate parental relationships are
   symptomatic of emotional involvement and immature functioning.
9) The interdependent interaction within the family triad remains
   inflexible and highly resistant to alteration from outside.
10) The functioning of family members within the interdependent
    interaction are constantly influenced, often quite strongly, by
    emotional pressures deriving from the extended family.

In the theoretical discussion which follows, we will regard these
conclusions as general guide lines for evaluating theory. They can
also serve as key points which any acceptable theory of family function and dynamics should explain.

CRITIQUE OF CURRENT THEORY

At this transition point in our consideration, I am reminded of
the Kantian dictum to the effect that thoughts without content are
blind, and perceptions without concepts are empty (69). The following
considerations are necessary in order that the perceptions we have
rehearsed in the first part of this paper might not remain empty, just
as the preceding development of some of the evidence concerning the
family was required in order that our theoretical reflections might not
be completely blind. It is important to remember, in any event, that
theoretical formulations are useless unless they are closely tied to the
empirical data. But even more important, we must remember that the
very meaning of the theory has its roots in the available evidence.
Consequently a theory which ignores or discounts available evidences
or which fails to consider crucial questions cannot be regarded as an
adequate theory. Our purpose in this discussion will be to critically
survey presently available conceptions of family functioning with the
intention of determining what precisely is being explained or not
being explained in the various approaches. It is hoped that by a
dialectical appraisal of theories in reference to general empirical findings we can reach some clarification of current problems and enigmas
in the understanding of family processes. Thus we have no intention
of forming theory; we are aiming only at a prolegomenon to a future
theory.

The Family Unit

More than a decade ago, Talcott Parsons wrote in a somewhat prophetic vein (108) that "...the sociological aspects of the family as a social system have understandably not been explicitly considered by psychoanalysts because they have concentrated on the particular relations of each patient to each of the members of his family in turn. There has been little occasion to consider the total family as a social system, though this might well yield insights not derivable from the 'atomistic' treatment of each relationship in turn." In the dozen or so years since then, there has been ample occasion to consider the total family as a functioning organism (14, 15). The common conviction of theorists of family behavior today is that the family must be conceived as a functioning unit and that the functioning of individual members of the family can be understood in reference to the overall structure of the family (1, 2, 3, 19, 20, 54, 55, 63, 72, 118, 131, 135). This represents the primary apperception of family theory and constitutes the principle point of divergence from the traditional, individual-oriented framework of psychiatric thinking. The shift from an individual to a family orientation is not without its pitfalls (15), but it would seem to be necessary for the family approach.

Within this general consensus, however, there are differences in perspective and approach, and different theorists stress different aspects of family functioning. The predominant orientation today sees the family as an interactional, or better transactional, system. The overwhelmingly complex nature of the family interaction has promoted a considerable fragmentation of research effort and conceptualization. Interest has centered for the most part on the nuclear family and most intensely on the father-mother-child configuration. Differential interests approach the analysis of the family system at different levels with the result that conceptualization of the family system is expressed in terms of analyses of interactional processes (10, 54, 55, 63, 65, 131, 134), pattern analyses (61, 81, 82, 83, 84, 85), analyses of structure (1, 2, 3, 4, 72, 118, 127, 134) and functional analyses (14, 15, 16).

Personality Development

On the positive side, it is agreed that the family provides the context of personality development and that it serves as the mediating agency for the influences of the larger cultural context. The process of personality growth is envisioned as constituting a progression from a condition of infantile dependence upon the parents to a condition of relative adult independence (3, 4, 16, 81, 115). There are certain nuances in the descriptions of the process which reflect differential interests. Lidz (81, 84, 85) places the emphasis on identity formation through interaction with parental figures. The ego develops specifically in relation to objects, and the child's world of objects is created by the parents in mutual interaction (80). By introjection and identification with the parental figures, the child moves normally toward increasing independence, achieving full identity toward the end of adolescence (84). The emphasis falls on identification and the mechanisms of interaction. Thus the defect in development is described in terms of defective establishment of object-relations, inadequate separation from early symbiotic objects, lack of healthy and culturally useful identification patterns, and disturbances in role-taking and identity formation within the family environment (6, 44), all of which reflect the dominant interest in patterns and mechanisms of interaction. Development is a function of experience (learning), action, and reaction (80), on the level of process analysis as proposed by Parsons and Bales (109).

Along the same lines, Ackerman (1, 3, 4) and Wynne (118, 134) place greater emphasis on identity formation as a process of integration of role-functions. Ackerman speaks of separation and differentiation from the parental matrix (4), but his emphasis is more operational and perceptual in the sense that the developing child becomes more aware of himself as distinct from the mother and later becomes aware of differentiations in the respective roles of mother and father. Identification follows upon the recognition of these distinctions. Wynne (118) places emphasis on the integration of these roles in the formation of a mature identity, not only within the individual himself but also within the total structure of the family (134). This conception of the developmental process reflects the concern of these theorists with the relation of interactional processes to the structure of the family in terms of roles.

A somewhat different emphasis is struck by Bowen (14, 16). He regards the primary symbiosis as constituting an "emotional oneness," which he describes as the "undifferentiated family ego mass." The process of personality development is correlatively a process of differ-

entiation of self from the family ego mass (16). The term "undifferentiated family ego mass" is unwieldy and perhaps confusing, but it
points to a level of family organization which is left unarticulated in
other approaches, namely a primitive emotional stratum in which
the fusion of emotionality makes the family more of an organic unit
than its transactional relations would imply. It is not clear how
identity formation proceeds in this theory, but it is intimately involved with the process of differentiation. Bowen is more concerned
with the failure of differentiation, which is of greater clinical concern
since it underlies and provides the context for overt symptoms. It is
clear, however, that the emphasis in this approach is not on the family
as an interactional system, nor on the structure of the family as a
group; rather it brings into focus a quite different level of family
emotional organization.

Family Pathology

On the negative side, it is generally agreed that the family itself is
the locus of resident pathology and that the patient is somehow externalizing and expressing symptomatically the underlying disturbance within the family (2, 7, 13, 14, 15, 19, 20, 53, 54, 80, 83, 84, 85,
115, 118, 122, 124, 135). Differences again emerge in the attempts to
specify the precise operations or mechanisms within the family system which are involved in designating or "making" the patient the
sick one. Identification is often appealed to in this context, in the
sense that the patient's failure to achieve mature development is
influenced by his identification with inferior parental figures or in the
sense that he introjects and internalizes parental values (13), ambivalent and antisocial impulses (48), and immature parental narcissism
(85). In this sense, the child can be said to identify with the unconscious, repressed, and conflictual aspects of the parental imagos (2,
3, 53).

Communication and Homeostasis

In explaining the assimilation of unconscious elements within the
family much has been made of communication theory (10, 117).
Contradictory patterns of verbal and nonverbal communication have
been described for phobic symptoms (35), antisocial acting-out (48),

and schizophrenia (83). The most influential formulation of the breakdown of communication in schizophrenia is that of Bateson's double bind hyopthesis (10). Normal human communication takes place at a number of levels, in which primary communications are continually qualified or "labeled" by mode-identifying signals. This discrimination is poorly developed in terms of language, so that its rich complexity is conveyed predominantly by nonverbal media (gesture, expression, intonation, context, etc.). Bateson sees the basic difficulty of the schizophrenic in his inability to discriminate communicational modes in the messages he receives from others, in the messages he emits to others, and in his own thoughts and sensations. Bateson argues that the family interaction must have provided a context in which unconventional communication habits would be appropriate. The double bind characterizes this developmental context and involves the following characteristics: (1) interaction or communication between two or more persons, (2) repeated experience sufficient to make the double bind structure an habitual expectation, (3) a primary negative injunction at one level of communication, involving a threat of punishment (arousal of anxiety), (4) a secondary injunction conflicting with the first at another level of communication and similarly reinforced with the threat of punishment, and (5) a tertiary injunction prohibiting escape from the field of interaction. It is impossible for the schizophrenic to discriminate, or correct his discrimination, of what order of message he is expected to respond to, i.e., he cannot communicate metacommunicatively (about his communications). There is thus a twofold demand pervading the patient's interaction with his family (10) which Bowen has expressed as an emotional demand to remain a child together with a typically verbalized demand to become a mature person (14). Consequently, in the schizophrenic family, there is a consistent incongruence between what they say and how they qualify what they say. Each member actively disqualifies the communications of the other members; the pattern is intermittent, but seems to be activated whenever any family member infringes the prohibitive rules of noninfringement which govern the family relationships (54, 63).

This approach evidently approaches the problem of dysfunction from a fresh avenue. The traditional psychiatric framework would dictate that the message was to be regarded as simple and the people receiving or sending it more or less confused. The communication theory, however, perceives the message as complex and incongruent. This viewpoint requires that the family behavior be perceived as circular rather than linear, as governed by homeostatic patterns of interaction which operate within the transactional system to preserve the balance of forces and needs (61, 131). The primary law of interaction in such a system seems to be that "when an organism indicates a change in relation to another, the other will act on the first so as to diminish and modify that change." (55) The family system evolves into a self-reinforcing and mutually destructive network of interaction in which the primary emphasis is on the preservation of existing patterns. The family system is consequently highly resistive to external change (106, 115). The operation of such homeostatic mechanisms has been observed by other family therapists (2, 3, 7, 14).

The communication theory and particularly the double bind hypothesis is aimed at providing an explanation of paralogical patterns of thinking and the obviously disturbed communication of the schizophrenic patient. The combination of this approach with Jackson's notion of homeostatic mechanisms not only helps to explain thought disturbances in the schizophrenic, but it also provides an excellent descriptive analogy for the comparatively "fixed" relations within the schizophrenic family. There remain certain gaps in the theory, however, which restrict its applicability. The double bind itself does not explain the differences between prepsychotic communication and psychotic communication, nor does it seem to make any provision for the fact of the psychotic break. There does not seem to be any explanation offered of the phenomenon of selective involvement among members of the same family (see conclusion 4 above). The theory should account for the fact that one or other child is caught up in the double bind and the others are not. Similarly, one wonders how the double bind can explain the presence in the same families (or in other families for that matter) of nonschizophrenic disturbances which do not manifest the thought disturbances characteristic of schizophrenia. Furthermore, Bateson himself (10) recognizes that the development of the double bind situation rests upon the antecedent impossibility of the patient's making a direct, clarifying metacommunication. The possibility is not open to him because his intense dependency prevents him from communicating about his mother's communicative behavior (10, p. 259). It seems, then, that the double bind itself needs explanation, both as regards its existence and as regards its direction.

It is important to keep in mind what the double bind hypothesis does explain. Given the operation of other factors to put it in effect, the double bind contributes to our understanding of some of the mechanisms involved in determining the form of schizophrenic symptoms. Similarly, the notion of homeostatic processes brings into focus the transactional nature of the family interrelations. Neither the double bind nor homeostatic processes can be understood without an underlying emotional involvement, yet both of them can be regarded as techniques evolved within the family group to maintain the balance of emotional forces. Incongruent communication and statement disqualification may thus be the preferred patterns of interaction in any relationship in which congruent communication carries with it the risk of a negative response or of a nonresponse in the other. This risk must be avoided because the communicator "needs" the relationship with the other in order to maintain his own functioning. Emotionally he is caught between the need to communicate in order to preserve the relationship and the need to avoid clarifying communication with its associated risk. He resolves the dilemma by so masking and qualifying his communications that the possibility of a rejecting response from the cocommunicator is diminished. At the same time, this same maneuver diminishes the probability of a clear positive response from the other. The range of communications tends to gravitate to a "safe" middle ground in which neither party is effectively communicating but from which neither party will run the risk of deviating. The same thing can be said for homeostatic processes, since the pattern of action and reaction is aimed at preserving the existing balance and counteracting any deviation from the existing pattern of implicit rules and expectations governing the relations of the members. In either case, such a system comes about because of a prior emotional involvement and is kept in operation by the demands of the continuing involvement. It is this emotional involvement within the family system which requires explanation and which remains at present an operative but implicit presumption of communication theory.

Role Structure

Another prominent approach to the understanding of the genesis of pathology within the family looks to the role structure of the family as the medium of analysis (1, 2, 3, 72, 122, 127, 134). The primary structural component of the family system is the role, i.e., the functioning form the individual assumes in reacting to a specific situation in which other persons or objects are involved. The role concept, therefore, incorporates personal and collective elements (99). Responses within the system are directed by role expectations which are learned through reciprocal transactions, typically within the family transactions involving the parents. Role behavior both satisfies individual needs and regulates the pattern of interaction within the family system (72). The orientation which this approach gives to therapy has been expressed in the following terms:

> From all this it is apparent that an appropriate frame of reference has not yet been designed, within which it is possible to integrate the therapy of an individual with the therapy of a family group. The treatment of a mother of a disturbed child is the treatment of a role, a highly specialized family function. It is not identical with the therapy of a whole woman, but rather of the personality of that woman integrated into a special social function, that of mothering (1).

Thus therapy aims at defining the interdependence of individual homeostasis with the homeostatic balance of role relations in family pairs and in the family as a whole, and specifically to support constructive forms of complementarity in role relations (2).

Complementarity in role relations is the normal family pattern (127). Ackerman (3) has defined complementarity as the "specific patterns of family role relations that provide satisfaction, avenues of solutions of conflict, support for a needed self-image and buttressing of crucial forms of defenses against anxiety." Complementarity is positive when family members experience mutual fulfillment of need in a way which promotes emotional growth of the relation and the interacting members; it is negative when it serves as a defense against pathogenic anxiety but does not foster positive emotional growth.

Within the family system, the sources of pathogenic disturbance can be found in the conflict or disequilibrium of role relations (2). Sources of tension can be related to differences in cultural value-orientations and social role expectations (127). The disturbed child becomes involved frequently in the conflictual role relations of the parents, which are accompanied by elevated levels of tension and anxiety. Therapy is usually directed to re-establishing patterns of complementarity in which the new equilibrium relieves the anxiety. Within the family structure, the patterns of role relations are divided according to sex and generation, i.e., male-female, parent-child (109).

The role uncertainties of the parents in schizophrenic families, especially regarding sex and parental roles, create an unstable family structure which apparently accentuates homosexual and incestuous tendencies in the children (44, 84).

In the schizophrenic family, attention has been called to the relatively rigid and inflexible role structure (115, 118, 134). Family roles are grossly condensed and stereotyped, complex experiences are reduced to simplified formulae, the family evolves a rigid conception of itself which defines the roles to which members adhere. Members collaborate in enforcing adherence to the shared role structure and any attempt to modify this structure must contend with repressive forces in the other members (118). Thus the collusively maintained family role structure exercises a tremendous influence on the child's identity formation. The family picture is dominated by a fixed organization of a limited number of roles with fluidity in the designation of which member fills which role at any given time. In a normal family, the role structure is continually undergoing modification in terms of the needs and expectation of family members, but in the disturbed family the sameness of the role structure is preserved despite changes. The shared mechanisms, by which deviations are excluded from recognition or delusionally reinterpreted, act to prohibit any meanings that might enable an individual family member to differentiate his personal identity either inside or outside the family role structure. As Wynne (134) perceives this situation, the structure is maintained by what he calls "pseudo-mutuality", which is based on an emotional need to maintain a sense of reciprocal fulfillment of expectations, but which emphasizes a predominant absorption in fitting together at the expense of the differentiation of the identities of the persons in the relationship. Consequently, the characteristics of the schizophrenic patient (fragmentation of experience, identity diffusion, disturbed modes of perception and communication) are derived from the family role structure by internalization (134). The internalized family role structure and its associated family subculture operate in the individual as a kind of primitive superego, and effect a reciprocal investment on the part of the child in preserving the family role structure which forms the basis of his personality equilibrium. Family members thereby satisfy the need to achieve a sense of relatedness, but they do so at the expense of personal identity, by destruction of meaning, by the fragmentation of experience and the chronic elimination of broad areas of felt experience

(122). The family has thus failed to present a context within which the meaningful integration of roles is possible. The schizophrenic has consequently failed to make the essential transition from the mere assimilation of roles, through the mechanism of identification, to a mature and functioning identity, through the process of identity formation (37, 118).

The general approach to understanding the family in terms of role structure and role functions obviously strikes at a different level of family organization than the communication type theory. Consequently, the analyses provided by each can be regarded as complementary and the analysis of communicative behavior within the respective family roles would undoubtedly serve a useful function. However, role theory also leaves some significant gaps. It does not give an account, for example, of why each individual assumes his respective role; given these respective roles, it provides a systematic framework for describing their interaction. It also does not explain why the internalization of the family role structure on the part of one child should make him schizophrenic, but on the part of another child it should make him neurotic or even normal. It provides the means for describing these relations once they have been brought into existence, but it does not explain how they came into existence. Even Wynne's excellent treatment of pseudo-mutuality (134) would seem to present this same difficulty. Pseudo-mutuality describes a type of relationship which helps to explain certain characteristics of the family role structure in schizophrenic families, but we are not told how this type of interaction came about or why it exists.

We are more or less forced to search out other factors than those provided by the role analysis to account for the impact on the family system. This does not mean that the influence of these factors is not mediated through the family role structure, although it would suggest that without such factors the role structure itself could not have its pathogenic effect. We must answer the question, why do family roles become stereotyped and what motivates the absorption in preservation of the family role structure in its rigid inflexibility? We are again confronted with an underlying emotional involvement which must be presumed to account for the operation of the mechanisms provided by the theory (pseudo-mutuality) but which is more or less presumed by the theory. It is as though the role structure were operating at one level of analysis, while the group was functioning in terms of another level of analysis which was at once more primitive and less organized, but which determined the effectiveness of the role structure. We are undoubtedly dealing here with a phenomenon similar to that described by Bion (11) in dealing with groups: the twofold level of group inter- action, one more conscious and governed by tendencies to work, the other more primitive and undifferentiated and governed by tendencies to emotionality.

This raises a more general question which can be asked about the types of transactional analysis we have been considering. The problem is one of deciding where to lay the burden of etiological significance. The theorist can search out an explanation for the facts of family functioning and disturbance at one of several levels. Communication theorists hypothesize that the significant variables can be discovered at the level of behavioral interaction. Role theorists hypothesize that the significant variables will be found in the definition of specific patterns of role interaction which would be associated with forms of pathology. Further removed from the behavioral pole, the significant variables can be sought at a more primitive level of emotional involve- ment. The lack of identifiable patterns of interaction (conclusion 6 above) and the apparent indifference of behavioral elements (conclu- sion 7 above) would tend to reinforce the persuasion that the signifi- cant etiological variables should be sought at the more primitive emo- tional level. Bowen's (14) observation that when the parents in his families were emotionally invested or close to their children, the chil- dren automatically regressed and all management approaches were equally unsuccessful, and that when the parents were not emotionally invested in the children, the patient improved and all varieties of man- agement technique proved successful, is a striking confirmation of this possibility.

Family Mechanisms

Other authors have discussed separate mechanisms within the fam- ily structure. Brodey (19, 20) has described externalization (projection plus the selective use of reality for the verification of this projection) and the narcissistic relationship (relation with a projected part of the self as mirrored in the other's behavior). In the narcissistic relation- ship, each member acts in such a way as to validate the expectations of the other derived from the projected image. In family relations of this sort, the unexpected is so reduced that each member can predict the behavior of the other family members. Along the same line, Bowen (14) has described the mother-child relation in terms of the mechanisms of projection and introjection. According to this conception, the mother denies her own feelings of helplessness and immaturity by projecting them onto the child. She is able to function more adequately by perceiving the child as helpless and in need of mothering. The mother, the child, and even the entire family accept this perception as a reality in the child, so that what began as a feeling in the mother becomes a reality in the child. The mother's projection is reciprocated by an introjection on the part of the child of the mother's inadequacies. As Bowen perceives this interaction, the child is drawn into it by automatically protecting his own interests by acting in such a way as to insure a less anxious mother. Similarly the father accepts and reinforces this situation because it stabilizes the mother emotionally and thus permits the father to have a less anxious relationship with the mother. Such mechanisms have a definite value, but the same criticism must be brought against them as was brought against communication and role theory, namely that they are unintelligible without a substratum of emotional involvement.

Another facet of family interaction which demands better understanding is the manner in which the extended family influences the dynamics of the nuclear family. Most of the current theories treat the interaction in preceding generations in terms of the formative influence on the personality of the parent in the present generation. It is as though the influence of the prior generation ceased to be a significant factor as soon as the child marries and forms a family unit of his own. Even Bowen's three-generational idea of the development of the schizophrenic process traces the process discontinuously from generation to generation (14). This may allow for a concurrent and contemporary influence derived from the extended family, but it does not provide the explanation for it. This is one direction in which fruitful investigation and thinking can be extended.

Toward a Family Theory

The fundamental insight of family therapy and the basic premise of family theory is that the family is the basic unit of conceptualization. The patient is thereby only externalizing through his symptoms an illness which is inherent in the family itself. He is a symptomatic organ of a diseased organism. To put it another way, there is a stage in the family process in which the emotionally involved family members are all more or less susceptible of becoming "the patient." It is essential, therefore, that family theory express and explain this undifferentiated equipotentiality; that it articulate a concept which represents the functional unity of the family system. It can be questioned whether any of the transactional theories of family functioning achieve this purpose. It can be questioned, for example, whether the transactional system is so linked to the patterns of interpersonal action and reaction that it must by its nature remain a composite concept whose meaning can be spelled out only by reductive explicitation of its component interpersonal interactions. Or, putting it another way, is the transactional concept so closely tied to the level of individual interaction that it can not be effectively raised to the more comprehensive level of the family as a unit? For the moment, we can go no further than the question.

From what has been said thus far, it is apparent that we have only begun to explore the complexity of family organization and functioning. Reflection on the available data and on current theoretical orientations makes it obvious that we are dealing with disparate levels of family functioning in the real order and with disparate levels of analysis in the theoretical order. Current theories tend to arrange themselves at various levels of "depth" in the description and understanding of family processes, namely, the level of behavioral analysis, the level of transactional analysis, and finally the level of emotional analysis. It is important to realize that each of these levels of analysis is concerned with different levels of operation within the family system and that each focuses on and gives emphasis to different aspects of the overall family organization and function. It is as though we were able to put the family under a microscope and were able to focus on several levels of the family and observe its processes at each level. We observe different facts at each level, but we know that we are in fact studying a single organism. If the microscope of theoretical formulation is still very rough so that we can only focus it at a few stages, we can have the confidence that the development of a more refined instrument will enable us to see better the interplay between the various levels. The instrument will be refined, of course, by a continued sharpening of present concepts and the progressive elaboration of more adequate concepts which will permit greater flexibility in achieving an understanding of the reality of the family.

But at the same time, the work of focusing at any given level is accomplished by certain techniques which are proper to that level. There are a great many available methods for the study of the family (28), but it is well to remember that methods are selective and that, in terms of our analogue, they are by their nature relevant to specific levels of family interaction. Mere behavioral observation will not gather any evidence or shed any light on the inner emotional dynamisms which permeate the family functioning, but behavioral observation will shed a great deal of light on the detailed patterns and sequence of interaction which take place between family members. Similarly, the family history approach will not shed much light on behavioral interaction or on intrapsychic or even interpsychic mechanisms; but this same approach is really the only available means for studying the broad sweep and significant conjunction of events within the extended family.

Consequently, in an area in which research and thinking are more exploratory (131) than definitive, the student of family dynamics must not confine the scope of his thinking about the family, even though he commits himself to an intensification of research effort in relation to a specific level of family interaction and in terms of a pertinent set of investigatory techniques. It is important, therefore, that he keep clearly in mind what kind of question he is asking, what specific facts and aspects in the family he is trying to explain or understand, what the limitations and relevance are of the instruments he chooses and the methods he employs to explore the family organism. As we have tried to suggest, each variable has an explanatory capacity in that it helps to understand some dimension of the family and therefore can be discarded only when it can be replaced functionally within the theory by another variable which offers better insight or which can be more systematically anchored within the overall theory.

At the present time, there are no clear cut indicators as to where in the various levels of family functioning and analysis the significant etiological and pathogenic variables are to be located. This is an important question because it is the identification of such variables which determines the link between theory and therapy. The analysis of data which we have presented above and the significant explanatory gaps in prevailing theories have suggested to us that the significant variables concerned with family dysfunction and decompensation are to be found at a more primitive level of emotional involvement in which the fusion of emotionality within the family attains a unitary condition by which it is a function of the family unit itself, independent but not divorced from the emotionality of its component individuals. This undifferentiated emotional system retains involvements with the extended family principally through parental figures, who are concurrently involved in both the nuclear family and their respective families of origin. While such a conception offers the possibility of giving greater unity to the fragmentary and fragmented approaches we have been discussing, it too would have its limitations and specificity of explanatory power. The articulation of this deeper level of conceptualization and the other pertinent levels of analysis remains a work of the future. So also the integration of family dynamics with the understanding of individual intrapsychic dynamics remains a challenging area to family theorists. We can hope that the cross-fertilization of diverse methods, interests, techniques and theories will yield in time a better understanding of the ways in which the human person comes to be what he is and to function in the way he functions within the context of the complex and often perplexing family organism.

REFERENCES

1. ACKERMAN, N. W., "Interpersonal Disturbances in the Family: Some Unsolved Problems in Psychotherapy," *Psychiatry*, 17, 359–368, 1954.
2. ACKERMAN, N. W., "Toward an Integrative Therapy of the Family," *Amer. J. Psychiat.*, 114, 727–733, 1958.
3. ACKERMAN, N. W., *The psychodynamics of family life*, New York, Basic Books, 1958.
4. ACKERMAN, N. W. and BEHRENS, M. L., "Child and Family Psychopathy: Problems of Correlation," in Hoch, P. H. and Zubin, J. (Eds.) *Psychopathology of childhood*, New York, Grune & Stratton, 1955. Pp. 177–196.
5. AGRAS, S., "The Relationship of School Phobia to Childhood Depression," *Amer. J. Psychiat.*, 116, 533–536, 1959.
6. ALANEN, Y. O., "Some Thoughts of Schizophrenia and Ego Development in the Light of Family Investigations," *Arch. Gen. Psychiat.*, 3, 650–656, 1960.
7. ALBERT, R. S., "Stages of Breakdown in the Relationships and Dynamics between the Mental Patient and His Family," *Arch. Gen. Psychiat.*, 3, 682–690, 1960.

8. ARONSON, J. and POLGAR, S., "Pathogenic Relationships in Schizophrenia," *Amer. J. Psychiat.*, 119, 222–227, 1962.

9. BACH, G. R., "Father-fantasies and Father-typing in Father-separated Children," *Child Develpm.*, 17, 63–80, 1946.

10. BATESON, G., JACKSON, D. D., HALEY, J. and WEAKLAND, J., "Toward a Theory of Schizophrenia," *Behav. Sci.*, 1, 251–264, 1956.

10a. BELL, N. W., "Extended Family Relations of Disturbed and Well Families," *Fam. Proc.*, 1, 175–193, 1962.

11. BION, W. R., *Experience in groups*, New York, Basic Books, 1961.

12. BOSSARD, J. H. S. and BOLL, E. S., "Adjustment of Siblings in Large Families," *Amer. J. Psychiat.*, 112, 889–892, 1956.

13. BOSZORMENYI-NAGY, I., "The Concept of Schizophrenia from the Perspective of Family Treatment," *Fam. Proc.*, 1, 103–113, 1962.

14. BOWEN, M., "A Family Concept of Schizophrenia," in Jackson, D. D. (Ed.) *The Etiology of Schizophrenia*, New York, Basic Books, 1960. Pp. 346–372.

15. BOWEN, M., "The Family as the Unit of Study and Treatment. 1. Family Psychotherapy," *Amer. J. Orthopsychiat.*, 31, 40–60, 1961.

16. BOWEN, M., "Out-patient Family Psychotherapy," paper read at St. Elizabeths Medical Society, St. Elizabeths Hospital, Washington, D.C., April 21, 1961.

17. BOWEN, M., DYSINGER, R. H. and BASAMANIA, B., "The Role of the Father in Families with a Schizophrenic Patient," *Amer. J. Psychiat.*, 115, 1017–1020, 1959.

18. BOWLBY, J., "Childhood Mourning and its Implications for Psychiatry," *Amer. J. Psychiat.*, 118, 481–498, 1961.

19. BRODEY, W. M., "Some Family Operations and Schizophrenia. A Study of Five Hospitalized Families Each with a Schizophrenic Member," *Arch. gen. Psychiat.*, 1, 379–402, 1959.

20. BRODEY, W. M., "The Family as the Unit of Study and Treatment. 3. Image, Object and Narcissistic Relationships," *Amer. J. Orthopsychiat.*, 31, 69–73, 1961.

21. CARLSON, H. B., "Characteristics of an Acute Confusional State in College Students," *Amer. J. Psychiat.*, 114, 900–909, 1958.

22. CLARK, A. N. and VAN SOMMERS, P., "Contradictory Demands in Family Relations and Adjustment to School and Home," *Hum. Relat.*, 14, 97–111, 1961.

23. COLM, H. N., "Phobias in Children," *Psychoanal. and Psychoanal. Rev.*, 46, 65–84, 1959.

24. COOLRIDGE, J. C., WILLER, M. L., TESSMAN, E. and WALDFOGEL, S., "School Phobia in Adolescence: A Manifestation of Severe Character Disturbance," *Amer. J. Orthopsychiat.*, 30, 599–607, 1960.

25. CUMMINGS, J. H., "The Family and Mental Disorder: An Incomplete Essay," *Milbank Mem. Fd. Quart.*, 39, 185–212, 1961.
26. DAVIDSON, S., "School Phobia as a Manifestation of Family Disturbance: Its Structure and Treatment," *J. Child Psychol. Psychiat.*, 1, 270–287, 1961.
27. DAY, J. and KWIATKOWSKA, H. Y., "The Psychiatric Patient and his 'Well' Sibling," *Bull. Art Ther.*, Winter, 51–66, 1962.
28. DELAY, J., DENIKER, P. and GREEN, A., "Le milieu familial des schizophrenes. II. Methodes d'approche," *Encéphale*, 49, 1–21, 1959.
29. DELAY, J., DENIKER, P. and GREEN, A., "Le milieu familial des schizophrenes. III. Résultats et hypothèses," *Encéphale*, 51, 5–73, 1962.
30. DYSINGER, R. H., "The Family as the Unit of Study and Treatment. 2. A Family Perspective on the Diagnosis of Individual Members," *Amer. J. Orthopsychiat.*, 31, 61–68, 1961.
31. EASSON, W. M., "Murderous Aggression by Children and Adolescents," *Arch. Gen. Psychiat.*, 4, 1–9, 1961.
32. EHRENWALD, J., "Neurotic Interaction and Patterns of Pseudoheredity in the Family," *Amer. J. Psychiat.*, 115, 134–142, 1958.
33. EHRENWALD, J., "Neurosis in the Family: A Study of Psychiatric Epidemiology," *Arch. Gen. Psychiat.*, 3, 232–242, 1960.
34. EISENBERG, L., "The Fathers of Autistic Children," *Amer. J. Orthopsychiat.*, 27, 715–724, 1957.
35. EISENBERG, L., "School Phobia: A Study in the Communication of Anxiety," *Amer. J. Psychiat.*, 114, 712–718, 1958.
36. EPSTEIN, N. B. and WESTLEY, W. A., "Parental Interaction as Related to the Emotional Health of Children," *Soc. Probl.*, 8, 87–92, 1960.
37. ERIKSON, E. H., *Identity and the Life Cycle*, New York, International Universities Press, 1959.
38. FALLDING, H., "The Family and the Idea of the Cardinal Role," *Hum. Relat.*, 14, 329–350, 1961.
39. FARINA, A., "Patterns of Role Dominance and Conflict in Parents of Schizophrenic Patients," *J. Abnorm. Soc. Psychol.*, 61, 31–38, 1960.
40. FINCH, S. M. and HESS, J. H., "Ulcerative Colitis in Children," *Amer. J. Psychiat.*, 118, 819–826, 1962.
41. FISHER, S., BOYD, I., WALKER, D. and SHEER, D., "Parents of Schizophrenics, Neurotics and Normals," *Arch. Gen. Psychiat.*, 1, 149–166, 1959.
42. FLECK, S., "Family Dynamics and Origin of Schizophrenia," *Psychosom. Med.*, 22, 333–344, 1960.
43. FLECK, S., CORNELISON, A. R., NORTON, N. and LIDZ, T., "The Intrafamilial Environment of the Schizophrenic Patient. II. Interaction Between Hospital Staff and Families," *Psychiatry*, 20, 343–350, 1957.

44. FLECK, S., LIDZ, T. and CORNELISON, A., "Comparison of Parent-child Relationships of Male and Female Schizophrenic Patients," *Arch. Gen. Psychiat.*, 8, 1–7, 1963.

45. GARMEZY, N., CLARKE, A. R. and STOCKNER, C., "Child Rearing Attitudes of Mothers and Fathers as Reported by Schizophrenic and Normal Patients," *J. Abnorm. Soc. Psychol.*, 63, 176–182, 1961.

46. GERARD, D. and SIEGEL, J., "The Family Background of Schizophrenia," *Psychiat. Quart.*, 24, 47–73, 1950.

47. GIBSON, R. W., COHEN, M. B. and COHEN, R. A., "On the Dynamics of the Manic-depressive Personality," *Amer. J. Psychiat.*, 115, 1101–1107, 1959.

48. GIFFIN, M. E., JOHNSON, A. M. and LITIN, E. M., "Specific Factors Determining Antisocial Acting Out," *Amer. J. Orthopsychiat.*, 24, 668–684, 1954.

49. GLIDEWELL, J. C., MENSH, I. N. and GILDEA, M. C. L., "Behavior Symptoms in Children and Degree of Sickness," *Amer. J. Psychiat.*, 114, 47–53, 1957.

50. GREENE, B. L., "Marital Disharmony: Concurrent Analysis of Husband and Wife," *Dis. Nerv. System*, 21, 73–78, 1960.

51. GREGORY, I., "Studies of Parental Deprivation in Psychiatric Patients," *Amer. J. Psychiat.*, 115, 432–442, 1958.

52. GREGORY, I., "Selected Personal and Family Data on 400 Psychiatric Inpatients," *Amer. J. Psychiat.*, 119, 397–403, 1962.

53. GROTJAHN, M., *Psychoanalysis and the Family Neurosis*, New York, Norton, 1960.

54. HALEY, J., "The Family of the Schizophrenic: A Model System," *J. Nerv. Ment. Dis.*, 129, 357–374, 1959.

55. HALEY, J., "Family Experiments: A New Type of Experimentation," *Fam. Proc.*, 1, 265–293, 1962.

56. HALEY, J., "Whither Family Therapy," *Fam. Proc.*, 1, 69–100, 1962.

57. HILGARD, J. R., NEWMAN, M. F. and FISK, F., "Strength of Adult Ego Following Childhood Bereavement," *Amer. J. Orthopsychiat.*, 30, 788–798, 1960.

58. HIRSCH, R., "Group Therapy with Parents of Adolescent Drug Addicts," *Psychiat. Quart.*, 35, 702–710, 1961.

59. HITSON, H. M. and FUNKENSTEIN, D. H., "Family Patterns and Paranoidal Personality Structure in Boston and Burma," *Int. J. Soc. Psychiat.*, 5, 182–190, 1959.

60. HOLLINGSHEAD, A. B., "Class Differences in Family Stability," *Ann. Amer. Acad. Polit. Soc. Sci.*, 272, 39–46, 1950.

61. JACKSON, D. D., "The Question of Family Homeostasis," *Psychiat. Quart. Supp.*, 31, 79–90, 1957.

62. JACKSON, D. D., BLOCK, J. and PATTERSON, V., "Psychiatrists' Conceptions of the Schizophrenogenic Parent," *Arch. Neurol. Psychiat.*, 79, 448–459, 1958.

63. JACKSON, D. D., RISKIN, J. and SATIR, V., "A Method of Analysis of a Family Interview," *Arch. Gen. Psychiat.*, 5, 321–339, 1961.

64. JACKSON, D. D. and WEAKLAND, J. H., "Schizophrenic Symptoms and Family Interaction," *Arch. Gen. Psychiat.*, 1, 618–621, 1959.

65. JACKSON, D. D. and WEAKLAND, J. H., "Conjoint Family Therapy: Some Considerations on Theory, Technique, and Results," *Psychiatry*, 24, 30–45, 1961.

66. JACOBS, E. G. and MESNIKOFF, A. M., "Alternating Psychoses in Twins: Report of 4 Cases," *Amer. J. Psychiat.*, 117, 791–797, 1961.

67. JENSEN, S. E., "Five Psychotic Siblings," *Amer. J. Psychiat.*, 119, 159–163, 1962.

68. KANE, R. P. and CHAMBERS, G. S., "Improvement—Real or Apparent? A Seven Year Follow-up of Children Hospitalized and Discharged from a Residential Setting," *Amer. J. Psychiat.*, 117, 1023–1027, 1961.

69. KANT, I., *The Critique of Pure Reason*, London, 1929.

70. KAUFMAN, I., FRANK, T., FRIEND, J., HEIMS, L. W. and WEISS, R., "Success and Failure in the Treatment of Childhood Schizophrenia," *Amer. J. Psychiat.*, 118, 909–915, 1962.

71. KAUFMAN, I., FRANK, T., HEIMS, L., HERRICK, J., REISER, D. and WILLER, L., "Treatment Implications of a New Classification of Parents of Schizophrenic Children," *Amer. J. Psychiat.*, 116, 920–924, 1960.

72. KLUCKHOHN, F. and SPIEGEL, J. P., "Integration and Conflict in Family Behavior," Topeka, Kansas, GAP Report No. 27, 1954.

73. KOHL, R. N., "Pathologic Reactions of Marital Partners to Improvement of Patients," *Amer. J. Psychiat.*, 118, 1036–1041, 1962.

74. KREITMAN, N., "Mental Disorder in Married Couples," *J. Ment. Sci.*, 108, 438–446, 1962.

75. LAKIN, M., "Assessment of Significant Role Attitudes in Primiparous Mothers by Means of a Modification of the TAT," *Psychosom. Med.*, 19, 50–60, 1957.

76. LANE, R. C. and SINGER, J. L., "Familial Attitudes in Paranoid Schizophrenics and Normals from Two Socio-economic Classes," *J. Abnorm. Soc. Psychol.*, 59, 328–339, 1959.

77. LEVENSON, E. A., "The Treatment of School Phobias in the Young Adult," *Amer. J. Psychother.*, 15, 539–552, 1961.

78. LEVITT, M. and RUBENSTEIN, B. O., "The Fate of Advice: Examples of Distortion in Parental Counseling," *Ment. Hyg.*, 41, 213–216, 1957.

79. LICHTENBERG, J. D. and PAO, PING-NIE, "The Prognostic and Therapeutic Significance of the Husband-wife Relationship for Hospitalized Schizophrenic Women," *Psychiatry*, 23, 209–213, 1960.

80. Lidz, T., "Schizophrenia and the Family," *Psychiatry*, 21, 21–27, 1958.
81. Lidz, T., Cornelison, A. R., Fleck, S. and Terry, D., "The Intrafamilial Environment of the Schizophrenic Patient. I. The Father," *Psychiatry*, 20, 329–342, 1957.
82. Lidz, T., Cornelison, A. R., Fleck, S. and Terry, D., "The Intrafamilial Environment of Schizophrenic Patients. II. Marital Schism and Marital Skew," *Amer. J. Psychiat.*, 114, 241–248, 1957.
83. Lidz, T., Cornelison, A., Terry, D. and Fleck, S., "Intrafamilial Environment of the Schizophrenic Patient. VI. The Transmission of Irrationality," *Arch. Neurol. Psychiat.*, 79, 305–316, 1958.
84. Lidz, T. and Fleck, S., "Schizophrenia, Human Integration, and the Role of the Family," in Jackson, D. D. (Ed.) *The etiology of schizophrenia*, New York, Basic Books, 1960, p.p. 323–345.
85. Lidz, T., Fleck, S., Cornelison, A. and Terry, D., "The Intrafamilial Environment of the Schizophrenic Patient. IV. Parental Personalities and Family Interaction," *Amer. J. Orthopsychiat.*, 28, 764–776, 1958.
86. Lidz, T., Parker, B. and Cornelison, A., "The Role of the Father in the Family Environment of the Schizophrenic Patient," *Amer. J. Psychiat.*, 113, 126–132, 1956.
87. Long, R. T., Lamont, J. H., Whipple, B., Bandler, L., Blom, G. E., Burgin, L. and Jessner, L., "A Psychosomatic Study of Allergic and Emotional Factors in Children with Asthma," *Amer. J. Psychiat.*, 114, 890–899, 1958.
88. Lu, Yi-chuang, "Mother-child Role Relations in Schizophrenia: A Comparison of Schizophrenic Patients with Nonschizophrenic Siblings," *Psychiatry*, 24, 133–142, 1961.
89. Lu, Yi-chuang, "Contradictory Parental Expectations in Schizophrenia: Dependence and Responsibility," *Arch. Gen. Psychiat.*, 6, 219–234, 1962.
90. McCord, W., Porta, J. and McCord, J., "The Familial Genesis of Psychoses: A Study of the Childhood Backgrounds of Twelve Psychotics," *Psychiatry*, 24, 60–71, 1962.
91. McGhie, A., "A Comparative Study of the Mother-child Relationship in Schizophrenia. I. The Interview," *Brit. J. Med. Psychol.*, 34, 195–208, 1961.
92. McGhie, A., "A Comparative Study of the Mother-child Relationship in Schizophrenia. II. Psychological Testing," *Brit. J. Med. Psychol.*, 34, 209–221, 1961.
93. Martin, P. H. and Bird, H. W., "A Marriage Pattern: The 'Lovesick' Wife and the 'Cold, Sick' Husband," *Psychiatry*, 22, 245–249, 1959.
94. Mason, P., "The Mother of the Addict," *Psychiat. Quart. Supp.*, 32, 189–199, 1958.

95. MEISSNER, W. W., "The Family Context of Psychosomatic Illness," in preparation.

96. MEISSNER, W. W., "The Family Context of Sex Deviation. I. The Male Homosexual," in preparation.

97. MILLAR, T. P., "The Child Who Refuses to Attend School," *Amer. J. Psychiat.*, 118, 398–404, 1961.

98. MOHR, G. J., JOSSELYN, I. M., SPURLOCK, J. and BARRON, S. H., "Studies in Ulcerative Colitis," *Amer. J. Psychiat.*, 114, 1067–1076, 1958.

99. MORENO, J. L., "The Role Concept, a Bridge between Psychiatry and Sociology," *Amer. J. Psychiat.*, 118, 518–523, 1961.

100. MORRIS, JR., H. H., ESCOLL, P. J. and WEXLER, R., "Aggressive Behavior Disorders of Childhood: A Follow-up Study," *Amer. J. Psychiat.*, 112, 991–997, 1956.

101. MURRAY, E. J. and MIRSKY, M., "Social Class, Family Structure, and Personality," Syracuse Univ., Mimeographed Report, 1961.

102. OBERNDORF, C. P., "Psychoanalysis of Married Couples," *Psychoanal. Rev.*, 25, 453–457, 1938.

103. O'NEAL, P. and ROBINS, L. N., "Childhood Patterns Predictive of Adult Schizophrenia: A 30-year Follow-up Study," *Amer. J. Psychiat.*, 115, 385–391, 1958.

104. OPLER, M. K., "Schizophrenia and Culture," *Scient. American,* 197 (2), 103–110, 1957.

105. OPLER, M. K., "Cultural Perspectives in Research in Schizophrenias: A History with Examples," *Psychiat. Quart.*, 33, 506–523, 1959.

106. OPLER, M. K. and SINGER, J. D., "Ethnic Differences in Behavior and Psychopathology in the Italian and Irish," *Int. J. Soc. Psychiat.*, 2, 11–23, 1956.

107. PARLOFF, M. B., "The Family in Psychotherapy," *Arch. Gen. Psychiat.*, 4, 445–451, 1961.

108. PARSONS, T., "Psychoanalysis and the Social Structure," *Psychoanal. Quart.*, 19, 371–384, 1950.

109. PARSONS, T. and BALES, R. F., *Family Socialization and Interaction Process.* Glencoe, Ill., Free Press, 1955.

110. PULVER, S. E. and BRUNT, M. Y., "Deflection of Hostility in Folie-a-Deux," *Arch. Gen. Psychiat.*, 5, 257–265, 1961.

111. REICHARD, S. and TILLMAN, C., "Patterns of Parent-child Relationships in Schizophrenia," *Psychiatry*, 13, 247–257, 1950.

112. REXFORD, E. N. and VAN AMERONGEN, S. T., "The Influence of Unsolved Maternal Oral Conflicts upon Impulsive Acting-out in Young Children," *Amer. J. Orthopsychiat.*, 27, 75–87, 1957.

113. ROBERTS, B. H. and MYERS, J. K., "Schizophrenia in the Youngest Male Child of the Lower Middle Class," *Amer. J. Psychiat.*, 112, 129–134, 1955.

114. ROBERTS, B. H. and MYERS, J. K., *Family and Class Dynamics in Mental Illness*, New York, Wiley, 1959.

115. ROSENBAUM, C. P., "Patient-family Similarities in Schizophrenia," *Arch. Gen. Psychiat.*, 5, 120–126, 1961.

116. RUBENSTEIN, B. O. and LEVITT, M., "Some Observations Regarding the Role of Fathers in Child Psychotherapy," *Bull. Menninger Clin.*, 21, 16–27, 1957.

117. RUESCH, J. and BATESON, G., *Communication: The Social Matrix of Psychiatry*, New York, Norton, 1951.

118. RYCKOFF, I., DAY, J. and WYNNE, L., "Maintenance of Stereotyped Roles in the Families of Schizophrenics," *Arch. Gen. Psychiat.*, 1, 93–98, 1959.

119. SANUA, V. D., "Sociocultural Factors in Families of Schizophrenics: A Review of the Literature," *Psychiatry*, 24, 246–265, 1961.

120. SARVIS, M. A. and GARCIA, B., "Etiological Variables in Autism," *Psychiatry*, 24, 307–317, 1961.

121. SARWER-FONER, G. J., "Patterns of Marital Relationship," *Amer. J. Psychother.*, 17, 31–44, 1963.

122. SCHAFFER, L., WYNNE, L. C., DAY, J., RYCKOFF, I. M. and HALPERIN, A., "On the Nature and Sources of the Psychiatrists' Experience With the Family of the Schizophrenic," *Psychiatry*, 25, 32–45, 1962.

123. SEARLES, H. F., "Positive Gefühle in der Beziehung zwischen dem Schizophrenen und seiner Mutter," *Psyche*, 14, 165–203, 1960.

124. SERRANO, A. C., McDONALD, E. C., GOOLISHIAN, H. A., MacGREGOR, R. and RITCHIE, A. M., "Adolescent Maladjustment and Family Dynamisms," *Amer. J. Psychiat.*, 118, 897–901, 1962.

125. SOBEL, D. E., "Children of Schizophrenic Parents: Preliminary Observations on Early Development." *Amer. J. Psychiat.*, 118, 512–517, 1961.

126. SOLOMON, R. and BLISS, E. L., "Simultaneous Occurrence of Schizophrenia in Identical Twins," *Amer. J. Psychiat.*, 112, 912–915, 1956.

127. SPIEGEL, J. P., "The Resolution of Role Conflict Within the Family," *Psychiatry*, 20, 1–16, 1957.

128. TOWNE, R. D., MESSINGER, S. L. and SAMPSON, H., "Schizophrenia and the Marital Family: Accommodations to Symbiosis," *Family Process*, 1, 304–318, 1962.

129. TOWNE, R. D., SAMPSON, H. and MESSINGER, S. L., "Schizophrenia and the Marital Family: Identification Crises," *J. Nerv. Ment. Dis.*, 133, 423–429, 1961.

130. WAHL, C. W., "Some Antecedent Factors in the Family Histories of 568 Male Schizophrenics of the United States Navy," *Amer. J. Psychiat.*, 113, 201–210, 1956.

131. WEAKLAND, J. H., "Family Therapy as a Research Arena," *Fam. Proc.*, 1, 63–68, 1962.
132. WEAKLAND, J. H. and FRY, JR., W. F., "Letters of Mothers of Schizophrenics," *Amer. J. Orthopsychiat.*, 32, 604–623, 1962.
133. WINCH, R. F., KTANES, T. and KTANES, V., "The Theory of Complementary Needs in Mate-selection," *Amer. Sociol. Rev.*, 19, 241–249, 1954.
134. WYNNE, L. C., RYCKOFF, I. M., DAY, J. and HIRSCH, S. I., "Pseudomutuality in the Family Relations of Schizophrenics," *Psychiatry*, 21, 205–220, 1958.
135. WYNNE, L. C., "The Study of Intrafamilial Alignments and Splits in Exploratory Family Therapy," in Ackerman, N., Bateman, F. L. and Sherman, S. H. (Eds.) *Exploring the Base for Family Therapy*, New York, Family Service Assoc. of America, 1961.

11

The Family Therapy
Situation as a System

ANDREW E. CURRY

IN SUPERVISION OF and consultation to family therapists, there is a
consistent linguistic peculiarity used when the therapist discusses
the case—particularly problem areas of the case. Frequently used are
such phrases as: "I feel they're trying to get us to . . . ," ". . . they've
maneuvered me into . . . ," ". . . It's like getting sucked into their way
of talking . . ." "Their communication patterns are so seductive I get
caught up in it myself . . .". The implication in these comments is that
there is a powerful matrix of forces operating in the family unit and
that the therapist cannot, without great caution and skill, avoid being
literally caught up in the processes of the family unit.

This paper will attempt to describe processes which occur between
a family unit and the family therapist. It can be said that these processes are "initiated" by the family to disrupt the overall family therapy situation, to neutralize the effectiveness of the therapist, and to
re-establish and maintain the family's pretherapy equilibrium.

BASIC CONCEPTS

When a family member is hospitalized and the family is involved in the patient's treatment program (1, 2), the situation may be described as follows. The family therapist and the family unit engaged in the process of family therapy constitute a complex behavior system. A *complex* system, in contradistinction to a *simple* system, is one in which some of the coordination and control functions required for the simple system to operate are taken over by a sub-unit (i.e., the therapist, ward personnel, etc.), so that aspects of coordination and control become, in part, extrinsic to the ongoing activity process of the simple system (i.e., the family).

Systems have both a structure and a process. The former may be defined as the arrangement of the system's components in three-dimensional space at a given moment in time. Process may be defined as all change over time; or, more precisely, all transmissions among subsystems within the complex system (5, 6, 7, 10).

The family therapy situation, itself, may be defined as a region of structured behaviors. These behaviors are attempts to introduce change-provoking agents into the simple system, family; while the family, at the same time, has the capabilities of accepting or rejecting the introduced agents. The effectiveness of these agents is unpredictable (8).

Within any complex behavior system, we may conceptualize three types of forces operating on the components of the system; these are (a) forces deriving from the components, (b) forces deriving from the system, and (c) forces that have their source in the environment of the system (5, 6). Translated to the family therapy situation, we may say that the three types of forces operating are those deriving from each subsystem—i.e., from the therapist, or from the family and its subgroupings; forces deriving from the total complex system; and, forces that have their source in the environment of the total complex system (i.e., the ward, the hospital, nurses, consultants, and supervisors).

Although a family may enter a treatment program and express a desire to work for change, there is a powerful urgency permeating the family unit to maintain the *status quo*, to go on interacting the way the family always has (9). When this powerful urgency becomes predominate in the family therapy situation, the family will resort to various tactics which disrupt the family therapy. These disruptive

behaviors are in sharp contradistinction to the ways a family explicitly rejects the therapy. The following discussion will focus on
"therapeutic failures" wherein the interactions between therapist and
family, therapist and one family member, and/or therapist and some
outside force, once triggered, drastically alter the family therapy situation.

In the examples to be cited, it will be relatively easy to conclude that
an "experienced therapist" would have been able to handle these disruptive manipulations and that the therapists involved are obviously
beginners. The examples are derived from the clinical experiences of
beginning and experienced therapists. In the teaching and supervision
of family therapy, as with all forms of psychological treatment, the
most instructive cases are those unsuccessful ones—recalled with
greater difficulty than the successful ones.

SYSTEM DISRUPTION

In the situation of family therapy, the therapist can be caught in
a combination of disruptive processes; these are (a) processes of *coalition* with one family member against another; (b) processes of *coalescence* with any one, or combination of family members; and (c)
processes of rapid change after which the complex system *coagulates.*
These groups of processes, for purposes of this discussion, are roughly
equivalent to the three forces, conceptualized by Herbst (5), that derive from the components of the complex system, the complex system
itself, and the environment of the complex system.

This discussion, in no way intended to be exhaustive, considers only
a few of the many processes used by a family unit or a member to
neutralize the effectiveness of a therapist. A family member may use
"helplessness," "putting-down (the therapist)"; or, even, "flight-to-
recovery." ". . . Just schuckin' that fool" (i.e., the therapist) is another
process described by a teenager in most colorful terms. On hearing
what is herein called "seduction," a family therapist working with con-
victs and their families called it "cooling-the-mark (i.e., the therapist)-
out."

Processes of Coalition

Two frequently seen coalition processes are related to the therapists's having been either surprised or seduced. Occurring early in

treatment, these coalitions are brief, temporary relationships in which the therapist is used in some capacity *against* another family member. In the following example, Mr. B. and his son, John (the patient), enter the office. Mr. B. is discussing very heatedly some subject from the previous session. His speech is pressured, urgent. The therapist, who had assumed that Mrs. B. would enter the room shortly, attempts to calm Mr. B. in order to find out what he is concerned about.

Father: ...And that's why...uh...I can't talk about it. You'll have to understand...and...I can't talk about it...that's all!

Therapist: Now, now ... let's find out what you're talking about ... uh ...

Father: ...What I just said...uh...uh, I've been telling you all along. It's from...uh...last week, you know. She's oversexed...we can't talk about that...

Therapist: ...Who's the she? (Here, the therapist has assumed that "she" is making reference to someone other than Mrs. B., whom he expects to enter the office momentarily, as usual.)

Father: ...Grace (i.e., Mrs. B.). She could...uh...we could never talk about this stuff...uh...sex, here. Not in front of him (looking toward John).

Therapist: ... Now, you'll recall, Frank (Mr. B.) that we're to have no secrets in these meetings ... and ... uh ... what we say here has to be ...

Father: ...No sir, Doc., we can't talk about these things...no (emphatically)...not here. I...uh...uh...I wouldn't have told you if we could. That's why Grace isn't here today!

Therapist: (Aware that Mrs. B. is not going to be present) ...Where's Mrs. B.?

John: (Laughing) She's at the doctors...um huh...

Father: ...And she's been very upset since last meeting...uh...*very* upset, uh...and it's...er...that's why I'm telling you about the sex business now...These meetings will make only worse...

Therapist: We're to have no secrets...

Father: I only told you about the...er...uh...sex business in confidence ...uh...well, it was in confidence...and I'll not have her come back here...er, no sir...

The therapist has been given considerable information that Mr. B. feels cannot be talked about when Mrs. B. is present. He knew that his wife would not be present in this session, but this information was withheld. Rather than mention this fact first, Mr. B. initiates a series of surprise communications which witness the therapist "responding" himself into a coalition with a demanding, threatening father, against the absent mother. Subsequent sessions witnessed the therapist allowing Mr. and Mrs. B. to retreat to superficial discussion of the patient's behavior, improvement, and gossip about the ward life.

Coalitions based on the therapist's having been seduced are frequently seen in therapy with marital couples. In settings where the family therapist is also the individual therapist for one of the marital partners, the therapist can be easily "seduced" with the help of his over-identification with "his patient." Seduction can take the form of manipulating the therapist into discussions of complicated intellectualizations; of shaming the therapist, who is a social worker, into explaining why the "doctor is not treating our case." When the family therapist is relatively young, or is treating a family one member of which is a prominent person, the therapist may be intimidated into a role of "supervisee" to the prominent and/or older family member. In the following example, the husband skillfully maneuvers the therapist into defending his Ph.D.

Therapist: How long has Jane's sleepiness been a subject of argument during her passes home?

Husband: ... Ever since she's been here ... er, er ... maybe ... it's the ... uh ... pills ...

Therapist: ... The pills?

Husband: Yea, I think it's the pills ... She's just so dopey at home! I don't know but I ... er ... uh ... maybe the MAO inhibitors would be much better in this case. Don't you think so, doctor ... it's er ... worth a try, I think ...

Wife: He (the therapist) knows which pills to give, Fred ... besides ... well ... er ... the arguments ... we've always had.

Husband: ... He's just the psychologist (emphatically). He's not a M.D. doctor. He's a Ph.D. one ... and there's a ... a difference, you know ...

Wife: But he's still a doctor ...

Therapist: ... Uh ... uh ...

Husband: A psychologist doesn't give the pills ... he doesn't ... er ... and how do I know he knows about the pills ... uh ... you (to wife) never consider anything ... any of the things that ... er ... are ...

Therapist: This concern about the pills: any ideas why it comes up ... now ... right now, after ...

Wife: (Shaking head) ... um ... um ...

Husband: ... I'm concerned about the wrong pills ... that's all! Do psychologists know about the pills ... uh ... er ... any thing about the pills? ...

Therapist: (With a slight rise in voice) ... Look, I ...

Husband: ... Well, do you?

Therapist: ... I ... er ... we know about the pills as much as anyone ... but ... uh ... why the concern, now ...
Husband: (Sighs exasperatedly) ... Oh ... uh ...

The remainder of the session was taken up with similar exchanges, as were the next several meetings. The therapist proved unable to get the discussions refocused. He was seduced into justifying his Ph.D. He was finally to say, in near desperation during a later session, that psychologists are just as "qualified" to do therapy as doctors.

Processes of Coalescence

These processes of coalescence may be differentiated from those of coalition in both *temporal* aspects and in terms of the *psychological* factors involved. As the definition of the word implies, there is a growing together, a psychological uniting into pathological interactions, taking place subtly over time. We may roughly categorize the processes of coalescence under four headings: (a) those in which the therapist has the "same" problem as a member of the family, (b) those in which the therapist and the family do not share the same perception of the therapist but the complex system continues to operate *as if* they do, (c) those in which the therapist projects his own family situation onto the family he is treating, (d) those in which the therapist is overwhelmed and immobilized by the family's pathology.

Examples of coalescent relationships cannot be gleaned from excerpts from tape recorded sesions. These relationships become evident, however, in supervisory sessions with family therapists. Consider the following example: In the supervision of a relatively long course (40 weekly sessions) of family therapy, the supervisor had repeatedly pointed out the need to explore the apparent stresses between Mr. and Mrs. A., as husband and wife. The therapist easily agreed, taking copious notes on the several techniques one might use to transfer the content focus from father-mother-child to that of husband-wife. But through several subsequent supervisory sessions, the therapist never brought any questions or comments on the subject. When the supervisor noted that the therapist had stopped wearing his wedding band, the therapist could say that he had been having severe marital difficulty for most of the previous year—concurrent with the course of therapy.

In another long term course of unsuccessful family therapy with a

Negro family, the consultant noted that the patient's mother continually called the therapist by the wrong name. The therapist (a Negro) was frequently being called by the name of the Caucasian doctor who was the patient's individual therapist. The tape recordings of this happening proved very disconcerting to the therapist, who was unable to understand these lapses. He was finally able to discuss his feelings about race but with great difficulty (3).

On another occasion, the supervisor and the consultant noted a marked alteration in the tone and steadiness of the therapist's voice each time one of the family members made some reference to suicide or death. Although the therapist minimized these observations, he was to prove unable to continue as therapist for the family, explaining that he had become severely depressed in reaction to the suicide of someone dear to him.

These examples would appear to suggest that one pathological system, over time, slowly dovetails into another. Because this phenomenon occurs outside the family therapist's awareness, the analysis of it is almost always confined to the supervisory sessions. The use of a "co-therapist" can serve to minimize processes of coalescence.

There is the anecdote of the family therapist who refused to accept the supervisor's notions that the therapist had been maneuvered into a coalescent-type relationship with a family member "because it would have had to have happened unconsciously . . . and those freudian concepts are no good in conjoint family therapy!"

Coagulated States Following Change

We have differentiated processes of coalescence from coalition by emphasizing the time and psychological factors operative in the family therapy situation. Coalitions manifest themselves very early in the therapy. We will now focus upon processes peculiar to well established courses of therapy which can be greatly affected by forces extraneous to the complex system itself.

Following a rapid change from one state to another ("oscillation") (4), we may say that the complex system can become coagulated. A course of therapy that has progressed in a liquid, "flowing" manner suddenly displays a complete reversal. The therapy bogs down into a mire of disorganization. The therapist will usually express an inability to explain or understand what has happened. It can be very profitable to look at other influences on the complex system, rather than to focus on the subsystems therapists or the family unit.

The rapid change can be said to be directly related to some variety of occurrence very much external to the family therapy situation itself. Almost always, the influence emanates from some other important person, thing, or factor. For example, the therapist may find himself caught between hospital administrative directives and the treatment needs of the family (4), as when the overall hospital philosophy changes from a definite service orientation to that of research. A more prevalent example may be found in situations where the therapist is caught between conflicting theories of supervisors, or conflicts between nursing and psychiatric staff. The therapist, in other instances, may have some need or very good reason to rebel against the case supervisor or consultant; or he may be reacting to certain aspects of his own family, professional, or personal situation.

A most vivid example was that of a small psychiatric clinic that hired a consultant to help the staff with what appeared, at first glance, to be a series of poorly handled and disastrous family therapy cases. On closer examination, the staff seemed to be most competent and well trained; enthusiasm was high, and the specific family units did not appear to be so complicated as to be the source of each therapist's difficulty. The consultant finally discovered that the clinic had had three "acting directors" over the previous year, and that each of them had espoused a different philosophy of treatment and commitment to family therapy.

In regard to the family unit itself, the place of employment of the father, for example, may be producing the source of strain on the therapy situation. Although this example perhaps stretches to make the point, one family was greatly effected upon discovering that many of their friends were also in treatment, but in individual analysis (a status factor in that particular area). There was not only a rapid change in the therapy itself, but in the way the family reacted to the therapist—respect and fondness gave way to condescension.

Specific to family therapy being done in a hospital setting is the effect of other families' progress, or lack of it, on the course of therapy with a family. Even more curious, the overall "milieu" of the ward plays an important role in producing changes in a course of therapy, for often nursing personnel are left out of the direct treatment, although they may spend a considerable amount of time with the family before and after a family session. Any force, external to the complex system, that can be conceived of as a threat of annihilation, real or imagined, to the system can produce a process of rapid change. After such changes, we are suggesting that the system "coagulates" rather than disintegrates.

In the above examples, there is an apparent crossing between two distinct complex systems that may be in conflict—implicit or explicit (4, 8). One of these complex systems, because of power, authority, and/or status, exerts an extraordinary amount of intrusive influence on developments within the family therapy situation. It can be mentioned, without elaboration, that such factors as staffing, budget, and even janitors (who have traditionally cleaned offices during after-hours, offices that are now used after hours for family meetings) have a profound effect on the family therapy situation.

DISCUSSION

We have described some of the processes which come into being as a result of forces operating in the situation of a complex behavior system, i.e., family therapy. This complex system is composed of two distinct simple systems: the therapists and the family unit. Using some concepts of behavior systems theory, an analysis of three categories of relationship has been attempted, on the premise that a complex system, by definition, must operate so as to maintain some type of steady state (9). If we postulate that an introduction of agents of change into any component part of a complex system generally results in complicated changes and adjustments in other parts of the system, then it would follow that the subsystem family can have change-producing effects on the subsystem of the therapists. We may even go so far as to suspect that the therapist has more opportunities to *be* effected by the family unit, than conversely, because he will have many more sources of stimulation and influence to respond to than will the family.

The potential for disrupting the family therapy situation can be understood as one way for the family to regain an aspect of control. Reabsorbing the control function, which was made extrinsic to the family system as a result of hospitalization of a family member, could then be conceived of as a reaction to the situation itself. For example, the demands and the intrusiveness of the hospital personnel could be said to constitute a stress producing strains in the internal functioning of the family system. In a phenomenological sense (2a), what the family unit is doing is related to the situation in which it is done.

The implications of this for teaching and supervision of family therapy are several; but, primarily, we are in a position to concentrate on enabling the family therapist to develop a model—a conceptualization of *situations* in behavior terms. There will be little need for us to argue about "resistance" or "lack of motivation." The potential for system disruption, for example, can be said to be inherently related to the complex behavior system, i.e., therapist - family unit - situation. The boundaries of this complex system cannot be conceived of as being as firm as the boundaries of the system that is the family unit; and, more importantly, the system boundaries of the family unit are undoubtedly very much more firm than those of the subsystem therapist. Were this not so, our ability to change families would be far greater than it is. The difficulty we meet in changing families can be attributed to the nature of behavior systems. The therapist's susceptibility to being maneuvered into relationships that disrupt, or at least stalemate, the progression of the therapy, can be understood in terms other than those of what is the best version of family therapy.

The teaching and learning of family therapy is made easier, moreover, if we recall that the family therapist cannot predict the effectiveness of the agents of change that he will introduce into the simple system, family, whereas a family may know very well that "it's only a matter of time before you give up on us, too . . ." One of the most striking aspects of the family therapy situation is the persistence of those relationships between family members that creates a static, seemingly unchanging equilibrium. It can be very helpful for the student of family treatment to consider that family units change slowly, if at all, not so much because of what he does or does not do, or how, from which theoretical orientation; but because of the structure and functions of the specific family. The task for him, then, is to learn more and more about the structure of situations and the elements of behavior systems.

SUMMARY

This paper has described processes which occur between a family unit and the family therapist, and has suggested that this relationship constitutes a complex behavior system. We have discussed three categories of disruptive processes which can effect the family therapy situation. The discussion was illustrative rather than exhaustive.

REFERENCES

1. BLINDER, M., COLMAN, A. D., CURRY, A. E. and KESSLER, D. R., "MCFT: Simultaneous Treatment of Several Families," *Amer. J. Psychother.*, 19, 559–569, 1965.
2. CURRY, A. E., "Therapeutic Management of Multiple Family Groups," *Internat. J. Grp. Psychother.*, 15, 90–96, 1965.
2a. CURRY, A. E., "Group Psychotherapy: Phenomenological Considerations," *Rev. Existen. Psycholo. Psychia.*, 6, 63–69, 1966.
3. CURRY, A. E., "Some Comments on Transference When the Group Therapist is Negro," *Internat. J. Grp. Psychother.*, 13, 363–365, 1963.
4. HALEY, J., Personal Communication.
5. HERBST, P. G., "Situation Dynamics and the Theory of Behavior Systems," *Behav. Sci.*, 2, 13–29, 1957.
6. HERBST, P. G., "Analysis and Measurement of a Situation—The Child in the Family," *Hum. Rel.*, 6, 113–140, 1953.
7. HERBST, P. G., "A Theory of Simple Behavior Systems: I & II," *Hum. Rel.*, 14, 71–94; 193–239, 1961.
8. HERBST, P. G., "The Analysis of Social Flow Systems," *Hum. Rel.*, 7, 327–336, 1954.
9. JACKSON, D. D., "The Question of Family Homeostasis," *Psych. Quart.* (Suppl.,) 31(1), 79–90, 1957.
10. MILLER, J. G., "Living Systems: Basic Concepts," *Behav. Sci.*, 10, 193–237, 1965.

12

The Process of Humanizing Physiological Man

EDWARD A. TYLER, M.D.

How MAN, THE physiological animal, becomes man, the social human is presented here as a social theory of human behavior. New born man is basically an animal who first relates to other men because of his physiological helplessness. Through his physiological dependency on sophisticated members of his species, he learns to also become psychologically dependent, but further growth introduces a struggle for autonomy. The establishment of an autonomous existence sets the stage for development of reciprocal relationships between autonomous individuals of roughly equal status. This humanizing process follows an orderly pattern from birth to death and any "normal" or "abnormal" human behavior can be explained or predicted by this parsimonious theory. Also presented is a superficial consideration of some physiological concepts which make the development of human psychological behavior not only possible, but extremely probable.

It is obvious that if no human infants were able to survive, the human species would soon disappear. In this theory psychosociological behavior is considered to be a special case of adaptive behavior designed specifically for human survival in an environment of other humans. *The physiological dependency of the infant man on an adult human for his individual, as well as species, survival is the crucial factor in development of those behaviors which we term social and psychological i.e., the humanizing process.* Reared by monkeys, wolves, or porpoises, he would become psychosociologically a monkey, a wolf,

182

or a porpoise with marked physical limitations if he survived at all (15).

Being a living organism, man has the basic characteristics of any protoplasm plus those unique to his species. In addition to the uniqueness of his anatomy and vital physiology, man inherits a potential repertoire of "human" behaviors. These potentials are passed along to him by his ancestors in the form of information stored in his genes. (Recent work (18) (25) suggests this information storage is an active process related to the metabolism of ribonucleic acid (RNA).) To be ever more than potential, this stored information must first be activated and developed by environmental stimuli (2, 12, 22). The time-space factor of being born in a certain geographic location, at a certain period in time, to a certain family, etc. so limits the available stimuli that any individual develops only a small segment of this potential.

Those traits of man which we refer to as "human" are the result of the interaction between his inherited (species and individual) potentials and his environment of other humans (37). Infant man is slowly taught how to become an adult man with "human" characteristics by those who have already learned how to behave as humans (5). Whereas the time-space variables in his human education account for his group or cultural uniqueness, his individual uniqueness depends on his personal environment experiences to stimulate and develop his personal inherited uniqueness.

There is a wide range in the variation of "human" behaviors in individuals. In adults this can be conveniently conceptualized as a continuum with a range from A to Z. Although the psychosocial experiences of the developing child have the greatest influence on shaping these characteristic behaviors, potential differences exist from the moment of conception but with a small range—A to C. Intrauterine experiences expand these potentials—A to F (44, 45).

Although individuals markedly differ in the way they perceive and respond to stimuli, the patterns of any individual are rather fixed and quite predictable. Each of his experiences is recorded by irreversible structural changes within himself. The patterns so imprinted (22) can be offset or balanced by newer spontaneous or induced (therapy) experiences, but no memory is ever lost without structural damage to the memory storage apparatus.

The structural changes induced by experiences so influence future experiences (through choices as well as interpretations) that no two children can possibly be exposed to the same interpersonal relationship experiences (not even identical twins intentionally reared "alike" by the same adults). Each individual is channeled into his own personal and unique sequence of experiences by that which he has already learned.

The adult human intermittently reinforces certain patterns of the infant's behavior with life-maintaining physiological gratification. In so doing he teaches the child that certain behaviors have social and psychological meaning as well as physiological survival usefulness. By simultaneously ignoring and/or negatively reinforcing other behaviors, he channels the experiences of the individual child (37). The adult who has already learned to assign psychosociological meaning to all of his own behavior does not even bother to consider that the behavior of the newborn may not yet have any psychosociological intent (ie., meaning, to the infant). The adult behaves as if there is as much psychosociological meaning, need or intent in the infant's behavior as in his own. Likewise, he behaves as if the child understands the psychosociological intent of the adult's behavior. Since all of the adult's behavior is endowed with some cultural and/or personal psychosociological meaning, the adult constantly implicitly and explicitly, consciously and unconsciously, intentionally and accidentally channels the potential behaviors and experiences of the child by reinforcing (i.e., responding to) those which have the most significant psychosociological meaning to this particular adult (5, 33). Thereby, the child learns the meaning of behaviors, perceptions, things, and symbols. What he learns through these experiences becomes his only way of judging and measuring reality (31). What is reinforced and/or extinguished, the rationalizations for this, and the resultant patterns of behavior vary greatly with the time-space orientation of the individual, but the principles concerning the initial dependency and later attempts at an autonomous existence are probably universal and timeless.

One of the problems of social science has been defining abstract terms and concepts. In this theory, man's entire life cycle is discussed by repeatedly using a same small number of concepts introduced to explain infant and preschool behavior. Every new, overlapping, or apparently unclear concept is defined with the simplest possible words, and the fewest number of terms compatible with retaining the richness of the "surplus" meaning in our more conventional abstract terms for "explaining" human behavior are used (21).

Human behavior as used in this article refers to any and all potential behaviors of the species *homo sapiens*. To be complete, this must include cellular behaviors, organ behaviors, individual behaviors, group behaviors, and society behaviors (26, 42). It includes the range from physiological processes to abstract thinking. However, the focus in this paper is on those behaviors of man interacting with an environment of other men. The ideas are presented *only* as a useful way of conceptualizing, as a correlated whole, this writer's clinical observations, social observations, personal feelings and thoughts, as they have been influenced by earlier and contemporary authors. As a theory, it can only become useful if it generates empirically testable hypotheses and/or more useful therapeutic techniques (13).

MOTIVATION AND SOME PHYSIOLOGICAL CONSIDERATIONS

An adequate theory of human behavior must take into account the motivation of the behavior (40). Admittedly it is here that one becomes most speculative because, as yet, our techniques for investigation have provided so littel useful data. This has led to highly imaginative theories on the one extreme (9, 16, 20, 23) and a denial of the relevance of studying motivation on the other (37).

The theory presented here makes the assumption that the motivation for behavior in all living substances is the same, namely, survival of the individual and perpetuation of the species (35). Based on the information available (past, current and anticipated) a living organism constantly makes choices of how to accomplish this motivational drive. His choices may appear appropriate or inappropriate in terms of "the true best choice" (i.e., "absolute reality") but to the behaving organism they appear to be the choices he must make. The preservation of the living state of protoplasm is not a static process. Protoplasm is an open energy system with delicately balanced intermittent intakes and outputs (11). Imbalances in this system beyond the rather narrow limits of its tolerance cause its breakdown, (i.e., permanent loss of these properties exclusive to living substances). The phenomenon of living substances maintaining themselves within their physiological limits has been termed homeostasis or steady state (3, 36). A shift in any direction away from the usual state of the organism calls forth a response (i.e., behavior) designed to counter this shift and return the organism to its familiar position between the two potential extremes. Living systems depend upon mechanisms to perceive, "recognize," and record experiences which are then used as the basis for directing immediate and future behavioral and structural changes enhancing the probability of an adaptation compatible with survival (13). Inability to behave in a way tending to reverse the trend toward increasing homeostatic imbalance is experienced as anxiety. The ever changing internal and environmental variables which threaten the organism's maintenance of his homeostasis have been usefully termed stress (31). Initially stresses occur only to the physiological system, but the physiological survival of the human infant immediately becomes dependent upon the social and psychological systems of other more mature humans. Thus the physiological and psychosociological survival of the human becomes inseparably intertwined starting at the moment of birth.

In order to survive, a living organism must adapt itself to the existing environmental variables. These variables within the environment and within the organism itself must be explored. The information gathered in these exploring experiences must be stored in such a way that it will be available to guide future behavior (17, 28). The future behavior ranges from simple repetitions to elaborate variations which are essentially original creations of the behaving individual. Deviations in the exploring-storing apparatus and/or the opportunities for learning how to utilize this apparatus will significantly alter the very functions upon which the development of a socialized human being so crucially depends. In human survival it becomes essential not only to reverse homeostatic imbalances but also to predict how the environment will respond to one's own behavior. Awareness of one's inability to make such predictions is also experienced as anxiety. Anxiety then is defined as the painful belief that one's survival has been, is, or will be seriously threatened and one has reason (real or fantasied) to doubt his ability to respond in a way to prevent this disasater (36).

It seems pertinent to digress for a moment and superficially consider the human information processing apparatus. In a single cell animal, the one cell has in its repertoire all the behavioral responses necessary for survival, within the limits of the adaptability of the particular species. Animals born without this minimal repertoire do not survive and reproduce. This amounts to a selectivity in that only those members of the species with certain inborn patterns of response and/or the capability for learning specific additional responses, can survive and mature.

As animals become multicellular and move into more complex environments, groups of cells become specialized and excel in only certain functions. The groups of specialized cells become dependent on each other. The single cell of a complex organism is no longer capable of surviving independently. This specialization of parts of organisms into tissues and organs with highly specialized but limited functions improves the species' adaptability to the environment. On the other hand, it increases the probability of survival of individuals handicapped in their adaptability by structural and/or acquired deviations. The more highly specialized a tissue and its functions, the more serious threat to the organisms' adaptation are any deviations. Some are incompatible with mere physiological existence and the organism dies. Others only handicap adaptation and the organism survives but must remain dependent upon other less deviant organisms. Man's most highly specialized tissue, the central nervous system, is his information processing center. It perceives, responds, and learns, i.e., seeks, stores, identifies, and recalls information necessary for survival (10).

By rank ordering the biological world on the basis of its ability to process information, one must consider man the most highly developed species in the animal kingdom. Man has developed an elaborate neurophysiological system in which speed of a stimulus-response reaction has been sacrificed for the ability to make choices. His apparatus makes but little use of the simple reflex arc where a single fiber transmits the stimulus on a fixed pathway with no decision points, little or no increment or decrement, and with one stimulus evoking one response. Although a reflex response is more speedy, there is no possibility of making a decision—stimulus A always evokes response A. An animal primarily dependent on this primitive reflex arc type of neurological apparatus cannot use judgment (i.e., time lag between stimulus and response) nor anticipate and respond to seek or avoid the desired and feared future. Man, on the other hand, has a most elaborate anatomical apparatus for the processing of information. He has roughly ten billion cells arranged in networks of approximately twenty to thirty cells. Within a given network all cells are believed to be connected with all other cells and each network connected with several other networks. Anatomically, there are elaborate feedback loops which can modulate the volume or time of the information-carrying process. Extremely fine discriminations can be made, and elaborate, highly individualistic patterns of response can be learned and created. Anatomically this difference appears dependent upon the synaptic junction, i.e., the points at which the fibers from two cells connect. These provide decision points. Information can be passed along, withheld temporarily or even indefinitely, incremented or decremented as it is passed across these synaptic junctions (11).

Any animal is exposed to a tremendous mass of raw, unprocessed information received as stimuli from its experiences. There is more information than the processing system can handle. Information is selectively filtered, grouped, generalized and given priorities (27). Some of the potential information is apparently lost, having been filtered out or not fitting the animal's coding system. The information can apparently be temporarily or permanently stored for future use. Now, one stimulus can evoke no responses with the energy being absorbed in the system. One stimulus can produce a single delayed response, the energy being stored until a more favorable set of circumstances presents itself. One stimulus can evoke a series of responses, the increment coming from the energy stored during previous stimuli (23). These earlier stimuli may or may not be the same as the one evoking the current series of responses. The efficiency of the delayed and substitute responses depends upon the use of a value judgment decision based on many previous specific and general learning experiences. In order to utilize the incoming information, the organism must learn what meanings these stimuli have in the world to which he is trying to adapt. Initially, a stimulus calls for a response without specificity of either. Learning involves discrimination between the different stimuli and correlating these with the different, appropriate (i.e., useful) behavioral responses (28). Maturation is now defined as an increasing ability to discriminate incoming stimuli, correlate these with the best choice behavioral responses and use judgment of when and whether to respond. Increasing maturity increases the probability of adaptation and survival.

The energy input which programs the memory storage apparatus is derived from the young animal's perceptions of his experiences. In man, a large number of these experiences have human psychological and sociological significance. These experiences program the patterns of interpersonal relationship which will be available to the individual as he grows and matures. Each new experience is capable of structurally altering the organism (11). Thereby identification and storage of each new experience is heavily influenced by that which is already known. Each new experience is compared and contrasted as a variation of similar or dissimilar previous experiences (9, 17, 33). The degree of apparent urgency to survival will significantly influence the weight and tenacity these earlier experiences will exert in the formation of the habitual patterns the individual uses relating to his environment (9).

PERSONALITY DEVELOPMENT

The rest of this paper is devoted to an examination of the relationship between the child and his environment of other humans, based on an assumption that each experience influences future performance (5, 9, 28, 33, 41).

The child *in utero* is not only dependent upon the adult for his physiological existence, but is actually a physical appendage of that adult. Although this anatomical attachment to the adult will be severed at birth, the child has no choice, compatible with survival, but to remain a physiological appendage of an adult until he is physically and psychologically developed and experienced enough to direct his own survival behaviors.

There is no reason to believe that the new born infant seeks anything other than physiological survival from his adult. Almost immediately, however, the adult unintentionally begins to condition him to seek psychosociological survival as well. So, at this very early period in the child's experiences, when his actual physical survival hinges on an adult's behaviors, an inseparable inter-weaving and confusion of what is physiological and what is psychological begins. Little by little as he becomes more physically mature he becomes less and less a physiological appendage and more and more a psychological appendage. Within the limits of his homeostatic mechanisms the infant can temporarily accept interchangeably physiological or psychological gratifications (6). A crying, hungry child can temporarily accept body contact, warmth, being cuddled, or gentle words even though he actually needs food. After the infant has become conditioned to "need" companionship of his adult, he can temporarily accept a bottle of milk as a substitute for his familiar adult companion, even though he has no physiological need for food. The child is now beginning to give significance to the apparent intent of as well as the actions of his adults. This growth in concern with intent will continue as he matures (32).

Dependency Relationships

The newborn child and his adults must initially adapt to each other in a mutually dependent relationship (4). The physical helplessness of the newborn human sets the stage for this original human interpersonal relationship, dependency (29). This is defined as a relationship in which one organism feels that his leaning upon another is essential to his well being and survival.

As the human infant's perceptive ability improves, he begins to recognize his own physiological needs and that they originate within himself. Next he learns that behavior will alter these needs. Initially any perception of a developing homeostatic imbalance leads to a gross unrefined behavioral (motor-secretory) response. Each specific physiological need is slowly isolated from the whole and appropriate specific behavioral responses correlated with them. He then believes that the behaviors themselves alone can always gratify his needs (6). By painful experiences he begins to recognize that gratification of these needs (and therefore his survival) is more dependent upon his communications to an adult than any of his other behaviors (33). He begins to recognize that his survival is only possible through a dependent interpersonal relationship. Because of his physical and experience limitations, he tends to over-evaluate the capabilities of his adults, and his need for dependency upon them. Correction of this error in judgment is essential for the attainment of psychological maturity.

When he first becomes aware of his dependency, he accepts it with any available adult, but as he is able to more discretely discriminate, he begins to believe that only one (or a few familiar substitutes) can provide the dependency essential to his survival. His limited, personal, but gross communications convey more meaning to his "teacher" than to a stranger. The feedback from the stranger is unfamiliar or inappropriate. Anxiety now becomes associated with a fear that the special adult upon whom his survival depends may not be available when stress appears (30). Only after he trusts the dependency relationship can he progress toward further psychological maturity (5, 32). Indefinitely, however, the usual human response to the perception of a threat to his integrity is to regress to a dependent relationship with another human (29). This regression is frequently the immediate and always the ultimate response, when he feels incapable of handling the threat (stress) alone (38). This is the normal adaptive process of regression which is used daily by all humans. The difference between the "healthy" and "unhealthy" use of regression is measured by the rate of recoverability to the type of relationship existing prior to the time the stress was perceived.

Autonomous Relationships

To adapt, a living organism must become familiar with his environment through exploration. In spite of his adults' careful channeling, his experiences are personal and his explorations throw him into conflict with the adult upon whom he has been dependent (1). This conflict causes the infant to explore the possibility of whether or not he can survive independent of the adult upon whom he has become psychologically dependent (19). Whereas the establishment of a trusting dependency relationship was the child's preoccupation during his first year, testing his autonomy remains in the foreground during his second and third years.

This constant attempt to prove his autonomy followed by regression to reaffirm dependency becomes the prototype of all psychosociological behavioral responses to stress (5, 6). He finds his dependent and autonomous interpersonal relationships are in direct competition with each other. Considering them at opposite ends of a continuum one increases as the other decreases. Any sudden or wide moves in either direction are experienced as a potential threat to the other relationship.

Initially the child tries to imitate the patterns of behavior he has observed being used by his adults. Because of the grossness of his discriminations, his copying is clumsy, awkward and inexact. First he experiments behaving without the supervision of the adult. He attempts to direct himself in activities for which he previously depended on mother rather than continue to wait for her to direct his behavior. He is in a "do it myself" stage. As his proficiency and confidence in directing his own interactions with his environment improve, he starts to copy that part of the adult's behavior with which he is currently most familiar—channeling, (i.e., helping by directing and controlling his behavior). In copying adult patterns, he attempts to control first his own and then their behavior. Just as they attempt to keep him from exploring what they consider to be within the realm of their own rights and privacy, he reciprocates by protesting their interference.

First the child says no to himself as he starts to do what mother usually forbids, taking over the direction she usually provides. As he gains more security he directs his "no" at mother when she tries to interfere with the privacy of his explorations (even though they may be in her personal belongings). The speed and firmness with which he can say "no" hinges upon the mother's attitude toward his explorations and attempts to control her (39).

The child's effort to establish his autonomy is primarily aimed at the adult upon whom he has been most dependent. When this adult seems displeased, the child experiences this displeasure as a threat to his survival. He regresses and seeks a dependency relationship with the adult he has just displeased. If the adult offers a token of willingness to accept the dependent, protective relationship, the child is ready to again explore their autonomous relationship. This occurs in a situation such as the child reaching to touch a vase on a table and the mother expressing her displeasure in actions and words. She scolds, spanks, or banishes the child. The child may or may not initially react with overt anger and rage, but ultimately he responds with fear and tears. He then seeks a token (tender words, cuddling, food, play, etc.) from the same adult as her recognition of his need to again be in a dependent role. When the *possibility* of his dependency has been reaffirmed, the child again explores touching of the forbidden object and the cycle is repeated. Anxiety now becomes associated with a second fear that he cannot correctly predict the response of the environment to his behavior (30, 32).

When someone other than the primary dependency adult is perceived as a threat, the child turns to his primary dependency person (usually mother) for reassurance, but he needs the availability of an alternate source of potential dependency to comfortably continue the stress of his autonomous explorations with his primary dependency person. In the American culture, the alternate source is usually the father but may be any adult or even an older sibling (12). The child's maturation as an autonomous unit depends upon his having opportunities for triangular experiences whereas dependency had needed only dual experiences (24).

To clearly differentiate himself as an independent being, the child needs uncompromising "no's" as well as "do it himself" experiences. There are three possible classes of experiences. Both child and adult say yes—child plays with toys while mother prepares a meal. Mother prefers no but can allow child to decide—child pulls out pans while mother prepares a meal. Mother says no and refuses to compromise— child tries to climb up on hot stove while mother prepares a meal. When his adults cannot accept a likely consequences of his behavior, they can not give him a choice. The child's acceptance of these no's is not initially based on his comprehension of adult values but rather on his fear of losing his potential dependency source. A child must also experience the opportunity of making choices of his own, and these come when the adult can accept any likely consequence even though it may not be preferred. To gain the true sense of autonomy essential to continuation of his psychological maturation, the child must gradually have a chance to depend more and more upon his own decisions and experience the consequences of these decisions.

Reciprocal Relationships

When the child has had sufficient experiences to begin to believe that he can at times, if not always, exist as an autonomous unit, he seeks interactions with other autonomous units. The experience of interacting with another autonomous unit serves to enhance his belief in his own autonomy.

Autonomous individuals are capable of interacting with each other in reciprocal interpersonal relationships. These are characterized by an intent to give and take as equals (32). But the young child's limited abilities and experiences make his relationships more reciprocal in intent than in fact. There is considerably more take than give on the part of the child, but his intent is reciprocal. This give and take as equals is either cooperative or competitive. Cooperative behaviors involve two individuals whose final accomplishment depends on their mutual participation because of their dissimilarities. Competitive behaviors involve two individuals trying to eliminate the necessity of the other's continued participation because of their similarities. In general, there are more cooperative behaviors between persons of the opposite

sex and more competitive behaviors between persons of the same sex
(9). Just as dependency and autonomy were placed on one continuum,
cooperative and competitive relationships fall at opposite ends of a
second continuum. In all reciprocal relationships both cooperative and
competitive behaviors are occurring simultaneously, but by intent one
or the other is in the foreground necessitating a diminution in its opposite.

Initially the child seeks merely a reciprocal relationship with
another autonomous individual without consideration of whether the
other individual is different from himself. By reversing roles and relating to other individuals as he has perceived adults were relating
to him, he attempts to establish a measure of his equality with other
autonomous individuals.

His adults are not long willing to accept his type of reciprocal relationship. They become quite concerned about the sex of the child and
project this into its future implications. The adults insist that the
"neutral" child choose "sides." He must declare and identify himself
as either a potential male or female (i.e., potential future, competitor
or cooperator). This forced choice is intiated by the adults not the
child. Although the parents take a major role, most, if not all, the
adults with whom the child comes in contact will reinforce this necessity of the child to "declare himself." Although the child is still many
years away from being a real competitor or cooperator, the adult is
more comfortable relating to him once his sex is established (i.e., is he
a potential cooperator or competitor?).

The positive aspect of this forced choice is that it encourages the
child to identify with the behaviors appropriate for his continued
maturation (9). This is another channeling experience which allows
him to make further refinements in his discriminations of the meanings of his world. Once this choice is made, it strongly influences all
other future choices. When the child is allowed or forced to make a
choice not consistent with his anatomical structure or is discouraged
from making any choice, the stage is set for a life-long conflict between
what he is and what he wishes to be (6).

When the child first seeks reciprocal relationships, his belief in his
own autonomy is still very tenuous. Although he may initiate a competitive play, a loss in the play is frequently perceived not only as a
stress in the reciprocal relationship, but as a threat to his autonomy
or even his dependency upon the adult. The behaviors and feelings

necessary to direct a successful competition are rarely appropriate for seeking dependency. Even in a cooperative reciprocal relationship the child frequently perceives his being asked to assist or share as a threat to his own dependency needs. When he feels he is being asked or expected to give more than he is capable or willing, he regresses and becomes unwilling to give anything. The giving has become such a threat that he attempts to return to a position of only taking (32).

The adult is always ahead of the child in recognizing and correctly responding to the relationship existing between the two of them (5). Recognizing the infant's helplessness, he arranges for the child to be dependent upon him. He also recognizes that he and the infant are autonomous units and so distinguishes between their independent physiological needs. The alert adult does not feed the child because the adult himself is hungry nor feed himself when the child is hungry. Recognizing their anatomical autonomy, he also introduces reciprocal relationships between himself and the young infant. Mothering behaviors cannot be carried out except in an interpersonal relationship in which another autonomous unit responds to being mothered. Even the competitive aspect of the reciprocal behaviors exist as the adult competes with the child, not only for the affection and attention of others but even for the use of the adult's own time and energy.

By the time the child is of school age he will have experienced all the possible types of relationships that he can ever have with another human being, a) dependency, b) autonomy, c) competitive reciprocal and d) cooperative reciprocal. The patterns he has learned strongly channel and influence all his future experiences. Whatever he learns is superimposed on his earlier experiences, and can only be variations of his original four relationships. One type of relationship may be in the foreground with individual A at the same time another is in the foreground with individual B. Neither is fixed and each changes as he perceives apparent or real changes in his psychological homeostasis.

Peer Group Relationships

During his pre-school period the child began to seek peer group contacts. However, his first serious efforts to become a member of his contemporary world at the expense of his adults' world (i.e., home) occurs when he finally decides that there is no possibility of his establishing an appropriate pair (i.e., reciprocal) relationship for himself within his own family unit. His reciprocal relationship experiences with his familiar adults have forced him to recognize that he is physically and psychologically inadequate to successfully participate as either a cooperator or a competitor in an adult world. He therefore, turns his explorations for continued growth and maturation towards his contemporary group (5).

Since his youthful contemporary companions are, at best, able to offer only sporadic and unreliable dependency at times of stress, he misses the support (i.e., potential dependency) of his adults. So the child still regresses to some level of potential or actual dependency on his parents while he attempts to strengthen his reciprocal relationships in the world of his contemporaries. He is now utilizing two differing levels of interpersonal relationships with two different individuals or groups. Competitive relationships with adults were perceived to be more stressful than cooperative relationships. Therefore, when he has any choice, he seeks a same sex peer group in an effort to establish competitive reciprocal relationships with less formidable opponents. Since he still perceives the greatest threats in the competitive area (9), he finds the parents of the same sex as the more suitable dependency source. To regress to dependency on the opposite sex parent still leaves the child in competition with the same sex parent and does not reduce the potential stress. The child establishes a dependency relationship with the parent of the same sex and a competitive reciprocal relationship with a peer group of the same sex. This strengthens his abilities and identifications in the area he perceives most urgently stressful to his continued maturation and survival.

The intensity of competitive behaviors differs in male and female children. This is also true in other species and must be considered to have, in part, an inherent biological basis. Another likely factor is that the female child finds herself in competition with her original dependency person (mother), and it is more difficult for these two individuals to compete. Always remembering the helpless infant's dependency upon her, the mother is less threatened by her female child competitor. On the other hand, to the father any child has been in competition with him for the mother's time and interest since birth. Always remembering this, the father is more threatened and threatening to his male child competitor.

Under circumstances in which the same sex parent is not available, is too passive, and/or the opposite sex parent is too seductive or dominant, the child is not encouraged to form the relationship which will best facilitate his maturity and identification with an appropriate role in his society. Obviously there are very few children that have the same balanced experiences. So we find a wide variation still compatible with a mentally healthy sex-generation identification and appropriate adaptive behavior (7).

As the child matures and becomes more secure in his own ability—now as a competitor within his peer group—he again makes an effort to gain autonomy from the person upon whom he is dependent. This time he seeks to establish his autonomy from the parent of the same sex. This begins to make itself quite evident in the prepubescent and pubescent period. Although this behavior may appear to be competitive, its intent is to establish autonomy from the same sex parent and is more a defiance than a competition.

This second major effort to establish an autonomous relationship is greatly strengthenend by the potential dependency now available from the contemporary same sex peer group rather than from a second adult as had been the case when the child established his autonomy from his original dependency person.

This same sex group period of the child's life is in the foreground from the beginning of school until puberty. It is one in which the child is consolidating his adaptive patterns of behavior for effectively relating to individuals of his same sex. Only as he feels somewhat secure in his abilities to establish competitive reciprocal relationships with his same sex contemporaries is he willing to seek out cooperative reciprocal relationships with his contemporaries of the opposite sex (5, 41).

Adolescent Relationships

At puberty there is a biological impetus of physiological and anatomical changes within the individual. He is rapidly approaching a point at which he can potentially participate in perpetuation of the species as well as his own individual survival. Although he is physiologically and anatomically ready, he needs further psychological maturing before he is able to establish an opposite sex relationship which will provide the opportunity for him to utilize this potential.

In his initial efforts he continues to use those patterns with which he has most recently gained proficiency, i.e., competitive reciprocal relationships. Although these patterns are useful in establishing contact, they are not useful in maintaining an opposite sex relationship or meeting the increased biological drives of puberty. The conflict of being unable to establish and maintain reciprocal relationships with contemporaries of the opposite sex is perceived as a stress. As always in the face of stress he regresses but now seeks dependency from his same sex peer group. No one is consistently dependent upon any one individual; rather all are dependent on the strength of the group. The group provides the opportunity for the exchange of information gained from the experience of others both in and out of the group. This information strengthens his possibilities of establishing a successful cooperative reciprocal relationship with an opposite sex contemporary. However, this dependency also threatens the autonomy which the individual has struggled to gain twice before. As he begins to establish a cooperative relationship with an opposite sex contemporary, he uses his new one-to-one relationship as a potential source of dependency to become autonomous from his contemporary same sex group (5, 41).

The economy and the social institutions of our American culture present a serious handicap to the adolescent's further development. A relationship for which he is now ready must be delayed because he does not simultaneously have the opportunity and responsibility to become an economically autonomous and productive member of the society. As the life span has been progressively increased, the length of the adolescent relationship has also been increased. This individual, now ready for a competitive reciprocal relationship in a world of adults, is not welcome.

If the adolescent insists on going ahead with an adult role, he risks being indefinitely penalized as he compares himself with his contemporaries who delayed taking on the adult role. So he must again regress to dependency on his adults. This time his dependency is economic and psychological rather than physiological and psychological. His ultimate adult adjustment will be somewhere between using this latest dependency as a means toward attaining economic autonomy, and accepting this dependency as a permanent way of life. In the latter case, he reluctantly admits to himself that the attainment of autonomy will never be possible for him. In this submission he seriously limits his ability to ever set up lasting adult reciprocal relationships with his parents, his contemporaries, or his own children. At a time when he should primarily be involved in reciprocal relationships with occasional temporary regressions to the dependency-autonomy struggle, he is obsessing in this latter struggle.

ADULT RESPONSES TO STRESS

Events which place a perceived stress on the reciprocal relationships cause temporary regression even in very mature adults. Some hypothetical examples are presented as typical of what happens in situations which are perceived as stressful.

In his job a man is engaged in a cooperative reciprocal relationship. A possibility of there being fewer jobs available is perceived as a stress. A mature person initially regresses to a more competitive reciprocal relationship with his fellow workers. As the stress continues he sees continued reciprocal relationships as a threat to his autonomy and attempts to produce as an individual rather than as part of the team. If the stress continues he seeks a dependent relationship with his boss, or relative, or some social institution designed to provide a dependent relationship to those in need of this regression. As the stress disappears the mature individual again seeks to establish his autonomy from the person or agency upon whom he has become dependent. He then moves back into a competitive, and later as the stress completely disappears, a cooperative relationship with his fellow workers.

As a second example let's see how the birth of the first child can effect the relationships of a married couple. If mature, they have primarily a cooperative relationship with some competitive aspects, and either is able to serve the other for temporary periods of dependency-autonomy regression. Even the anticipation of adding a third member to this family twosome changes their relationship. When the newborn arrives, one of the adults, usually the mother, must temporarily shift a major part of her relationship from her spouse to her child. The amount of time involved in relating to her dependent infant markedly alters her previously balanced reciprocal relationships with the father. Either mother, father, or both regress because they perceive the child as a stress. The father's regression is primarily related to the mother's part withdrawal from her reciprocal relationship with him. The father now finds himself in competition with the child for dependency on the mother. He deals with this by seeking more tokens of dependency from the mother, his own parents, his secretary, a waitress, his contemporaries or where ever it seems to be offered. He must eventually deal with the situation by establishing a modification of his old reciprocal relationship with the mother and fill the gap with a new relationship with his child.

Whether he is ever successful in this solution is tied in with how the mother handles the changing situation (and vice-versa). Depending on her previous experiences with learning mothering behavior, she feels more or less inadequate to give the dependency sought by the child. She, too, attempts to regress and seeks dependency from the husband. If he is unable to supply it, she turns to her physician, her mother, or even the child. She eventually must find time for a reciprocal relationship with the father plus a dependency relationship with her child. Only when the two parents are able to recover from this stress and establish a new pattern of reciprocal relationships with each other can they offer the child the experiences which he will need to become a mature adult (4, 5, 41).

Other physiological or sociological events which call for behavioral changes are handled in a similar manner. At menopause there is physiological stress as well as psychological stress. However, the psychological stress may precede or follow, by quite some time difference, the actual physiological changes of menopause. The psychosocial implications as well as the awareness of differences in physiological feelings are preceived as stress (5, 43). As always the individual handles the stress by regression to dependency. She then moves towards establishing altered reciprocal relationships, but her flexibility for establishing new relationships is beginning to diminish. This leads her to attempt using her old patterns with new, appropriate or inappropriate, individuals. A mother who has permitted and encouraged a great deal of dependency upon herself may be able to establish reciprocal relationships only in the role of a mother. When her children grow up, she may try mothering her husband where it is inappropriate or baby sitting where it is quite appropriate. She may sense her own daughter's giving birth to children as a severe competitive threat and handle this by insisting upon usurping her daughter's role with the grandchild or placing herself in competition with her grandchild or her son-in-law. The degree and speed of recoverability in establishing new reciprocal relationships determine the end result.

Old age is usually perceived as a more serious threat. There are anatomical, physiological, economic, new learning, sexual, and psychological limitations. Regression occurs, and depending on the way in which the individual has previously handled stress and the degree of impairments, is followed by attempts to again become autonomous and establish new reciprocal relationships. As the realistic handicaps to adaptation increase, it is frequently impossible for a senile person to exist except in a relationship where he predominantly seeks dependency.

Mental health, then, hinges upon two factors. A chance to learn how to establish reciprocal relationships with other autonomous human beings and the ability to use the regression to dependency and/or the dependency-autonomy struggles as a temporary adaptive mechanism which can be given up or used in direct relationship to the realistic stress the individual faces.

REFERENCES

1. ADLER, A., *Practice and Theory of Individual Psychology*, New York, Harcourt, 1925.
2. BOWLBY, J., "Critical Phases in the Development of Social Responses in Man and Other Animals," *New Bio.*, 14, 25–32, 1953.
3. CANNON, W., *The Wisdom of the Body*, New York, Norton, 1939.
4. DEUTSCH, H., *The Psychology of Women*, 2, New York, Grune & Stratton, 1945.
5. ERIKSON, E., *Childhood and Society*, New York, Norton, 1950.
6. FENICHEL, O., *The Psychoanalytic Theory of Neurosis*, New York, Norton, 1946.
7. FLECK, S., CORNELISON, A., NORTON, N. and LIDZ, T., "Incestuous and Homosexual Problems," in Masserman, J., *Individual and Familial Dynamics*, New York, Grune & Stratton, 1959.
8. FREUD, A., "Adolescence," *Psychoanalyt. Stud. Child.*, 13, 255–278, 1958.
9. FREUD, S., "Sixth Impression," *Collected Papers*, London, Hogarth, 1950.
10. GALAMBOS, R. and MORGAN, C. T., "The Neural Basis of Learning," *Handbook of Physiology, I, Neurophysiology*, 3, 1471–1499, 1960.
11. GERARD, R. W., "Neurophysiology: An Integration," *Handbook of Physiology, I, Neurophysiology*, 3, 1919–1965, 1960.
12. GRAY, P. H., "Theory and Evidence of Imprinting in Human Infants," *J. Psychol.*, 46, 155–166, 1958.
13. HALL, C. and LINDZEY, G., *Theories of Personality*, Philadelphia, Wiley, 1957.
14. HALSTEAD, W., "Thinking, Imagery, and Memory," *Handbook of Physiology, I, Neurophysiology*, 3, 1669–1678, 1960.

15. HARLOW, H. F., "The Heterosexual Affectional System in Monkeys," *Amer. Psychol.*, 17, 1–9, 1962.

16. HARTMAN, H., "Notes on the Theory of Sublimation," *Psychoanalyt. Stud. Child*, 10, 9–29, 1955.

17. HILGARD, E. R., *Theories of Learning*, New York, Appleton, 1956.

18. HYDEN, H., "Satellite Cells in the Nervous System," *Scient. Amer.*, 205, 62–70, 1961.

19. JOSSELYN, I., *The Adolescent and His World*, New York, Fam. Serv. Assn. Amer., 1952.

20. JUNG, C. G., *Modern Man in Search of a Soul*, New York, Harcourt, 1933.

21. LEVITT, E. E., *Clinical Research Design and Analysis in the Behavioral Sciences*, Springfield, Ill., Thomas, 1961.

22. LORENZ, K., "Imprinting," as discussed by Gerwitz, J., in Foss, B. M. (ed.), *Determinants in Infant Behavior*, New York, Wiley, 1961.

23. KRIS, E., "Neutralization and Sublimation," *Psychoanalyt. Stud. Child*, 10, 30–46, 1955.

24. MAHLER, M. S. and GOSLINER, B. J., "On Symbiotic Child Psychosis," *Psychoanalyt. Stud. Child*, 10, 195–212, 1955.

25. McCONNELL, J. V., JACOBSON, A. L. and KIMBLE, D. P., "The Effects of Regeneration upon Retention of a Conditioned Response in the Planarian," *J. Comp. Physiol. Psychol.*, 52, 1–5, 1959.

26. MILLER, J. G., "Toward a General Theory for the Behavioral Sciences," *Amer. Psychol.*, 10. 513–531, 1955.

27. MILLER, J. G., "Information Input Overload and Psychopathology," *Amer. J. Psychiat.*, 116, 695–704, 1960.

28. MILLER, N. E. and DOLLARD, J., *Social Learning and Imitation*, New Haven, Yale, 1941.

29. NURNBERGER, J., *Introduction to the Science of Human Behavior*, New York, Appleton, 1963.

30. OTTINGER, D., "Some Effects of Maternal Inconsistency and Emotionality Level upon Offspring Behavior and Development," unpublished doctoral dissertation, Purdue, 1961.

31. PIAGET, J., *The Construction of Reality in the Child*, New York, Basic, 1954.

32. PIAGET, J., *The Moral Judgment of the Child*, Glencoe, Ill., Free Press, 1948.

33. REUSCH, J. and BATESON, G., *Communication: The Social Matrix of Psychiatry*, New York, Norton, 1951.

34. SCOTT, J. P., "Critical Periods in Behavioral Development," *Science*, 138, 949–958, 1962.

35. SELYE, H., "Stress and General Adaptation Syndrome," *Brit. Med. J.*, 1383–1392, 1950.

36. SELYE, H., "The Alarm Reaction," *Canad. Med. Asso. J.*, 34, 706, 1936.

37. SKINNER, B. F., *Science and Human Behavior*, New York, Macmillan, 1953.

38. SPITZ, R:, "Anaclitic Depression," *Psychoanalyt. Stud. Child*, 2, 313–342, 1948.

39. SPITZ, R., *No and Yes*, New York, International Universities, 1957.

40. STELLAR, E., "Drive and Motivation," *Handbook of Physiology, I, Neurophysiology*, 3, 1501–1527, 1960.

41. SULLIVAN, H. S., *The Interpersonal Theory of Psychiatry*, New York, Norton, 1953.

42. VON BERTALANFFY, L., "An Outline of General Systems Theory," *Brit. J. Philos. Sci.*, 1, 134–165, 1950.

43. WEISS, E. and ENGLISH, O. S., *Psychosomatic Medicine*, Philadelphia, Saunders, 1943.

44. FRIES, M. E., "Some Basic Differences in the Newborn," Film Library, New York Univ., 1942.

45. THOMPSON, W. R., "Influence of Prenatal Maternal Anxiety on Emotionality in Young Rats," *Science*, 125, 698–699, 1957.

13

Extended Family Relations of Disturbed and Well Families

NORMAN W. BELL, PH.D.

I T HAS LONG BEEN RECOGNIZED that the mental health of individuals is related to the family. However, until recently there has been a failure to conceptualize the family *qua* family; studies of individual pathology have usually reduced the family to individual psychodynamic terms (1). Beginning with Richardson's (2) pioneer attempts to characterize the family as a group with properties in its own right, considerable changes have taken place. Numerous investigators have developed conceptual schemes to describe the subtle and complex processes in families. Such reformulations involve a shift away from the view that mental illness is a characteristic of an individual toward the view that disturbance in one member is a symptom of the functioning of the whole family. Concomitantly, different therapeutic approaches to families as groups (3) or to individuals (4) as family members have been developed.

These reconceptualizations produce a needed corrective to earlier tendencies to overemphasize the significance of an individual's innate tendencies or of isolated segments of relationships in which he may be involved. However, to the family sociologist, there appears a danger that the fallacies of oversimplification and reductionism characteristic of the focus on the individual are being repeated again at the family level. Family psychiatrists seem, by and large, to view the family as a self-contained, invariable unit (5) existing in a social and cultural vacuum. The significance of a grandparent[1] or an extra-family activity of a parent may be recognized as incorporated in one member's pathology in particular instances. But systematic consideration of the interdependence of the nuclear family and related families of orientation, or of the nuclear family and the surrounding society as a universal structural principle have been lacking.[2] Both on theoretical (7) and empirical (8, 9) grounds it is difficult to find justification for neglecting the frameworks within which families function.

PROBLEM

This paper will explore only one segment of the total web of relationships in which families exist, namely relationships with extended kin. Every society recognizes and patterns the relations of successive generations (10). The breaking or changing of old ties and the formation of new ties through marriage are always transition points with potential stresses. As Radcliffe-Brown has expressed it ". . . Marriage is a rearrangement of social structure. . . . A marriage produces a temporary disequilibrium situation. . . . The establishment of a new equilibrium after a marriage requires that in certain types of kinship or family structure there is a need felt for emphasizing the separateness of the two connected families. . . . The principal points of tension created by a marriage are between the wife and the husband's parents and the husband and the wife's parents." (11, pp. 43–58 passim). The thesis of this paper is that disturbed families are ones in which this "disequilibrium created by marriage" has not been resolved but continues to provoke and maintain conflicts and the underlying discrepancies that cause them, and that well families have achieved some resolution of the problems of ties to extended kin so that these kin are neutral or even positive forces in the resolution of family problems.

---

[1] The first volume of *The Psychoanalytic Review* in 1914 includes abstracts of articles on the "grandfather complex" by Jones, Abraham, and Ferenczi.

[2] Ackerman (6) is one of the few who have advanced into this area and he puts the stress mainly on the emotional and attitudinal aspects.

BEFORE PRESENTING DATA relevant to this thesis it may be helpful to review briefly the nature of family processes which lead to individual pathology and some features of the American kinship system, two domains not previously related to one another.

In common with various other family researchers I assume that functional disturbances arise from and are maintained by family interaction, including the emotional dynamics associated with overt behavior. Different researchers have focused upon different aspects of the patterns of interaction, some emphasizing the persistent structural features, others the nature of communication processes, still others the discordance between overt behavior and inner feelings. Common to all appears to be some conception that, as a group, the family must try to adapt to the discrepancies within and between individuals and reach some equilibrium. Unless the underlying issues are resolved there will be a strong tendency to act out the problems by involving others in biologically, psychologically or socially inappropriate roles. Such processes lead to disturbances of ego identity. The disturbance, so dysfunctional for the individual, serves positive functions for the family in its efforts to secure or preserve some sort of integration (12). Removal of, or change in, the disturbed individual upsets the "pathological equilibrium" and leads to changes throughout the system. Much less work has been devoted to well families, but conversely it might be formulated that to cope with discrepancies they adopt mechanisms which actually resolve the discrepancies or at least contain them in ways that are not pathogenic for individual members.

THE FAMILY PROCESSES associated with mental illness or health have been described by others in some detail (13) with focus on the operations within nuclear families. But any nuclear family is part of a larger "family field" and must cope with the establishment and structuring of ties to two families of orientation. Some kinship systems stress the continuity of generations by subordinating the younger generation to the authority of the elder and stress the preference of one lineage over the other. The American kinship system (14) emphasizes the structurally isolated nuclear family and is bilateral. The emphasis on the isolated nuclear family means that there is discontinuity and relative independence of adjacent adult generations. The characteristic of bilaterality means that both the husband's and wife's families are potentially of equal importance in reckoning descent, controlling property, giving support and direction and so on. Since neither side of the family receives a culturally prescribed preference, each family must work out its own balance of the ties to, and independence of, two extended families. This task is further complicated by the tendency to define the maintenance of kinship ties as a feminine rather than masculine role.[3]

DATA

The data which is to be cited here are drawn from a long-term study of disturbed and well families. The broader project, directed by Drs. John Spiegel and Florence Kluckhohn, is concerned with the interrelation of cultural values, family roles and the mental health of individuals.[4] Details of the population studied have been presented elsewhere (1, 15, 16); here it is sufficient to note that intact working-class families with at least three generations available for interviewing were studied intensively for periods ranging from two to five years. The families were of varying ethnic backgrounds. Half of them had a functionally disturbed child (here called "disturbed families"); half had no clinically manifest disturbance (called "well families").

Contact with the "sick" families was mainly in the office setting; the child and both parents, at a minimum, were seen in weekly therapy sessions. Occasionally parents or a parent and child were seen jointly. Family behavior before and after interviews was observed. Eventually all families were visited in their homes on several occasions, and relatives were interviewed where possible or at least were met during visits. With the "well" families there was similarly extended, regular contact by teams of a child psychiatrist, a psychiatric social worker and a sociologist. The bulk of these contacts was in homes. Clearly the meaning of the contact for these well families was different, but we were reasonably satisfied that comparable data were obtained for both groups.

FINDINGS

Four aspects of how extended kin articulate with nuclear families will be discussed. The first two (extended families as countervailing forces and extended families as continuing stimulators of conflict) deal

[3] I do not mean to imply that the American kinship system presents more, or more intense, problems than other kinship systems. Other systems engender problems too (e.g. the daughter-in-law in traditional China) but the focal problems are different.

[4] Sponsored by the Laboratory of Social Relations, Harvard University and the Children's Medical Center, Boston, and supported by grants from the National Institute of Mental Health and the Pauline and Louis G. Cowan Foundation.

with the dynamics of intergroup relationships. The second two (extended families as screens for the projection of conflicts and extended families as competing objects of support and indulgence) deal more with the social-psychological qualities of the relationships. Distinguishing these four aspects is, of course, an analytic device; empirically they are intertwined.

Extended Families as Countervailing Forces

The ability of the nuclear family to contain its conflicts and control the impact of its discrepancies by means of a child is limited. Adult members in particular may experience guilt about the child, particularly when his condition is defined by outside agencies such as schools, courts and neighbors. But even short of this step, parents are capable of experiencing guilt or anxiety through identification with the child, a necessary but often neglected correlate of the child's identification with the parent.

Mr. Costello, for instance, brought his younger son for medical attention when this son began to stutter seriously. The father had suffered from a speech problem himself in childhood. He "understood" his son's stuttering as something learned from an older brother, although it was more closely related to the chronic stool-retention problems this younger child had, the physical symptom for which medical attention was sought. The older son's stuttering had not affected the father deeply; this symptom in the younger son with whom the father was so closely identified was intolerable.

Aging of the child may shift the child's capacity to absorb family tensions so that he is able to escape parental pressures more and get support for himself from the peer group (17). Maneuvers within the family are not always adequate to restore the pathogenic equilibrium. At such times there may be a resorting to the extended family to shore up crumbling group defenses. Typically this process includes a seeking for support from the natural parents and an attack upon the in-laws. In the full form this becomes reciprocal with the other spouse drawing upon his family for reserves and attacking his in-laws. As the vicious circle progresses, the whole family becomes split. A day in the life of the McGinnis family will illustrate this:

Mr. and Mrs. McGinnis lived in a state of armed truce. Mrs. McGinnis domineered the family in an irrational, active way. Her domination of their oldest son, perceived by herself as maternal devotion, was extreme. Mr. Mc-

Ginnis had developed set patterns of schizoid withdrawal from the family and persistent needling of the 12-year old son to grow up before he was drafted into the army or was thrown out of the family to go to work. The bane of Mr. McGinnis' life was his old, unreliable car which in its weaker moments he used to kick and curse. For Mrs. McGinnis and her son this car was the proof of the father's stupidity and the family's low status. Mr. McGinnis was continually harassed to get a new car. One day, independently, he did go out and buy a second-hand station wagon. When Mrs. McGinnis was told of this she conjured up an image of a high, homely, small bus. In the telephone conversations with her family, which quickly followed, this distorted image was elaborated. They soon gathered around to "kid" Mr. McGinnis about running a jitney to New York. Their perverse pleasure was short lived when they saw a quite ordinary station wagon. By this time Mr. McGinnis was bitterly attacking his in-laws and soon after paid a rare visit to his aged mother who was nearly indigent and in a nursing home. His visit reawakened Mrs. McGinnis' suspicions that her mother-in-law had money hidden away which should be given to them. When Mrs. McGinnis' spinster sisters came under fire from Mr. McGinnis, she defended them in exaggerated terms and returned with interest comments about Mr. McGinnis' paranoid sister.

For the McGinnises this schismogenic process was not conscious. Mrs. McGinnis called her various family members every day so there was nothing unusual in her telling them of the "bus" her husband had bought. In other families the process is quite conscious and deliberate. The Manzoni's, for example, knew that visits to their own families made their partners wildly jealous, and knew just at what point to call or visit a relative.

Even children become sensitive to the familial tensions regarding extended families and disappear to visit grandparents, insult visiting relatives, or engage in other operations to crystallize the parents', and eventually, the whole family's, split feelings about in-laws.

The mechanisms by which extended families are brought into conflict situations may be conscious or, at least apparently, unconscious. Frequently the sequence is initiated by what seems to be a casual and innocent conflict. Until we are able directly to observe the initiation of this spreading of conflict, it is difficult to be specific about the mechanisms involved. I feel fairly sure that the process is a subtle one, that no direct reference to conflicts in the nuclear family or direct request for allies has to be made. Rather both or all parties to the relationship are sufficiently sensitized that the spreading process can begin, or flare up, through minimal cues in tone of voice, timing of contacts and so forth. In all, I believe these mechanisms are not different from those observed in the families of schizophrenics, where therapy teams (18), and hospital staff can become drawn into family conflicts (19).

In the light of Bott's findings (8) regarding the nature of the social network and intrafamilial role allocation, it is important to inquire into the relationships between the extended families. When they are drawn into family conflicts do they themselves echo those conflicts, as Brodey finds that therapy teams do? None of our families had been geographically mobile to any large extent, so most extended families did have superficial acquaintance with each other. The frequency of active relationships was low, being clearly present in only one out of eleven cases. Since the frequency of active relationships in the general population is unknown, it is difficult to be sure of the significance of this. Of course, in our society the respective parental families stand in no particular relationship to each other and there is no term to denote it.[5]

Well families also have conflicts, but they differ in several respects. The open conflicts that occur are incidents on a foundation of basic integration, are self-limiting, and do not compromise a wide range of interaction in the future. In striking contrast to the disturbed families, active engagement in disputes was kept within the family by well families. This does not come about by the kin being unaware of the conflicts. Indeed they often seem quite well-informed about them, but these kin groups are not drawn into the pattern of balancing off one side of the nuclear family against the other.

In some well families there was evidence that the extended families not only did not become drawn into and amplify the conflicts, but even acted in benign ways to reduce conflicts and restore family functioning. An interesting example of this occurred in the DiMaggio family:

One summer Mr. DiMaggio's mother wanted to visit a nephew who had recently migrated to Canada from Italy. Over Mrs. DiMaggio's protests it was decided that the grandparents and four of their five sons, including Mr. DiMaggio, would make the trip; Mrs. DiMaggio would stay at home with her youngest child. During the absence of her in-laws, Mrs. DiMaggio became mildly depressed, and developed fantasies that her husband was having a gay time. Though her own family was living nearby, her contact with them did not increase markedly. The night before arriving home, Mr. DiMaggio phoned his wife. Though she did not complain openly, he sensed her state of mind. He felt guilty and when they arrived home, he managed to arrange it so that the rest of the family entered the apartment before he did. In their first contacts the brother-in-law and parents-in-law were attentive to Mrs.

---

[5] Other languages do have a term for this relationship, e.g. the Jewish word *Machatenen*

DiMaggio. One brother-in-law, a priest, took her aside and talked to her about the obligations of marriage and informed her of how unhappy her husband had been while away. When Mr. DiMaggio did come in, his wife put aside her complaints, brightened up and was genuinely glad to see her husband. Mrs. DiMaggio remained aware of her reactions but resumed a normal, close relationship with her in-laws.

Extended Families as Stimulators of Conflict

Extended families are not always passive elements in the situation, and in some instances the initiative for provoking conflict seems to rest with them. Extended families may be responding to discrepancies in their family structure in the same ways, thereby inducing conflicts within the nuclear families we have in focus.

The Mozzarellas had for some time had the father's unmarried brother living with them and their three children. At one point this brother took or stole a small amount of money from the Mozzarellas. Mrs. Mozzarella was furious and began to fight with her husband. The conflict grew and the brother moved out. Rather than abating, the conflict between husband and wife widened and deepened. Finally Mr. Mozzarella moved out for a few days, but did not stay with his brother. After a few weeks absence the brother also moved back in with the family.

In all such instances it is likely that the action of the extended family has to fall on prepared grounds in the nuclear family. Often these actions are appropriate—almost uncannily so—to the weak spots in the family organization. In themselves the actions of the extended family may appear innocent enough, but their effects are widespread. Frequently the triggering incident is a gift.[6]

Mrs. McGinnis' mother gave her grandson gifts of money just at the times when Mr. McGinnis was berating his son for his failure to earn his own spending money. The money mitigated the economic problem, but increased the father-son conflict and eventually the whole family was at odds.

In some instances the precipitating incident seems to be more genuinely innocent, with the problem being the inability of the family to develop or employ mechanisms for insulating themselves or for controlling conflicts once they have begun.

---

[6] The gift, as Marcel Mauss has shown (20), creates an obligation of the receiver to the donor. Normally this cements the social structure. As I shall discuss presently, for conflicted families the assuming and discharging of obligations is problematic and tends to break down the social structure.

Mrs. Manzoni's brother was in an army basic training camp about 40 miles away. He often visited the Manzonis when on leave. His visits were agreeable to the Manzonis who even looked forward to them since their uncontrollable son responded well to direction from this uncle. One weekend, however, he brought a buddy along with him. Mrs. Manzoni tried to be hospitable, but father and son both reacted sharply to this shift. Bitter arguments about the invasions and demands of Mrs. Manzoni's family ensued. Mrs. Manzoni retaliated with accusations that her husband did many favors for his family.

Whether conducted in an innocent or calculated way, extended families frequently do provoke conflicts in the nuclear families. The impact is not always the open conflict described in these examples. Often the impact is at the latent level, exaggerating the discrepancies that already exist.

At the well end of the continuum extended families do not intervene in their married children's lives in ways which set off the trains of reaction described above. The interventions which do occur do not cut to the bone and are not reacted to in a stereotyped way. To illustrate:

Mr. McNally's brother was a heavy drinker and had served time for theft. Occasionally he would come around to the McNally home, presumably looking for food and money. Mrs. McNally would refuse to let him into the house. Mr. McNally, though he had some interest and sympathy for his brother, supported such responses on the part of his wife. At times he sought out his brother and tried to help him, but these approaches were not timed and carried out so as to reflect on his wife or compensate for her rejection of the brother. On her side, Mrs. McNally did not interfere with her husband's attempts to rehabilitate his brother, though she expected little to come of them. Both husband and wife had mixed feelings about this relative but their attitudes toward him appeared to be appropriate.

Rather than acting as *agents provacateurs*, the extended kin of well families are able to remain neutral and respect the boundaries of the nuclear family. For their part, the well families are not hypersensitive to the actions of kin.

Mrs. Flanagan's parents lived nearby. They were old and somewhat infirm. Periodically heavy demands for help were made on Mrs. Flanagan. Even though the whole family was preoccupied with being cared for and had much physical illness, these demands were accepted as a necessary sacrifice, even by the children. Mr. Flanagan accommodated himself to the demands on his wife by being helpful at home and at his parents-in-law.

Extended Families as Screens for the Projection of Conflicts

The extended family need not be an active or even potentially active element in the conflict situation. In all cases there was some evidence that the extended family served as a screen onto which a family member could project sentiments which referred more immediately to a spouse, child or parent. This process, which I have labelled the *overgeneraliza-tion of affect* is mainly of negative sentiments. Positive sentiments are also involved as a reciprocal tendency, though they are not so conspicu-ous. The overgeneralization spreads over social space and time. In the extreme cases an impervious dichotomy of good and bad occurs and ra-tionalizes a wide range of avoidance behavior and expression of dislike.

Mrs. Donovan, in her first therapy sessions, painted a picture of the many deficiencies of her oldest son and her husband. She felt that they were no good and were just like her husband's family, all of whom were no good and never had been any good. Her own father, who died in her adolescence, was com-pletely different, having been intelligent, sensitive, liberal, sophisticated and unprejudiced. Her mother, concerning whom she had more mixed feelings, came in for little comment at this time. Mrs. Donovan had had, since her marriage, minimal contact with her husband's family. Contacts which did occur substantiated her view of her in-laws.

The families in which pathology was highly integrated tended to show a pattern of each spouse directing his or her negative sentiments towards the in-laws and directing positive sentiments toward the natu-ral parents. Reality sometimes makes such splitting difficult. However, grandparents who can in calm moments (or in therapy) be evaluated realistically, tend to be defended when they are criticized by the partner, and part of the defense is an attack upon the partner's side of the fam-ily. The reverse picture, of one person directing negative sentiments to his own parents and positive ones to his in-laws seems infrequent. In our cases it was noted only in one family and in this case the tendency was mild.

This sort of conflict involves, naturally enough, parents more than children. Still it is not restricted to them. The children are quite likely to assimilate the parental sentiments and to align with one rather than the other or "slide" between the two.

Jackie McGinnis, for example, could echo all of his mother's feelings and suspicions of his paternal grandmother and condemn the paternal grand-father who had died many years before his birth. At such times he was posi-tive about and in close contact with maternal relatives. To a lesser degree he could reverse the roles if he was in conflict with his mother and wanted to get something from his father.

Again, projection of feelings through space and time need not emerge in overt conflict. The projection may be a stable characteristic of an individual's psychological functioning within the family which magnifies the discrepancies which do exist.

Mrs. McGinnis occasionally used her suspicion that her mother-in-law had money secreted in a Canadian bank in her arguments with her husband, insisting it was money which they had a right to. Even when she was not attacking her husband on this account, it was part of her fantasies about giving her son the education her husband was convinced he should not have and was incapable of getting. Buttressed by this projection, she was able to push her son and herself in directions which took them farther and farther from the father.

I hope that it is clear that there is more to this pattern than the pathological functioning of individuals. Individuals, children as well as parents, utilize the structure of the family and the extended family as arenas in which to express their ambivalent feelings. Reciprocally the schisms of the family and the extended family reinforce and perhaps even stimulate complications in their feelings about parent figures. Individuals who may have been able reasonably well to integrate their ambivalent feelings toward their parents may have difficulty in adapting to the existence of parents *and* parents-in-law.[7]

Members of well families, as material cited earlier suggests, do not develop such polarized feelings about kin. There certainly were mixed feelings and, on occasion, strong negative feelings about kin, but these could be handled and even if not fully expressed, the tendency to split feelings and maintain them in a rigid fashion was not present. This lack of overgeneralization of affect was true of positive feelings as well as negative ones. In contrast to Epstein and Westley's (22) normal families, we did not meet the pattern of "adoration" which they observed in the wife-husband relationship. This difference in findings regarding normal families may be a genuine difference in the sample of families studied or may be a function of different methods of investigation used. In our group there was also no "adoration" spreading to the extended families.

---

[7] Cf. Parsons' (21) proposition that socialization involves the internalization not simply of separate parent figures but also the internalization of the *relationship between* the parents.

Extended Families as Competing Objects of Support and Indulgence

I have chosen to treat separately a theme closely related to all the above. My feeling is that this theme is a central and basic one. It is this: that extended families become competing sources and objects of the support and indulgence for the nuclear family. In American society the norm is for nuclear families to be independent.[8]

The disturbed families we have seen almost universally presented problems of this sort. When the loyalty and commitment of some members can no longer be implicitly assumed and is called into question, processes are set in motion to generate and amplify conflicts. In some instances the medium of conflict is money, as with Mr. McGinnis:

He had an ambulatory paranoid sister who journeyed about the country taking skilled clerical jobs. Invariably she would develop suspicions that she was being watched and plotted against and quit her job. In desperate financial straits she would wire Mr. McGinnis for money. Though recognizing her as ill, Mr. McGinnis would usually get money somewhere and send it to her. He maintained that he kept this secret from his wife, though she was well aware of what was going on. (Both, incidentally, silently assumed that all this was kept secret from the children, which was also inaccurate.) For Mrs. McGinnis this justified her suspicions that her mother-in-law was holding back and in derivative and half-recognized ways complicated the family fights over money.

The diversion of material goods as well as money to the extended family can be the precipitant of conflicts. For the Manzonis it was the cost of food which was consumed by Mrs. Manzoni's family. Mr. Manzoni felt that the food served his in-laws was better than that served *his* family if they visited, and more of it was consumed.

In other cases the questioned commodity was affection and attention. Mr. McGinnis was preoccupied with the amount of time his wife spent talking to her family on the telephone and compared it to the neglect of his own mother, a neglect of which he himself was guilty. The Man-

---

[8] Legally the situation is confused. Marriage is recognized as a legal union which obligates the husband to support his family, and both parents to support their minor children. Similarly a legal marriage (and even in some circumstances a common-law union) entails the right to pass property onto family members and the right of family members to claim property of a deceased member. At the same time we still have laws, occasionally enforced, that children, even married children, are obligated to support indigent parents (23). This vagueness of our laws and our mores, together with our bilateral kinship system, presents the possibility of conflict. Family resources—whether they be money, goods, affection or services, are not unlimited. There are always alternative directions in which they may be allocated. Even comfortably situated families may have problems in the allocation of wealth and contain "poverty-stricken" members (24).

zonis were continually suspicious that the other was seeing his own family and being influenced by them. Children too were perceived as liking one side of the family more, paying more heed to one side, and even of resembling, physically or in personality, one side of the family rather than the other.

In the Costello family such a pattern was developed to the extreme. Their first son was a "mother's boy," the second a "father's boy," and they moved in largely separate interactional spheres. When Mrs. Costello wanted to visit her parents, which she felt obliged to do weekly, her older son would not tolerate being left behind while her younger son protested strongly about going. Each visit was thus a struggle for Mrs. Costello and sufficient proof to Mr. Costello that she should stay at home.

Whatever the resource being contended about, the pattern of real or perceived favoritism for part of the extended family structure can arise. The pattern seems to serve multiple functions; it externalizes the internal conflicts of any given individual and allows him to rationalize his own shortcomings (as with Mr. McGinnis), for his own shortcomings pale into insignificance in the light of the others' misdeeds. At the same time it preserves the conflicts within the family. Being external they are beyond influence of any one person or combination.

Once again well families stand in contrast. They too have problems about the allocation of resources but diverting them to one family of orientation, as the earlier illustration of the Flanigans suggests, does not stimulate feelings of deprivation and resentment. Correspondingly resources from extended families, even when the differential between the contributions of the two sides of the family is considerable, do not become foci of conflict.

To summarize the material presented above, it may be said that disturbed families have difficulties in solving the problems of how to relate to two sets of "parents" and of establishing family boundaries. The absence of boundaries allows family conflicts to spread to extended kin and means a deficit of ability of the nuclear family to insulate itself from the vagueness of the outside world. Thus extended kin are drawn into, or play into the conflicts of the nuclear family so that underlying discrepancies are not resolved but are spread and made more rigid. In this family setting individual members have difficulty in taking roles as representatives of the whole family. *Vis à vis* the outside world of kin they act as individuals; what they give to or receive from kin casts them as competitors with other members rather than as collaborators with the whole family. This interpersonal situation appears to foster the awakening and acting out of ambivalent feelings with a consequent circular effect.

IMPLICATIONS

The thesis has been advanced here that the extended families are, or become, involved in family pathology and that different patterns of relationship with extended families are set up by disturbed families than by normal or healthy families. In conclusion I should like to explore some of the implications of such findings for theories of the relationship between family processes and mental illness, and for therapeutic efforts at diagnosis and treatment.

Several years ago Ackerman complained of etiological theories in dynamic psychiatry that they "... hypothesize a relation between a piece of the child and a piece of the parent." (25, p. 182) His evaluation was that these were inadequate and that we had to evolve theories which related to the integrity of the individual to the family as a whole. A great deal of progress in this direction has been made but the question may be raised again with regard to family-centered theories. The point is not that they are incorrect but that they are only part of the picture. Families are seldom, if ever, isolated from kin. If ties to extended families are present and involved in the family processes must we not at some level include this in our theory? The findings presented, though based upon a small and selected population and derived from studies of neurotic children rather than psychotic adults, seem to me to argue in this direction.

The issue can be posed in a more general form. The systems we deal with are not closed, they are always embedded in and to some degree derive their rationale and patterning from, broader systems. For some purposes we may treat them *as if* they were closed but we must never paint them as the whole truth. In this I have tried to look outward from the family system to its kin. One might equally well take cognizance of the fact that the family is involved in many other networks of relationships and that these too may function to stimulate and maintain conflicts or alternatively to contain and correct them.[9] Ultimately we must refer our finding to the general patterns of values which characterize cultures and subcultures and which have a pervasive influence

---

[9] For brief comments on how work associates, neighbors and professionals may be assimilated to pathological family patterns see (4, 12).

in shaping personality, family role patterns, and the whole family field extending through space and time, indeed the whole fabric of society. Florence Kluckhohn has devoted her major attention to the analysis of these patterns of value orientations (26). It is, I believe, possible to show that the type of issue which comes up in this process of re-equilibrating the imbalance associated with marriage, the pathological ways of coping with discrepancies, and the available alternatives for resolving the issues can be deduced from the variations in value orientations characteristic of different groups.

Our work is vastly complicated by such a theoretical position but I see no alternative to dealing with reality as it is. If a broader range of variables can be dealt with precisely and adequately, we may develop theories with more specificity than our current conceptions. In an earlier era it was popular to attribute mental disturbances to broken homes. I daresay there are 100 papers in the literature reporting such findings. It is only part of the problem of these studies that they report inconsistent findings and that they seldom have adequate control groups. A more serious problem is that broken homes seem to be related to delinquency, neurosis, schizophrenia, and various psychosomatic disorders. An agent so nonspecific is of little help or at best is merely the first step. Most studies of families have also lacked control groups. It is not clear whether the presumably pathogenic processes detected in the families of schizophrenics are really absent in families with less seriously disturbed individuals and perhaps even families without disturbance. Tracing out how pathology is integrated in a broader network than the nuclear family may give some added specificity.

There might also be advantages to paying close attention to the history of families. It is striking that we have not developed models of the developmental processes of families that compare to our models of individual development. For example, in the Donovan family many shifts in group and individual dynamics coincided with changes in the closeness of the nuclear family to the wife's mother.

After their marriage the Donovans lived with the wife's mother, and had a fairly happy marriage. Acute difficulties arose after they moved to their own dwelling; Mrs. Donovan's sentiments about her in-laws became more negative, and Mr. Donovan's contacts with his family, which were more rigidly pursued, became more threatening to the wife. The problems were heightened after Mrs. Donovan's mother remarried. During the course of therapy the two family units jointly purchased a two-family house and lived close to each other again. Many conflicts abated following this move.

If we can learn to listen to the histories patients give, not individual but familial, we can learn much about the dynamics of the group and how the family has got to its present state. Such findings as have been reported may also have implications for our therapeutic endeavors. To the extent that we misplace the causal forces which have led to, and maintain pathology, we may misjudge the potentials for change and how to bring it about. Systematic consideration of patterns of relationships with extended families can give us added leverage in the diagnosis of particular problems with which we are confronted.

Treatment strategies may need rethinking in the light of this view of pathology as a process broader than the individual family. In our research work we saw relatives, not because we had any systematic program or good rationale to intervene therapeutically with them, but in pursuit of our research interests. This was not always readily agreed to by members of the nuclear family but in many cases it had a salutary effect, for the family members, for the relatives, and for their relationships. Relatives were seldom ignorant of the difficulties in the nuclear families or of the involvement with the psychiatric clinic. Nuclear families often preferred to believe that their problems and attempts to get help were unknown to kin, but on close examination, this was another example of "open secrets."

In several cases it was a significant turning point when the person being seen could allow his relatives to be seen by the therapist.

Mr. Donovan was resistant to therapy in many ways but dead set against his family being seen. After a year with very limited progress (and incidentally some time after the family had moved back into a house shared with Mrs. Donovan's mother), he was able to discuss his discomfort with authority figures unless he could be on close friendly terms with them. A little later, Mr. Donovan offered to take the therapist to visit the rest of his family. Subsequent to this social visit, there took place meaningful discussions of Mr. Donovan's feelings of loyalty to and sympathy with his own family, and his resentment at his wife's depreciation of them, him, and his son.

While such techniques are regarded by many as unorthodox, dangerous and/or unnecessary, I believe a case can be made that there are instances in which therapy fails unless the therapist can understand and involve himself into the fabric of meanings and the network of relationships the patient knows as natural (4).

As for the relatives, seeing them legitimizes their interest in the nuclear family, but brings this interest under some control. We found they were sometimes able to neutralize their involvement in the nuclear families and get for themselves a broader perspective on the nuclear family. It was also profitable to get, by seeing a relative, a fresh perspective on a case. Just as Brodey sees the advantages of seeing married partners to get a "stereoscopic view" of the relationship, so seeing members of several families offers the advantages of a stereoscopic view of families.

We have not included relatives in therapy on a systematic and regular basis and I can only conjecture about the advantages and problems that "kin group therapy" might bring. There are no logical grounds for stopping at the boundaries of the nuclear family, boundaries which are very permeable and shifting.[10] At one level, movement in therapy consists of changes in the sentiments about and interaction with extended families. To cite the Donovans once more:

> Mrs. Donovan's depreciation of her son, husband and all her husband's family gradually gave way during therapy. In the space of three years, they altered sufficiently to lead her to buy a small Christmas gift for her mother-in-law. Contact of the whole family with her husband's siblings increased. Eventually, she visited her mother-in-law and found that she had good qualities as well as bad, and that it was not unpleasant to visit her. As her sentiments were mitigated, her relationship with her husband expanded and changed and shifts even appeared in the whole family constellation.

It is possible that this central process in the whole family might have been speeded up if both partners could have been influenced simultaneously, as indeed we do in treating mother-child pairs.

SUMMARY

This paper has taken up the issue of whether our understanding of functional disturbances can afford to stop at the boundaries of the nuclear family. It has been argued, and some evidence has been presented, that disturbed families are distinguishable from well families in terms of their patterns of relationships with extended families. Disturbed families have a deficiency of family boundaries which leads them to involve extended kin in their conflicts and makes them sensitive to influence from extended kin. Directly or indirectly a considerable segment of kindred systems become part of a pathological drama, until pathology

---

[10] One wonders what family therapists would do if they attempted to treat matrifocal families such as exist in the south and around the Carribean.

is a characteristic of the system, not of individual persons or families. Such findings require replication with larger samples, but do raise questions about the adequacy of our theories of family pathology and our treatment techniques.

REFERENCES

1. SPIEGEL, JOHN P. and BELL, NORMAN W., "The Family of the Psychiatric Patient," in Silvano Arieti (Ed.), *American Handbook of Psychiatry,* New York, Basic Books, 1959.
2. RICHARDSON, HENRY B., *Patients Have Families,* New York, Commonwealth Fund, 1945.
3. BELL, JOHN E., *Family Group Therapy,* Pub. Health Mon. No. 64, U. S. Dept. of Health, Educ. and Welfare, 1961.
4. BELL, NORMAN W., TRIESCHMAN, ALBERT and VOGEL, EZRA F., "A Sociocultural Analysis of the Resistances of Working-Class Fathers Treated in a Child Psychiatric Clinic," *Amer. J. Ortho.,* 31, 388–405, 1961.
5. LEICHTER, HOPE, "Boundaries of the Family as an Empirical and Theoretical Unit," in Nathan W. Ackerman, Frances L. Beatman and Sanford N. Sherman (Eds.), *Exploring the Base for Family Therapy,* New York, Family Service Assoc. of America, 1961.
6. ACKERMAN, NATHAN, "Emotional Impact of In-laws and Relatives," in Samuel Liebman (Ed.), *Emotional Forces in the Family,* Philadelphia, Lippincott, 1959.
7. BELL, NORMAN W., and VOGEL, EZRA F., "Toward a Framework for the Functional Analysis of Family Behavior," in Norman W. Bell and Ezra F. Vogel (Eds.), *A Modern Introduction to the Family,* Glencoe, Free Press, 1960.
8. BOTT, ELIZABETH, *Family and Social Network,* London, Tavistock Publications, 1957.
9. ZIMMERMAN, CARLE and CERVANTES, LUCIUS, *Successful American Families,* New York, Pageant Press, 1960.
10. APPLE, DORRIAN, "The Social Structure of Grandparenthood," *Amer. Anth.,* 58, 656–663, 1958.
11. RADCLIFFE-BROWN, A. R., "Introduction," in A. R. Radcliffe-Brown and Daryll Forde (Eds.), *African Systems of Kinship and Marriage,* London, Oxford Univ. Press, 1950.
12. VOGEL, EZRA F. and BELL, NORMAN W., "The Emotionally Disturbed Child as a Family Scapegoat," *Psychoanalysis and the Psychoanalytic Review,* 47, 21–42, 1960.
13. SANUA, VICTOR D., "Sociocultural Factors in Families of Schizophrenics," *Psychiatry,* 24, 246–265, 1961.

14. PARSONS, TALCOTT, "The Kinship System of the Contemporary United States," in Talcott Parsons *Essays in Sociological Theory*, Glencoe, Free Press, 1954 (revised edition).
15. KLUCKHOHN, FLORENCE R., "Variations in the Basic Values of Family Systems," *Soc. Cswk.*, 39, 63–72, 1958.
16. SPIEGEL, JOHN P., "Some Cultural Aspects of Transference and Countertransference," in Jules H. Masserman (Ed.), *Individual and Familial Dynamics*, New York, Grune & Stratton, 1959.
17. PITTS, JESSE R., "The Family and Peer Groups," in Norman W. Bell and Ezra F. Vogel (Eds.), *A Modern Introduction to the Family*, Glencoe, Free Press, 1960.
18. BRODEY, W. M. and HAYDEN, M., "The Intrateam Reactions: Their Relation to the Conflicts of the Family in Treatment," *Amer. J. Ortho.*, 27, 349–355, 1957.
19. BOWEN, MURRAY, DYSINGER, R. H., BRODEY, W. M., and BASAMANIA, B., "Study and Treatment of Five Hospitalized Family Groups with a Psychotic Member," paper delivered at the American Orthopsychiatric Association Meetings, Chicago, 1957.
20. MAUSS, MARCEL, "Essai sur le don," in Marcel Mauss *Sociologie et Anthropologie*, Paris, Presses Universitaires de France, 1950.
21. PARSONS, TALCOTT and BALES, R. F., *Family, Socialization and Interaction Process*, Glencoe, Free Press, 1955.
22. EPSTEIN, NATHAN B. and WESTLEY, WILLIAM A., "Grandparents and Parents of Emotionally Healthy Adolescents," in Jules Masserman (Ed.), *Psychoanalysis and Human Values*, New York, Grune & Stratton, 1960.
23. SCHORR, ALVIN L., *Filial Responsibility in the Modern American Family*, Washington, D. C., U. S. Dept. of Health, Educ. and Welfare, 1960.
24. YOUNG, MICHAEL, "The Distribution of Income Within the Family," *Brit. J. Soc.*, 3, 305–321, 1952.
25. ACKERMAN, NATHAN W. and BEHRENS, M. L., "Child and Family Psychopathy: Problems of Correlation," in P. H. Hoch and J. Zubin (Eds.), *Psychopathology of Childhood*, New York, Grune & Stratton, 1955.
26. KLUCKHOHN, FLORENCE R., STODTBECK, FRED, and others, *Variations in Value Orientations*, Evanston, Ill., Row, Peterson, & Co., 1961.

14

Adaptive, Directive and Integrative Behavior of Today's Family

MARVIN B. SUSSMAN, PH.D.

T HE INCESSANT THRUST of social change and alterations in the structure and function of modern institutions prompts a critical review of various tenets of the social sciences. In need of particular reappraisal is the assumption that the family and its kin network are largely dependent upon and continuously adjusting to other societal institutions wielding superior potency, that in essence, the family must either respond with appropriate adaptive behavior or be destroyed as a substantive concern.

Such a notion lacks validity since it does not give sufficient consideration to the independent side of the family's behavior. The theoretical posture of this paper is that dependent, integrated, and independent conditions of the family in its relationships with other social institutions can be demonstrated. The urban family and its kin members, through varied activities, influence or are influenced by the activities of educational, health, economic, welfare, and other societal institutions. In some instances its influence is felt directly by producing specific changes in the policy, structure, and activities of these institutions. In others, influence is less directional but more reciprocal and blends the normative requirements of the family-kinship structure with other societal institutions; and, in certain situations, the family has minimal influence and is, in fact, dependent upon other social realms for its existence.

In this analysis two basic themes are discussed. The first is that the majority of American nuclear families are active with other units within a kin-related network which is capable of providing for its members' economic, emotional, educational, welfare, and other supports complementary or competitive to those furnished by other societal institutions. This condition affects intra-family relationships and the individual's or his family's relationships with other kin-related nuclear families and societal institutions. The kin network is a voluntary social organization and like all voluntary ones competes for the interest and participation of its members (1, 2, 3, 4, 5, 6, 7, 8, 9).

The second theme involves a rejection of the prevalent assumption that the modern urban family, whatever its structure, is dependent upon other social institutions and must adjust to their normative demands in order to survive.

Since a decade and a half of research on the structure and activities of the family have resulted in a reconceptualization of family theory in sociology, it is no longer necessary to prove the nuclear family is active with other units within a kin-related network and that this network provides economic and emotional supports and carries out other activities complementary to those of other societal institutions. The establishment of the viability of a kin-related family system refutes certain allegations concerning the isolation and autonomy of the nuclear family. What now require attention are the theoretical bases for such a network and the meaning and significance of inter-family activities for the concerned individuals and nuclear units.

Numerous studies have indicated the nature of the give-and-take between nuclear related families in urban environments. But what is the rationale for this exchange? Given a number of alternative strategies of voluntary associations—capable of furnishing financial aid, emotional support, and social services—what are the bases for continuous interaction between nuclear-related families within a kinship network? It becomes obvious that the urban kinship network in modern society is a voluntary structure, and that a theoretical explanation of its continued existence can be derived from studies of social organization.

The Concept of Reciprocity

One of the key concepts for explaining the bases of the network is reciprocity (10, 11, 12). Studies of marital interaction deal with role complementarity, role expectations, and the implied assumption that successful marital relations require a give-and-take, an exchange whereby the individuals in the dyadic relationship do things for one another and which is a commonly shared expectation. Yet, the notion of reciprocity has not been used extensively in family research; the most significant theoretical work on reciprocity and exchange has occurred in analyses of large-scale organizations and small groups. Numerous studies in these two areas have come to the nub of the problem by indicating that individuals engage in reciprocal acts because they expect to be rewarded, i.e., receive some payoff. In the family field, in contrast, there pervades a certain alarm and fearfulness about talking so blatantly, because it is contrary to the romantic myth and hard to believe that marital partners engage in activities that result in payoffs for themselves. Rather, many prefer to believe that individuals in a marriage relationship act according to some moral code which requires each partner to be completely "other" oriented. It becomes obvious to the serious student of social behavior that the kinds of interaction and reasons for such interaction which exist in one societal system must exist in all others.

Reciprocity is based upon activity for which one is rewarded; and, as George Homans (13) has suggested, the more the individual is rewarded as a consequence of his action in any situation, the more likely he is to engage in the same or similar related activities later on. In contrast, as the individual engages in activities for which he is unrewarded, he disengages himself from or reduces the frequency or intensity of meaning of these activities. In the parlance of the marketplace, people should help and not injure those who have helped them.

Unequal Exchanges

One common misunderstanding about reciprocity is the implied assumption that exchanges between two individuals must be equal or approach equality. The assumption is that eventually there is a reckoning and that if the exchanges are unbalanced then there results a severing of the relationship. Undoubtedly each individual in any relationship with another person or with a group makes such an evaluation, but in all probability it is not a closely calculated one. A reckoning should not be discounted in evaluating the bases for reciprocity; however, the majority of reciprocal relationships which exist among individuals are based upon exchanges which are unequal and often involve unspecified, perceived obligations for which the individual giver can never be certain of the appropriate returns.

The bases for this unequal exchange are the powers of attraction which relate individuals to one another and the existence of social structures based upon differentiation of influence, power, status, and prestige. Attraction implies that one individual desires to be associated with another and that from this association the individual will be rewarded. In some instances a person may stay in a relationship where he must give more than he receives because this is his best available alternative. Rewards may come not only from the other person in the reciprocal relationship but from others outside who confer status based on the association. The attractive person has some qualities or resources which can be released if there develops a mutually attractive relationship.

A corollary principle is the voluntary behavior of the individual who is attracted to another person. He enters into this relationship on his own volition and consequently in subsequent exchanges has a legitimate right to expect an exchange of equal quantity. However, in this relationship his desires and expectations may not be in consonance with reality. He may be in a subordinate position and giving a great deal more to the attractive person than he is receiving; yet he is satisfied and motivated to continue this exchange.

Another element of the reciprocity process is that exchanges need not be made in the same genus. An individual receiving financial reward in an exchange may give in return deference, honor, prestige, and respect to the individual. In other words, there is little expectation that individuals will reciprocate in the same order or with an equal amount.

The Process of Bargaining

Related to reciprocity is the process of bargaining, which has as its objective getting some advantage in a transaction with another individual. It is difficult to delineate the specific motivations for the bargaining process while, by the same token, it is obvious that each interaction involves some degree of bargaining. Each party to the interaction consciously, or more often subconsciously, directs his behavior in relation to his perception and expectations of what the other individual will accept in order to reach an agreement. The interesting feature of the bargaining process is that the individual has perceptions and expectations of what the other person will accept but never is completely certain of what is an acceptable arrangement. Consequently, bargaining which ensues is actually an effort to determine what are acceptable expectations and to give to the other person a minimum concession in order to obtain a greater advantage. Mechanisms of bargaining involve not revealing one's real intentions; often the verbal communication is expressed to indicate that the individual is thinking primarily of the other person rather than of himself.

Familiarity with the bargaining process has developed through observations of the relationships between formal structures such as industrial firms and unions, or school systems and teachers. In such settings the bargaining process has been formalized so that every participant is aware of the steps one must take in order to reach an accord. Bargaining which occurs in relationships between individuals or between families is less formal and visual, but it does take place in a very real and significant way. The husband in taking an adamant position on an issue evaluates his wife's initial response in order to determine what mileage he can get by standing firm or making concessions. His wife, in turn, is trying to find the bases for his demand, to evaluate his expectations, and to give minimal but sufficient compliance so that she in turn can bargain more effectively on another issue or situation. It is obvious, as Shelling points out (14), that the continuous process of bargaining guided by expectations and knowledge that the other is also guided by expectations results in the compounding of expectations and becomes the source of conflict and tension among individuals.

The use of expectations in discussing both reciprocity and its correlate of bargaining needs clarification of one point. Expectation is very closely linked with reciprocity and bargaining. However, in those instances citing reciprocal relationships, the expectation of reciprocity is not expressed; whereas in common usage of bargaining such as between formal structures, the expectation is expressed.

Processes of Power and Influence

A discussion of reciprocity cannot be concluded without some reference to the processes of power and influence. It has already been demonstrated that reciprocal relationships may be asymmetrical in that individuals in subordinate or superordinate positions are in a reciprocal relationship engaging in exchanges of unequal quantities and of different items. The location of individuals in a structure where they can command a larger share of the exchanges indicates, as Simmel (15) suggests, an active reciprocity with orientation and influence even in the apparently one-sided superordinate-subordinate relationship. It is helpful, especially in discussing reciprocity between family members or between families, to differentiate the terms "power" and "influence." Influence as exercised by an individual is his ability to persuade individuals to do things in such a way that benefit is accrued to the person who is wielding the influence. Power, on the other hand, implies a legitimate use of force to compel a one-sided reciprocity. Influence has little effect upon anyone except a receptive person and is in this sense a voluntary reciprocity rather than a compulsory one. It is apparent that reciprocal relationships among family members and among families are based more upon the subtle expression of influence than the outright effects of power.

Reciprocity and the Kin Network

The existence of social exchange or reciprocity in human relationships cannot be disputed, and there is no question that this fundamental and pervasive process is a basic element in integrating member nuclear family units within the urban kin family system. In the relationships between member units on intergenerational or bilateral kin lines, reciprocal relationships emerge partially out of tradition and feelings of familial responsibility and partially out of opportunity and the rewards that ensue from effective bargaining. Exchanges between member family units are not equal, nor do they occur, nor are they expected to occur, about the same time. In looking at intergenerational exchanges, one can make a case for serial reciprocity. Parents will do a variety of things for their married children and grandchildren with the expectation that at a later time when they are in their declining years these young married children, now middle-aged and established, will take care of their needs as they become less and less independent. In turn, the middle-aged couple taking care of aged parents engage in all sorts of activities to launch their young children into marriage and careers, expecting in turn when they reach their three score and ten that they will be looked after by their children.

Exchanges which involve aid in time of need, maintaining communication and visitation patterns, sponsoring the job or career of the child of one's siblings, etc., are a subtle and less visible form of bargaining.

Influence, attraction, and desire to achieve a preferred position in any relationship are being exercised continuously. Participants are perpetually faced with the task of handling apparently contradictory norms, those pertaining to behaviors guided by notions of familial responsibility and those directed by self-interests, namely, to take advantage of the opportunity to be rewarded in a given relationship. The resolution of this conflict is not easy, and some individuals are more motivated to participate in reciprocal relationships because of the filial responsibility norm than the self-interest norm.

It is suggested that one cannot continue indefinitely in a reciprocity relationship without receiving some reward in return. The service perspective can be followed only so far, after which it loses its ability to sustain the individual in the relationship. In a study currently being completed concerned with the distribution of property after the death of a family member, it is found that kinship relations are undisturbed when dispositions of property go according to traditional patterns. In our society, upon the death of the male head of the household, property is usually distributed to the surviving spouse and the couple's progeny. Perhaps 90 percent of the property settlements are of this kind. However, in those cases which do not follow this typical model, because there is no surviving spouse or the testator decided for his own good reasons to disenfranchise certain potential heirs and legatees, it is found that kinship relations are severely disturbed and dismembered. Potential heirs and legatees have specific views on who should be rewarded, according to the reciprocities based upon services rendered to the deceased. The child who has labored long and hard to care for the aged parent discovers that another favored child or nephew or some distant relative is given the legacy, and the consequence is dismemberment of kinship relations because of the failure to fulfill expectations in this instance. The point of this illustration is that the service orientation must in time become integrated with the self-orientation in order to sustain a reciprocal relationship. Obviously both the service and self-interest motives exist. Just how important they are and how they work are still unknown quantities.

In any network the individual or family unit can choose to be involved in kinship relations and theoretically can withdraw from the network. In actual practice, involvement on a voluntary basis takes on the trappings of tradition and commitment in a very short time. The more involved one becomes, the more one builds credits and debits and the more one becomes cemented to the viable and functioning kinship network. As this problem is studied more carefully, one will detect parallels to the commitment process of novices going into a profession or religious order; it becomes easier to extricate oneself from reciprocal relationships of the kin network earlier in development of the network than later on. With each transaction the individual becomes more and more committed to the structure, while the relationships take on more and more meaning and significance for him.

To summarize this point, the basis of the kin network in modern urban society is reciprocity where exchanges occur via bargaining. Rewards—or payoffs—of unequal amounts and of different genus are received by the interacting individuals or groups. The network is one of several alternative social structures and becomes preferred when it provides real or perceived payoffs for participating individuals superior to those offered by other societal institutions. It is likely that participants who find this a preferred alternative cannot so freely withdraw from the tradition- and commitment-laden relationships of the nuclear family and related kin. Thus, while reciprocity is fundamental to the kinship network, voluntary exchange is tempered by increasing commitments to the system.

Adaptive and Integrative Postures

The acceptance of this theoretical posture of family organization and behavior leads one to question further popular notions concerning the organization of society and to seek evidence which establishes the multi-postures of the family (integrative, independent, dependent) in different situations and in different time periods of its own life cycle.

A current popular position is that as a consequence of industrialization there emerges a "mass" society with specialized institutions providing educational, health, welfare, recreational, economic, political, and social services for the family. Today's family in being served in this fashion, must adapt to the normative demands of these societal institutions; it thus becomes an "adjusting" enterprise and its success as a family measured by the payoffs it receives is predicated on developing skills to manipulate these outside bureaucratic structures and their varied occupational systems. This condition of the family's dependence and the need to rely on manipulation in dealing with other societal institutions, especially formal ones, is almost true but not completely true.

For example, educational activities are performed today primarily by the school; however, if education is conceived not only as learning a body of accumulated knowledge but also as learning new roles, then the family is in the business of education because it is carrying on vital socialization activities. In many societies the family-kinship network decides which of its children will be educated; how much financial support it will give the educational system, what type of educational system it wants, and so on. If the family finds the curriculum of the school not to its liking or the values espoused in the school in conflict with its own, there follow complaints, lack of support and cooperation, strikes, and even violence—expressions of power and direct influence upon the educational system.

Influence of the family upon the school is expressed further in a more diffuse manner. The school's educational program (teaching methods, curriculum, objectives and hardware) is related to the social class of the family, its patterns of socialization and home environmental conditions. Schools must cater to the demands, needs, faults, and expectations of their clients. Unequal reciprocities develop between the two structures at different stages of their respective development in relation to their specific needs and in given situations. Consequently one cannot generalize about the adjusting or dominating posture of the family or for that matter other societal institutions with which it is interacting. At best, one can identify problems involving interaction, the positions assumed, and the mechanisms employed to achieve accommodation between the two. Other examples of inter-institutional reciprocities, the postures assumed and mechanisms employed can be presented readily. The task now, however, is to indicate the meaning and significance of kin network involvements for its individual members.

It is impossible to detail the variety of situations in which the family and its kin network influence directly the behavior of their members in dealings with other societal institutions. One point of departure is to examine an area of behavior in which there is almost universal agreement, at least among scholars, that the family and kinship network influences are largely absent and if present are only minimal.

Occupational mobility is such an area. Robert Lynd wrote many years ago on the subject of the "long arm of the job." Implied in his analysis and those of the students who followed him is the view that in a highly differentiated bureaucratized society economic opportunities are not confined to any one geographical area, segment or class of the society. An open class system requires social and geographic mobility of its members. Moreover, the job determines a man's position and the family's status in the society. The decision to make a job change is arrived at after employing scientific principles, i.e., it is a rational decision. Occupational mobility implies movement along a career line which provides increased payoffs as one climbs a higher rung of the ladder. Hence one takes those jobs which provide the best opportunities and to a large degree business and industrial corporations have evolved policies and practices of promotions incorporating this stance of occupational mobility.

A similar condition is believed to exist among the professions. Mobility should occur not primarily for financial and status payoffs as in the case of the corporation executive but because of increased opportunities for rendering service and behavior in keeping with the ideology of a service orientation. One cannot neglect or deny the increase in economic position and status as the individual moves to more responsible positions in his profession. Most professionals prefer to think of this, however, as a consequence of motivation rooted in an "other" oriented service tradition rather than a marketplace ideology.

Whatever may be the rationale underlying mobility for specific classes of workers and their families, many still hold to the notion that the economic system not only creates the conditions of mobility but also determines the stages and patterns of occupational movement.

However, it is a common phenomenon that decisions concerning, for example, whether to accept or reject a job offer are substantially influenced by familial elements. A spouse's preference for a geographic region and the residence of either partner's kin network may confound the model of rational decision making in reference to occupational choice and mobility. Consider a professor refusing a midwestern job offer—in terms of work conditions and salary surpassing his incumbent position—because his wife desires to remain near her New England parents; or another eastern-based faculty member turning from a lucrative offer to seek a California university in follow-up of his affinal kin's western migration. There is no doubt that the wishes, concerns, and advice of one's family members are evaluated along with other pushes and pulls emanating from the economic and work systems and one's profession.

These observable departures from rational decision making have probably always existed, but are today more overt because of modernization and affluence. Modernization has prompted changes in family role structure, increased participation in decisions by both spouses and their issue, and greater utilization of the kin network as one of several available alternative systems which can provide payoffs for individuals and their families. Affluence has produced more positions than takers, thus lessening the importance of economic considerations. In the occupational, as well as the educational realm, the independent force of the family is evident.

Summary and Conclusions

A reappraisal of the modern urban family shows that the kin-related network assumes multiple postures, both dependent and independent, in interaction with other societal institutions. As a voluntary system, the family competes for members with other social realms, also offering emotional, educational, economic and other supports. Based upon reciprocity with exchanges, often of an unequal nature, occurring through bargaining, the kin network acquires commitments by providing rewards perceived as superior to those offered by alternative social structures. Once preferred, the kinship system rapidly instills tradition-laden obligations in its members.

In many instances the family directly influences its members' behavior in dealings with other social institutions. This influence is particularly marked in such areas as occupational mobility and education. Rather than responding with subordinate, adaptative measures, the familial system may act to alter a job decision or school policy according to its own orientation. Changes in family role structure wrought by modernization and expanded job opportunities produced by affluence further serve to broaden the independent scope of family behavior.

It is increasingly difficult in studying a social, health, welfare, or economic problem to ignore the family and its kin network structure and activities as factors affecting outcome. The resources, postures, power, and actions of this social system have relevance for other societal institutions. One example is the medical field, affected by professorial manpower shortages, changing concepts and practices of therapy, increased demand for services, shortage of institutional facilities, and limited funds; here, the family looms as a basic resource and therapeutic community for its ill members.

From whatever theoretical stance the family is viewed, no appraisal is adequate unless it is recognized that the modern kin network can influence and direct as well as be influenced and directed.

REFERENCES

1. SUSSMAN, M. B., "The Help Pattern in the Middle Class Family," *Amer. Soc. Rev.*, 18, 22–28, 1953.
2. SUSSMAN, M. B., "Family Continuity: Selective Factors Which Affect Relationships Between Families at Generational Levels," *Marriage and Fam. Liv.*, 16, 112–120, 1954.
3. SUSSMAN, M. B., "Activity Patterns of Post-Parental Couples and Their Relationship to Family Continuity," *Marriage and Fam. Liv.*, 7, 338–341, 1955.
4. SUSSMAN, M. B., "The Isolated Nuclear Family: Fact or Fiction," *Soc. Prob.*, 6, 333–340, 1959.
5. SUSSMAN, M. B., "Intergenerational Family Relationships and Social Role Change in Middle Age," *J. Geront.*, 15, 71–75, 1960.
6. SUSSMAN, M. B. and BURCHINAL, L. G., "Kinship Family Network: Unheralded Structure in Current Conceptualizations of Family Functioning," *Marriage and Fam. Liv.*, 24, 231–240, 1962.
7. SUSSMAN, M. B., BURCHINAL, L. G., "Parental Aid to Married Children: Implications for Family Functioning," *Marriage and Fam. Liv.*, 24, 320–332, 1962.
8. SUSSMAN, M. B., "Relationships of Adult Children with their Parents in the United States," in *Family, Intergenerational Relationships and Social Structure*, E. Shanas, G. Streib, (eds.) Englewood Cliffs, New Jersey, Prentice Hall, 62–92, 1965.
9. SUSSMAN, M. B., "The Urban Kin Network in the Formulation of Family Theory," The Ninth International Seminar on Family Research, Tokyo, Japan, forthcoming in *Yearbook of International Sociological Association*, Rene Konig (ed.)
10. SUSSMAN, M. B., "Theoretical Bases for an Urban Kinship Network System," paper given at the annual meeting of the National Council on Family Relations, October 29, 1966, Minneapolis, Minnesota.
11. MAUSS, MARCEL, *The Gift, Forms and Functions of Exchange in Archaic Societies*, trans. by Ian Cunnison, London, Cohen and West Ltd., 1954.
12. LEVI-STRAUSS, C., "The Principle of Reciprocity," in *Sociological Theory*, L. A. Coser and B. Rosengerb, (eds), New York, McMillan Co., 204–294, 1957.
13. HOMANS, G., *Social Behavior: Its Elementary Forms*, New York, Harcourt, Brace and World, 53–59, 1961.
14. SHELLING, T. C., "An Essay on Bargaining," *The American Economic Review*, 46, 281–306, 1956.
15. SIMMEL, G., in *The Sociology of Georg Simmel*, K. H. Wolff, (ed), New York, The Free Press of Glencoe, 182, 1950.

15

Interdisciplinary versus Ecological Approach

EDGAR H. AUERSWALD, M.D.

THE EXPLOSION of scientific knowledge and technology in the middle third of this century, and the effects of this explosion on the human condition, have posed a number of challenges for the behavioral sciences that most agree are yet to be met. The overriding challenge is, of course, the prevention of nuclear holocaust, but such problems as crime and delinquency, drug addiction, senseless violence, refractive learning problems, destructive prejudice, functional psychosis and the like follow close behind.

Practically all behavioral scientists agree that none of these problems can be solved within the framework of any single discipline. Most espouse a putting together of heads in the so-called "interdisciplinary approach." The notion is not new, of course. The "interdisciplinary team" has been around for some time. Some new notions have emanated from this head-banging, but there have been few startling revelations in the last decade or so.

However, a relatively small but growing group of behavioral scientists, most of whom have spent time in arenas in which the "interdisciplinary approach" is being used, have taken the seemingly radical position that the knowledge of the traditional disciplines as they now exist is relatively useless in the effort to find answers for these particular problems. Most of this group advocate a realignment of current knowledge and re-examination of human behavior within a unifying holistic model, that of ecological phenomenology. The implications of this departure are great. Once the model of ecology becomes the lattice-work upon which such a realignment of knowledge is hung, it is no longer possible to limit oneself to the behavioral sciences alone. The physical sciences, the biological sciences, in fact, all of science, must be included. Since the people who have been most concerned with constructing a model for a unified science and with the ingredients of the human ecological field have been the general systems theorists, the approach used by behavioral scientists who follow this trend is rapidly acquiring the label of the "systems approach," although a more appropriate label might be the "ecological systems approach."

These terms are currently being used metaphorically to describe a way of thinking and an operational style. They do not describe a well formed theoretical framework as does the term "general systems theory." It is with the former, the way of thinking and the operational style, that I am concerned in this paper.

The two approaches described above differ greatly. Let us examine why the difference is so profound. The ongoing accumulation of knowledge and its application to practice follows a well known sequence. This might be broken down into steps as follows: the collection of information or data, the ordering of that data within a selected framework, analysis of the data, synthesis of the results of analysis into hypotheses, the formulation of strategies and techniques (methodologies) to test the hypotheses, the construction of a delivery plan for use of these strategies and techniques, the implementation of the plan, and the collection of data from the arena of implementation to test its impact, which, of course, repeats the first step, and so on.

The key step in this sequence is the second one, the ordering of data within a selected framework, because it is this step, and this step alone, that gives structure to the rest, all of which are operational. Not only does the nature and outcome of subsequent steps depend on this structuring framework, but so does the prior step, the collection of data. What data among the infinite variety of available natural data are considered important, and are, therefore, collected in any given arena, will depend on the conceptual framework used. It is here that the difference between the two approaches is to be found.

The "interdisciplinary" approach maintains the vantage point of each contributor within his own discipline. While it has expanded the boundaries of the theoretical framework of each discipline to include concepts borrowed from other disciplines, only those concepts which pose no serious challenge or language difficulties are welcomed. More importantly, I think, the interfaces between the conceptual frameworks of different disciplines are ignored, and, as a result, the interfaces between the various arenas of systematic life operation (e.g., biological, psychological, social or individual, family, community) represented by different disciplines are also ignored.

The structural aspects and the clarity of context of the data collected are lost as a result. The precise source, pathway, and integrating functions of messages passing between various operational life arenas in the ecological field cannot be clearly identified. Analysis of such data depends almost entirely on the *content* of these messages, and much distortion can and does take place.

The "systems" approach, on the other hand, changes the vantage point of the data collector. It focuses precisely on the interfaces and communication processes taking place there. It begins with an analysis of the *structure* of the field, using the common structural and operational properties of systems as criteria for identifying the systems and sub-systems within it. And by tracing the communications within and between systems, it insists that the structure, sources, pathways, repository sites and integrative functions of messages become clear in addition to their content. In my opinion, this, plus the holistic non-exclusive nature of the approach, minimizes the dangers of excessive selectivity in the collection of data and allows for much more clarity in the contextual contributions to its analysis. And the steps which follow, including prescription and planning of strategies and techniques, gain in clarity and are more likely to be rooted in concrete realities.

There are some very practical advantages that accrue as a result of the above. At the level of *theory,* for example, the ecological systems model, by clarifying and emphasizing the interfaces between systems, allows for the use of a variety of theoretical models which have to do with interactional processes and information exchange. These models form bridges between the conceptual systems of single disciplines. Information theory, crisis theory, game theory, and general communications theory for example, represent some of the bodies of research and knowledge which become useable in an integrated way.

Knowledge that has been accumulating from the study of specific ecological systems, such as the family and small groups, the development of which lagged until recently because the systems did not fit neatly into the bailiwick of any one traditional discipline, can also be included without strain. And the developmental model of the life cycle of the individual man and of various larger human systems as they move through time in the ecological field of their environment assumes meaning in a larger context.

In addition, the use of this model in planning has demonstrated its many implications for the design and operational implementation of delivery systems, especially for community programs (e.g., "comprehensive community health" programs). The ecological systems approach insures that the entire process of planning for a community is rooted in the realities and needs of that community. The organized identification of the ecological systems making up a target community allows for the planned inclusion of information collection stations in each key system and at primary interfaces which provide feedback to the planning arena, thus setting up a servo-system which assures that planning will remain closely related to changing need. Over a period of time, as a picture of a target community emerges from such data, it will emerge as an idiosyncratic template of the structural and operational configurations of that community. It will not, as in the "interdisciplinary" approach, emerge as a predetermined template of the theoretical structure of the dominant discipline.

As a result, program designs constructed in this manner are deeply imbedded in the target community. They will develop as another ecological system among the many, thus greatly clarifying the context in which any program can be integrated into the life of the community as a whole. Furthermore, the delivery organization itself becomes viewed as a system with assigned tasks made up of sub-systems performing sub-tasks including intra-organizational tasks. This allows for more clarity in the selection of staffing patterns, in the definitions of staff role functions, in the construction of communication systems and data collection (record-keeping) systems, and of the assignment of tasks within the organizational structure to staff members best equipped to handle them. Of special import to community programs is the fact that with the clarification of specific tasks to be performed comes the increased possibility of identifying those tasks that can be carried out by staff members or volunteers who need relatively little training.

At the *operational* level the strategies of evolution and change can be more clearly designed. More important, perhaps, use of the ecological systems approach allows for the development of a whole new technology in the production of change. Many techniques have, as a matter of fact, already appeared on the scene, largely within organized movements aimed at integration in its broadest sense, such as the Civil Rights Movement and the "War On Poverty." Some community organization and community development programs, techniques using economic and political pressure, and techniques which change the rules of the game such as the non-violence movement, all represent a new technology, and all have their relevance to the broadly-defined health needs of socially isolated individuals, families, and groups.

In service programs working with individual people and families this new technology is also emerging, more slowly perhaps. Many new ways of coping with familiar situations are being developed. Techniques of treating families as systems, for example, represent one advance. In particular, an emphasis which stresses the organization of events in time and traces the movement of the developing infant-child-adolescent-adult-aged individual's degree of participation versus his isolation in relation to his family and to the flow of surrounding community life—such an emphasis makes it possible to determine with much more clarity in what life arenas the individual, the family, or a group of individuals needs assistance, and thus to more effectively combat the anomie and dehumanization characteristic of our age. The result is that the targets of therapeutic activity are much clearer and therapeutic work is more clearly focused on forces and situations that are truly etiological in a given problem situation. Techniques of producing therapeutic change can be brought to arenas much larger than the therapy room or even the home. I think that a single story will serve to illustrate more concretely what I mean.

In the story I wish to tell, two therapists, one a "systems" thinker, the other a member of an "interdisciplinary" team, became involved in the case of a runaway girl.

To give you some initial background, I should explain that I have been involved in designing and implementing a "Neighborhood Health Services System" for provision of comprehensive biopsychosocial care to a so-called "disadvantaged" community. The main aim in setting up this unit was to find ways to avoid the fragmentation of service delivery which occurs when a person's problem is defined as belonging primarily to himself, and he is sent to a specialist who is trained to deal primarily with that type of problem. The specialist naturally sees the problem not only as an individual matter, but defines it still further according to the professional sector he inhabits. He is not accustomed to looking at the total set of systems surrounding the individual with the symptom or to noticing the ways in which the symptom, the person, his family, and his community interlock, and he is often in the position of a man desperately trying to replace a fuse when it is the entire community power line that has broken down. Furthermore, the specialist's efforts to solve the problem are apt to be confined to arbitrarily chosen segments of time called "appointments." And finally, there is that unfortunate invention, the written referral, a process of buck-passing that sends many a person in trouble from agency to agency till he finally gives up or breaks down. As a beginning we decided that we would have to pilot some cases in order to gain some experience with the different approach we felt was needed.

At this point, a case providentially dramatizing the points we had in mind fell into our hands. (We have since found that almost every case that falls into our hands providentially dramatizes these points.) One of our psychiatrists was wandering about the neighborhood one day in order to become better acquainted with it and to explore what sort of crises and problems our neighborhood program must be prepared to serve beyond those we already anticipated. I should say here that this psychiatrist,[1] by virtue of several years of pioneering work with families, including the experimental use of game theory and games in diagnosing and treating them, was particularly well qualified to handle the situation I will describe. His explorations that day had brought him to the local police station, and while he was talking to the desk sergeant, a Puerto Rican woman arrived to report that her twelve year-old daughter, Maria, had run away from home. This was apparently not the first time. She described the child to the police, who alerted their patrols to look for her and assigned two men to investigate the neighborhood. Our psychiatrist, whom I will refer to from now on as our "explorer," was intrigued and decided to follow up the situation himself.

He first identified himself to the mother as she left the police station and asked if she would be willing to allow him to help her with her current difficulty. She agreed. He learned that she lived a few blocks away with her now absent daughter and another daughter, aged 14. Her own parents lived nearby, and she had a paramour who also lived in the neighborhood. The father of her two children had long since deserted his family, and she was uncertain as to his whereabouts. The exploring psychiatrist learned also that the runaway girl had been see-

---

[1] Dr. Robert Ravich. I am indebted to Dr. Ravich for the case material reported.

ing a psychotherapist at the mental health clinic of a local settlement house. In addition, he ascertained the location of her school.

He then decided that his behavior might appear unethical to the child's therapist, so he proceeded to the mental health clinic, a clinic which prided itself on the use of the "interdisciplinary" team approach. The original therapist turned out to be a social worker of considerable accomplishment and experience, who agreed to cooperate with him in his investigation after he explained what he was up to and that he had the mother's permission. He read the child's case record and discussed the girl with the therapist at some length. He learned that at a recent team case conference, the diagnosis which was originally assigned to the girl, that of childhood schizophrenia, was confirmed. The team also decided that in the light of repeated episodes of running away from home, her behavior was creating sufficient danger to indicate that she be placed in a situation where that danger would be alleviated while her therapy continued. For a twelve year-old Puerto Rican girl in New York City, especially one carrying a label of schizophrenia, this almost always means hospitalization in the children's ward of a state hospital. Accordingly, the arrangement for her admission to the state hospital covering the district had been made and was due to be implemented within a few days.

The next stop for our explorer was the school, where Maria's teacher described her as a slow but steady learner, detached from most other children in the class, vague and strange, but somehow likeable. The guidance counselor reported an incident in which she had been discovered masturbating an older boy under the school auditorium stairs. This behavior had led the school authorities to contemplate suspending her, but since they knew her to be in treatment they decided to hold off, temporarily, at least.

The exploring psychiatrist also learned at the school that Maria was involved in an after-school group program at the settlement house. He returned there and got from the group worker a much more positive impression of the girl than he had previously encountered. She participated with seeming enthusiasm in the projects of the group and got along very well with the other children. The group worker, by way of providing evidence that Maria had much potential, showed the therapist a lovely and poignant poem she had contributed to a newspaper put out by the group. It was never ascertained whether the girl had written or copied the poem. She had, nevertheless, produced it, and there was general agreement that its theme of isolation was one which was expressive of her.

Back at Maria's home, our explorer talked to Maria's sister, who at first grudgingly, but then with some relish, admitted that she knew where the girl had gone during her previous runaway episodes. She was the sometime mascot of a group of teenage boys with whom she occasionally traveled for two or three days at a time. The sister did not know where she went or what she did during the junkets, but she suspected that sex was somehow involved. She also volunteered the information that neither she or her mother had ever found it easy to communicate with her sister, and that if the therapist really wanted to talk to someone who knew her, he should talk to her grandfather. So off to the grandparents' apartment he went.

The grandmother turned out to be a tight-lipped, highly religious Pentecostalist who was at first unwilling to say much at all about the girl.

The grandfather, however, was a different kettle of fish. Earthly, ebullient, jocular, bright, though uneducated, his love for Maria was immediately apparent. He spoke of her warmly, and bemoaned the lack of understanding that existed in her home. Remembering a passing reference in the case record at the mental health clinic to a suspicion that the grandfather may have engaged in seductive play with the girl, if not open sexual activity, our explorer raised the issue of the girl's emerging adolescent sexuality. This brought an outburst from the hitherto silent grandmother that confirmed the mutually seductive quality of the grandfather's relationship with the girl, followed by a return blast from the grandfather who revealed that his wife had refused to sleep with him for several years. He readily admitted his frustrated sexuality and the fact that he was at times aroused by his budding granddaughter.

I have presented only a sparse picture of the rich amount of information collected by our explorer up to this point. In a continuous five hour effort, without seeing the absent Maria, he was able to construct a picture of her as a child who had grown up in relative isolation in a home where she received little support and guidance. Communication between herself and her mother had become more and more sparse over the years, most likely because of efforts of her older sister to maintain her favored position in the home. She had turned to her grandfather, who, feeling frustrated and himself isolated in his own marriage, brought his sexually-tinged warmth willingly into a relationship of mutual affection with her. Furthermore, it seemed clear that with someone like the group worker who liked her and who, because the group was small, could spend time with her, Maria could respond with warmth and exhibit an intelligence that otherwise remained hidden. But, and this was, of course, speculative, the tools she perceived as useful in her search for a response from others would most likely be limited to infantile techniques of manipulation developed in early years prior to the need for verbal communication or, based on the relationship with the grandfather, some form of seduction where the currency of acceptance was sex. And, at the age of puberty, having been shut out of the female world of her mother and sister, she was using this currency full blast in the world of boys.

The next day our explorer talked again to the mother, who told him that the girl had been found by the police on the street and had been hospitalized at a large city hospital on the adolescent psychiatric ward. Before visiting her, he briefly questioned the mother about her paramour. It turned out that the subject of marriage had come up between the two of them, but because he earned a limited income, both he and the mother had decided against living together or getting married. Either action would result in loss of the support the mother was receiving from the Department of Welfare for herself and her two children.

All that had been predicted the day before was corroborated when our explorer visited the girl in the hospital. Her behavior with him, and, as it turned out with the resident physician on the ward, alternated between childish manipulation and seductive behavior of a degree which appeared bizarre in a 12 year-old. But she was, at the same time, a lithely attractive girl with a lively wit which blossomed once she felt understood. She was ambivalent about the alternatives of going home or of going to a state hospital, mildly resisting both.

Our exploring psychiatrist then returned to the mental health clinic to discuss what he had observed with the child's therapist and the consulting psychiatrist. He suggested a plan of action as an alternative to hospitalization. By targeting on key issues in various systems surrounding this child, it seemed theoretically plausible that the conditions which held her fixed in a pattern of behavior that had been labeled as sick and crazy might be changed, thus freeing her to accept new coping patterns which she could be helped to learn. An effort to re-establish communication between the child and her mother, who had shown with her other daughter that she could raise a child with relative success, would be one step. It might not be feasible to work with the grandparents' unsatisfactory marriage, but an explanation to the grandfather, who had already tentatively understood his contribution to the girl's dilemma, might be useful. If the Department of Welfare were willing, and if the boyfriend's income could be enhanced by at least a little supplementary public assistance, the mother and her boyfriend might be induced to marry. Teacher and guidance counselor could be helped to understand the girl's behavior more fully and might cooperate on a plan for helping the girl learn new ways of relating in school. The group worker's investment in the girl could be used to a good effect in this joint effort to help her grow. And the original therapist, instead of concerning herself with defense systems and repressed conflict could concentrate on helping the family provide the maximum of support and guidance possible, or, if she wished, could still work with the girl herself. With these suggestions, our exploring psychiatrist bowed out.

A month later, a follow-up visit to the mother revealed that the girl had been sent to state hospital on the recommendation of the resident on the adolescent ward who agreed with the diagnosis and felt that, since she was "a schizophrenic," she should be in a hospital. No one had made any counter-move and contact between all of the helping people except the state hospital doctor and the girl's family had been terminated. This outcome had occurred *despite the fact that the mother and her boyfriend had, after a conversation stimulated by our therapist-explorer, presented themselves at the mental health clinic and expressed their willingness to marry if it seemed wise, their wish to have Maria come home, and their hope that someone at the clinic would help them learn what they must now do for her as parents.*

I have, I realize, presented an unusual situation. Reasonable question could be raised, I suppose, as to how often this sequence could occur. And my own bias is obvious in the manner of my presentation. But I think the case illustrates the radical difference between the two approaches under discussion. The approach of the therapist from the interdisciplinary clinic and that of our exploring psychiatrist are not merely two points on a continuum of techniques. The "ecological systems" approach literally changed the name of the game. By focusing on the nature of the transactions taking place between Maria and the identifiable systems that influenced her growth, it was possible for the "systems" psychiatrist to ascertain what strengths, lacks, and distortions existed at each interface. Two things happened when this was done.

The first was that Maria's behavior began to make sense as a healthy adaptation to a set of circumstances that did not allow her to develop more socially acceptable or better differentiated means of seeking a response to her needs as a developing child. Thus, the aura of pathology was immediately left behind.

The second was that the identification of lacks and distortions in the transactional arena of each interface automatically suggested what needed to be added or changed. Thus the tasks of the helping person were automatically defined. Rigidity of technique in accomplishing these tasks could not, under those circumstances, survive. Flexibility, ingenuity, and innovation were demanded.

The implications of what can happen if this approach is used universally are obvious. If proper data is kept, it seems inevitable that new clusters of data will occur to add to our knowledge, and a new technology of prevention and change develop.

The case of Maria has a certain uniqueness that separates it from most similar cases across our country. The uniqueness is not to be found in the "interdisciplinary" approach used, but rather in the quantity of skilled people who were trying to help her. Despite their dedicated efforts, all they managed to accomplish was Maria's removal from the only system that could be considered generic in terms of her growth and socialization—her family—and her removal from the school and community which should provide the additional experience she needed if she were to become a participant in the life of her society. In addition, they succeeded in stamping a label on the official records of her existence, a label which is a battleground of controversy among diagnosticians, but which means simply to the lay public that she is a nut.

By chance, Maria wound up in a mental hygiene clinic where her behavior was labeled as sick. She might just as easily have joined the many girls showing similar behavior who wind up in court and are labeled delinquent. Either label puts her in a category over which various members of "interdisciplinary" teams are in continued conflict. The needs of the girl, which are not clearly apparent, in either arena, become hopelessly obscured. Decisions made by those charged with the task of helping her are likely to be made without cognizance of those needs, since they depend for their outcome too often on the institutionalized procedures and momentary exigencies in the caring organization or person.

As a final point, let me explore the nature of the communications breakdown that occurred between the two therapists.

In his explorations, our "systems" psychiatrist collected a good deal of data that was not known to the "interdisciplinary" therapist and team in order to insure that he understood the operations that had been going on at each interface in which he was interested. This additional data only supplemented the data previously collected and agreed with it in content. Thus the two agreed substantially as long as they confined their communications to content and to inferred construction of the internal psychodynamics of the persons involved, Maria and the individual members of her family. And, as it happened, this was all they discussed until the exploring "systems" psychiatrist returned for a final chat. At that time, having ordered his data in such a way as to clarify the transactions which had been taking place at the interfaces between Maria and the various systems contributing to her growth, his suggestions flowed from a plan designed to affect those interfaces. The "interdisciplinary" team, including the original therapist, had not ordered the data in this way. Since the dominant disciplinary framework used in their arena was psychiatric, they had ordered the data around a nosological scheme for labeling illness. The outcome of their plan of action, therefore, was to apply a label signifying the nature of Maria's illness, and to decide, reasonably enough within this framework, that since treatment of her illness on an outpatient basis had not been successful, the next step was hospitalization, a decision backed by the assumption that her runaways were dangerous.

It was literally impossible, at the final meeting, for the suggestions of our "systems" therapist to have meaning to the "interdisciplinary" team. They fell on ears made deaf by a way of thinking which could not perceive them as meaningful. They came across as a dissonance which had to be screened out. Communication between the two approaches thus broke down completely.

This instance of breakdown is characteristic of efforts of communication between people from the two arenas. Conversations I have had with a variety of people who take the ecological systems view, backed by my own experience, seem to add up to the following:

There seems to be no serious problem of communication between the systems thinker who emphasizes structure and the experimental behavioral scientist who does basic research in his laboratory or even the researcher who is attempting to deal with a wide range of natural data. Such researchers have selected and defined the structure of the theoretical framework in which they wish to work and are the first to admit that the outcome of their research carries the label of validity within that framework alone.

The clinical scientist, whose emphasis is more on the content of his data, is for the most part a different animal. Most clinical theorists, planners, and practitioners, regardless of discipline, seem caught in the highly specialized sequence of their own training and intradisciplinary experience, upon which they seem to depend for the very definition of their personal identity. Generally speaking, a situation seems to exist in which the integration of the cognitive apparatus of the clinician is such as to exclude as a piece of relevant data the notion that his intra-disciplinary "truths," which he carries to the interdisciplinary arena, are relative. He most often will hear and understand the notion when it is expressed. But, again speaking generally, he treats it as unimportant to his operations, as peripheral to the body of knowledge he invests with meaning. Why should this be?

I think it is because the clinician is a product of the specialized fragmentation of today's world of science. To him, admission of this fact would mean that he would have to rearrange his cognitive style, his professional way of life, and, all too often, his total life style as well, if he were to maintain a sense of his own integrity. Not only would he have to renounce his idols, but he would have to go through a turbulent period of disintegration and reintegration. He would have to be willing and able to tolerate the fragmentation of identity boundaries such a transition entails. He would have to leave the safety of seeming truths, truths he has used to maintain his sense of being in the right, his self-esteem, his sense of values, and his status in the vertical hierarchies of his society. He would have to give up the games he plays to maintain his hard-won position in his discipline, games such as those which consist of labeling persons from other schools of thought as bright but limited, misguided, or insufficiently analyzed. More often than not, he would rather fight than switch.

I imply, of course, that he should switch. Thus the question must reasonably be asked: Why should he? Why should he attempt such a fundamental change? After all, he can point with pride to the many accomplishments and successes of his discipline and his own work within it.

But to rest on his laurels, in my opinion, is to abdicate responsibility.

It is like crowing over the 70% or so of juvenile delinquents who become law-abiding citizens and, ignoring the 30% who do not. The major responsibility of today's behavioral scientist is to those who don't or won't make it, not those who do, to Maria, not to Little Hans, whom he already knows how to help.

The least he can do is examine his labels and how he uses them. In the life-space of Maria's world, there is a serious question as to which system deserves the prefix, *schizo*.

16

Non-Verbal Cues and Reenactment of Conflict in Family Therapy

MURRAY H. SHERMAN, Ph.D.
NATHAN W. ACKERMAN, M.D.
SANFORD N. SHERMAN
CELIA MITCHELL

W HEN an entire family is seen together in therapy, there is the opportunity to observe a reenactment of the specific conflict which has brought the family to treatment (1). This enactment of conflict is attributable to many factors, among which is the family's need to demonstrate their emotional turmoil to the therapist in order to gain his help in resolving the family neurosis. However, the family conflict also has a static, perseverative quality which leads to its continuance in all sorts of situations in and out of treatment. One of the major advantages of family therapy is the opportunity afforded the therapist to observe and intervene in these perseverative enactments *in situ*, on the very scene of battle.

Within any given session it is often difficult to detect the specific origins of a particular conflict enactment at the very moment it is occurring. These origins are doubtless of a multidimensional sort, but among them the significance of non-verbal cues has been noted with increasing frequency (5, 9). As a matter of fact, the significance of such subtleties of non-verbal communication as tonal inflections and fleeting facial expressions has long been noted as characteristic of the psychoanalytic situation (8, 10, 11), but only now are these data being explored in a systematic, scientific fashion. The development of such

249

scientific recording devices as the tape recorder and motion picture camera has undoubtedly been a major factor in the study of fleeting aspects of non-verbal expressions. The scientific description of the startle pattern (6) and its diagnostic significance was made possible by examination of individual frames of motion picture recording.

The traditional role of the psychotherapist has tended to include relatively less attention to these non-verbal behaviors than to the verbal content that is communicated. Moreover, the specific relationships between non-verbal cues and the psychodynamics of family conflict have not yet been demonstrated in detail with illustrative case material. The problems of this type of study have been explored from the standpoints of kinesics (4) and of paralinguistic analysis (7), but our intent here is to deal with more molar cues that could be detected in ordinary therapeutic interaction, were the therapist to pay particular heed to these minute behavioral expressions.

The basic therapeutic data are exceedingly hard come by. It is only too well known that a therapist's own report of his sessions will often omit much of the most vital interaction, even where there is a sincere effort to communicate this material. Tape recordings lose much of the subtle interaction and communication of therapy, and non-verbal cues are often totally missed in taped transcriptions. Sound films are undoubtedly the most satisfactory form of recording of both verbal and non-verbal behavior, despite the almost prohibitive expense involved. Even these sound films require transcription if they are to be scientifically analyzed, and the transcription, if conscientiously done, is a most time consuming task.

One gets the impression that something is transpiring in the therapeutic process which has almost its own resistance to deeper understanding. There seems to be an exceedingly subtle intercommunication that transpires at a very basic and even primitive level, and this process somehow eludes us when we try to translate it into verbal form. An almost transcendent, secretive quality becomes attached to the subtleties of a therapeutic relationship, which defies even the most searching and strenuous efforts at explicit description. It seems likely that non-verbal cues do play a most significant role in this tenuous process and a detailed investigation of their functions in the re-enactment of family conflict may cast some light upon the more general problem of therapeutic communication.

The B. Family

It was decided to investigate a filmed sample of non-verbal behavior as this emerged within the context of family therapy. We were interested both in the therapeutic use that could be made of non-verbal behavior and also in the specific forms in which this behavior reflected the total family conflict.

The B. family was chosen for this investigation because a preliminary viewing of a sound film of one of their family therapy sessions indicated a plentitude of non-verbal behavior.

The B. family consisted of Mr. Jack B., aged 52, whose occupation was that of half-owner of a hardware business;[1] Mrs. Joan B., aged 43 and a school teacher; Sam, aged 16; and Ann, aged 10. The incident precipitating this family's coming to the clinic occurred about two months prior to the filmed session. Ann had become very angry and excited and had gone into a temper tantrum in which she had taken a large knife and threatened Sam with it. Sam was overcome by a fit of fear, ran into his parents' bedroom to tell them what was happening and had then apparently collapsed on the bed in a cold, perspiring faint.

This incident was the culmination of a long series of conflicts in which Ann had continually intimidated and manipulated the entire family. Mrs. B. was almost totally unable to discipline Ann and would resort to various manipulative strategems to make her eat or behave as she should; these strategems were admittedly ineffective. Mrs. B. would then make periodic efforts to draw up lists of preemptory rules of family behavior, which were soon ignored. Mrs. B. attributed her inability to discipline Ann to her relationship with her own mother, whom she described as overbearing, overprotective and highly demanding. Mrs. B.'s own father was described as passive and ineffectual; she called him a "horror," a term which she also applied to Sam as a difficult infant.

Sam's relation with his mother was a highly ambivalent and inconsistent one. Mrs. B. was overly solicitous about Sam's health and he would resent this and withdraw from it. On the other hand, when Mrs. B. got angry with Sam, he would become very disturbed, would reassure his mother that he loved her very much and plead that she not be angry with him.

---

[1] Names and other identifying data have been disguised.

Mr. B.'s parents had been divorced when he was seven, and he had lived with his mother who tried to encourage him to be "independent." In his own marriage Mr. B.'s work often kept him away overnight, and he generally took a passive and unassertive role. A particular incident well illustrates the lines of control and interaction in this family. Ann had become angry with Sam and wanted to poke him in retaliation for something he had done. She asked her parents each to hold one of Sam's arms so she could poke him. Mr. B. refused to do this but stood by as Mrs. B. held both of Sam's arms, and Ann obtained her revenge.

For several years prior to coming to therapy at the agency Mrs. B. had had a severe case of torticollis and had consulted a number of psychiatrists and other medical specialists. She had finally been cured by massive injections (nature undetermined) and used this as evidence that there had been no psychological meaning to the symptom. Sam's symptomatic picture included a bizarre masturbatory ritual in which he would telephone hospitals and ask them for information on how to feed a resistant infant. Sam would provoke his informant into telling him to use force if necessary, and this was highly exciting to him.

There is an interesting confluence of symptoms among the three generations. Mrs. B.'s own mother had had the habit of continually passing wind. Mrs. B.'s belching, as will be evident in the session below, was a highly significant aspect of her relationship to her husband. Sam, when emotionally disturbed, was prone to vomit. All three individuals apparently converted their aggression into an involuntary eruption through a bodily orifice.

The B. family was seen in family therapy by a caseworker over a period of one year and there were also periodic interviews (eight) by Dr. A. Ann's behavior became much improved. She was more controlled and the temper tantrums receded. Mrs. B.'s preoccupation with Ann's eating habits also receded but was replaced by an obsession with her school work. On one occasion Mrs. B. so annoyed Ann by inquiring whether she had done her homework that Ann deliberately tore it to shreds before her mother's eyes.

There was some active inquiry and handling of the sexual relationship between Mr. and Mrs. B. Mr. B. complained that his wife was not active enough in sex and said that he felt certain wives could learn a good deal from some prostitutes, whom he had known before marriage. Mrs. B. complained that her husband was an inadequate lover and did not satisfy her. She said that his demands, if she acceded to them, would make sex much too mechanical for her. During the course of therapy Mr. B. became more active in sex, but there was not a great deal of improvement.

Family therapy was hindered by a number of resistances which developed. When anger was expressed by the children during the sessions, Mrs. B. felt that this was very bad because it was just what she was coming to therapy to prevent. Mr. B. objected to the explicitness of sexual discussion. Various family members would become ill, which prevented the family's being seen together. There were also fee difficulties; the parents felt the fee was too high and they were frequently behind in payments. Nevertheless, despite all these difficulties, it was felt that therapy had made certain significant gains and that much had been accomplished in family understanding and improved relationships.

A Family Therapy Session

In order to develop the accompanying transcript of a sound film of family therapy, a tape recording was made from which the dialogue was taken. Then the film itself was watched approximately one dozen times to fill in the visual and other contexts. Many minute aspects of family communication, such as subtle facial expressions and small bodily movements, have nevertheless been lost, despite considerable effort to include some of the most essential and noticeable ones. One wonders whether the return from such effort merely to transcribe and communicate yields a commensurate reward. On the other hand, the very difficulty of this task leads one to believe that a special secret must somehow be buried in these mountains of words and gestures.

TRANSCRIPT OF SOUND FILM

1. Dr.: Jack, you heaved a sigh as you sat down.
2. Mr. B.: Just physical, not mental.
3. Dr.: Whom are you kidding?
4. Mr. B.: Kidding no one.
5. Dr.: (warningly) Jack!
6. Mr. B.: I'm tired because I put in a full day.
7. Dr.: Well, I'm tired every day. When I sigh, it's never purely physical.
8. Mr. B.: Really?

9. Dr.:	Yes. What's the matter?	
10. Mr. B.:	Nothing. Really.	
11. Sam:	(laughs)	
12. Dr.:	Your own son doesn't believe that.	
13. Mr. B.:	Well, I mean nothing, nothing caused me to sigh specially today, or tonight.	
14. Dr.:	Well, maybe it isn't so special, but—uh—How about it, Sam?	
15. Sam:	(shakes head no)	
16. Dr.:	You wouldn't know? All of a sudden you put on a poker face. You do it very knowingly.	
17. Mr. B.:	(laughs)	
18. Sam:	I really don't know.	
19. Dr.:	Well, do you know anything about your Pop?	
20. Sam:	Yeah.	
21. Dr.:	What do you know about him?	
22. Sam:	Well, I don't know except that I know something about him.	
23. Dr.:	Well, let's hear.	
24. Sam:	Well, I (laughs nervously)—he's a man.	
25. Dr.:	He's a man?	
26. Mr. B.:	(makes beckoning gesture with his hand to Sam) Come on, come on, come on. Dr. A. wants some information from you.	
27. Sam:	All right, I'll tell you, Dr. A.	
28. Dr.:	Your father uses his hand (referring to beckoning gesture), you know. Not like mother. She has another gesture. Give, give, give (demonstrates). Mother's gesture is this (shows). Pop's gesture is give. (Father laughing loudly all this while.)	
29. Sam:	I don't have much to say about Dad. He's just a normal man. He's my father. He's a good guy, that's all.	
30. Mrs. B.:	May I make a suggestion?	
31. Dr.:	What's your suggestion?	
32. Mrs. B.:	Well, I have been keeping an anecdotal record of the time that has elapsed since we were here. Not every minute of the time, but anything that I think is important enough to relate. Now, I think this is good for many reasons. When you read, you sort of get a better view of things, and if you'd like me to read it, I will. If you feel you'd rather ask questions, you can. But—uh—that's my suggestion.	
33. Dr.:	Well, I'm glad you called my attention to that notebook that's in your lap. You come armed with a notebook, a record.	
34. Mrs. B.:	I've been doing this in school, as a matter of fact.	
35. Dr.:	I see.	
36. Mrs. B.:	And I've been keeping this record since last week, because I think it's very important. You forget very quickly what	

people say and how they say it, unless you write it down right away. Now, this is something that I do for children in the class that I have to have their case histories. And I think it's a wonderful idea.

37. Dr.: Well now, what have you there? A case history on your whole family?

38. Mrs. B.: Yes.

39. Dr.: Marvelous! How long is it?

40. Mrs. B.: It's not that long. I just started it. (Jack starts to read over Joan's shoulder.) There's something here that you didn't see last night.

41. Mr. B.: Oh, you cheated!

42. Mrs. B.: I didn't cheat. I just didn't tell you there was more to it, that's all. You read the front of the book, but—

43. Mr. B.: That's cheating.

44. Mrs. B.: No, it isn't. So, if you would like me to read it. It's sort of a little resume of my thinking in the last week. I was quite disturbed last week in the middle of the week, very disturbed. So much so that on the last day of school, a little girl in my class gave me a pin, a four leaf clover pin. Now I never told this little girl anything. She said, "Maybe this will change your luck." So I was very disturbed and that's what made me do this. I felt it's better to come with exact words and phrases rather than remembering things.

45. Dr.: Now—uh—is this a four leaf clover? Is that what you've got?

46. Mrs. B.: Yes.

47. Dr.: That change your luck?

48. Mrs. B.: No, not yet it hasn't, but—

49. Dr.: Have you got it on you?

50. Mrs. B.: No. I didn't wear it tonight but it was very sweet and I, I cried for a little while after she left, because I was so—

51. (Mr. B. picks at his finger and Dr. notices.)

52. Dr.: Your finger hurting?

53. Mr. B.: No, I was—had a little hangnail.

54. Mrs. B.: That's a nervous ailment of his. He picks at his feet, at a rash there and he picks at his fingers. That's a nervous ailment of *his*.

55. Sam: Pretty disgusting (laughs amusedly).

56. Dr.: Pretty disgusting, is it?

57. Sam: (to mother) What about your nervous habits?

58. Mrs. B.: I have quite a few.

59. Sam: Like sitting and—never mind. Quite a few.

60. Mrs. B.: I said I have a few.

61. Sam: Yeah, and they're pretty bad, because when I—

62. Dr.:   Are you sore at mother because she's picking pieces out of Papa's uh—

63. Sam: Yeah.

64. Dr.:   Fingers?

65. Sam: Yeah; so what? So he has nervous habits. So don't we all?

66. Dr.:   What kind of a piece would you pick, like to pick out of Mama?

67. Sam: Huh? She has some pretty disgusting habits.

68. Dr.:   Well, what are they?

69. Mrs. B.: I'll tell you what they are.

70. Dr.:   Now wait a minute. Sam is talking.

71. Sam: Uh—(laughs nervously).

72. Mrs. B.: Well, Sam, you don't have to be bashful. This is to give information. You don't have to be—

73. Dr.:   He's not bashful.

74. Mrs. B.: —embarrassed, in my mind.

75. Dr.:   Hold it, hold it, hold it. Now, Sam.

76. Sam: I don't know how to put it, if you want the truth.

77. Mrs. B.: That's why I was going to put it for you.

78. Sam: Yeah, well I, maybe she has some better words for the thing.

79. Dr.:   No, no, no, no, now. This is, is that same old give, Sam, here to me (repeat father's gesture as above), the same old insincere ritual, you first Alphonse. Let's not be scared around these here parts. You started something. Finish it.

80. Sam: Mom—uh—she belches.

81. Dr.:   She belches.

82. Sam: Consistently, repeatedly, and disgustingly.

83. Mrs. B.: That's right. I swallow air. I went to a doctor many years ago about it. It's a nervous habit, and when I'm very upset, evidently I swallow—

84. Sam: Why were you so upset tonight?

85. Mrs. B.: Tonight was not for that, Sam.

86. Dr.:   Sam, when Mama belches, whom does she, whose face does she belch into?

87. Mr. B.: Mine mostly.

88. Sam: His! (laughing and pointing vigorously to father)

89. Dr.:   His. (all laugh)

90. Mr. B.: Mine, if you like, or anybody else who happens to be around.

91. Sam: Only with her choice friends she refrains (sic) herself. Somehow she doesn't swallow air when her good friends are around, her high class friends (sarcastically).

92. Mrs. B.: That's right. It's not high class, Sam.

93. Sam: Yes, it is.
94. Mrs. B.: No, I wouldn't call it high class.
95. Sam: But you manage not to swallow air—
96. Mrs. B.: Well, let me read what's in here (picks up notebook). Maybe this will give you a better idea—
97. Dr.:   Well, one moment now. Is that the only—
98. Sam: That's about the worst habit she has.
99. Dr.:   —habit, in your eyes?
100. Sam: Yeah, that's about the worst of it.
101. Dr.:   That's the worst? No others?
102. Sam: (giggles) No, I haven't got the nerve.
103. Dr.:   Come on, come on.
104. Sam: No, no, really. That's about all.
105. Mrs. B.: Now I don't know what else he has reference to.
106. Dr.:   You know you're only playing a game now. That isn't fair.
107. Sam: I'm sorry. I'm not going to say anything else.
108. Dr.:   Now he's tensing up because he knows all about Mama's habits.
109. Sam: Then ask him (points to father, laughing embarrassedly).
110. Dr.:   No, I want to ask you first. You started this.
111. Sam: I'm sorry. I'm not going to tell you.
112. Dr.:   (perceiving Ann smiling broadly) Ann, Ann's got a trick up her sleeve, too.
113. Sam: I can't tell you that, Dr.
114. Dr.:   Oh, come on.
115. Sam: I'm sorry, I can't.
116. Mr. B.: He doesn't want to embarrass his mother.
117. Mrs. B.: I don't know what he has reference to so I don't—
118. Dr.:   You're a teaser, Sam—
119. Sam: I'm sorry, I—
120. Dr.:   —a teaser.
121. Sam: I can't.
122. Dr.:   You start to begin to commence to say something about your Ma. You make a big promise and all of a sudden you fade out. That's not cricket.
123. Sam: No, well, that's about the worst thing.
124. Dr.:   I know you Ma is impatient. She's looking at her—
125. Mrs. B.: No, I was just—
126. Dr.:   —at her record.
127. Mrs. B.: No, that's not impatience. I was just—looking at it (the notebook). But he's not saying anything so I've nothing to listen to.

128. Sam: No, I'll tell you the truth. I really don't have anything—I'm
               not going to say.
129. Mr. B.:   Might as well ask somebody else.
130. Dr.:   If you don't say, it's going to come out in the wash anyway.
131. Sam: So let it come out.
132. Dr.:   It might as well come out where it started.
133. Sam: I'm sorry. I will not do it (emphatically)!
134. Dr.:   (again noticing Ann) Ann, do you want to speak up ahead of
               Pop?
135. Mr. B.:   Come on, Ann.
136. (Ann hides head in her arms. Sam puts his arm around Ann in a friendly
     way and whispers to her.)
137. Mrs. B.: Oh, look now, you're wasting—
138. Sam: Come on, Ann.
139. Ann: I'm finished. Mommy's a nut. Daddy's a nut.
140. Sam: I'll say they are!
141. Dr.:   Always belching in Pop's face.
142. (Mrs. B. and Ann laugh.)
143. Dr.:   Oh, Mom likes that! Look at her giggle!
144. Mrs. B.: You know why I'm giggling?
145. Dr.:   Why?
146. Mrs. B.: I asked Jack as a favor to me, when I realized that I was going
               to do this, that he should keep some kind of a record of our
               relationship. I feel there's lots to be desired in it. Maybe if
               we can get it down on paper, you can help us with it. So—
               he—did do it for several days. Last night, I said, *"Please*
               write that thing for me. Because I want to know." I knew I
               had written it down. So he did write it down. And there were
               several things he wrote that were mostly about things that
               I don't care to discuss in front of the children. However, one
               of the things was about the belching. And I giggled because
               I refuse to take it seriously. I know it's nothing terrible. It's,
               it's a nervousness. And so I, I giggle. Now as a result of that
               giggling, evidently, it put him in a different frame of mind.
               And after he said he wouldn't let me see his paper until after
               I let him read what I had written. Well, some of this stuff is
               pretty—rugged. I mean, it's, it's what I think and it's not
               complimentary in some respects. But he read it and for the
               first time since we're married, which is twenty years, he
               didn't get—
147. Mr. B.:   More, dear.
148. Mrs. B.: All right, it's a little more than twenty. He didn't get angry.
               And I can honestly say that's the first time that he ever acted

like the kind of man I hoped he was. (Father sighs deeply.) He didn't get angry with, with it—at this notebook. Well, of course he didn't—

149. Dr.: Oh, my, my. That's quite a bit of progress. Last week, you said he wasn't no man at all.

150. Mrs. B.: Most of the time he, he does not react the way I would like him to. I can honestly say this is the first time he acted the way I would like him to and the way I would expect him to, the first time since we're married. It was a pleasure to see him *not* get angry at something that was the truth, and he, and it was, there was a sense of humor in it, and it just lovely. And I, I would appreciate so much—

151. Dr.: You mean Jack has a temper with you?

152. Mrs. B.: Yes; he's either too good or too bad.

153. Dr.: Too good or too bad. (Notices Jack protruding his tongue.) Look at his tongue.

154. Mrs. B.: He can be a son of a bee or he can be an angel. And he doesn't always follow the middle course. Either he's too easy to get along with or for nothing he'll—

155. Dr.: I asked you to look at his tongue.

156. Mrs. B.: Well, I didn't see his tongue.

157. Dr.: Why don't you look?

158. Mrs. B.: Well, I was talking to you so I was looking at you.

159. Dr.: Why do you have eyes for me only? What about Jack?

160. Mrs. B.: Well, I think that when you talk to somebody, you should look at him, which is something he doesn't do. Which I have criticized—

161. Mr. B.: (noting Mrs. B.'s pointing finger) Did you see that finger go? (laughs loudly)

162. Mrs. B.: Which is something I have criticized him for many times. I think—

163. Dr.: Well, what did you want to talk about that he had his tongue in a very special position?

164. Ann: (gestures) Like this.

165. Mrs. B.: Well, I don't know why. I don't know why at all. He was laughing to himself. I don't know why.

166. Dr.: (to Jack) Did you see what happened?

167. Mr. B.: No, no. I would really appreciate it if you'd tell me.

168. Dr.: (to Ann) How do you feel about that tongue of his?

169. Ann: I though it was funny.

170. Dr.: (to Jack) What were you about to do with your tongue?

171. Sam: What a family!

172. Mr. B.: It happens that my putting my tongue out is a habit (all

laugh). It's a habit of maybe forty or forty-five years. Whenever I write, I can just sign my name, my tongue will be out.

173. Dr.: You mean you stick your tongue out whenever you concentrate?

174. Mr. B.: Whenever I do anything—

175. Ann: I know something I could say, but Sam would kill me and so would my father, so I can't.

176. Mrs. B.: Nobody is going to kill you, Ann.

177. Mr. B.: Nobody will kill you.

178. Ann: Sam will, Sam will.

179. Mrs. B.: Sam won't kill you either. Nobody kills around here.

180. Dr.: All right, spit it out, Ann. Let's hear.

181. Mrs. B.: Come on, Ann.

182. Ann: Sam, Sam—

183. Dr.: What were you going to say?

184. Mrs. B.: Go ahead.

185. (Sam turns completely away from group, so that his back is turned to the camera and to the group members. He maintains this position for most of the remainder of this session, until the interaction noted in items 334 through 340.)

186. Ann: Today, he had a date with a girl and he locked the door, and when I was at the door, he said, "You're going to be in so much trouble!" And I think he likes the girl more than he does me, because whenever I have a date, he, I never lock the door. When I, I had to get something in the kitchen—and he, and it was locked when I—knocked. And he said, "I have to tell her that I don't like her." And then I found out that he was lying about that. And I don't think it's right to lock the door—because—Renee and Helen, we had to go around the back way and he wouldn't let us in.

187. Dr.: Shows what your brother, Sam, did to you.

188. Mrs. B.: That's another thing about Sam. He, he's like his father in that respect. He's either too good or too bad. Either he's an angel and, and a *doll;* or, for no reason at all, he'll blow his top and simply not be fit to live with.

189. Dr.: (notices Ann grinning, making faces, and bidding for attention) See, as you were concentrating, you didn't see what Ann was doing with *her* top.

190. Ann: (giggles)

191. Mrs. B.: Now, I hope Sam isn't angry after this session.

192. Mr. B.: I was going to say that in my opinion, this is the case with most people, although Joan seems to think that this is a problem

that we have a corner of the market on. I think that most people tend to go to either of two extremes. I think it's the unusual person who steers a steady, middle-of-the-road course constantly. I haven't yet met that person.

193. Mrs. B.: Well, I think that's true, "constantly." But to get unduly upset over *nothing*, and, and raise the roof, and get really nasty and mean—

194. Dr.: How does he do that?

195. Mrs. B.: Well, if I read these notes, you'll know how he does it. Otherwise, I can't really describe it to you, my inner feelings. That's the only way—

196. Dr.: Before you read your notes now, I'd just like to ask Jack one question. When you belch in Jack's face—

197. Mrs. B.: (interrupting) Well, I don't deliberately do that.

198. Dr.: Excuse me.

199. Mrs. B.: I don't deliberately do that.

200. Dr.: How does, how does it feel?

201. Mr. B.: Well, her belching does something to me that, that I just can't explain, with as good a command of English that I think I do have. It is just like waving a red flag in front of my face. And has for years to the point where we went to doctors in Woodmere and with no satisfaction.

202. Ann: (interrupting) Sam—

203. Mr. B.: And the thing that aggravates me more than anything is that with certain company, although she pleads that this is uncontrollable, and that she has no control over it, with certain company in the house, she can control it beautifully.

204. Dr.: Well now, when was the last time she belched in your face?

205. Mr. B.: Last night.

206. Mrs. B.: No, no, no.

207. Mr. B.: Please don't say "no," because you belched—

208. Mrs. B.: (interrupting) Most of the time—

209. Mr. B.: —when I— The minute she gets into bed, she starts belching like mad.

210. Dr.: In bed?

211. Mr. B.: Yes.

212. Mrs. B.: Yes, I think it's psychological.

213. Mr. B.: Yes, the minute she gets into bed. Yes.

214. Mrs. B.: I really think there is something psychological. I'm not feeling now. When I lie down, I begin to swallow air. I don't know why. And there are some times I don't do it, but on the whole, when I—

215. (Sam turns to Ann while his mother is talking. He smiles with Ann, puts his arm around her, whispers something, and then again turns away from group.)
216. Ann: (interrupting) Excuse me, but just now he—
217. Mrs. B.: All right (trying to resume).
218. Ann: He said, "If you tell about that lipstick mark, I'll kill you!"
219. Mr. B.:   Oh, stop it now!
220. Mrs. B.: Sam, you're being as silly as, as I would expect you to be now.
221. Ann: I'm going to bring it out.
222. Dr.:   As soon as I begin concentrating on the love life between Ma and Pa, you two kids start cutting up.
223. Sam: I'm sorry, but I don't like it one bit. (still turned away from group)
224. Ann: (raises hand) He—
225. Dr.:   (to Sam) Would you rather talk about your love life?
226. Sam: No. I'd rather talk about nobody's love life.
227. Ann: I'd like to say something.
228. Dr.:   Yes, Ann.
229. Ann: Well, he has a mark on his neck. And I was teasing him and saying it was lipstick from his girlfriend. And he said, "If you say that in front of Dr. A., I'll murder you." And I didn't like that—what he said.
230. Mrs. B.: Sam has not got a sense of humor when it comes to things he's touchy about. He doesn't want to discuss his report card, which I said I would discuss tonight. And he said, "You'd better not, or else." And I think it's a very important thing to discuss.
231. Dr.:   Sam—
232. Mrs. B.: (interrupting) Would you mind turning around and acting like a man?
233. Mr. B.:   Sam.
234. Dr.:   He's angry. It's—
235. Mrs. B.: (interrupting) I can see he's angry at me, too, now.
236. (Ann whispers with her mother and changes places with her.)
237. Mrs. B.: Now, please turn around. (Sam continues facing away.)
238. Dr.:   Now, we were—
239. Mrs. B.: Yes.
240. Dr.:   —talking about his special date with his girlfriend and Ann felt *so alone*. Because, after all, Sam's your boyfriend, isn't he?
241. Ann: No.
242. Dr.:   No?
243. Ann: No. Never had one.
244. Dr.:   Is it bad? But Sam is also sore at me because he doesn't like it when—

245. Ann: (interrupting) He doesn't like it because—
246. Dr.:   —when we talk about, talk to Ma and Pa here about their love life. He doesn't like that at all. He wants to pretend like he knows nothing at all about their love life.
247. (Mother puts arm on Sam's shoulder and tries to turn him back to group.)
248. Mrs. B.: Will you—?
249. Sam: Stop touching me!
250. Mrs. B.: Well, will you turn around and act like—
251. Sam: I don't feel like it.
252. Mrs. B.: I know you don't feel like it, but turn around anyway.
253. Sam: (makes barely audible, objecting sound)
254. Dr.:   Sam, you're angry at me, not Ma.
255. Sam: No, I'm not angry at you. I'm angry at my sister and my mother.
256. Ann: Just because I told the truth.
257. Sam: Why don't you learn to shut up for a change?
258. Ann: Why don't you shut up?
259. Dr.:   Ann, when you changed seats, you wanted to get away from you brother. Are you angry at him?
260. Ann: Yes.
261. Mrs. B.: You see—
262. Dr.:   (interrupting) You didn't like it when he had that girl in the apartment?
263. Ann: No.
264. Dr.:   What were you so sore about?
265. Ann: Because I had nothing to do. And I wanted to get something out of the kitchen, and he told me to go out.
266. Dr.:   Well, he wanted a little privacy with his girlfriend.
267. Ann: In a smooch.
268. Dr.:   Smooch. Well, what's wrong with a smooch?
269. Mr. B.:   What's wrong with that?
270. Ann: Because he had marks on his neck.
271. Sam: Will you shut up!
272. Mrs. B.: Sam, you're acting so babyish.
273. Sam: Will you, will you, please, too.
274. Dr.:   Don't you think a guy like Sam can smooch a little bit with a girl, and get some lipstick on his neck.
275. Ann: (whispers) It's wrong.
276. Dr.:   What? It's wrong? It's bad?
277. Ann: (whisper) Yes.
278. Dr.:   The only thing I know that's bad about it is that he got the lipstick on his *neck*.

279. Ann: Yeah, so it's evidence.
280. Dr.:   Oh, you want to hang the man on evidence.
281. Ann: When we leave, he's going to murder me.
282. Dr.:   You're not going to smooch?
283. Ann: No.
284. Dr.:   What are you going to do?
285. Ann: Nothing.
286. Mr. B.:   What was that game you were playing at your dance, with a bottle in the middle of the room spinning around? Huh?
287. Dr.:   Anyhow, anyhow you two kids just—
288. Ann: I didn't get lipstick.
289. Dr.:   You two kids just pulled us right out of your parents' bed. We were in there in the double bed. Mom was belching in Pop's face and that's where you interrupted the story. Now, Joan, you say it's psychological.
290. Mrs. B.: I felt—
291. Dr.:   The moment you go to bed with Jack—
292. Mrs. B.: Not the moment. I wouldn't put it quite so—uh, like that. But I do—uh—begin to swallow air and I don't know why. I really don't. Now, maybe what I have written here will have some bearing on the subject.
293. Dr.:   Well, you can read that in just a moment. Seems you hurt Jack's feeling, torment him no end. He can't stand it when you belch in his face. Is that right?
294. Mr. B.:   Did you ever try, or think that you wanted to kiss a woman, and just when you're about to do it, have her belch in your face?
295. Ann: (giggles loudly)
296. Dr.:   I'm terribly sympathetic with you.
297. Ann: (giggles again)
298. Mr. B.:   I mean—
299. Dr.:   It's really not what I would call kissing.
300. Mr. B.:   I mean—this is something!—Unless you wear a gask mask!
301. (Mrs. B. and Ann giggle together almost uncontrollably.)
302. Dr.:   Smells bad?
303. Mr. B.:   Blows your head to one side and it's really very unhealthy. And I just hope you never have, have the—
304. Dr.:   Exposure to gas?
305. (Mrs. B. and Ann continue to giggle, even louder now.)
306. Mr. B.:   Yes, specifically.
307. Dr.:   At the very moment you wanted to kiss her.
308. Mr. B.:   Well, you're afraid. I'm serious. I—

309. Mrs. B.:   Well, I think this is just part of an excuse on his part, really. Because I don't do it that often, or every night.

310. Ann: Just now!

311. Mr. B.:   You do it that often and you do it—

312. Mrs. B.:   Believe me when I tell you I don't. I, I cannot—it does not happen every night or anything like that. There are nights—

313. Mr. B.:   I didn't say it happened every night.

314. Mrs. B.:   All right.

315. Mr. B.:   There are nights when you will blame it on what you've eaten. There will be nights when you'll blame it on what you've drank. There'll be nights when you'll blame it on being upset. And other nights, you'll blame it on not sleeping enough the day before. (Joan and Ann are giggling.) And you will not always have an excuse, but the belching is there.

316. Dr.:   Ann, she just loves this. (Ann giggles.) Oh, boy, does she love it!

317. Mr. B.:   I'm not saying it was done deliberately, but—

318. Dr.:   (to Ann) You raised your hand. What did you want to say?

319. Ann: I want you to see the marks on Sam's neck.

320. Sam: Oh, never mind!

321. Ann: You want to stop it, I know. But I want to get him as mad as he got me today.

322. Dr.:   Now, just a minute. We're in your parents' bed. Can we stay there a few minutes? Or won't you let us? (brief silence) Now, (to Ann) suppose you move over again next to Sam, because we've got a problem between Ma and Pa here. We got to know what to do with this gas.

323. Ann: I don't want to go near him. (But she moves back, next to Sam.)

324. Mrs. B.:   Well, I'll leave out anything that has to do with bed. Because if it's going to disturb them, then I think it should be left out.

325. Sam: (angrily) It disturbs me.

326. Dr.:   I notice—

327. Sam: It's disturbed me for the last ten minutes.

328. Dr.:   I know that. You're mad at me. Because last week you said you didn't want to be here and we had to stop. Would you rather leave the room? (no answer) Sam?

329. Sam: I wouldn't like to answer that.

330. Dr.:   It isn't really that you don't know about this stuff. You just want to make out you don't know about this stuff.

331. (Mrs. B. whispers to Ann.)

332. Sam: (still turned aside from group) I don't want you to talk about it in my presence. I'm willing to talk about anything you want, which I think is wrong, if anyone else is present, but I don't want to be present.

333. Mrs. B.: Well, why don't you leave?
334. Sam: All right, I'll leave. (Gets up and moves toward door.)
335. Mrs. B.: It's perfectly all right. You can wait outside.
336. (All talk at once. Dr. restrains Sam as he is leaving.)
337. Mr. B.:   Wait a minute. Wait a minute. Let Dr. A. decide whether Sam is to leave or not.
338. Mrs. B.: Well, I'm sorry. I thought—
339. Dr.:   Okay. Sit down.
340. (Sam then takes his chair and now faces group.)
341. Dr.:   If we come to a point, Sam, where it seems really sensible for both children to leave, I'll ask both of you to leave. If we want to deal with the *very* private part in the relations between Ma and Pa. But I want to know what bothers you so much.
342. Sam: It bothers me.
343. Dr.:   I know it bothers you.
344. Sam: I don't know why; it just bothers me.
345. Ann: I don't want to go out of here even at the private part because, because he's going to kill me if I go out.
346. Dr.:   (to Sam) Why so much?
347. Sam: I don't know; it just bothers me.
348. Dr.:   Yeah, but it would be very interesting to, to try to understand—
349. Sam: I really, I really wouldn't mind—
350. Dr.:   —why you act so terribly—
351. Sam: Well, I don't know. It just, it just bothers me.
352. Dr.:   You know that every Ma and Pa kiss.
353. Sam: I certainly do, but that—
354. Dr.:   So what's the trouble?
355. Sam: It bothers me. I don't know what the trouble is. It bothers me.
356. Dr.:   Do you think, since we're all here together—
357. Sam: No, I'll tell you why it bothers me, if you want to know—
358. Dr.:   —that you make an attempt with us and see—
359. Sam: No, I'll tell you exactly why it bothers me. Because just like it bothers me that Ann is citing my private business, which I entrusted to her to just mind her own business. I didn't even ask her to, to bother me, when she, she insisted on bothering me. I told her something about, you know I wanted to tell the girl that I didn't like her, so she should please leave me alone. But what I do is my business and I think that what my parents do is their business. I may be very wrong. I—maybe it's everyone else's business. But I don't like it and I, I would rather not be present if you, or whoever wants it, wants to discuss it.
360. Dr.:   Now, Sam—

361. Ann: Just now—

362. Dr.:   —you don't want to be in on a thing that we talked about, the private love life between Ma and Pa, because if you are, you're afraid that Ma and Pa, and I, too, might invade your private love life.

363. Sam: No, that, that isn't possible, because I do not feel that way. Because *nobody* knows about my private love life except me. And—

364. Ann: And me.

365. Sam: —and that's the way it's going to stay as far as I'm concerned.

366. Dr.:   You insist on your privacy.

367. Sam: That's right.

368. Dr.:   Well, all right. Look, I can't keep you here. The door is wide open, but I would prefer, if you can tolerate it, that you stay with us, because I'm interested in helping the whole family. Even if it bothers you—

369. Sam: As long as you don't let Ann know, that's all I care about. As long as you know it annoys me.

370. Dr.:   —just to hear something.

371. Sam: Well, all right. Whatever you say, Dr.

372. Dr.:   Now, that's very good. Now, you let me know if it's too much for you because—

373. Sam: Well, as far as I'm concerned, the second it began was too much for me, because I don't like it. But if, as far as if you want me to stay—

374. Dr.:   I'd prefer it.

375. Sam: Okay. Whatever you say.

376. Dr.:   Good. (Ann raises her hand.) Ann.

377. Ann: Well, I, I don't want to go home tonight because he's gonna—

378. Sam: (in great exasperation) I, I—did I ever hit you or harm you?

379. Ann: Oh, today.

380. Sam: Well, I never did. So just be quiet.

381. Dr.:   Well, do you think he ought to kill you because of what you did, talking about his smooching?

382. Ann: Well, I—

383. Dr.:   Do you think he ought to kill you?

384. Ann: Well, I saw those marks on his neck all right. Look if they're not lipstick.

385. Dr.:   Well, I already saw them. So what? What's terrible about that?

386. Ann: And telling me that story that he doesn't do anything. And — and — and he — and Sam was so mean to me. He, he, he, he was mad at me. He wanted me to call up my friend when he heard that she was coming, so that we wouldn't peek in on

him, and so that he would have privacy with his girlfriend. And, and—

387. Dr.: Well, now, don't you think when, when you're Sam's age, you'll want a little bit of privacy with your boyfriend?

388. Ann: Yeah, but if, if I had a little brother that had a date, and I wouldn't tell him to break the date.

389. Mr. B.: Because he can't be sure you wouldn't invade his privacy. That's why.

390. Dr.: Well, we'll, we'll settle this later, but he didn't do anything terrible.

391. Ann: And he locked the door. And when I knocked, he, he came out stamping his feet and yelling at me.

392. Dr.: I think you're just jealous of that girl he had in there. That's all.

393. (Sam laughs)

394. Ann: I'm not jealous of that ugly girl.

395. Dr.: Oh! She was ugly, was she?

396. Ann: Yes.

397. Dr.: You mean you're better looking?

398. Sam: I'm going to smack her right in the face if she doesn't shut her mouth. Look (to father), do you mind if I leave?

399. Mr. B.: No, I don't mind.

400. Sam: (gets up and starts to leave)

401. Dr.: Wait a minute. (Sam leaves room.)

402. Mrs. B.: You see, what Sam is doing now is what he does at home, which I think is inexcusable. I feel that this child should have a great deal more control over himself than he has.

403. Dr.: Well, you're a good preacher. I agree he ought to, but he doesn't. There are—

404. Mrs. B.: That's right.

405. Dr.: —reasons for that—

406. Mrs. B.: I'm disturbed about what he just did.

407. Dr.: —It's about Ann. (to Ann) You say his girl was ugly. Are you much prettier than she?

408. Ann: I think so.

409. Dr.: Oh, you're pretty jealous of her.

410. Ann: I am *not* jealous of her.

411. Dr.: Oh, you're teasing now.

412. Ann: I'm not.

413. Dr.: You're a pretty good romancer yourself. Like to tease a lot, you and Sam both. Well, anyhow, let's be back to Ma and Pa. Is that all right with you, Ann? Hm? Well now, what did you

do last night when she belched in your face? You wanted to kiss her and she belched.

414. Mr. B.: No, I didn't want to kiss her. I merely said that that is my reaction. You asked what my reaction is and why I resent it, or why it upsets me, and I merely said it is very unhappy to kiss a woman and have her belch in your face.

415. Dr.: Hmm.

416. Mr. B.: Now, that doesn't mean that every time I attempt to kiss my wife she does it. But—it can happen more often than not.

417. Dr.: Well, you know, you, you sound so reasonable right now that I don't believe a word that's coming out of your mouth. You're not that reasonable when you get belched at. Are you?

418. Mr. B.: Well, it annoys me to the point where I have—

419. Dr.: It does.

420. Mr. B.: Yes. I have turned around and I have at times left the bed and gone inside and read the newspaper, and read a magazine or done other things. I've criticized her for it.

421. Ann: Can I please go out now?

422. Dr.: Well we're going to bring Sam back in here in a little bit.

423. Ann: I'll come back if he starts to hit me.

424. Dr.: You want to be with him?

425. Ann: No, I want to go out. (leaves room)

426. Dr.: All right, folks, here's your chance to talk plain English.
(From here the session continues without either of the children present.)

The Interaction of Verbal and Non-verbal Behavior and Its Therapeutic Significance

Within the context of our script there are certain relationships between verbal and non-verbal expressions which are evident. Perhaps the most obvious relationship is that of the inverse relationship between overt speech and non-verbal expression.

The verbal productivity of the group members is given in Table I. Three separate indices are used. The total number of words used gives a general indication of total verbal output. The number of items may indicate the proneness to intervene verbally or to respond to the therapeutic intervention. The number of items with twenty-five or more words may reveal the member's ability to hold the floor, so to speak, and the number of words in these twenty-five or more word items could indicate the member's tenacity in floor-holding.

TABLE I

Verbal Productivity of Group Members

	Total Number of Words	Total Number of Items	No. of Items with 25 or More Words	No. of Words in 25 + Items
Dr. A.	1593	153	13	511
Mr. B.	679	52	7	370
Mrs. B.	1480	78	17	933
Sam	720	79	4	229
Ann	559	58	3	234

Table I demonstrates that Mrs. B. is more productive verbally than any other family member. Dr. A. does produce more words and also more items. His productivity, however, consists to a large extent of brief therapeutic interventions. Mrs. B. is the most determined "floor-holder" and produces the largest quantity of words in this capacity. These data do thus support the inverse relationship posited between verbal productivity and non-verbal expressiveness. Mrs. B., who makes the fewest gestures (see below), does most of the talking. Since we are mainly concerned with the specific non-verbal expressions in their clinical context, the data of Table I will not be analyzed in more detail.

Let us focus now upon the interaction between verbal and non-verbal behavior for each individual in the family, especially as this is responded to by the therapist. Look, for example, at Item 28, where Dr. A. reacts to the father's gesture rather than to Sam's remarks of the moment. Mr. B. responds to Dr. A.'s interpretation with a loud laugh, which in itself contains both release and defiance.

At Item 51 Mr. B. picks at his finger and the therapist immediately uses this gesture to open up an entire channel of inquiry. The whole subject of "disgusting habits" stems from this single observation, although the object of attention shifts from Mr. B. to Mrs. B. Mr. B. seems quite expert at averting inquiry, while Mrs. B. apparently takes on a scapegoat role (2) most readily at this point. Mrs. B.'s belching, another non-verbal expression, becomes the fulcrum about which the remainder of the session revolves.

Sam's attitude of provocative reticence is the channel through which the therapist is able to approach the parents' sexual conflict. It is of interest to note that the subject of belching and sex is again opened by a gesture interpretation (see Item 79). Sam exhibits two basic behavioral gestures in this session. The first is that of pointing vigorously to his father (Items 88 and 109). This gesture has both accusation and warmth, a kind of laughingly pointing to the perpetrator of the deed. It is as if Sam wants to turn the spotlight on the masked hero (or villain) and induce him to remove his disguise.

Sam's second gesture is that of turning entirely away from the group. He actually spends the major part of this session with his back turned to his family (Items 185 to 340) and soon after he does turn back to the group, Sam gets up and leaves the room. It is clear that Sam wants to remove his name entirely from the cast of players. And yet there is a kind of pretense to Sam's withdrawal. Despite his apparent wish to leave he both attracts attention and provokes anger by turning his back. Sam's very efforts to flee make him conspicuous and a topic of family concern.

In addition, Sam's apparent withdrawal has a hidden face. Although his verbal expressions to his sister are angry accusations, his behavioral gestures are warm and affectionate. He smiles warmly at Ann and puts his arm around her in a friendly fashion (Item 215). This behavior is quite contradictory to overt verbalization and would probably not be detected without motion picture recording.

Mr. B. has a number of small gestures. He sighs (Item 1), beckons with his hand (Item 28), picks at his finger (Item 51) and sticks out his tongue (Item 153). None of these escape the attention of his therapist. It is as if Mr. B. is trying to remain unnoticed, but is betrayed by involuntary cues, which demonstrate his instigatory role in the family circle.

Ann's gestures are not yet so definitively developed. She demonstrates with her whole body and by facial grimaces. Ann makes faces (Item 112), raises her hand (Item 134), hides her head (Item 136) or merely interrupts (Item 175). She cannot fully express herself in words and must take her part by actions and facial masks; this is primitive drama.

It is of interest that Mrs. B., who during this session reveals almost no behavioral gestures but sits rather stiffly and with frozen facial expression, speaks far more than any other family member. It is as if words take the place of actions that cannot come forth. Nevertheless, such suppressed activity has come out in the secret family life. Mrs. B. belches and is unable to control this involuntary betrayal of hostility. When the subject of belching is discussed, Mrs. B. and Ann go into uncontrollable giggles (Items 301, 305 and 315), which may demonstrate a conspiratorial alliance between the women of the family. In one sense Mrs. B.'s frozen face is itself a form of non-verbal expression, as is the entire gamut of facial expressions and mannerisms. Mrs. B. is the only family member who does not laugh on her own, and she communicates a sense of emotional isolation which may be related to her lack of non-verbal expressiveness.

There are numerous interpretations that can be made of the individual gestures and in fact the major therapeutic movement in this session arises from Dr. A.'s reflecting of gestures (Items 28 and 79) and calling attention to them. Thus Sam's frequent laughing may be a clue to his repressed aggression and inability to assert himself. Mr. B.'s sighs and movements with his tongue reveal his frustrated oral cravings.

Perhaps the most significant behavioral gestures are those of Sam putting his arm around Ann in a friendly way and whispering to her. His affectionate attitude in this behavior is quite at odds with the overt verbal communication, since the friendliness between the siblings is contradicted by their bitter quarreling. By analyzing the total behavioral sequence one can see that Sam provokes his sister into instigating his own aggression. He seems to provoke Ann's first contribution to the session (Items 136, 139: "Mommy's a nut; Daddy's a nut!") and then feels free to corroborate her comment (Item 140).

Later (Item 215) he smiles broadly at Ann, while threatening to kill her if she gives away his secret. Of course Ann complies with Sam's wish to interrupt the proceedings and, as Dr. A. notes, the children succeed in steering the conversation away from the topic of parental sex.

The most significant non-verbal behavior is that occurring outside this session: (1) Mrs. B.'s belching, (2) Mrs. B.'s notebook, and (3) Sam's lipstick mark. Therapeutic progress has already brought all of this behavior into treatment process.

Non-verbal Cues and the Re-enactment of Conflict

Let us turn from interpretations of gestures and behavior to some structural relationships within these data. It is our impression that the verbal communications among family members are *cued* by certain key gestures. On a relatively overt level we have seen how Sam cued Ann to interrupt an unwelcome topic of conversation. However, what about the gesture where Mrs. B. puts her hand on Sam's shoulder to persuade him to turn back to the family circle (Item 247)? This gesture, as seen on the film, seems more studied and artificial than spontaneous. Sam's immediate reaction is one of intense annoyance, but his only expression is a grunt. Dr. A. tries to clarify Sam's anger but then Ann again lends herself as a target of displaced hostility. In this sequence we can perceive (1) inadequate mothering, (2) reactive anger from Sam, and (3) Ann's provocative drawing of the anger from Mrs. B. to herself. The sequence thus illustrates the crucial traumatic interaction of this family in encapsulated miniature.

Let us examine Mr. B.'s tongue gesture (Item 153) and the behavior in which it is embedded. Mrs. B. and the therapist are engaged in an analysis of her husband's behavior, and she is expressing her pleasure at "the first time he ever acted like the kind of man I hoped he was." Mr. B. sighed deeply at this comment, and Mrs. B. went on to say that her pleasure arose mainly from her husband's lack of anger at reading what she had written about him. Dr. A. interprets Mr. B.'s manhood and his temper, and then the tongue emerged.

It is clear that Mrs. B.'s concept of masculinity is a significantly inverted one. Acceptable masculinity to her means compliance to her own wishes and a lack of aggression, but in twenty years of marriage she has been unable to get Mr. B. to accede completely to the passive role she would like to assign. Now Mrs. B. feels that therapy has succeeded in getting her husband to see the light. This was "the first time that he ever acted like the kind of man I hoped he was. He didn't get angry. . . ."

Mr. B.'s tongue gesture is soon mimicked by Ann, who also sticks her tongue out. When Dr. A. tries to clarify this interaction, Ann again evades him. She says merely that she thought her father was being funny, and then changes the subject back to Sam (Item 175). It is at this point that Sam turns his back on the family group.

Here we see a series of role inductions that starts with a conflict of role definition (masculine assertiveness) expressed by the mother, is transmuted into a gestural displacement by the father, which in turn is mimicked and sidetracked by the daughter, which then leads to the withdrawal from the family by the son. Again we have the total family conflict triggered and illustrated in miniature by a brief family exchange of non-verbal gestures.

Mr. B. is unable to take the appropriate role of assertive paternal responsibility. His wife expresses her dissatisfaction in terms of the fact that "he does not react the way I would like him to." Mr. B.'s inner conflict is unverbalized, but comes out in a gesture of his tongue. Ann mimics and makes fun of her father's plight, and then turns the spotlight on her brother. She verbalizes her father's latent rage and expresses it in terms of "Sam would kill me and so would my father." Sam is immediately provoked to leave the scene. *This sequence may well reproduce the conflict that originally brought the family to treatment.* That is, the daughter embodies the unexpressed but violent antagonisms of her parents. When she confronts her brother with this violence, he suddenly fades out of the scene. Does this not recall the incident in which Ann threatened Sam with a knife and he then fell in a dead faint in the parents' bedroom?

We could use these instances of *miniature re-living* of the family conflict as a way of conceptualizing one mode of effectiveness of family therapy. That is, family treatment offers the opportunity to mitigate the traumatic effects of conflict by re-inducing them in therapy and gaining insight into their origins and effects. In this process there is no doubt that the role of the family therapist is paramount and we turn now to an analysis of the therapist-family interactions.

It is clear that Dr. A. is the most active member of the group. He is continually trying to impart meaning to the behavior that takes place and he confronts each family member with the implications of the material that emerges. In addition, there is therapeutic effort to improve communication among the family and to permit each member to express opinions and feelings that have lain dormant. The subject of belching is a good example of behavior that has emerged for examination and discussion as a result of Dr. A.'s direct prompting and encouragement.

It is significant to note that Dr. A. is interested both in specific material that is being withheld and also in improving the over-all efficiency of family communication. These two factors are interrelated, and it is a therapeutic challenge to attend simultaneously to both of them. The way in which this task is accomplished is well illustrated quite early in the session, at Item 28. Dr. A. had been prompting and encouraging Sam to express his feelings about his father. However, at the moment that Sam seems ready to reveal some material, the therapist interrupts to call attention to a gesture on Mr. B.'s part and he compares this to Mrs. B.'s gesture. This therapeutic maneuver brings Mrs. B. into the session for the first time. She brings up the "anecdotal record" that she has been keeping, and this is the material that later in the session leads to her comments about the "kind of man" she wants her husband to be. Thus, by attending to both non-verbal cues and reluctance to be direct in expression, the therapist is able to uncover the subtle structure of family communication.

If we put all of this material together, we can see a unity to the family therapy session that emerges. There are various cues, verbal and non-verbal, that prompt each family member to re-enact the traumas and conflicts that led the family to seek treatment. We see the family drama re-lived in miniature scenes, each of which reproduces the family conflict and the member's place in it. The therapist may then be seen as a kind of director or stage manager, who sets the scene and elicits the dialogue and stage action.

The factor that seems to lend most unity to the session is the total family interaction, which seems to have a quality of dramatic destiny. It is as though each family member is taking a role determined by an underlying plot design that has its own independence and intention. Thus, Mrs. B. comes into marriage and must then participate in a husband-wife team. She wants her husband to "act like a man," but her concept of this role has been conditioned by her father, who "was a horror." Soon there is a son, who also seems to Mrs. B. to be "a horror," and later there is a daughter, who does not take the role her mother assigns to her and thus becomes a discipline problem.

Mr. B., who came from a divorced home, was raised to be "independent." Now, as a father, he tends to remain aloof from the battle. He assigns the role of disciplinarian to his wife, but at the same time mocks her (Item 161) in order to call attention away from his own role inadequacy (Item 153) and to undercut her authority, which he senses should belong to him.

Sam and Ann reproduce the provocative inconsistencies of their mother and father. Thus Sam incites Ann to antagonize him, and he in turn withdraws from the family in the same way his father abdicates his role. Ann similarly follows her mother in making fun of the masculine image of aggression ("Sam's going to kill me.") but at the same time is overcome by her own aggressive impulses that she cannot control.

Non-verbal cues during this family session also illustrate a kind of hypocrisy on the part of the parents. Mr. and Mrs. B. have, on the surface of things, demanded certain forms of behavior from their children. Thus Mrs. B. asks Sam to act "like a man" and rejoin the family circle (Item 232), but her act of touching him has the actual effect of reinforcing his apparent rejection of the family (Items 247–

253). Sam is quite "touchy" (Item 230) in his relationship with his mother, and here it is clear that her non-verbal behavior plays a direct role in instigating his touchiness. Mrs. B.'s words ask for one form of behavior but her actions elicit another. In some respects this contradiction resembles the "double-bind" situation, as described by Bateson and others (3, 12).

Mr. B., on the other hand, often makes perfunctory efforts to appear as the authority and disciplinarian of the family. Thus he insists that Sam respond to Dr. A.'s question (Item 26). However, at the same time that he makes this presumably authoritative demand, he simultaneously makes a hand gesture (Item 26) which betrays his own need to be given to rather than to direct the actions of others. When this need of Mr. B. is interpreted by the therapist (Item 28), Mr. B. laughs his acknowledgement and Sam merely continues his provocative withholding.

There is thus a power vacuum in this family, attributable to a mother with a distorted concept of masculinity and a father who partly fits the emasculated role assigned him and partly rebels from it. The vacuum plus the inconsistency of role prevent any true stability in the family structure. Perhaps, if Mr. B. were more totally accepting of the role his wife would assign him, the family would be more stable and perhaps also more distorted in their personality patterns. The nuclear problem might be resolved if Mr. B. could assume the role of dominant and just father, but this does not seem within his present capability.

Before summarizing, some qualifying comments regarding the interpretative significance of non-verbal expressions should be mentioned. These non-verbal cues seem generally to derive from motivations which are less conscious than do verbal expressions, and they are therefore relatively less subject to deliberate control. Nevertheless, non-verbal cues may also to some extent be used in a defensive and perhaps deceptive sense. Sam responds to his mother's gesture of touching him on the shoulder (Item 247) as if it were a manipulative and controlling action, and this type of non-verbal behavior can be as contrived as any verbal expression. Non-verbal behavior may dramatize, deceive, disguise, express or betray; and each expression must be evaluated accordingly.

Also, the hypothesis positing an inverse relation between verbal and non-verbal expressions most likely obtains mainly in reference to verbalizations which are ineffective and fail to express true feeling. Non-verbal expressions must be judged in the context of the total family structure and alongside of verbal communications. They must not be judged solely in isolation but rather in the total context of which they are a part.

Summary

(1) Non-verbal expressions tend to occur in inverse proportion to verbal expressions which are ineffective or fail to express true feeling. Family members who suppress their opinions tend to give vent to more non-verbal forms of expression than do family members who express themselves more fully in words.

(2) Non-verbal expressions may give clues to attitudes or traits which are directly contradictory to expressed verbal opinions. Thus, if the therapist is guided solely by verbalized responses, he may often miss the crux of what is occurring in therapy.

(3) The non-verbal expressions tend to act as hidden cues whereby the total family is prompted *continually to re-enact miniature episodes of shared emotional conflict*. This re-enactment of crucial role conflicts may have a cathartic effect and seems oriented toward discharge of accumulated tension. However, its perseverative quality reveals a helpless, repetitive aspect that requires therapeutic intervention.

(4) The therapist elicits suppressed opinions and attitudes of family members by direct challenge and confrontation of preconscious material. In addition, he may pay particular attention to non-verbal expressions, and by calling attention to them be able to reach and formulate some central aspects of the dramatic conflict of the family.

REFERENCES

1. ACKERMAN, N. W., *The Psychodynamics of Family Life*, New York, Basic Books, 1958.
2. ACKERMAN, N. W., "Prejudicial Scapegoating and Neutralizing Forces in the Family Group, with Special Reference to the Role of 'Family Healer'," Mimeo., 1962.
3. BATESON, G., JACKSON, D. D., HALEY, J. and WEAKLAND, J., "Toward a Theory of Schizophrenia," *Behav. Sci.*, 1, 251–264, 1956.

4. BIRDWHISTELL, R. L., "Kinesics Analysis in the Investigation of the Emotions," Address to the A. A. A. S., Dec. 1960, Mimeo.

5. EHRENWALD, J., *Neurosis in the Family and Patterns of Psychosocial Defense*, New York, Hoeber, 1963.

6. LANDIS, C. and HUNT, W. A., *The Startle Pattern*, New York, Farrar and Rinehart, 1939.

7. PITTENGER, R. E., HOCKETT, C. F. and DANEHY, J. J., *The First Five Minutes: A Sample of Microscopic Analysis*, Ithaca, New York, Paul Martineau, 1960.

8. REIK, T., *Listening with the Third Ear*, New York, Farrar, Straus & Co., 1948.

9. RUESCH, J., *Therapeutic Communication*, New York, Norton, 1961.

10. SCHROEDER, T., "Psycho-therapeutics: From Art to Science," *Psychoanal. Rev.*, 18, 37–56, 1931.

11. SHERMAN, M. H., "Peripheral Cues and the Invisible Countertransference," *Amer. J. Psychother.*, to be published.

12. WEAKLAND, J., "The 'Double-Bind' Hypothesis of Schizophrenia and Three-Party Interaction," in Jackson, D. D. (ed.) *The Etiology of Schizophrenia*, Basic Books, 1960, pp. 373–388.

17

Convergent Internal Security Systems—A Rationale for Marital Therapy

SHELDON H. KARDENER, M.D.

INTRODUCTION

The purpose of this paper is to emphasize a theoretical frame of reference within which interventions may be made in the treatment of couples. The purpose of any such system is to facilitate active participation on the part of the patients in the process of understanding what their behavior or symptom means, what purpose it is designed to serve, why it was once important, and how it may no longer be adaptive. With such an understanding, choices can be conceived and options exercised by the couple which previously had not been considered possible.

DESCRIPTION

Man is, if nothing else, a social being who seeks fulfillment within a field of human relatedness. The concept of an "independent adult" should be replaced by, and understood as, the desire for a state of mature dependence. This is a condition of being wherein mutually growth-enhancing interpersonal interactions occur. It differs from a state of immature dependence, existing normally only when we are very small children; the infantalization of one or both partners is antithetical to growth enhancement.

279

However, we all start off in the immature dependent state with our parents—and therein lies the rub! The nature of relating becomes learned by the way those significant adults interact with each other and with important others. The child is, in a sense, an understudy in the drama of human intercourse portrayed by a man and a woman who simultaneously define by their behavior the roles of man-husband-father and woman-wife-mother.

This parental home scene becomes a valued and needed system which, when operant, creates the only sense of security and assurance for survival the child knows. An all or none mode exists, and options are non-existent. This need system becomes incorporated within the child part of the self and serves as the basis for an emotional criteria which defines home and family. It is the internal security system which becomes sought after in the face of change or decision making in order to reestablish a sense of status quo.

Simultaneously, within the growing adult part of the self, there develops a conscious awareness of what the individual wants in a mutual adult relationship. This may be defined by either emulating a good parental relationship, or by cultural standards and mores, or by peer and others' examples of behavior. We all want good healthy, growth-enhancing relationships—we all need a sense of security. When what one wants as an adult is compatible with what one emotionally needed as a child, one can operate on "automatic Pilot" in the selection of a mate.

However, when what one wants is discordant with the internal security system, a remarkable skill develops in selecting mates who fulfill the criteria of the once survival-imbued internal security system—no matter how distressing the outcome. Beyond our conscious awareness and based probably largely on non-verbal communication, we carefully screen potential partners who, by their own familiarity with the old roles, provide exactly what is needed to restage the old parental play. "Be it ever so miserable, there is no place like home."

This helps to explain why it is that partners who divorce often turn right around and marry either exactly the same kind of person they divorced, or someone who superficially seems to be just the opposite, ending up with a repetition of the same nature of relatedness as that which they don't want. Underlying this behavior is the fulfillment of the needs of their internal security system. A word about opposites is in order. To the extent an individual is repelled by the roles portrayed by the parents, but nonetheless feels totally dependent upon them, an emotional dilemma of needing what is not wanted develops. An individual tricks himself into feeling the resolution of that dilemma follows if he behaves "just the opposite," or selects a mate who seems just the opposite of the heterosexual parental model. But, just as mirror images are the identical though opposite images, so too does the relationship end up, for all its oppositeness, identical in the nature of relatedness.

It follows too that the old adage "opposites attract" is a more superficial commentary whereas "birds of a feather flock together" describes more accurately the process of mate selection. This phenomena of sameness is, however, a mixed blessing. The hope is that a mate who so clearly can appreciate exactly what it was like to be a child growing up within the parental home, would share the desire to prevent the repetition of those behaviors adjudged bad and growth inhibiting. This is a realistic hope and provides therapeutic leverage in helping to define reasonable goals in treatment. However, the couples must be helped through awareness to understand that they also share a mutual need to keep things just as the parents had done in order to gratify their internal security system. To do otherwise would break with precedent and follow an uncharted course with which they have no experience, a frightening prospect indeed when viewed from the perspective of the child within the adult.

In a troubled marriage that has lasted any length of time, it follows that each partner is equally responsible for actively working at keeping the marriage miserable. It should be amply clear at this point that the goal striven for is not misery, but security. This is a security based upon the childlike (never childish) perception that there are no alternatives. The misery, pain, and unhappiness simply become the unfortunate price to be paid, as in childhood, to gain some semblance of safety in a relationship. Those feelings also serve as signals to the child within the adult, that he is indeed home. We can, on this basis, put to rest such biologically and psychologically unreasonable concepts as finding pleasure in receiving or giving pain. It is a concept which, masquerading under the rubric of sado-masochistic relationships, has clouded our understanding of, and appreciation for, the desperate, albeit paradoxical, search for a familiar sense of internal security. Also put to rest should be such concepts as a person not wanting to get well or foolishly making repetitive mistakes. These are statements viewed from only an adult perspective which totally ignores the motivating emotional force stemming from the child's perspective. It is after all the very nature of this latter perspective that dictates that no options are available.

The role of the therapist becomes one of helping the adult part of each partner in a marriage to recognize what the child part unnegotiably demands in order to feel secure; and to emphatically acknowledge that at one time such had to be the case; and, most importantly, acknowledge that while options then were absent, it is not so now. Following the clear identification of the mutual, child-like, internal security systems, and elucidating their origin in the behavior patterns of each respective parental pair, treatment then consists of exploring and encouraging the exercise of options now available to the adults. Initially, also, the therapist must be prepared to reinterpret the reemergence of the former diadic interaction. After all, not only was the method of interacting imbued with security needs, it also is the most familiar way of relating. As the couple understands this and gains experience and comfort with behaving differently, they can themselves take over the role of the therapist in guarding against the children within from interfering with the emerging adults.

CLINICAL ILLUSTRATIONS

Mr. and Mrs. A.

Mr. A., now 30 years old, grew up in a family where, when he was two years old, his real father disappeared and was replaced two years later by a passive, compliant, opinionless stepfather whose only expression of unique individuality occurred when he played golf by himself. The mother seemingly dominated the home and made all the decisions. The real father was never discussed. Mr. A. began to develop the feeling that men seemed superfluous in a relationship with a competent, aggressive woman. The stepfather, by his behavior, did nothing to counter the boy's feelings which only lent support to a deeper, frightening fantasy that his real father must have been destroyed by such a woman.

He grew up with the unconscious resolution that the way to appear as a strong, capable, viable man in a relationship was simply to choose a "safe" wife, and this he did. His first wife was both intellectually and culturally inadequate. She was raised in an environment that dictated complete subservience to the man, and she barely graduated last in her high school class. When he graduated college, he found that the marriage was a dull and unrewarding drag and that they shared nothing in common. He wondered why he ever married such a girl for she was not at all what he wanted. Their first and only child was two years old when Mr. A left his wife, and she then filed for divorce after four years of marriage. Two years later, he found the "right girl": a young lady who had graduated college, shared his political, cultural, and ethical values, and who seemed capable and competent. Unbeknownst to the young man and woman, the little girl within her and the little boy within him had sized each other up through whatever verbal and non-verbal cueing existed, and found they shared the same internal security system values. The adults had already decided they shared the same wants in a relationship. The only problem, which became evident five years later when their first and only child was two years old, was that these systems which matched each other were mutually discordant.

Mrs. A. was the only child of a couple who, when she was about two years of age, began to have severe financial difficulty. The mother had to go to work and constantly blamed the father for the family's insecurity. She would nag him to action on the one hand but berate, belittle, and predict doom for any action he then half-heartedly undertook. Mrs. A. felt her mother was a "destructive bitch" who never gave her father a chance, and, although pitying father, she despised him for his weakness in not confronting mother. Instead, he would either run off to the golf course or bury himself in reading a pile of newspapers to escape her attacks. She resolved she would never be like her mother and would never marry a weak, passive, insecure man. However, her sense of internal security dictated that the only home possible was one in which the woman "took over" in a way that rendered the man useless and superfluous.

Her husband, as already described, basically felt useless and superfluous by the role model his parents' behavior set—for which he had compensated by avoiding a relationship with a capable, competent woman. Once they were married, the wife absorbed any and all blame for faults or problems in their life situation. She abandoned any plans for graduate school and, although funds were needed, was unable to bring herself to get a job. She steadily became more and more dependent upon him. When he became aware of how little she was using her capabilities, he would constantly cajole her to function at her real level, but would either absent himself from the house when she did (often to go play golf) or undercut what she did. One of his suggestions was for her to go to a sensitivity training course. As a result, she became aware of how "he was keeping me from growing." What she was not then aware of, however, was how much she needed him to do so in order for her not to become a "bitch" (i.e., competent, capable, aggressive) who would destroy him.

The couple came to therapy only after they had started filing for divorce, and she was living in her own apartment. Although the rationalization of his growth-inhibiting function was initially given as the reason for her move, that proved only a superficial reason. The additional factor was that she left in the same shared belief that to grow was to become a "bitch" and destroy him.

They functioned *as if* the only role choice possible in a marriage was for the woman to destroy the man by her capability to function autonomously. They thought they would counter this horrible, but necessary, criterion by doing just the opposite of their gender-linked parental patterns. It became a "teeter-totter" marriage in that the man was "up" and viable only so long as the woman was "down" and helpless. They had mutually tricked themselves into thinking their wants were fulfilled (i.e., a viable, strong, confident man in a relationship—"nothing like father"; a non-destructive woman—"nothing like mother") when actually they were satisfying their need to reestablish the same kind of hubsand-wife relationship that their parents had exemplified. The cruel hoax was that in a "teeter-totter" relationship, it does not really matter who is up or down, the paucity of mutual adult togetherness is the same.

Mr. and Mrs. E.

Mrs. E., a 24-year-old graduate student, married 11 months, presented with the onset of a moderately severe agitated depression following the successful completion of a research project. She complained that the symptom threatened to mar her first year of marriage. She had one prior episode one and one-half years earlier, also following the successful conclusion of her first year of graduate work, and at the time she started to go steadily with her future husband. At that time, she made a suicide gesture by taking a barbiturate overdose.

She is the third daughter of four children, born to an Eastern European Orthodox Catholic immigrant family. The only work the father was able to obtain was as a manual laborer which financially necessitated her mother's also going to work. Although verbally encouraging all of the children to go to college, there was a prevailing mood in the family that no matter what one ever did, things would always go badly. The patient's aunt (mother's youngest sister) was the only one in the family to get a higher education. The aunt was never able to accomplish anything in life because of recurrent depressions which often necessitated hospitalization and always disrupted the family. The patient's mother was (and is) involved in caring for this aunt and her family and would constantly lament as to what a waste the aunt's schooling efforts were, for they ended in no good result. This was added to her general complaints that things were never going to go right. Mrs. E. was the only child to go to college, which accomplishment was greeted by the family's saying that these days, that's not enough and graduate work was necessary. The patient's father, like her aunt's husband, portrayed the role of a long-suffering, helpless man who was trapped by circumstances he could only tolerate but never alter. The patient's suicide attempt was angrily greeted by the mother with "Next time you'd better do it right." Mrs. E. describes her siblings as all being very unhappy people who feel unfulfilled.

Mr. E. is the eldest of two boys in a lower middle class Jewish family. His father graduated from professional school during the depression and was only able to get a civil service clerical job which, however, he continued to maintain—without advancement. His mother had always wanted to go to professional school and continues to regret not being able to do so because of the paucity of funds. Mr. E. was very much aware of a feeling of inadequacy and uncertainty about himself, expressed by profound doubts that he could ever find anyone who would love someone as ugly and incapable as he felt himself to be. He concluded graduate work and now engages in scientific professional work, but always with the nagging feeling that he may fail at his endeavors. This is resolved by the conscious self-statement: "Oh well, I can always do something else if I fail." "Something else" was defined as that which would be at a lesser level of performance.

Mrs. E. bitterly berated herself for seemingly destroying her beautiful relationship with her husband which had been going so well for the prior 11 months. (Her mother had predicted the marriage wouldn't last a year because she had married out of her faith to a man who "obviously" was the cause of Mrs. E's original depressive episode.) Mrs. E. could not understand why she was putting her husband through such "hell," nor why he so patiently and, almost obsequiously, supported her. She felt there was no hope for her in that she was, and would only be, just like her aunt. Initial interviews were punctuated by her frequent statements, "what difference does it make," "nobody can help," or "can't you see I'm sick." She was upset when her husband's background was focused upon, saying, "He isn't the sick one, I am."

It was pointed out to them *both* that they were doing exactly what they felt they needed to do in order to negotiate their relationship about the mutually and once validly held mythology that a family is that close group of people who "always try harder"—as long as they carefully remained second! Security for Mrs. E. was to live up to the role model of the youngest female sibling in her mother's family, and have a long-suffering husband with whom she could establish the only kind of real relationship thought possible as mutually modeled by their seemingly very different parental pairs. Even if the mortar of the relationship had to be misery and chronic failure, it became a cheap price to pay if indeed the alternative were no relationship at all. They could begin to sense how they both—she, by active symptomatology and he, by passive compliance—were busily engaged in fulfilling their needed, albeit worst, expectations—all as though there were still no options.

CONCLUSION

The family has long been recognized as that least divisible social unit necessary for the transmission of cultural values from one generation to the next. It is in a sense the social chromosome by which individual, familial, and cultural identity is "inherited" by the offspring. To the extent that identity is a meaningful, adaptive, positive one, the process of "psychological intermarriage" intensifies and reenforces such traits. Security and a sense of well being stem from a couple's ability to recreate such a home. Paradoxically, but reasonably so, the same "psychogenetic" process occurs—for the same desired purpose—when the identity is a maladaptive, negative one. Common to both is the desire to achieve a sense of internal security by fulfilling those needs which once characterized the only nature of relating existent.

This absolutely remarkable capacity by which couples "find each other" and intricately interact in order to reestablish a home and family just like the parental one they each left, is explored as a rationale for marital therapy. It becomes an exciting therapeutic interaction when the couple can explore together their internal security systems. This permits them to recognize how they mutually contribute an interdigitating part to fulfilling old needs learned from childhood, even if the outcome is no longer that which is wanted in a relationship. The couple incorporates the role of the therapist in helping each other avoid returning to old ways of relating by understanding their needs once fulfilled by these roles. They can then exercise new options neither of them previously felt were possible.

REFERENCES

1. BERNE, E., *Principles of Group Treatment,* Oxford University Press, New York, 1966.
2. FAIRBAIRN, W. R. D., *An Object-Relations Theory of the Personality,* Basic Books, New York, 1954.
3. KARDENER, S. H., "The Family: Structure, Patterns, and Therapy," *Ment. Hyg.,* 52 (4), 524–531, 1968.
4. KARDINER, A., KARUSH, A. and OVESEY, L., "A Methodological Study of Freudian Theory," *Int. J. Psychiat.,* 2, 489–544, 1966. Reprinted from *J. Nerv. Ment. Dis.,* 129, 1959.

Part Two

RESEARCH

EDITOR'S INTRODUCTION

Research in the area of family behavior, family development, and family change presents some extraordinary hardships. Here, our expertise is limited. We are still far from being able to conceptualize the breadth, depth, and complexity of the challenge of research on the human family. The most we can do at this stage is pose some relevant questions and identify particular difficulties.

What kinds of investigation of family dynamics do we dignify with the term "research"? The closer we come to the essence of family relationship processes, the less sure we are as to how to study them. The more we learn, the sharper is the conviction that research on family life calls urgently for new approaches, for the discovery of a whole new set of research principles and methodologies appropriate to the unique character of this challenge. In all research, the nature of the problem predetermines the method of study and the search for a solution. Since the family phenomenon is, in fact, a slice of life, the question is how we research a piece of living experience.

Under the rubric of family research, do we embrace descriptive methods of study—"naturalistic observation," or do we confine the category to what is called "systematic research"? And if the latter, do we restrict ourselves to vigorous experimental design and quantitative studies? What do we include and what do we exclude in the connotation of the word "research"?

Studies of behavior are influenced by a hereditary tradition concerning the standards of research in the physical sciences. Investigation of physical events identifies dependent and interdependent variables. The constancy of one variable is preserved while we observe the effect of altering another. The model is that of careful, precise, experimental design with the establishment of reliable controls. There is the further criterion of replication of the findings. Across the years these standards became deeply entrenched. In gradual stages, however, as the understanding of scientific method grew, we interpreted their meaning in a more flexible, creative manner. Even in the physical sciences there is a discernible shift of emphasis to relationship processes and to system properties.

The very nature of the family phenomenon necessitates a study design which gives full respect to dynamic relationships, systems theory, and ecological context. It is not possible to experiment with family dynamics in the way we do with physical processes. Precise controls cannot be established. One is unable to reproduce, in any exact way, a single family experience; for instance, the death of a parent. "Hard data" are difficult to come by in this field. It seems important in this context to distinguish between what is scientific and what is merely scientistic. The first priority is to understand the nature of the problem; the question of one or another method of study, important in its own right, is nonetheless secondary. A whole range of methods of study can be molded to fit the requirements of a particular problem. For physical events, biological events, and for social and psychological events, the standards of scientific investigation must necessarily be different.

In the area of family behavior, the more we narrow the field of investigation, the more precise are the findings, but often at a great cost. We court the danger of excluding too much of the essence and thus twisting the problem we are examining. On the other hand, the broader the study and the more we encompass within it, the less quantitative are the findings. The one thing we cannot afford to do is tailor the family phenomenon to what we can easily measure by conventional methodologies. There is always the risk of measuring wrong events, insignificant events, or somehow arbitrarily perverting the problem to fit it to a given methodology. It is the sad truth that we have a plethora of published statistical studies which, at the least, are trivial and, at the most, misleading. Often the problems that are easily examined are the less important ones. By contrast, the crucial problems are, by their very nature, complex and difficult subjects of research.

Thus, there are many questions: (1) what problems should be studied; (2) by what means; (3) how do we conceptualize the relations between problem and method, between the observed and the observer; (4) how do we interpret the findings? Here many factors come into play: questions of bias, context, the influence of preconceived ideas, the idiosyncratic slant of different classes and cultures. Consider, for example, the challenge of doing research on the results of family psychotherapy. We do not yet know how to approach the problem. Past efforts to do research on the effects of other forms of psychotherapy have failed ignominiously. How should we conceptualize the task of studying the outcome of family treatment?

It seems clear that we cannot apply old methodologies to new problems. There are the special difficulties of attempting to study family behavior with contrived situations as against following the model of an experiment in nature. There are the special complications of our conceptualization of the temporal factor, the examination of family dynamics in the here and now as against the emphasis on the past. There is the limitation imposed by our inability to replicate family experience. Finally, there is the interpretation of the role of the observer; he not only affects the observed but becomes part of what he is himself investigating.

Admitting all this, the prospects are not really as dim as they first appear. There is, in fact, reason for hope and cheer. In this field, more and more, we are discovering new, imaginative principles of investigation. We are inventing a whole new set of methods of research appropriate to the nature of the problem. Among these, we are discovering new dimensions of descriptive study, we are learning to capitalize on a wide range of "experiments in nature," and we are becoming more adept at the applications of systems theory to the special problems of family interaction.

18

Methodological Issues in Family Development Research

REUBEN HILL, PH.D.

M ANY OF THE problems of method and technique encountered by researchers attempting to study families developmentally stem from the primitive state of the conceptual frame of reference in use and still others from the special requirements of the longitudinal method of data collection which has been linked to the developmental approach to family study. I have accordingly organized my presentation around these two axes beginning with a description of the family development frame of reference and the problems involved in operationalizing its chief concepts, followed by a delineation of the research situation of researcher and cooperating families in longitudinal studies, and I will conclude with a listing of some of the solutions which have been devised in recent years.

THE CONCEPTUAL FRAMEWORK OF FAMILY DEVELOPMENT

The developmental approach is the youngest of seven conceptual frameworks used in family study identified by Hill and associates (13) through their Inventory of Research in Marriage and Family Behavior from the content analysis of several hundred pieces of research on marriage and the family published in America during the past 30 years. The analysis included search for the key concepts used, the foci peculiar to the approach and the definitions of the family implied (if not explicitly given) by those using the approach. A recent article (14) describes in some detail five of these frameworks, their properties and the assumptions on which they have been built. A basic shortcoming of all of the frameworks analyzed to date, except the developmental, has been their failure to cope systematically with the social time dimension. Where process concepts dealing with the dynamics of change were utilized, they failed to specify time in units appropriate to families and therefore had limited value in assembling generalizations about family change. This is not surprising since with the exception of the developmental framework each of the approaches originated in domains of social science other than family sociology: (1) The institutional, the structure-function, and the situational approaches developed out of the effort to understand society and culture; (2) The learning-theory and the psychological habitat frameworks both developed out of the study of personality development; (3) The symbolic-interactional approach similarly was organized to cope with issues of the development of personality, primarily with the processes in the growth of "self" and the phenomenon of socialization; it was only years later that this approach was adopted for the study of the family; finally (4) The household-economics approach originated in the analogy of the household as an economic firm and still uses many of the concepts of management and of the economics of consumption in its balance sheet approach to family living—it is quite marginal to family study because of its almost complete lack of concepts of family organization. The family-development approach is the only framework which has been formulated from its beginning by students of the family with the conceptual demands of family research in the forefront of concern.

Properties of the Family Developmental Approach

The family-development approach emphasizes the time dimension neglected by the other conceptual frameworks dealing with the family but its focus is on the family as a small group association, the nuclear family occupying a common household. The time units employed encompass the family life span expressed in stages of development but subdivided into years of marriage.

The approach is eclectic in its incorporation of the compatible sections of several other approaches to the study of the family. From rural sociologists, it has borrowed the concept of stages of the family life cycle. From child psychology and human development have come the concepts of developmental needs and tasks. From the sociologists engaged in work on the sociology of the professions have been borrowed the concept of career as a series of role sequences and the view of the family as a convergence of intercontingent careers of husband and wife, later of children. From the structure-function and interactional schools have been borrowed the trio of concepts: position, role and norms, particularly as these involve age and sex roles, and plurality patterns. The many concepts associated with the family as a system of interacting personalities find their place in the modifications of the concept of role seen in role playing, role taking, reciprocity of roles, and role differentiation. These several concepts are assembled together in a frame of reference that furnishes an opportunity for accretion of generalizations about the internal development of families from their formation in the engagement and wedding to their dissolution in divorce or death. I have elsewhere attempted to state the scope and organization of this framework succinctly:

> The family development approach views the family as a small group system, intricately organized internally into paired positions of husband-father, wife-mother, son-brother, and daughter-sister. Norms prescribing the appropriate role behavior for each of these positions specify how reciprocal relations are *to* be maintained, as well as how role behavior may change with changing ages of the occupants of these positions. This intimate small group has a predictable natural history, designated by stages beginning with the simple husband-wife pair and becoming more and more complex as members are added, with the number of interpersonal relations reaching a peak with the birth of the last child, stabilizing for a brief period, to become less and less complex subsequently with the launching of adult children into jobs and marriage as the group contracts in size once again to the dyadic interactions of the husband-wife pair. As the age composition of the family changes, so do the age-role expectations for occupants of the positions in the family, and so does the quality of interaction among family members.
>
> Viewed social psychologically and developmentally, the family is an arena of interacting personalities, each striving to obtain the satisfaction of his desires. Parents often defer the satisfaction of their own immediate needs, however, in buliding complementary roles be-

tween themselves and their children. At some stages of development, parents and children are good company; at other stages, their diverse developmental strivings may be strikingly incompatible.

There can be identified by the use of these concepts, several stages of the family life cycle, each with its own peculiar sources of conflict and solidarity. Each of these stages may be seen in three dimensions of increasing complexity: (1) the changing developmental tasks and role expectations of the children as they age; (2) the changing developmental tasks and role expectations of the parents (largely complementary), in their capacities as providers, homemakers, spouses and parents; and (3) the developmental tasks of the *family as family*, which flow from the cultural imperatives laid upon it at each stage of growth, and the implications for the family of the personal developmental requirements of each child and adult. (12)[1]

Emphasis and Scope

Family development studies at the descriptive level place their emphasis less on *what* the behavior is than on *when* it occurs, more on the timing and sequences of family behavior than on the content of behavior alone. The charge is to discover what behaviors can be expected to change predictably over the natural history of families as against behaviors which are more or less constant, or which are adventitious and/or situational.

At the analytic level we go beyond the explanation of family behavior as a function of family characteristics to specify the relative contribution of developmental time to the formula of explanation. When the stages of family development have been sufficiently refined by hundreds of descriptive studies we should be able to pose and answer the question: Can a family's behavior be predicted by knowing its

---

[1] It is sometimes easier to conceptualize the first two of these dimensions; namely, the regularities in changing expectations for children and for parents which derive directly from age norms and their reciprocities, than to perceive the third dimension of imperatives for families as families. Let me illustrate somewhat concretely: Coping with the demands of the community and of family members, families develop policies that not only help in making choices in the present, but give direction and structure to the future. As the family develops in stature and competence from wedding date onward, it builds a history of problem solutions, a pattern of decision-making, and a set of rudimentary family policies by which choices can be made involving children and the family's future and by which actions can be judged. These policies, moreover, include the family's time schedule for reaching important goals and objectives—owning a home, completing the family, launching children into jobs and marriage, and retirement. These are the contents of the family culture with respect to timing and scheduling which, if we knew them, would make family behavior more or less predictable.

structural characteristics and the stage of development in which the family finds itself?

An immediate byproduct of this conceptual framework has been its sensitizing effect upon researchers utilizing the family as the unit of study. Any research which seeks to generalize about families without taking into account the variation due to the stages of family development represented in the sample will have tremendous variance unaccounted for, just as studies which ignore social class differences leave much unexplained. Buying patterns, saving patterns, and mobility patterns can be expected to vary greatly over the family life span, as will hundreds of other family behaviors as yet unassessed by family life cycle categories.

With this backdrop of the properties of the developmental approach and its emphasis and scope let us turn to the chief problems of method which need to be resolved if more theoretically relevant empirical research is to be carried out.

OPERATIONALIZING THE CONCEPTS OF THE APPROACH

The problem of operationalizing the concepts of the developmental framework is enormous since most of them are inferred rather than directly observed concepts. We must be content for the moment to name, describe, define and list our inferred concepts and seek more concrete observable concepts to stand as their indicators. An example of work undertaken of this order is found in the differentiating of stages of the family life span utilizing the basic developmental framework.

According to the developmental approach the quality of interaction over time would be best reflected by the combinations of role sequences occurring among the several positions within the family. At any given time the interactional pattern could be caught by analysis of the role clusters in each position in the family in reciprocity or in conflict with the role clusters in all other positions. This role content of the several positions in the family constitutes the *role complex* of the family at a given point in time. A stage of development would change, according to the framework, each time a fundamental change in the age role content in the positions making up the family occurs, or in other words each time the family's role complex changes.

Earlier work on differentiating stages of the family life cycle by empirically minded rural sociologists utilized very little theory in devising stages but worked rather from readily available demographic data about the changes in numbers in the family (plurality patterns), and changes in ages of children. It has been possible, however, to build on their empirical work, for example, to allow age composition to stand for the age-role content of the positions in the family and to utilize these data for differentiating stages of family development which have some theoretical relevance. Other data which are readily available include years married, birth of first and last child, and releasing of first and last child to jobs and marriage, which also suggest positional content for the family structure over time. The theoretically most sophisticated schemes for differentiating stages of the family life span today utilize three sets of data as indicators of change in the role complex:

A first criterion used for dividing up the life span is the observable "number of positions in the family" which permits inferring stages of "expansion", of "stability" and of "contraction" to be blocked off. Changes in stages of development (because fundamental changes in role complex occur) would be justified by the birth of the first child, launching of first child into marriage, and launching of last child.

A second criterion involves the age composition of the family which reflects indirectly the *family's complex of age role expectations in reciprocity* at any one time in the history of the family. To play fair with the conceptual framework a stage would be changed each time the role complex changed in any degree. If we were engaged in undertaking case studies of individual families this procedure would be most interesting to follow, but in seeking to differentiate stages of development for large numbers of families it would be highly impractical to designate a new stage each time the complex of age-role expectations changed since there would be almost as many different combinations of stages (family careers) as there are families in the study. Duvall (8), reflecting the judgments of the various committees working on the problem since 1948 chose a simpler solution to the problem in her text. She suggests that it is sufficient to change stages of development each time the oldest child shifts from one significant age category to another. Of all the children, to be sure, the oldest child's development is the most significant for the shift in role content in the parents' positions, since his experiences present new and different problems which as yet the family has not encountered and brings about the most modification of role content in all other positions in the family. The significant age categories in which changes would be expected to occur in our society include: infant, pre-school child, school child, adolescent and young adult.

A third criterion involves the change in the age-role content in the husband-father position which occurs with his retirement from active employment. For the mother who has not been gainfully employed her retirement from active mothering occurs with the launching of her last child into marriage and is captured in the shift in the family's role complex from the launching center to the postparental stage.

Employing these three sets of readily available data of numbers of positions in the family, age composition of the family and employment status of the father several stages of the family life span can be differentiated, each representing a distinctive role complex as follows: I Establishment (newly married, childless); II New parents (infant–3 years); III Preschool Family (child 3–6 years and possibly younger siblings); IV School Age Family (oldest child 6–12 years, possibly younger sibling); V Family with Adolescent (oldest 13–19, possible younger siblings); VI Family with Young Adult (oldest 20 until first child leaves home); VII Family as Launching Center (from departure of first to last child); VIII Postparental Family, The Middle Years (after children have left home until father retires); IX Aging Family (after retirement of father).

The scheme above has the advantages of simplicity, that it draws from data easily available, that it is relatively easy to code, that the number of categories is manageable statistically, and that it tends to be comparable from one study to another. The scheme also predicts quite well the timing of different kinds of family behaviors such as home ownership, purchase of automobiles, television sets and certain durable goods, changes in residence, and gainful employment of the mother (21). The scheme, however, has certain disadvantages. It masks the great variation among families in the middle stages of development and gives an illusion of smoothness of family development over time for all families, which empirical observations so far have failed to support (21). It is a true and accurate description of changes in role complexes of families with an only child, but it is not differentiating enough for families of various sizes and spacing of children.

Rodgers (21) has sought to improve on the Duvall scheme by shifting stages not only when the oldest child graduates from one significant age category to the next, but also when the youngest child makes these changes, increasing thereby for all families the number of possible stages to twenty-four, an unmanageable number to manipulate without more cases than the average research budget can afford to obtain. Making the much more rigorous test by applying his scheme of multiple stages to longitudinal rather than to cross-sectional data Rodgers demonstrates how heterogeneous are the middle stages identified by Duvall scheme. His data are drawn from the family composition histories of 300 families in the Twin Cities of Minneapolis-St. Paul, Minnesota consisting of a grandparent generation of 100 families, a parent generation of 100 families and a young married child generation of 100 families.

Using Roman numerals which correspond with Duvall's stages and adding subscripts for the modifications of these stages by the changes in role complex due to the youngest child changing age category, Rodgers provides a direct comparison year by year over the life span of the results using the two systems of classification. His youngest child designations are shown by the subscripts: a for infant; b, preschool child; c, school child; d, adolescent; e, young adult. As an example, Duvall's Stage V, Family with Adolescent has the following possibilities in Rodgers scheme: V Family with Adolescent (where only child is adolescent), Va Family with Adolescent (oldest is adolescent, youngest is infant), Vb Family with Adolescent (oldest adolescent, youngest preschool child), Vc Family with Adolescent (oldest adolescent, youngest school child), Vd Family with Adolescent (both oldest and youngest are adolescents). The differences between the two schemes are shown in Table I in the findings[2] for the 100 families of the grandparent generation over their life span as we move year by year from the first year of marriage to the last year.

Using Duvall's scheme of differentiating stages, the families make a nice movement from one category to the next right through the life span. At the beginning and at the end of the life span the two systems look the same but in the child rearing and launching years, the impression of homogeneity within the Duvall stages is rudely dispelled by taking into account role content changes with the youngest child's

---

[2] Rodgers arrived at his typical career progressions by defining as the "typical" category year by year that category in which 50% or more of the cases appeared, or if no category contained sufficient cases, then the categories with the most cases which together totalled 50% or more (for example in the 14th year of marriage, Va Adolescent Family with Infants, contained 36% of the cases and IVa—School Age Family with Infants contained 17%, permitting Rodgers to list both as typical of the 14th year of marriage of the grandparent generation).

TABLE I

Stages of Development Designated by Year of Marriage Utilizing Two Category Schemas from Longitudinal Data from 100 Families

Year of Marriage	Rodgers 24 Category Schema	Year of Marriage	Duvall's 9 Category Schema
Year 1	I	Year 1	I
Years 2–4	II	Years 2–4	II
Years 5–7	IIIa	Years 5–7	III
Year 8	IIIa, IVa	Years 8–13	IV
Year 9–13	IVa		
Year 14	IVa, Va	Years 14–20	V
Years 15–19	Va, Vc		
Year 20	Va, Vc, Vd		
Year 21	Vd, VIa, VIIa, VIIb, VIIc, VIId	Year 21	VI
Year 22	VIIa, VIIb, VIIc, VIId	Year 22–37	VII
Year 23–24	VIIa, VIIc, VIId		
Year 25	VIIb, VIIc, VIId		
Year 26–27	VIIb, VIIc		
Year 28	VIIc, VIId, VIIe		
Year 29–32	VIIc, VIId		
Year 33	VIIc, VIId, VIII		
Years 34–37	VIId, VIII		
Years 38–46	VIII	Years 38–46	VIII
Years 47–63	IX	Years 47–63	IX

development as Rodgers has done. Heterogeneity, or overlapping of stages, is especially apparent in the 21–25 years of marriage when parents are engaged not only in attending weddings of their oldest but are typically engaged also in rearing infants, preschoolers, school agers and adolescents. As late as the 24th year of marriage we have enough families engaged in caring for infants to be listed as a typical life cycle category in the Rodgers schema.

This analysis of longitudinal data suggests strongly that what we had earlier regarded as exceptional, namely the elongated spacing pattern which required parents to simultaneously address themselves to the cries of new infants and to arrangements for the weddings of their eldest, should not be treated as residual in the differentiating of life cycle stages as has been done in the past. Each of Rodger's typical career progressions promises subject matter for more detailed research to specify the similarities and differences in role sequences and of role complexes as these several age and spacing combinations are followed over time.

PROBLEMS AND COSTS OF THE LONGITUDINAL

To take full advantage of the conceptual framework of family development practically dictates a system of longitudinal data collection and analysis. But following couples from engagement period of wedding through their family life span to the dissolution of the family is fraught with many practical difficulties, not the least of which includes the possibility that the researcher won't live to see his project completed. There are the difficulties of sampling, of securing the couples' cooperation and commitment over such a long time period, of maintaining contact with the families for a long time, of committing oneself to a study of the necessary duration, and the many other organization and personal changes that lessen the chances of research continuity (15). There are the very real problems of morale maintenance as families tire of being studied and more seriously the possible effects on the families of being trained to be more planful, or more permissive with children, as a consequence of the questions asked until they no longer represent the population from which they were originally drawn. Researchers who have had the most experience in the past with this method are to be found in the fields of child development and public health where in recent years the costs of operating longitudinal studies have been carefully surveyed (18). Baldwin (1) makes a number of cogent points which might be applied to the use of the longitudinal study in family development without too much difficulty:

> Longitudinal studies, as they were originally conceived, seemed to have gambled on the existence of clear developmental trends that would shine through the welter of influence of uncontrolled events. In physical growth the gamble paid off quite well. Many measures of physical growth are relatively uninfluenced by the disturbances found in the normal life of the child . . .
>
> The most serious technical problem is the real inability to control the environment of a child over any reasonably long period . . . We must be content with very inadequate controls over the events in the child's life . . .
>
> When the interest of child development research shifted from the study of maturational process to the study of the effect of early childhood experiences, the famous longitudinal studies were caught in mid-stream. They were committed to a research design that involved the careful periodic description of a relatively unselected group of children from birth onward. The design was a reasonable

one for the purposes that guided its inception, but for the investigation of the effects of early childhood experiences it was not so well selected...

It should be apparent that a longitudinal study of the effects of one, two or three variables of childhood experience upon later personality is a big investment for relatively small return—quantitatively speaking. It behooves us, therefore, to precede such an undertaking with careful pretesting, study of cross-sectional differences, and cruder retrospective studies to establish the likelihood of major effects. *A longitudinal study is the last, not the first step in a research program. It is an absolutely essential research method if we are to get firm knowledge of psychological change, but paradoxically it is to be avoided whenever possible.* (Italics mine)

In family study the same unvoiced assumption is made that developmental trends will show through the mass of uncontrolled influences and it is only in the short run compromises on the longitudinal method that attempts have been made to control the events impinging on the family over time. Yet the major objection to the longitudinal method in family study has been the financial and organizational cost and awkwardness rather than the looseness of research design intrinsic in the method. This will be clearer as we examine the devices that have been developed to circumvent the disadvantages of the full application of the longitudinal method in family research.

ALTERNATIVES TO THE LONGITUDINAL METHOD

Alternatives to the longitudinal study in dealing with the time dimension are compromises of variable validity. Five are sufficiently differentiated to justify our attention; 1) the synthetic pattern of development constructed from cross-sectional data; 2) retrospective history taking; 3) segmented longitudinal study; 4) segmented longitudinal panels with controls; and 5) the intergenerational panel, combining retrospective histories (backward oriented) and panel interviews forward in time. Each of these several alternatives justifies individual attention since each seeks to minimize one or more of the enormous costs which one would have to pay if a truly longitudinal study were to be carried out.

Synthetic Patterns of Development from Cross-Sectional Data

This method is both the most frequent and the least defensible of the compromises in current use. A cross-section of the population is taken by sampling categories of "years married" and the data obtained on a given variable are treated as if they were longitudinal. For example, marital adjustment scores from cross-sectional samples have been used to advance the generalization that marital happiness declines over the life-span from the honeymoon through the childbearing and childrearing period to reach its lowest point when the children are adolescents and leave the home at which point the scores improve and remain higher than before on into old age (2, 3, 24). Each of these investigators was comparing couples of different durations of marriage but charting the results as if they were drawn from a cohort of married couples that had been followed over their family life span. Their work may be contrasted with that of Burgess and Wallin (4) which involves a truly longitudinal study of great cost which began with 1000 engaged couples and followed these with measures of their adjustment to each other in engagement, after three years of marriage, and again after 20 years of marriage. With three measures in time for every couple considerably firmer generalizations may be made. For most couples disillusionment between engagement and the third year of marriage was not characteristic but subsequent disenchantment during the childbearing and childrearing years is reported (20).

Cross-sectional studies are suggestive of hypotheses as to what is happening over time as couples age but may provide erroneous generalizations since they do not control for generational differences in value orientations and styles of life which have been influenced by historical circumstances. Take for example, the impressions one would get from cross-sectional data with respect to gainful employment of wife over the life cycle compared with longitudinal data on this question (17). The rapidity of social change has so effected behavior that the three generations reflected in cross-sectional data mask the tremendous changes that have occurred when each generation is studied longitudinally. Viewed cross-sectionally, wives begin the marriage with a majority in the labor force and the proportions employed declines to about one third during the child bearing years, turning up only slightly with the entering of the youngest children in school to drop off sharply in the later years to less than 20 percent gainfully employed.

Separating the three generations from each other and following each cohort longitudinally quite different generalizations can be made. Only 5% of the wives in the grandparent generation began marriage in the labor force and the number increased slowly from the second year of marriage to the 20th year when it was still less than 10%, rising sharply during the next decade to 20% employed where it remained for the balance of the life span. The parent generation begins marriage with 20% employed and drops progressively to less than 10% in the 5th year of marriage when the proportion employed climbs steadily and sharply to 60% employed in the 3rd decade of marriage and drops to 40% in the 4th decade. The married child generation begins marriage with 62% of wives employed dropping to 28% in the 5th year and returning to 40% in the 6–10 year period.

From the longitudinal data it is possible to see that in each successive generation more of the wives have worked during the first several years of marriage, and more have returned to work as their children grew up. Similar accelerations appear in the acquisition of homes, and in the acquisition of durable goods which are completely masked in synthesizing the life cycle through cross-sectional samples of years-married categories.

The cross-sectional study avoids many of the costs of the truly longitudinal study in the ease of sampling, of securing cooperation for only one interview and of manageability in analysis. Attrition and non-response problems are minimized. A poorly designed cross-sectional study can be interrupted and redesigned but the longitudinal study, once underway becomes difficult to change if the data are to be comparable from one wave of measurement to the next. Nevertheless, the synthetic pattern of development built from cross-sectional data can rarely be more than suggestive of developmental patterns—it is a poor substitute for the more costly longitudinal study.

Retrospective History Taking

This is a method for manipulating the time machine backward in time through the device of recall by the respondent. If the study is to cover the entire span of development, the informants will be in their sixties and seventies and not the most trustworthy of collaborators. Certain behaviors simply may not be successfully elicited back in time for such respondents: marital happiness, marital communication, value consensus, authority patterns and allocation of roles, parent-child and sibling-sibling relationships. On the other hand, from our Minnesota study, we have found residential histories, job histories, automobile and durable goods purchases, and family composition histories not impossible to obtain from our most aged respondents. When checked with the testimony of generations of the same line, the histories by the grandparents appeared substantially accurate.

To my knowledge there has been nothing comparable in family development to the study by Jayaswal and Stott (16) comparing the results of retrospective histories and longitudinal records on personality characteristics of children. They found high correspondence between the descriptions of their own personalities as children by adults now parents, with the descriptions by the aged parents of these adults when they were children. But they found little or no correspondence between the descriptions recorded for these children when at Merrill-Palmer as nursery school children based on what their parents and their teachers said about them and the present-day descriptions on which there is such high consensus between the two generations 20–25 years later. Do families construct myths slowly over time in the process of helping children develop identities on which there develops high consensus between parents and children? Is there likelihood of running into such distortions in using retrospective histories for longitudinal data in certain areas of family life?

An advantage of the method of retrospective history taking over some of the other compromises we will describe is that the data are not wedded to the stages of development established *a priori* by the researcher and so may be altered from analysis of the historical data obtained to discover new points of significant change in family development. It is also a relatively inexpensive way of operating the time machine since years and decades may be covered in a two-hour interview, but it does require families as respondents that are far enough along in the life span to have a history to record. Moreover, the method is limited to issues that can be studied in the past tense. Some of the most interesting variables involve data which should be carried forward in time; e.g., the spacing and controlling of fertility, or the creation of patterns for coping with children's needs in the absence of the mother in the labor force. The one variable has long run implications, the second may be studied in the short run, but both variables would be better suited to cohorts of young families moving forward in time than aged families reminiscing over the past.

Segmented Longitudinal Studies

In this category of solutions I place the many studies which deal with a segment of the family life span to test hypotheses about family change at selected points in developmental time. LeMasters (19) chose the interview and the retrospective method to test whether or not parenthood was a crisis for new parents. Goodrich (11) and his associates are moving forward rather than backward in time permitting them to determine a) whether or not pregnancy is a crisis (since they begin with newly married couples), b) whether or not the assumption of parental roles has an impact upon the husband-wife relationship, and c) whether there are basic changes in what I have termed the family role complex, with the separation of the preschool child from his mother in attending playschool. Note the wide range of methods of data collection employed by the Goodrich team, direct observation, interviews tests, and projectives. Gathering data at the rate this team is doing would soon inundate them and hamper later analysis if the study were to continue for the family's life span.

Other less dramatic examples of the segmented longitudinal study include several dealing with the later years of family development. Deutscher (6) selected couples shortly after their last child was married to discover retrospectively with them whether or not this was a critical period in their family development. Cumming and associates (5) have followed couples from the middle years into the aging years after the retirement of the breadwinners and have formulated from their data a theory of disengagement. Streib and Thompson (22) have added a contrast control group in comparing families of men who have retired (with before and after interviews) with those of the same age where the father continued to work, to arrive at generalizations about the impact of retirement upon a limited number of family and personal behaviors.

These studies have all employed the principles of the longitudinal method over short periods moving forward in time, as in the panel study, or backward in time by retrospective interviews. The losses due to attrition are less in these segmented longitudinal studies than in the long term type as are also the training effects from being studied over long periods of time. The returns contribute piecemeal to theories of the middle range about family development: indeed, this may be the way most of the hypotheses in family development will be tested in the near future, but many questions of theory can not be answered in this fashion. Do good parent-child relations in the adolescent years make for good relationships between middle aged parents and their married offspring as asserted by Dinkel (7) and questioned by Stryker (23)? Do families become more competent in dealing with critical situations over time? The questions of continuity and discontinuity of change in family development are also less likely to be adequately answered by these short-run longitudinal studies.

Segmented Longitudinal Panels with Controls

Ingenious and more promising than any of the other compromises I have listed to date is the design described by Feldman (10). When carried to its full term this approach could involve careful sampling of categories of the population according to the stage of family development in which they were located, undertaking interviews in two or more waves to capture the patterns characteristic of the stage of development in which they are presently located (in the first wave) then undertaking interviews in a second wave late enough so that many families would have changed stages. Those who have not changed would be treated as controls to be compared with the first set of families who have changed.

This design would be particularly useful for capturing changes in quality of interaction from the role complex of the childless companionate to the role complex of new parents (Feldman's current emphasis), from preschool to school age, from young adult to launching center, from launching center to postparental stage, and from postparental stage to aging family (after retirement of father). These are all stages in which developmental theory suggests some discontinuity in roles, and possibly sharp breaks in the role content of the positions in the family. By sampling families on the upper edge of each stage it should be possible to see enough of them make the shift during the study period to have enough *changers* to match with *nonchangers* to obtain excellent contrast data.

The design copes with the large issues of costs, of attrition, of tiring, of the so-called training effects of having been studied, better than the other compromises listed, but it depends heavily on the adequacy of the stage categories developed to date.

The intergenerational panel, combining retrospective histories, and panel interviews forward in time. This compromise on the longitudinal study was developed by Hill and Foote in 1958 for a study of changing patterns of family planning and decision-making where the focus was to be on long term financial planning and consumption (12). It was reasoned that attention to the careers of families up to the present (through retrospective interviews) and systematic recording of the planning and fulfillment of plans over a year's period (through waves of panel type interviews forward in time) would provide evidence of competence in planning and judgment in decision making (family consumership) of rare quality for family development.

An intergenerational sample of intact three-generation families representative of Minneapolis-St. Paul was selected despite the possibility of undue residential stability in such a sample. The advantages it offered for the family development framework were substantial. The population of families would be regionally homogeneous, largely urban, and intergenerationally linked, thus holding constant the variables of region, urbanity, and variations in private family culture. Moreover, it would offer depth historically and permit intergenerational comparisons in which continuity in the transmission of family culture could be noted. Such data permitted the researchers to take into account changes due to historical circumstances such as wars, depressions, and periods of inflation. Patterns of family spending and consumption change over time, partly because family members grow older and their needs change, and partly because historical circumstances shift. From intergenerational data it is possible to distinguish the continuities and changes that can be generalized as part of life cycle development from those that are adventitious or due to historical circumstances.

A sequential system of interviews in four waves, once every three months, enabled the interviewers to encompass a complete annual cycle, thus accounting for seasonal variations in routine. The repeated interviewing enabled the study to conform to the principles of a longitudinal study for the year of data gathering. To supplement this year's data with retrospective history taking, the study relied upon the respondents' memories and powers of verbalization, as assisted and checked by the testimony of prior and succeeding generations.

Interview content for successive waves of interviews divided in such a way that part was repeated at each wave and a part was different: The former dealt primarily with recent and immediately prospective purchase plans, or other changes in family status, and their fulfillment or modification, whereas the latter dealt with the intergenerational history of the family and its long-range financial goals and commitments. Thus in four waves a life cycle pattern for each family on residential mobility, family composition, occupational careers, and financial growth was obtained.

At each wave, expectations of purchases and any other changes in family status during the next three months were elicited and the extent of commitment to the proposed change probed. On the second and subsequent waves, changes in the family inventory and other areas being studied were noted and discrepancies between expectations and outcomes discussed. An account of the reasons for postponement, the change in importance now ascribed to the expected but postponed purchase or action, and the interplay of family members about the purchase (action) or failure to buy (act) was obtained. This concentration on *what happens between waves* distinguishes this longitudinal study of decision making from most panel studies, which merely observe changes in opinion on issues at different points in time or collect evidence of fulfillment or nonfulfillment of purchase plans at specified points in time. The advantage of taking soundings at different points of time is lost unless linkages of a process nature are made in between to account for change or non-change, wherever this is discrepant with expectations.

This fifth compromise on the truly longitudinal study happens to be one with which I am most familiar, and on which I have most information. It has many of the limitations of the truly longitudinal study in that there are potentially serious problems of attrition and training effects on the families being studied. By careful training of our interviewers we were able to keep attrition to an absolute minimum with only 28/1400 interviews lost from non-cooperation. The tests we used for capturing training effects did not reveal any evidence of interviewer impact in the decision making process, which may only mean, to be sure, that our tests were inadequate to capture the training effects.

The idea of studying a panel of families forward in time by means of waves of interviews evenly spaced has great merit but proved difficult to schedule in such a way that the time period between interviews was precisely the same for each family making it impossible to make many intra-wave comparisons. With a national panel following up on the Minnesota pilot study, a much larger staff has interviewed all families within a three week period to keep the distance between waves more uniform.

This intergenerational panel combining retrospective histories and panel interviews forward in time has many advantages over the truly longitudinal study with only a few of its disadvantages. It is, however, more costly than the other compromises listed. It elicits data which can test the categories of family development since it is not dependent *a priori* on the adequacy of the stages already identified; indeed

Rodgers' work (21) on developing new categories has been drawn from the Minnesota data. It avoids the organizational problems of the lifetime longitudinal study and successfully deals with the issues of attrition and possible training effects. By joining the theoretical interest of sociology in family development with its methodological interest in intergenerational comparisons, this design provides a device for obtaining the benefits of longitudinal study without having to follow families for thirty years. By comparing generations of the same lineal families over their histories from marriage to the present, and by observing their behavior over a twelve month period, an effective compromise or synthesis of the several considerations in longitudinal study has been at least partially achieved.

DO SIMULATION MODELS OFFER PROMISE?

In closing this piece I would like to raise the question for those familiar with the capacities of the digital computers about the feasibility of speeding up family development by computer simulating programs. I have in this piece maligned the propensity of colleagues to treat cross-sectional data as if they were longitudinal, but the associations between variables pointed up by cross-sectional data when ranged by years married (even if fictitious) might be utilized in programming a simulated family life span for a cohort of married couples to discover why and where the data are distorting of longitudinal patterns observed from the more time consuming longitudinal studies that have been completed. Similarly the simulation model lends itself, it would seem to me, to manipulation by altering the revenue of families, simulating thereby changes in economic conditions such as occur in recessions, and/or modifying the spacing patterns of births to discover what effects these would have on homogeneity and heterogeneity of stages of development.

Would simulation models be useful in throwing light on changing vulnerability to divorce by years married and age composition of the family, on the phenomenon of disillusionment and disenchantment with marriage over the childbearing and child rearing periods with the honeymoon-like increase in good relations in the postparental period, or throw light on the declining power of the father in decision-making over the family's life span (suggested by cross-sectional studies but not yet tested by longitudinal research), or enable us to understand better family performance variables such as residential mobility, financial growth, and acquisition of durable goods over the family's life span?

At the present date we know better what factors are statistically associated with each of these dependent variables than we know dynamically how these factors change in their explanatory power over the family's many stages of development. It is problems of this order to which we must turn if the promise of family development as a theoretical development in sociology and social psychology is to be realized.

REFERENCES

1. BALDWIN, A. L., "The Study of Child Behavior and Development" in P. Mussen (Ed.), *Handbook of Research Methods in Child Development*, New York, Wiley, 1960.
2. BLOOD, R. O., JR. and WOLFE, D. M., *Husbands and Wives*, Glencoe, Illinois, Free Press, 1960.
3. BOWERMAN, C. E., "Adjustment in Marriage," *Sociol. Soc. Res.*, 41, 257–263, 1957.
4. BURGESS, E. W. and WALLIN, P., *Engagement and Marriage*, Philadelphia, Lippincott, 1953.
5. CUMMING, E., DEAN, L. R., NEWELL, D. S. and McCAFFREY, I., "Disengagement—A Tentative Theory of Aging," *Sociometry*, 23, 23–25, 1960.
6. DEUTSCHER, I., *Married Life in the Middle Years*, Kansas City, Community Service, 1959.
7. DINKEL, R., "Parent-Child Conflict in Minesota Families," *Am. Soc. Rev.*, 8, 412–419, 1943.
8. DUVALL, E. M., *Family Development*, Chicago, Lippincott, 1957, rev. ed., 1962.
9. DUVALL, E. M. and HILL, R. (Eds.), *Dynamics of Family Interaction*, New York, National Conference on Family Life, 1948.
10. FELDMAN, H. and MEYEROWITZ, J. H., "The Personal Relations of Primiparous Couples," unpublished paper, September, 1962.
11. GOODRICH, W., "Developmental Patterns in the Infant and in the Young Family," Bethesda, Maryland: National Institute of Mental Health, 1961, mimeo.
12. HILL, R., "Patterns of Decision-Making and the Accumulation of Family Assets" in N. Foote (Ed.), *Household Decision-Making*, New York, New York Univ. Press, 1961.
13. HILL, R., KATZ, A. M. and SIMPSON, R., "An Inventory of Research in Marriage and Family Behavior," *Marriage Fam. Liv.*, 19, 89, 1957.

14. HILL, R. and HANSEN, D. A., "The Identification of Conceptual Frameworks Utilized in Family Study," *Marriage Fam. Liv.*, 22, 299–311, 1960.

15. HOFFMAN, L. W. and LIPPITT, R., "The Measurement of Family Life Variables" in P. Mussen (Ed.), *Handbook of Research Methods in Child Development*, New York, Wiley, 1960.

16. JAYASWAL, S. R. and STOTT, L. H., "Persistence and Change in Personality from Childhood to Adulthood," *Merrill-Palmer Quart.*, 47–56, Winter, 1955.

17. *Household Inventory Changes Among Three Generations of Minneapolis Families*, New York, Res. Serv., Marketing Serv., Gen. Elec. Co., 1962.

18. KODLIN, D. and THOMPSON, D. J., *An Appraisal of the Longitudinal Approach to Studies in Growth and Development*, Lafayette, Indiana, Soc. for Res. in Child Devel., 1958.

19. LeMASTERS, E. E., "Parenthood as Crisis," *Marriage Fam. Liv.*, 19, 352–355, 1957.

20. PINEO, P. C., "Disenchantment in the Later Years of Marriage," *Marriage Fam. Liv.*, 23, 3–11, 1961.

21. RODGERS, R. H., *Improvements in the Construction and Analysis of Family Life Cycle Categories*, Kalamazoo, Western Michigan Univ., 1962.

22. STREIB, G. F., "Family Patterns in Retirement," *J. Social Issues*, 14, 46–60, 1958.

23. STRYKER, S., "The Adjustment of Married Offspring to Their Parents," *Am. Soc. Rev.*, 20, 149–154, 1955.

24. TERMAN, L., *Psychological Factors in Marital Happiness*, New York, McGraw Hill, 1938.

19

The Patient's Family:
Research Methods

LESLIE Y. RABKIN, Ph.D.

THE FAMILY, as the chief agent of socialization, exerts its influence in myriad ways to make the child an extension of itself and of its cultural mileu. The extraordinary complexity of this interaction of child with family leaves great room for role confusion and distortion. And it is these distortions which we label as signs of mental illness.

Within the purview of the concern with family processes and mental illness there have been attempts to simplify the interactional nature of the family relationships and focus on but a single aspect of the child's inheritance. Researchers such as Kallman (52) and Slater (83), for example, have marshalled much evidence to bolster their belief that mental illness is primarily of biological origins, the genes transmitted through the parents being the cause of the child's emotional difficulties. A combination of the geneticists' intransigent theoretical views and Jackson's (50) incisive and critical reassessment of their evidence, has temporarily at least lessened the force of their argument.

The psychogenic notion of emotional and mental disorder, that early pernicious home experiences have a deep and lasting effect on the individual's psychological adjustment, postulates that there are family patterns of roles and behaviors which, presented by the parents and assimilated by the child, predispose him to one or another psychological disturbance. According to this point of view, it is the parents' attitudes and modes of behavior which are "inherited" by the child.

Much of the thinking about psychogenic causation has continued in the tradition of the early Freudian notions. Freud emphasized the etiological importance of specific parental behaviors (e.g., seduction, frustration) and stressed the psychological effects of these activities when they occurred at the earliest stages of the child's development. This "critical period" conception has led researchers to focus their attention on what will later be described as "trait" studies (87), attempts to correlate a specific parental attitude (e.g., overprotection, rejection) with a specific set of responses in the child (e.g., aggression, autism).

More sophisticated analyses have noted the insufficiency of a theory built on the notion of the "traumatic" event (49) and have pointed to two far more important etiological processes: (1) the chaining effect of these parental attitudes or "traits," interacting with the child's specific response pattern at different stages in the life cycle, and themselves changing as a result of both environmental and intrapsychic factors and the feedback their behavior elicits from the child, and (2) how the child himself perceives these attitudes and behaviors, what he is able to take in and respond to out of the countless stimulations presented by his parents. These kinds of interactive, dynamic formulations are a welcome and necessary move away from the earlier *tabula rasa* conceptions.

The history of our concern with the family of the psychiatric patient has been reviewed before (87). Such a history shows the cumulative influence of such fields as social work, child guidance, sociology and psychoanalysis in helping us move away from the 19th century organic conceptions of "insanity"—concepts which portrayed mental illness as the result of a hereditary taint, physical degeneracy, or the work of a parasitic infection, towards the psychological notions noted above.

There is little doubt that by the mid-twentieth century the notion that disturbed parent-child relationships was an important etiological element in all the emotional disorders, from schizophrenia to psychosomatic disturbance, has taken its place firmly beside the organic explanations. In addition, this psychological point of view has behind it 30 years of studies designed to delimit more clearly what are decisive elements in these relationships.

These innumerable studies have utilized a *pot-pourri* of methods and produced a varied group of findings—often contradictory. They have been essentially of two types: (1) those which seek to isolate some aspect of the parent's personality which is seen as the key pathogenic element in the parent-child relationship. These have been called "trait" studies (87), and have been in particular vogue since Frieda Fromm-Reichmann (31) coined the phrase "schizophrenogenic" mother; and, (2) those which see the *total* family unit as disturbed and attempt to describe the pathological patterns of interaction being developed within this small group, e.g., (59, 14, 1, 9).

The methods of examination have made use of every available psychological tool: (1) case history material; (2) psychological tests; (3) psychotherapy; (4) interviewing; (5) attitude scales and questionnaires and (6) observational methods. In surveying this jumble of material, one is struck by the wide range of methodological problems which appear, such as: inadequate or non-existent control groups, poor specification of such data as socioeconomic status, the use of unreliable and inappropriate instruments, and a particularly potent problem of experimenter bias.

Recent books and articles (77, 87, 63) have carefully examined much of the literature in the area of parent-child relationships in various psychiatric disorders and found it wanting. Sanua, focussing on the families of schizophrenics, culled nearly a hundred studies in this area and, after noting the deficiencies of most of these studies in dealing with such variables as ethnic group membership, social class, diagnostic category, age and sex, concluded:

> Although the evidence of the importance of family factors in the background of schizophrenics is quite compelling, the patterns of the home environments need to be more clearly defined and isolated from home patterns which lead to other types of psychoses, neurosis, and other antisocial behavior. (p. 265)

He found that many studies disregarded control groups, lumped both schizophrenic children and adults together, and made no attempt to use more parsimonious sociocultural explanations of their findings.

For example, two early and oft-quoted studies of the family of schizophrenics are those of Gerard and Siegal (33) and Tietze (90). In their interviews with schizophrenics and their families, Gerard and Siegal noted an extreme attachment to the mother, marked by an excessive babying, spoiling, and over-protectiveness. In 57% of the cases the schizophrenic was found to be the mother's favorite. Tietze, interviewing 25 mothers of schizophrenics, discovered that ten mothers overtly rejected their children, while the other 15 were also rejecting, albeit more subtly.

Sanua, submitting this data to closer scrutiny, found that nearly 70% of Gerard and Siegal's patients were of Jewish and Italian parenthood and came from lower and lower-middle class families, while 64% of Tietze's patients were Protestants of the professional and business classes. These differing social and ethnic backgrounds, Sanua feels, may explain the seeming contradiction between Gerard and Siegal's findings of overprotectiveness and Tietze's findings of rejection. He writes: "It would be expected that in Jewish and Italian families there would be more babying of children, while such practices may not be considered proper in Protestant families of higher classes." (p. 249) The overprotective Jewish mother has often been noted before. Wolfenstein (94), for example, writing of the Jewish mother of one of her adolescent patients, comments: "Mrs. S. continues to think of her adolescent son as a helpless infant who cannot be trusted to do anything for himself and who, if left to his own devices, will injure himself, probably irreparably." (p. 424)

Spiegel and Bell (87) set themselves a different task. They sought to examine the family of the psychiatric patient from many angles— as an etiological agent, the effect mental illness in one member of a family has on the other members, family-oriented treatment approaches, and the general nature of family pathology. Their analysis of some 85 studies of parent-child relationships in psychosis, neurosis, delinquency and behavior disorders, and psychosomatic conditions, led them to conclude:

> On the whole, the review of the trait studies produced the impression that none of the parental traits held up for investigation can be correlated with a distinct and predictable pathological outcome, and that, while they may constitute a necessary condition, they certainly do not constitute a sufficient condition for the appearance of a specific form of psychological disorder in the child. (p. 124)

They found, for example, that the concept of rejection is offered as a descriptive trait of the mothers of schizophrenics (75), the parents of neurotic children (13), the parents of delinquents (45), and the mothers of allergic children (66). The investigators were also struck by the methodological flaws in this array of studies—non-comparability of findings due to the use of different measures and populations, poorly delineated control groups, the haphazard choice for study of some partial relationship within the interdependent family group and, importantly, the lack of a coherent view of the family as a structural and functional unit.

McCord and McCord (63) focussed their attention on the problems of delinquency and psychopathy and extensively surveyed the literature on these subjects. They found that most authors agreed that these children had been rejected in childhood, had reacted with aggression, and displayed the so-called psychopathic syndrome: a lack of normal guilt feelings, impulsivity, pleasure-seeking, and an inability to relate to other people. However, in turning the causative tables upside down and posing the question, "Does rejection necessarily result in psychopathy?", they found such studies as that of Sears, Macoby and Levin (80) as evidence that rejection does not always increase aggression nor lead to delinquent and psychopathic behavior. Thus, beyond the vague and global notion of "rejection," there appeared no consistent pattern of parental traits which could be said to lead inevitably to aggressive outcomes.

These authors, as we have briefly noted, have made some telling general criticisms of the literature on parent-child relationships in the various physchiatric disorders. Sanua focussed on the poorly specified sociocultural factors in the studies of the families of schizophrenics; Spiegel and Bell pointed to the great overlap and non-specificity involved in the family "trait" studies; and the McCords pointed to the necessary but not sufficient aspects of a theory of delinquent behavior based on the "rejection" hypothesis.

CRITICISM OF METHODOLOGIES

The purpose of this paper is to extend these general criticisms of family research to the more specific methodologies which have been employed by these studies. In addition, we hope to present some guideposts for further research which will allow for a new approach to understanding the family of the psychiatric patient. The methodologies to be examined below are: (1) the case history, (2) psychological testing, (3) psychotherapeutic observation, (4) interviewing, (5) attitude and rating scales and questionnaires, (6) observational studies. Specific examples will be utilized but no attempt will be made to be comprehensive in our coverage of the literature.

Case History Studies

In this category fall those studies in which the authors, having access to a large number of hospital or clinic records, make a *post-hoc* investigation of the backgrounds of a specific clinical group, seeking to find significant events or patterns of occurrences which can be said to be characteristic of the group in question. Such factors as parental rejection and/or overprotection, e.g., (53), the incidence of broken homes, e.g., (62), or patterns of family relationship and the home environment, e.g., (26) have been particular focal points. Other studies, fewer in number, like that of O'Neal and Robins (70), have been entirely empirical in nature, seeking simply to sift the case records with no preconceived ideas as to what they might find, tabulating all data which showed a noteworthy trend.

Case history studies have always appealed to researchers in institutions with a large patient population. The material is readily available, the collating of data can be done by a secretary or graduate student, and this method of data gathering can claim to avoid the pitfall of subjective clinical impression, so notoriously unreliable. There appear, however, to be glaring methodological problems in studies utilizing this material.

The first difficulty is that these histories are not gathered for research purposes but are generally part of the clinical evaluation of the patient. Thus, only certain items tend to get tabulated, those considered by the social worker to be relevant to the etiology of the patient's disorder. This means that certain theoretical notions intrude into what gets recorded. For example, we know that Freudian theory postulates that the vicissitudes of sexuality play an overwhelmingly important part in personality development. Within this orientation, then, many questions may be asked about the patient's sexual development and behavior, and their findings later interpreted to show how sexual disturbances played a key role in the patient's pathological development. However, Hovey (47), for one, has shown that many self-referent items pertaining to sex (e.g., "I have had sexual experiences that make me feel ashamed") fail to significantly discriminate psychiatric patients from controls. Thus, incidence in the patient population and prevalence in the general population are not compared. Without this check, the results cannot be clearly interpreted.

Not only are histories collected for clinical purposes, but their source itself raises many questions as to their validity for research. For the most part, life history data is collected from a single informant, usually the mother of the patient. The exigencies of hospital and clinic time being what they are, little effort is made to cross-check and in some way to validate this historical data. This means that the patient's past life and his behavior soon begin to be described via the categories and phraseology of the informant. No wonder, then, as Goffman (34) points out, the patient in a mental hospital often imagines a "conspiracy" existing between his family and the medical staff. Note should also be made of the well-documented inability (97, 39) of mothers to accurately report on behavioral and developmental events, even when the report concerns their small child. Factors of conscious and unconscious forgetting and distortion enter here.

An example of the errors possible with this method of data collection, and one particularly pertinent to the results reported by many researchers concerned with the etiology of schizophrenia, concerns the phenomenon which Kasanin, *et al.* (53) pointed out many years ago—the overprotective mothers, because of this very trait, tend to remember and give the fullest amount of history material. Thus, if incomplete and inadequate records are discarded from the sample, as has invariably been the case, we will find ourselves left with just those records given by "overprotective" mothers. Reasoning from case material to etiology then becomes rather indefensible.

Once the records are chosen for analysis, what of control groups or some base-line for comparison? There has been an unfortunate tendency to choose control groups, if they have been used at all, more on the basis of their availability rather than their relevance to the study. Often these controls are staff personnel at the hospital where the patients are confined, an occasional attempt being made to match them with the patients on a number of "easy," demographic variables. The sometimes inappropriateness of such a group can be vividly seen in a study by Oltman, *et al.* (69) who sought to gauge the significance of broken homes and parental loss in schizophrenia. They chose, as a control group, hospital employees, and concluded that the incidence of broken homes in schizohprenia was no higher than in the control group. However, analysis of their data shows these controls to have an incidence of parental loss which is *twice* that of the population at large. This can hardly be said to be a normal control.

Having chosen a control, the researchers may then seek to rate certain aspects of the history—for example, the extent of parental rejection. While bare demographic data (age, sex, etc.) are straightforward enough to be reliably coded, this reliability often falls quite low when what is to be classified are more subtle behavior. McKeown (64), for example, found an inter-rater reliability among four judges of only 67.2% when their task was to set parental behaviors into four categories—demanding-antagonistic, superficial, protective, indulgent, and encouraging.

Nor is any cognizance taken of the factors of degree and timing of these occurrences, certainly not in any comparative way. The importance of this specification is pointed up by Despert (24), who writes, concerning schizophrenic children:

> Various degrees of rejection and ambivalent behavior are also frequently noted in parents of neurotic children. However, there again the factor of severity must be considered. The profound and complete rejection on the part of the mothers of these children was a conspicuous factor. (p. 201)

It may be just such variables as degree and timing of occurrences which can help reconcile the confusing finding that certain parental traits (e.g., rejection) crop up in the life histories of patients with all types of diagnoses. An approach based on such a "critical periods" notion of socialization should lead to a series of refined hypotheses.

Finally, all the data having been assembled and analyzed, results are reported and evaluated—a procedure which should be reasonably scientific and objective, but which tends to be strongly influenced by the clinician's theoretical point of view. Bender (10), for example, takes the view that:

> ... schizophrenia is a maturation lag at the embryonic level in all areas which integrate biological and psychological behavior; an embryonic primitivity or plasticity characterizes the pattern of behavior disturbances in all areas of personality functioning. It is determined before birth and hereditary factors appear to be important." (p. 512)

Within this framework, a study was carried out (11), which purposed to show that while the home and family environment of neurotic and asocial children is the specific etiological factor in their problems, schizophrenic children do *not* seem to come from such uniformly bad environments. This statement is not only counter to the findings of most other case history studies, but seems to belie the results which Bender herself obtained in a previous study (10). As Sanua (77) points out, an analysis of this earlier study shows that 42% of the sample of schizophrenic children *did* come from disturbed homes where they were abused, or lived in foster homes during infancy.

Interviewing Studies

These studies involve interviews of varying degrees of structure and intensity with the mothers of psychiatric patients, e.g., (90), both parents, e.g., (68), or the patients themselves, e.g., (55). The usual report is a composite of clinical impressions and quotes from an interview schedule. For the most part, these interview studies are conducted in the clinic or hospital where the patient is being treated, and only occasionally do they utilize a control group.

Assessing interview studies presents us with problems similar to those met in evaluating the case history method, as well as several new ones. An important point concerns the data which is not reported or, if reported, not clarified. Sometimes the interview focusses on specific aspects of the life history. An example is the well-designed study of Kohn and Clausen (55) which had carefully matched schizophrenics and controls focus their reports on family experiences occurring during their 13th year. This is an intentional narrowing of the data gathered. Often, however, the disregard for other historical and ecological variables (particularly social class and sex differences) simply leaves us with many unanswered questions.

In Tietze's (90) study, for example, in which she interviewed the mothers of 25 schizophrenic patients and characterized them all as overanxious, obsessive, frigid and domineering, she buttressed her clinical hypotheses about the parent-child relationship, as Gerard and Siegal (33) point out, with examples drawn only from the backgrounds of *female* patients. No attempt was made to spell out possible sex differences in background.

We are also faced, once again, with the problem of the validity of these accounts. There is every reason to believe that social desirability factors will operate in a situation so emotionally loaded for the participants, as well as the associated factors of blocking, selective recall, denial, etc. As Kohn and Clausen (55) noted about their interview material:

> We must assume that to some degree these reports must be inaccurate. Both patients and parents have undoubtedly failed to see significant aspects of their relationships; their reports are undoubtedly colored by

the experience of psychosis, and by the changes in the relationships since the period of childhood reported on. (p. 311)

Nor do the descriptions of the usual maternal informant (e.g., in Tietze), laced as they inevitably are with words like "narcissistic," "manipulative," "self-centered," offer much hope that the reports offered are accurate or even relatively unbiased accounts. Of course, the counterstransference elements exemplified by the very choice of these adjectives must also be weighed. Expectancy and need-perception are powerful factors!

In the case of the interview, as with all clinical studies of patients and/or families, we have the distortion involved in what can be called "self-selection" of cases, our sample always being limited to those individuals who offer themselves for treatment or survey. The differential rates across social classes and ethnic groups in seeking this help (46, 88) impose another source of bias on the data gathered.

Psychodiagnostic Studies

This method of research has been the special domain of psychologists, who have used various batteries of tests to unearth patterns of family behavior or the personality characteristics of the family members. For the most part, they have used those best known projective techniques, the Rorschach and Thematic Appercetion Test. The testees have sometimes been only mothers, e.g., (72, 92), other times the patients themselves (82) and occasionally the entire family group (67, 29). The more frequent type of psychodiagnostic study, however, has been in the nature of a "content analysis" approach to the records of patients drawn from the various diagnostic groupings, focussing on their individual psychodynamics and attempting to reconstruct some early relations with significant others.

The chief criticism which can be levied at the use of psychological tests to assess family interaction is our lack of knowledge concerning the connection between the material elicited and any sort of "real" behavior. This is true of course of some of the other techniques reviewed (e.g., how are attitude scale results related to behavior?), but interpretation of psychologicals involves an even higher order of inference because of their greater indirectness. Weinberger (93), for one, has critically discussed the problem of the relationship between psychological test analysis and behavior, concluding that:

... test reports generally stress intrapsychic dynamics and either ignore completely their relationship to overt behavior or else make tentative connections which are often unverifiable. (p. 6)

Perhaps the work of such researchers as Jackson and Weakland (51) in the area of the "schizophrenic family's" interaction patterns, will help to verify some predictions made from psychological test data. In any event, the controversy over the usefulness for prediction of psychodiagnostics has raged for many years (65) and the problems of validity are manifold (43).

There is also the interpretation bias involved in the use of tests, leading to the focussing on the pathological and conflictual areas of personality functioning, with little concern for signs of psychological health, defensive strength, or growing maturity. Family members assessed from this frame of reference naturally tend to appear in a rather negative light. Since the a priori bias of the investigators is usually toward uncovering parental pathology, a "freezing" of opinion takes place (84, 23) which can only lead to a distortion in interpretation.

Alongside these more theoretical problems is the problem of inadequate control groups. This is exemplified in a study by Prout and White (72), comparing the Rorschachs of the mothers of 25 schizophrenic patients and 25 normal young adults. As expected, the mothers of the schizophrenics were portrayed in negative terms, such as their excessive ambitiousness for their sons. The control mothers were seen as more energetic and maternally warm, as well as more accepting of their sons as individuals. What is important here, however, is that this control group consisted of a more intelligent and socially-minded group of mothers (such as hospital volunteers) than one could expect to find in the general population.

Thus, while interesting hypotheses often emerge from these studies, the great amount of overlap between groups which plagues the attempts to utilize psychological tests to describe family environments or parental personalities, lessens the research usefulness of this tool, at least as it has been used to this point.

Attitude Scales, Rating Scales and Questionnaire Studies

These methods, exemplified by the Parental Attitude Research Instrument (PARI), developed by Schaefer and Bell (78), and the

University of Southern California Parent Attitude Survey devised by
Shoben (81), attempt to elicit the attitudes of parents through a
series of scales each of which is theoretically relevant to the child's
personality development. The items used are generally in the form of
opinions ("children should be shown lots of affection") with which
the parent is asked to agree or disagree along a four-point scale of
intensity. To make these statements less threatening and avoid distortion, the items are usually presented in the form of a cliche or
truism. Originally designed to measure the attitudes of the mothers
of normal children, they were quickly taken over to help assess the
child-rearing attitudes of the mothers of deviant groups of children
and adults.

The proponents of this type of research have pointed to the greater
objectivity of such measures, and they have administered them in
various ways, both in person and through the mails. Although most
of these studies have sought to assess the attitudes of parents towards
their children, occasional attempts have been made to unearth the
child's attitude towards his parents, e.g., (17).

The most important factors which tend to vitiate the validity of
the questionnaire studies are (1) that what is measured here are
present attitudes, with unknown historical continuity, and (2) that
little is known about the relationship of expressed attitudes to actual
behavior even concurrently, much less retrospectively. What is known
(99, 38) suggests that these relationships are at best tenuous, and
more likely non-existent.

Because these are present attitudes, they are very much influenced
by present circumstances. And these present conditions tend to be
that one member of a family has been labeled as "sick," and another
member, often in the very clinic or hospital where the "sick" one is
being treated, is asked to tell of his or her attitudes towards child-
rearing or of incidents which occurred in the life history of the patient, particularly those in which the informant was involved.

It seems inevitable that such a situation will lead to defensiveness
on the part of the respondent. Much of this will stem from guilt
feelings called forth out of a sense of responsibility for the illness of
the patient. In addition, those parents whose conceptions of the origin of the patient's illness fall into what Korkes (56) calls the "Dis-
sociative-organic" or the "Dissociative-social" groups, will parade out
a wide series of ingenious defensive maneuvers. This defensiveness can
take many forms—suppression of information, justification of actions

and beliefs, repression of what actually occurred. Add to this the problem of actual forgetting, and the acquiescence (7) and social desirability sets (22) which color any such rating scale, and you have a vast array of distorting factors. It would appear that present attitudes, as reported, would have doubtful validity as an index of what actually occurred during the period of early childhood training.

Even if we assume that currently expressed attitudes can be valid indices of real behavior, the work of Gordon (37) and Leton (57), among others, casts doubt on the usefulness of the currently most widely used measures, the Shoben scales on the PARI. These researchers have found little relationship between what attitudes parents profess to have, as measured by these instruments, and what behavior they can be observed to engage in.

Two other problems which plague all studies utilizing such measuring instruments are those of "drop-outs" and demographic variables. Goldstein and Carr (35), for example, were unable to differentiate the child-rearing attitudes of the mothers of catatonic schizophrenics from those of the mothers of paranoid schizophrenics. What they found was that the mothers of the catatonics were more often unable or refused to fill out the questionnaire, and when they did so, left out answers. The problems of who volunteers for a study and the depletion of the experimental group through drop-outs, are as important in the area of attitude studies as they are in that of interviewing. The results of research such as that of Lubin, et al. (61) on the differential personality patterns of responders and non-responders to a questionnaire, should be carefully considered. They found, for example, that while responders were significantly higher (on the Edwards Personal Reference Schedule) for n-order and on the dependency ratio, non-responders were significantly higher on n-aggression.

In line with the problem of demographic variables, it has consistently been found (98) that obtained differences among various groups probably have little to do with the normalcy or deviance of the patient, but are a reflection of social class, religious, and age differences among the parents. Thus, unlike the other methods of study reviewed in this paper which purport to find startling differences among groups, even the most ardent attitude scale and questionnaire researcher has been hard put to unearth any significant and replicable group differences which cannot be readily interpreted as artifacts of these methodological problems.

Psychotherapy Studies

The many articles which fall under this rubric are generally the result of many years' work with one or another group of patients and consist of a series of clinical impressions. The descriptions of patients and parents are usually couched in a language different in quality from that which is used in the more "objective" studies. What one gets here is generally a psychodynamic formulation, sometimes based on therapy of the patient alone, e.g., (25), sometimes on therapy conducted with both parent and child, e.g., (85), and, more recently, on some form of "conjoint" family therapy (51), in which all available family members are seen together by a single therapist.

There have, of course, been many criticisms leveled at psychotherapy itself, from Eysenck's (27) complaint that it "doesn't work" to Aastin's (3) slightly tongue-in-cheek view of therapy's "functional autonomy." As a research tool there have been found an equal, though not so dramatic, number of difficulties inhering in this method.

First of all, the literature on the phenomenon of operant conditioning leaves us with some confusion as to the exact role of the therapist in influencing the production of material which arises in the course of psychotherapy. It would seem risky to lend complete credence to what is observed and collated out of this situation for the purposes of research until we can better understand the role of the therapist-observer, his influence and biases. When a patient's therapy is the specific focus of a research program, there is always the danger that simply collecting the data will distort the process and confound the results. This is the classic analytic argument against psychotherapy research and it remains a moot point.

More specifically, in terms of research design, none of these therapy write-ups are based on a comparison with control groups and, more often, little is specified about the patient beyond his or her age and sex. As Bateson (8) has pointed out, for example, the exact importance of the "double-bind" (9) in the family of the schizophrenic cannot be elucidated until this phenomenon is studied in other groups such as the families of delinquents. Nor can we overlook the ethnic variations, Bateson continues, considering the prevalence of this mode of communication in, for example, the middle class Jewish family.

Finally, considering the importance of social-class factors in the establishment of family behavior patterns (86), the fact that the majority of psychotherapy studies have been carried out on middle and upper class patients means that the results probably have an important class bias. Little has so far been done in this direction with Hollingshead and Redlich's (46) Class V group.

Observational Studies

These ambitious studies, grounded in a concern with the family as an ongoing, communicating group, involve, in intent, a radical departure from past investigations of family functioning. Theoretically, as Haley (41) notes, they have "shifted their focus to the family as a unit of study, as a system in itself, with an attempt to differentiate one type of family from another rather than an attempt to determine how a family influences a member."

The basic paradigm has been to bring together two or more family members, present them with a task of more or less structure to be worked out conjointly, and have observers classify and rate their behaviors, e.g., (60, 36, 79, 32, 28). The tasks presented in these sessions have included standardized questions or tasks (58), projective test stimuli (60), and questionnaires to be filled out and the different responses reconciled (89, 91). The behaviors measured (primarily verbal, but including non-verbal) have usually been rated along dimensions of conflict, dominance, intrusion, and influence patterns and, more rarely, those of support, encouragement, or other integrative behavior. Primarily, these studies have been content rather than process oriented, emphasizing the amount, for example, of maternal domination or parental conflict, rather than the ongoing "who-does-what-to-whom, when" sequence, although this latter type can also be found.

There are many problems in interactional, observational research, some specific to the study of families, others inherent in the methods themselves. On the general level are such factors as observer inference concerning the behavior veing coded (of particular moment when using such methods as the Bales system (6) where the observer's judgment of primarily verbal interaction is all-important), the representative nature of the situations observed, the relationship of observer to observed, the reliability of judgments, etc.

For the most part, experimental family interaction studies have not only failed to adequately solve these general problems, but have demonstrated methodological difficulties of their own such as the interference of preconceptions concerning the family of the psychiatric patient carried over from single-member studies, a focus on part-processes, mainly of a negative valence, and only scattered attempts at utilizing control groups, or a variety of families.

Most studies seem also to straddle the fence between examining what *individual* family members do and what the family does as a unit. For example, in a study carried out at The National Institutes of Mental Health, with families of normals, delinquents and schizophrenics, Stabenau, *et al.* (89), utilized a combination of projective and cognitive test devices administered individually to family members and a Revealed Differences technique in which the members performed conjointly. The family task revealed no significant differences between the groups, and the investigators were forced back to examining the individual protocols to assess parental perceptions of family relationships, while making "global" judgments (apparently with pre-knowledge of which families were which) about family transactions.

Another problem concerns the tasks presented to the families. Judging by the methods used so far in these studies, the realm of generalization of results would appear to be quite limited. A task like the color-matching technique of Goodrich and Boomer (36) is one, as they are quick to point out, which "is relatively simple, which involves judgments about physical reality rather than social reality, and which contains only one ambiguity" (p. 19). One might hazard a guess that, in reality, the conflicts which these couples will be forced to cope with as time goes on will be complex, concerned more with social reality, and be quite ambiguous. The fact that their's is a longitudinal study of family formation will result in some answers as to the connection between this laboratory task and reality tasks.

The inferential process in family interaction studies should be commented on. The categorization of family interchanges has been found to be highly reliable when observers are trained in a certain method. Yet, as Haley (40) cogently notes:

> ... (the use of several observers) is thought to be more scientific, and yet even if several raters agree, which is unusual unless they have been trained to look at the data in the same way, there is still doubt whether the family is actually doing that something or whether raters are merely making the same inference because they have a common point of view. (p. 44)

Given, for example, the backlog of "knowledge" concerning the schizophrenic's mother and her dominance, confused communication, etc., it is likely that raters' predispositions will interfere with their raw observational power. And, as noted above, most studies have had to end up relying on "qualitative" descriptions since attempts to order families in some other manner have failed.

Perhaps Haley's (40) demonstration of the viability of mechanical recording devices to take the most simple measurements of family interaction will lead to further adoption of this methodology. In its own way, this admittedly crude measure of family patterns is no more primitive than the kinds of evaluations being carried out by observers whose capacity for apprehending the intricate totality of interaction leaves much to be desired. How, after all, is an observer to be able to simultaneously evaluate verbal messages on the informational and symbolic level, vocal inflections, bodily movements, and the temporal relationship of events?

If the methodology of this important type of research is to be improved, two steps are of the utmost importance. First of all, is the development of a language of interaction, a conceptual system which can encompass the behavior of two or more people simultaneously, rather than in a cause and effect sequence. Secondly, is the further use of the complex experimental techniques suggested by Haley (42) for testing out the hypotheses drawn from observational research, which should, in turn, refine our observational abilities.

SOME GUIDEPOSTS FOR FUTURE RESEARCH

In the preceding pages, I have presented a resume of the most popular methods used to study the family of the psychiatric patient. These methods can be broadly classified as:

1. Those which rely on the report of others, of varying degrees of relationship to the patient—examples are the sampling of maternal attitudes through the PARI and the interviews held with relatives and friends—designed to gather a psychiatric history or to allow the clinician to assess the personality, attitudes and behavior of these "significant others."

2. Those which require a retrospective account from either patient or family, such as Kohn and Clausen's (55) request that the patients try to recall their early adolescent family experiences. These studies often make the same explicit assumption as do the "report" ones: that reported attitudes or behaviors are rigidly fixed and have not changed over time, through maturation or under the impact of the patient's

illness. Nor do these studies usually allow for the inevitable distortions of memory, both simple forgetting and the more psychologically determined repressions which color any retrospective account.

3. Those which rely on present observation of the family. These observations have generally been made in the course of psychotherapy, although more recent studies have relied on observational analysis of family interaction. In these studies, too, behavior has been classified according to *a priori* categories which portray for example, "domination" as bad, "sharing" as good, with little concern for how these behaviors *appear to the participants*. Also, as these studies are concerned with cause and effect relationships, to reason backward from what is presently observed in the family interaction appears to be an arbitrary dismissal of the all-too-real effect which the disturbed member's illness has on the present situation. In light of the literature on the reorganization of the family which occurs after some member has been identified as the "sick" one (20), it may be too early in family research to assume that any bit of reported or observed behavior is a causative element in the patient's disorder and not an effect of this very fact.

Quite often, in making statements concerning cause and effect from these data, researchers have fallen victim to what Benjamin (12) has called "predictive contaminants." These are the:

> possible determinants of a successful prediction which lie outside the inductive or deductive theoretical framework on which the prediction is presumably based and which, therefore, could partially or wholly destroy whatever validating significance might otherwise be attributed to the success of the prediction. (p. 27)

Some possible "contaminants" of family studies are easy to specify. For example, we may predict that a certain constellation of parental traits will lead to a certain pathological outcome, disregarding the possibilities that: (1) these attitudes may be the parental *response* to the patient's behavior and not its cause or, (2) the end result may be mental illness, but the cause may lie in genetic transmission, biochemical factors, etc. And this hardly exhausts the possible alternative explanations.

Even more pertinent is the "contaminant" which resides in the possibility that these "pathological" parental attitudes and behaviors lead to a certain outcome *not* as a *cause sui*, but because they are perceived and reacted to in a certain way by the child, a way perhaps unrelated to the manner in which both parents and researcher construe them.

There is, indeed, reason to believe that the influence of parental attitudes and behavior depends more on the *child's perception* of them than on what they "really" are. This hypothesis stems from work being conducted on at least three fronts:

1. The first of these is the "transactional" school of perceptual theory, epitomized by the work of Ames (2) and Hastorf and Cantril (44). Moving away from both the stimulus-ascendence orientation (the S-R school) and the nativism and apriorism of Gestalt theory, these researchers have established a phenomenological, functional approach to perception. What this represents is summarized by Ittelson (48).

> In short, the overall trend of contemporary perceptual studies has been away from the earlier stimulus orientation, based on the assumption that external stimuli determine perceptions, and toward the treatment of perceiving as essentially a creative process actively carried on by the organism. This trend is based on the assumption that the individual acts in any situation in terms of the way he perceives that situation. (p. 672)

There are, of course, echoes of this theoretical stand in the phenomenology of Combs and Sygg (21) and in the therapeutic philosophy of Carl Rogers (76). In the study of parent-child relationships, however, this trend has never had the number of adherents as has the straight S-R approach, e.g., (80). Its implication for the study of the family revolves around the fact that what occurs within the confines of this small group can be fully studied only from the viewpoint of the individual member's perception of these events and not in terms of some imposed *a priori* categories of the researchers. Hastorf and Cantril's (44) discovery that the fans of opposing sides at an athletic contest perceived what amounted to different situations, is parallel to what one finds in a family situation, where the divergence is even more dramatic due to the latter's heightened emotional arousal value.

2. Another approach which points to the importance of intra-individual processes is that of Chess, et al. (19). It has long been known (15, 71) that no isomorphic relationship exists between child-care practices and later personality development, and Chess and her co-workers have longitudinally studied 85 children seeking to ascertain

whether a definable, non-experiential, intra-individual reaction pattern was in evidence which would help account for the effects of child care practices.

They found (18), in line with the work of Fries and Woolf (30) and Klatskin, et al., (54), that:

> ...the individual, specific reaction pattern appears in the first few months of life, persists in a stable form thereafter and significantly influences the nature of the child's response to all environmental events, including child care practices. (p. 793)

This reaction pattern is composed of various categories of behavior, such as activity-passivity, regularity-irregularity, and approach-withdrawal, which, present from birth, permeate every aspect of the infant's and child's life—sleeping, feeding, bathing, playing, and toilet training. As an example, some infants have difficulty in establishing regular internal patterns of response to hunger and sleepiness, and cry irregularly and excessively. Thus, a demand feeding schedule would not be viable with this infant since its crying is an unreliable index of its hunger. They discovered too that babies with reaction patterns of a predominantly positive cast—positive responses to other people, easy malleability and/or distractibility—are those who can be easily and quickly disciplined.

The relevance of these findings here is that, as Chess, *et. al.*, (18) note: "...the omnipotent role of the parent in the shaping of the child is indeed a destructive illusion." (p. 801) On the contrary, children with different reaction patterns will react differently to what is objectively the same parental behavior. There may of course be certain reaction patterns which characterize special groups of children, the only possibility which would make parental "trait" studies an appropriate approach to family pathology. In any event, the invocation of the specific reaction pattern helps clear up some of the confusion arising from the discovery that such a factor as "maternal rejection" may be associated with any one of a number of possible outcomes, from the most pathological to the apparently benign.

3. A third converging approach has been the work of Ausubel (5) and his students. Ausubel, whose notions concerning ego development stress the role of perceptual variables, has operated from the following vantage point:

> ...although a child's role and status in his home and his parents'

behavior toward him are objective social events in the real world, they affect his ego development to the extent and in the form in which they are perceived. This does not imply that the perceived world is the real world but that perceptual reality is both psychological reality and the actual (mediating) variable that influences behavior and development. (5) (p. 276–277)

Ausubel has carried out research into the relationship of such factors as the child's perception of himself in the family along the continua of acceptance-rejection and intrinsic-extrinsic valuation, to various components of ego structure (4). He found that children who saw themselves as being *extrinsically* valued, that is in terms of their abilities or performance, conceived of their capacities in more omnipotent terms and were rated as being less independent and less able to postpone gratification. These factors are, of course, related to an immature state of ego development. This is a likely result of a parent's valuation of a child only for his potential "greatness," a parent who thus has a stake in maintaining infantile attitudes of omnipotence and grandiosity. In such a case, it is the child's *perception* of these parental behaviors and attitudes which mediates their effect on his personality structure.

On the basis of these various theoretical propositions, it seems highly important to assess the child's view of his parents and family life. An examination of these perceptions, utilizing different methods, should provide us with many leads for future family research and help clarify the effects of different family attitudes and "environments" on various types of children.

We have carried out some research (73, 74) as a first step in this direction. Utilizing a series of direct and indirect questions and a picture method on groups of normal, neurotic, schizophrenic, and behavior disorder children, it was found that the disturbed children differed from normals in their family role perceptions. Schizophrenic children, for example, tended to see mother as more dominant and punitive, father as more passive and less competent, than did normals, while behavior disorders saw father as far more hostile than did normals or any other group. Neurotics perceived a family environment akin to that of the schizophrenics, but with father a stronger, more assertive and competent figure than he was for the psychotic children. These differing perceived family role constellations were interpreted in terms of their effect on the children's identifications and symptomatic behavior. Presently, we are engaged in assessing the role perceptions of *all* family members, with an eye toward discovering the key areas of disagreement and conflict in each type of family.

Another area of relevant inquiry, still untapped, is this: assuming that there is, indeed, a communication of family pathology and that the child learns faulty habits of coping and distorted modes of thinking within this context, the question remains as to *how* this communication is carried out, *what* exactly is learned, and *how* this learning takes place.

The recent work of Singer and Wynne (95, 96) focussing on the links between differing patterns of family transactions and types of schizophrenic thought disorders in the offspring, is a beginning approximation towards understanding these problems. The type of common concern around which their research centers can be understood from the following statement (95):

> Although the isolated statements of individuals (in families of schizophrenics) may even appear 'normal,' nevertheless, viewed from beginning to end, the over-all transactional disorder in a family's communication sequences may be comparable stylistically to that found in the vagueness or fragmentation of a severely impaired schizophrenic. That is, the form or structure of these family-wide transactions is comparable to that of individual schizophrenic thought disorder. (p. 194)

This type of research, examining the entire family communication network, focussing on *structure* rather than *content*, is far more meaningful for our understanding of psychopathology than the multitudinous "trait" studies reviewed earlier. After all, as Bruner (16) has recently pointed out, the behaviors and modes of thought of humans, "reflect the routines and subroutines that one learns in the course of mastering the patterned nature of a social environment." (p. 2) So far, we know all too little about the different patternings which characterize the family environments of disturbed individuals, or for that matter, normal ones.

The problem is, of course, even more complex than this. We don't know, for example, how the child learns to "read" his parents, what cues he uses to assess mood, attitude, feeling, nor what effect these perceptions have. The child, despite our theoretical language, does not have access to the parents' "unconscious" attitudes and feelings, except as they are expressed in behavior, and as metacommunication studies have shown, this behavior may have a variety of relationships to the conscious messages being presented in any context. If this is the case, how does the child learn his own family signals, and how does he come to cognize their meaning?

In other words, as Bruner's quote makes clear, we learn "outside in." What our task should be in family studies is to find out what *is* "outside," in the immediate social environment, how it gets inside, and what happens then which leads to the individual's and family's difficulties in living.

REFERENCES

1. ACKERMAN, N. W., *The Psychodynamics of Family Life*, New York, Basic Books, 1958.
2. AMES, A. JR., "Visual Perception and the Rotating Trapezoidal Window," *Psychol. Monogr.*, 65, 1951.
3. ASTIN, A. W., "The Functional Autonomy of Psythotherapy," *Am. Psychologist*, 16, 75–78, 1961.
4. AUSUBEL, D. P., BALTHAZAR, E. E., ROSENTHAL, I., BLACKMAN, L. S., SCHPOONT, S. H. and WELKOWITZ, J., "Perceived Parent Attitudes as Determinants of Children's Ego Structure," *Child Developm.*, 25, 173–183, 1954.
5. AUSUBEL, D. P., *Theory and Problems of Child Development*, New York, Grune and Stratton, 1958.
6. BALES, R. F., *Interaction Process Analysis: A Method for the Study of Small Groups*, Cambridge, Mass., Addison-Wesley, 1950.
7. BASS, B. M., "Authoritarianism or Acquiescence?" *J. Abnorm. Soc. Psychol.*, 51, 616–623, 1955.
8. BATESON, G., Personal communication, 1961.
9. BATESON, G., JACKSON, D. D., HALEY, J. and WEAKLAND, J., "Toward a Theory of Schizophrenia," *Behav. Sci.*, 1, 251–264, 1956.
10. BENDER, "Twenty Years of Clinical Research on Schizophrenic Children, with Special Reference to Those under Six Years of Age," in Caplan, G. (ed.), *Emotional Problems of Early Childhood*," New York, Basic Books, 1955, pp. 503–515.
11. BENDER, L. and GRUGETT, A. E. JR., "A Study of Certain Epidemiological Factors in a Group of Children with Childhood Schizophrenia," *Am. J. Orthopsychiat.*, 26, 131–145, 1956.
12. BENJAMIN, J. D., "Prediction and Psychopathological Theory," in Jessner, L. and Pavenstedt E. (eds.), *Dynamics of Psychopathology in Childhood*, New York, Grune and Stratton, 1959, pp. 6–77.
13. BOLLES, M. M., METZGER, H. F. and PITTS, M. W., "Early Home Back-

ground and Personality Adjustment," *Am. J. Orthopsychiat.*, 11, 530–534, 1941.

14. BOWEN, M., "A Family Concept of Schizophrenia," in, Jackson, D. D. (ed.), *The etiology of Schizophrenia*, New York, Basic Books, 1960, pp. 346–372.

15. BRUCH, H., "Parent Education or the Illusion of Omnipotence," *Am. J. Orthopsychiat.*, 24, 723–732, 1954.

16. BRUNER, J. S., "The Course of Cognitive Growth," *Am. Psychologist*, 19, 1–15, 1964.

17. CASS, L. K., "Parent-Child Relationships and Delinquency," *J. Abnorm. Soc. Psychol.*, 47, 101–104, 1952.

18. CHESS, S., THOMAS, A. and BIRCH, H., "Characteristics of the Individual Child's Behavioral Responses to the Environment," *Am. J. Orthopsychiat.*, 29, 791–802, 1959.

19. THOMAS, A. *et al.*, *Behavioral Individuality in Early Childhood*, New York, New York Univ. Press, 1963.

20. CLAUSEN, J. A. and YARROW, M. R., "Mental Illness and the Family," *J. Social Issues*, 11, 3–65, 1955.

21. COMBS, A. W. and SNYGG, D., *Individual Behavior: A Perceptual Approach to Behavior*, rev. ed., New York, Harpers, 1959.

22. COWEN, E. L. and TONGAS, P., "The Social Desirability of Trait Descriptive Terms: Applications to a Self-concept Inventory," *J. Consult. Psychol.*, 23, 361–365, 1959.

23. DAILEY, C. A., "The Effects of Premature Conclusion upon the Acquisition of Understanding of a Person," *J. Psychol.*, 33, 133–152, 1952.

24. DESPERT, J. L., "Prophylactic Aspect of Schizophrenia in Childhood," *Nerv. Child*, 1, 199–231, 1942.

25. DESPERT, J. L., "Some Considerations Relating to the Genesis of Autistic Behavior in Children," *Am. J. Orthopsychiat.*, 21, 335–350, 1951.

26. ELLISON, E. A. and HAMILTON, D. M., "The Hospital Treatment of Dementia Praecox: Part II," *Am. J. Psychiat.*, 106, 454–461, 1949.

27. EYSENCK, H. J., "The Effects of Psychotherapy: An Evaluation," *J. Consult. Psychol.*, 16, 319–324, 1952.

28. FARINA, A., "Patterns of Role Dominance and Conflict in Parents of Schizophrenic Patients," *J. Abn. Soc. Psychol.*, 61, 31–38, 1960.

29. FISHER, S. and MENDELL, D., "The Communication of Neurotic Patterns over Two and Three Generations," *Psychiatry*, 19, 41–46, 1956.

30. FRIES, M. E. and WOOLF, P. J., "Some Hypotheses on the Role of the Congenital Activity Type in Personality Development," *Psychoanal. Stud. Child.*, 8, 48–64, 1954.

31. FROMM-REICHMANN, F., "Notes on the Development of Treatment of Schizophrenics by Psychoanalytic Psychotherapy," *Psychiatry*, 11, 263–273, 1948.

32. GARMEZY, N., CLARKE, A. R. and STOCKNER, C., "Child Rearing Attitudes of Mothers and Fathers as Reported by Schizophrenic and Normal Patients," *J. Abnorm. Soc. Psychol.*, 63, 176–182, 1961.

33. GERARD, D. L. and SIEGEL, J., "The Family Background of Schizophrenia," *Psychiat. Quart.*, 24, 47–73, 1950.

34. GOFFMAN, E., *Asylums*, New York, Anchor Books, 1961.

35. GOLDSTEIN, A. P. and CARR, A. C., "The Attitudes of the Mothers of Male Catatonic and Paranoid Schizophrenics toward Child Behavior," *J. Consult. Psychol.*, 20, 190, 1956.

36. GOODRICH, D. W. and BOOMER, D. S., "Experimental Assessment of Modes of Conflict Resolution," *Fam. Proc.*, 2, 15–24, 1963.

37. GORDON, J. E., "The Validity of Shoben's Parent Attitude Survey," *J. Clin. Psychol.*, 13, 154–156, 1957.

38. GREENBAUM, W., "Influence of Certain Maternal Attitudes on the Behavior of Rejected Children," Unpublished doctoral dissertation, University of Florida, 1954.

39. HAGGARD, E. A., BREKSTAD, A. and SKARD, A. G., "On the Reliability of the Anamnestic Interview," *J. Abnorm. Soc. Psychol.*, 61, 311–318, 1960.

40. HALEY, J., "Research on Family Patterns: An Instrument Measurement," *Fam. Proc.*, 3, 41–65, 1964.

41. HALEY, J., Personal communication, 1964.

42. HALEY, J., "Family Experiments: A New Type of Experimentation," *Fam. Proc.*, 1, 265–293, 1962.

43. HARRIS, J. G., "Validity: The Search for a Constant in a Universe of Variables," in Rickers-Ovsiankina, M. (ed.), *Rorschach Psychology*, New York, Wiley, 1960, pp. 380–439.

44. HASTORF, A. H. and CANTRIL, H., "They Saw a Game: A Case Study," *J. Abnorm. Soc. Psychol.*, 49, 129–134, 1954.

45. HEWITT, L. E. and JENKINS, R. L., *Fundamental Patterns of Maladjustment: the Dynamics of Their Origin: A Statistical Analysis Based upon Five Hundred Case Records of Children Examined at the Michigan Child Guidance Institute*, Springfield, Ill., State of Illinois, 1946.

46. HOLLINGSHEAD, A. B. and REDLICH, F. C., *Social Class and Mental Illness: A Community Study*, New York, Wiley, 1958.

47. HOVEY, H. B., "The Questionable Validity of Some Assumed Antecedents of Mental Illness," *J. Clin. Psychol.*, 15, 270–272, 1959.

48. ITTELSON, W. H. and CANTRIL, H., *Perception: A Transactional Approach*, Garden City, New York, Doubleday, 1954.

49. JACKSON, D. D., "A Note on the Importance of Trauma in the Genesis of Schizophrenia," *Psychiatry*, 20, 181–184, 1957.

50. JACKSON, D. D. "A Critique of the Literature on the Genetics of Schizophrenia." In D. D. Jackson (Ed.), *The Etiology of Schizophrenia*. New York, Basic Books, 1960, 37–87.

51. JACKSON, D. D. and WEAKLAND, J. H., "Conjoint Family Therapy: Some Considerations on Theory, Technique, and Results," *Psychiatry*, 24, 30–45, 1961.

52. KALLMANN, F. J., *Heredity in Health and Mental Disorder*, New York, Norton, 1953.

53. KASANIN, J., KNIGHT, E. and SAGE, P., "The Parent-Child Relationship in Schizophrenia. I. Overprotection-Rejection," *J. Nerv. Mental Dis.*, 72, 249–263, 1934.

54. KLATSKIN, E. H., JACKSON, E. B. and WILKIN, L. C., "The Influence of Degree of Flexibility in Maternal Child Care Practices on Early Childhood Behavior," *Am. J. Orthopsychiat.*, 26, 79–93, 1956.

55. KOHN, M. and CLAUSEN, J. A., "Parental Authority Behavior and Schizophrenia," *Am. J. Orthopsychiat.*, 26, 297–313, 1956.

56. KORKES, L., "The Impact of Mentally Ill Children upon Their Families," Unpublished doctoral dissertation, New York University, 1959.

57. LETON, D. A., "A Study of the Validity of Parent Attitude Measurement," *Child Developm.*, 29, 515–520, 1958.

58. LEVINGER, G., "Supplementary Methods in Family Research," *Fam. Proc.*, 2, 357–366, 1963.

59. LIDZ, T. and FLECK, S., "Schizophrenia, Human Integration, and the Role of the Family," in, Jackson, D. D. (ed.), *The Etiology of Schizophrenia*, New York, Basic Books, 1960, pp. 323–345.

60. LOVELAND, N. T., WYNNE, L. C. and SINGER, M. T., "The Family Rorschach: A New Method for Studying Family Interaction," *Fam. Proc.*, 2, 187–215, 1963.

61. LUBIN, B., LEVITT, E. E. and ZUCKERMAN, M., "Some Personality Differences between Responders and Nonresponders to a Survey Questionnaire," *J. Consult. Psychol.*, 26, 192, 1962.

62. MADOW, L. and HARDY, S. E., "Incidence and Analysis of the Broken Family in the Background of Neurosis," *Am. J. Orthopsychiat.*, 17, 521–528, 1947.

63. McCORD, W. and McCORD, J., *Psychopathy and Delinquency*, New York, Grune and Stratton, 1956.

64. McKEOWN, J. E., "The Behavior of Parents of Schizophrenic, Neurotic, and Normal Children," *Am. J. Sociol.*, 56, 175–179, 1950.

65. MEEHL, P. E., *Clinical versus Statistical Prediction*, Minneapolis, Univ. Minnesota Press, 1954.

66. MILLER, H. and BARUCH, D. W., "Psychosomatic Studies of Children with Allergic Manifestations. I. Maternal Rejection: A Study of Sixty-Three Cases," *Psychosom. Med.*, 10, 275–278, 1948.

67. MORRIS, W. W. and NICHOLAS, A. L., "Intrafamilial Personality Configuration among Children with Primary Behavior Disorders and their Parents: A Rorschach Investigation," *J. Clin. Psychol.*, 6, 309–319, 1950.

68. NUFFIELD, E. J. A., "The Schizogenic Mother," *Med. J. Australia*, 2, 283–386, 1954.

69. OLTMAN, J. E., McGARRY, J. J. and FRIEDMAN, S., "Parental Deprivation and the 'Broken Home' in Dementia Praecox and Other Mental Disorders," *Am. J. Psychiat.*, 108, 685–694, 1952.

70. O'NEAL, P. and ROBINS, L. N., "Childhood Patterns Predictive of Adult Schizophrenia: A Thirty-year Follow-up Study," *Am. J. Psychiat.*, 115, 385–391, 1958.

71. ORLANSKY, H., "Infant Care and Personality," *Psychol. Bull.*, 46, 1–48, 1949.

72. PROUT, C. T. and WHITE, M. A., "A Controlled Study of Personality Relationships in Mothers of Schizophrenic Male Patients," *Am. J. Psychiat.*, 107, 251–256, 1950.

73. RABKIN, L. Y., "The Disturbed Child's Perception of Parental Attributes," Unpublished doctoral dissertation, Univ. of Rochester, 1962.

74. RABKIN, L. Y., "The Disturbed Child's Perception of his Parents," *J. Indiv. Psychol.*, 20, 172–178, 1964.

75. REICHARD, S. and TILLMAN, C., "Patterns of Parent-Child Relationships in Schizophrenia," *Psychiatry*, 13, 247–257, 1950.

76. ROGERS, C. R., *Client-centered therapy: Its Current Practice, Implications, and Theory*, Boston, Houghton-Mifflin, 1951.

77. SANUA, V. D., "Sociocultural Factors in Families of Schizophrenics," *Psychiatry*, 24, 246–265, 1961.

78. SCHAEFER, E. S. and BELL, R. Q., "Development of a Parental Attitude Research Instrument," *Child Developm.*, 29, 339–361, 1958.

79. SCHULMAN, R. E., SHOEMAKER, D. J. and MOELIS, I., "Laboratory Measurement of Parental Behavior," *J. Consult. Psychol.*, 26, 109–114, 1962.

80. SEARS, R. R., MACCOBY, E. E. and LEVIN, H., *Patterns of Child Rearing*, Evanston, Ill., Harper, 1957.

81. SHOBEN, E. J., JR., "The Assessment of Parental Attitudes in Relation to Child Adjustment, "*Genet. Psychol. Monogr.*, 39, 101–148, 1949.

82. SINGER, J. L., "Projected Familial Attitudes as a Function of Socioeconomic Status and Psychopathology," *J. Consult. Psychol.*, 18, 99–104, 1954.

83. SLATER, E. "Genetic Investigations in Twins," *J. Ment. Sci.*, 99, 44–52, 1953.
84. SPERBER, Z., "Rigidity and Conformity Tendencies of Judges and Their Utilization of Autobiographical Material in Making Predictions," *J. Consult. Psychol.*, 26, 144–148, 1962.
85. SPERLING, M., "The Neurotic Child and His Mother: A Psychoanalytic Study," *Am. J. Orthopsychiat.*, 21, 351–364, 1951.
86. SPIEGEL, J. P., "The Resolution of Role Conflict within the Family," *Psychiatry*, 20, 1–16, 1957.
87. SPIEGEL, J. P. and BELL, N., "The Family of the Psychiatric Patient," in Arieti, S. (ed.), *American Handbook of Psychiatry*, New York, Basic Books, 1959, I, pp. 114–149.
88. SROLE, L., LANGNER, T. S., MICHAEL, S. T., OPLER, M. R. and RENNIE, T. A. C. *Mental Health in the Metropolis: The Mid-town Manhattan Study*, I, New York, McGraw-Hill, 1962.
89. STABENAU, J. R., TUPIN, J., WERNER, M. M. and POLLIN, W., "Comparative Study of Families of Schizophrenics, Delinquents and Normals," Paper read at the American Psychiatric Association, 1964.
90. TIETZE, T., "A Study of Mothers of Schizophrenic Patients," *Psychiatry*, 12, 55–65, 1949.
91. TITCHENER, J. L., D'ZMURA, T., GOLDEN, M. and EMERSON, R., "Family Transaction and Derivation of Individuality," *Fam. Proc.*, 2, 95–120, 1963.
92. TOMS, E. C., "Personality Characteristics of Mothers of Schizophrenic Veterans," Unpublished doctoral dissertation, Univ. Minnesota, 1955.
93. WEINBERGER, G., Unpublished manuscript, 1962.
94. WOLFENSTEIN, M., "Two Types of Jewish Mothers," in, Mead, M. and Wolfenstein, M. (eds.), *Childhood in Contemporary Cultures*, Chicago, Univ. Chicago Press, 1955.
95. WYNNE, L. C. and SINGER, M. T., "Thought Disorder and Family Relations of Schizophrenics. I. A Research Strategy," *Arch. Gen. Psychiat.*, 9, 191–198, 1963.
96. WYNNE, L. C. and SINGER, M. T., "Thought Disorder and Family Relations of Schizophrenics. II. A Classification of Forms of Thinking," *Arch. Gen. Psychiat.*, 9, 199–206, 1963.
97. YARROW, M. R., CAMPBELL, J. D. and BURTON, R. V., "Reliability of Maternal Retrospection: A Preliminary Report," *Fam. Proc.*, 3, 207–218, 1964.
98. ZUCKERMAN, M., RIBBACK, B. B., MONASHKIN, I. and NORTON, J. A. JR., "Normative Data and Factor Analysis on the Parental Attitude Research Instrument," *J. Consult. Psychol.*, 22, 165–171, 1958.
99. ZUNICH, M., "The Relation between Parental Attitudes toward Child Rearing and Child Behavior," *J. Consult. Psychol.*, 26, 197, 1962.

20

Normal Crises, Family Structure and Mental Health

T HERE IS A GROWING body of work in the social-psychiatric field known as "crisis" studies. Although these studies have been conducted by people with different approaches and different topics, with no single set of theoretical and clinical interests, there is a common factor among them in that the crises being considered are viewed as *turning points*—as points of no return (1, 2, 3, 4, 5, 6). If the "crisis" is handled advantageously, it is assumed the result for the individual is some kind of maturation or development. If the stresses engendered by the "crises" are not well coped with, it is assumed that old psychological conflicts may be evoked or new conflicts may arise and a state of poorer mental health may be the result. Further, it is suggested that persons undergoing the crisis are amenable to influence when skilled intervention techniques of relatively brief duration are applied.

In a program of Family Research recently initiated in the Community Mental Health Program at the Harvard School of Public

Health, there is an attempt to focus on the application of some of these ideas to a more prevalent type of crisis than in the studies referred to above. Our concern is with the critical transition points in the *normal, expectable* development of the family life cycle: getting married, birth of the first child, children going to school, death of a spouse, or children leaving home. These, too, are seen as points of no return. While both normal and expectable, these standard status transition points in the life cycle of the family always have elements attached to them that are novel for the individuals experiencing them. This is perhaps especially true in our society where *rites de passage* are limited, where anticipatory socialization for new familial roles tends to be minimal, and where the prescriptions for behavior expected in the new roles may be highly variable. Thus these critical turning points often provoke disequilibria both in the individuals concerned and in the family system. It is postulated that the way these normal "crises" or status transitions are handled or coped with, will affect outcome—both in terms of the mental health of the individuals and in terms of the ensuing family relationships. It is also assumed, in line with Lindemann's (2) and Caplan's (1) assumptions that, to the extent that these critical periods have a limited time of "acute" disequilibria, it may be possible to do preventive intervention in a limited time so as to improve outcome levels.

The Initial Exploratory Study

For this program of Family Research the initial exploration lasted nine months and was aimed at collecting data that would improve and alter our early conceptualizations about engagement, honeymoon and early marriage. It was undertaken, too, to map the field of our interest and to order it in such a way that it would be possible to make intelligent strategy decisions for future research.

Though we are interested in various developmental phases of the family, the study has so far focused systematically on the first phase, *getting married.* Some data has been obtained on the next phase— the first pregnancy and the critical point of having a first child—as some of the young couples we have worked with quickly enter this phase. In the "getting married" phase we have delineated three subphases: the engagement period which ends with the *rite de passage* of the wedding, the honeymoon period, and the early marriage period up to three months after the wedding. For each of these subphases we postulate a series of tasks inherent to it, and we will attempt to see how people have performed on these tasks and how this is related to outcome a year after marriage. The type of variables we are concerned with in outcome are (a) individual health status: this will include physical and psychological symptoms, feelings of satisfaction with the marital relationship and other spheres of life, and happiness; (b) state of interpersonal relationship: an evaluation of the "fit" between the couple and the degree of harmony in their relationship, and (c) the state of functioning of the couple as a social system, which includes the degree to which the functions of the family group are performed and the readiness of the couple for the next phase, that of having a child.

GAINING ACCESS to engaged couples presented a number of difficulties. For one reason or another it was not feasible to obtain couples from the local marriage registries, through newspaper marriage announcements or via public health nurses, all of which were explored. Finally, we obtained our initial subjects from the clergy, who were most cooperative. We worked with various denominations, making it a point to go from the top of the clergy hierarchy down. This was particularly helpful with our Catholic contacts. The Catholic Church runs a large pre-cana (premarital) counselling program which seemed to be a potential pool for later research subjects.

In the first instance, we were not very selective about the characteristics of the couples we obtained. We tried to obtain young, married couples, allowing them to vary in social class, religion and occupation. In the initial period we ended up with six couples, three having been referred by the Catholic clergy (1 engaged, 1 just married, 1 just pregnant and in second month of marriage); 1 Unitarian couple, and 2 Episcopalian couples. Both Catholic and Protestant clergy referred couples to us randomly from among those on their lists awaiting marriage. Among the Catholics, the sanction of the clergy was more effective in assuring participation in the research, with only one couple so referred (a mixed marriage) declining cooperation. Among the Protestant couples, the clerical referral was a much less decisive factor in determining individuals' responses to our approach, with about half the couples refusing to participate.

The initial sample of six couples was investigated in a relatively intense way. A great problem when seeking complex, intimate data is how to get meaningful material through relatively limited contacts with subjects. Unless this problem is solved, we cannot obtain sufficient numbers to test our hypotheses and we always remain with very tentative formulations. In addition, repeated intensive research contact with the same people increases the chances of affecting our subjects and altering the very phenomena we are studying.

Our interviews were relatively unstructured for this exploratory phase because we were experimenting with methods to obtain data about extremely complicated social and psychological phenomena where we are uncertain of the specific crucial dimensions. Many aspects of these complex phenomena are pre- or unconscious and differentially sensitive for different respondents. Also the data collected comes through an interpersonal relationship of interviewer and interviewee, the nature of which affects the data obtained. Furthermore, as we were dealing with concurrent processual material obtained by repeated contacts (approximately 12 interviews over a period of five months) there was the probability that we might actually change some aspects of the phenomena under study. In such a situation it was felt that the continued contact might set up expectations (counter-transference) in the interviewer that might affect his eliciting of subsequent data. One attempt to minimize the effect of the latter was to supervise each interview and deal both with counter-transference problems as well as data gaps from the research point of view.

While we still place high value on obtaining current data, it is also felt there is a definite place for retrospective data. In some instances we found retrospective data to be more accessible and accurate. This was especially true of certain events that were emotionally loaded at the time of the interview but which could be talked about with less anxiety later. For example, it seemed that most couples could only discuss details of the honeymoon sometime after the event.

The Conceptual Framework Developed

The original set of six couples were followed for varying periods after marriage. Some became pregnant, and we continued work with them in a relatively unstructured way up to six months after marriage. We then attempted to examine the data and order it into a more manageable form. The conceptual framework diagramatically represented in the chart indicates our over-all orientation to the data on the "getting married" phase. From this field of concern, we have selected a portion in which to do more systematic research in a later phase of the research.

FRAMEWORK FOR CONCEPTUALIZING "GETTING MARRIED" DATA

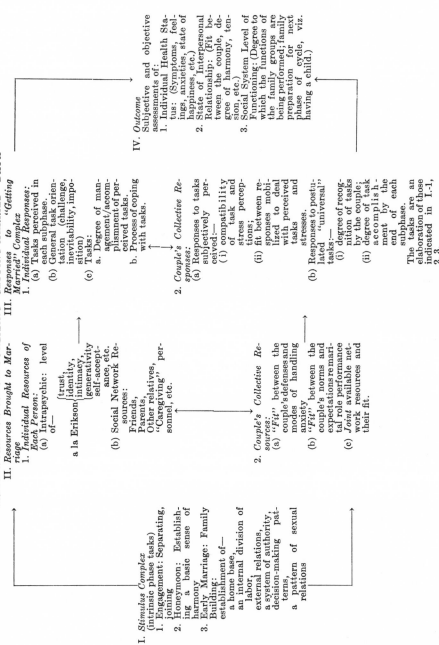

I. *Stimulus Complex* (intrinsic phase tasks)

1. Engagement: Separating, joining
2. Honeymoon: Establishing a basic sense of harmony
3. Early Marriage: Family Building: establishment of—
   a home base,
   an internal division of labor,
   external relations,
   a system of authority,
   decision-making patterns,
   a pattern of sexual relations

II. *Resources Brought to Marriage*

1. *Individual Resources of Each Person:*
   (a) Intrapsychic: level of—
   a la Erikson { trust, identity, intimacy, generativity self-acceptance, etc.
   (b) Social Network Resources:
   Friends,
   Parents,
   Other relatives,
   "Caregiving," personnel, etc.

2. *Couple's Collective Resources:*
   (a) *"Fit"* between the couple's defenses and modes of handling anxiety
   (b) *"Fit"* between the couple's norms and expectations re marital role performance
   (c) *Joint* available network resources and their fit.

III. *Responses to "Getting Married" Complex*

1. *Individual Responses:*
   (a) Tasks perceived in each subphase.
   (b) General task orientation (challenge, inevitability, imposition)
   (c) Tasks:
   a. Degree of management/accomplishment of perceived tasks.
   b. Process of coping with tasks.

2. *Couple's Collective Responses:*
   (a) Responses to tasks subjectively perceived:—
   (i) compatibility of task and stress perceptions;
   (ii) fit between responses mobilized to deal with perceived tasks and stresses.
   (b) Responses to postulated "universal" tasks:—
   (i) degree of recognition of tasks by the couple;
   (ii) degree of task accomplishment by the end of each subphase.
   The tasks are an elaboration of those indicated in I.-1, 2, 3.

IV. *Outcome*

Subjective and objective assessments of:

1. Individual Health Status: (Symptoms, feelings, anxieties, state of happiness, etc.)
2. State of Interpersonal Relationship: (Fit between the couple, degree of harmony, tension, etc.)
3. Social System Level of Functioning: (Degree to which the functions of the family groups are being performed; family preparation for next phase of cycle, viz. having a child.)

The chart presents a schematic organization of concepts that have been found useful in organizing the data on the process of "getting married" as a role-transitional crisis. At present, problems of carrying out research on these concepts and testing out our ideas about the ways in which they are interrelated are less fully worked out than the framework itself.

Research Strategy

It can be seen from the diagram that we are concerned with the personal and social resources that couples bring to a marriage, the way they cope with the tasks presented by the first phase of family life, how much their personal resources alter between engagement and the first few months of marriage, and how coping techniques and task accomplishment relate to outcome, say a year after marriage. These concerns imply at least five sub-studies. They are:

A study of the relation of couple's task accomplishment to outcome; a study of the relation of coping processes (individual and couple) to outcome; a study of the fit between the salient intrapsychic levels of each person of a couple and the relation of the various types of "fits" to outcome; a study of the relation of intrapsychic level of development of the individual to coping processes, to task accomplishment in each subphase, and to total outcome; a study of change in the level of intrapsychic development along salient dimensions, after one year of marriage.

We decided to begin with a study of the *relation of couple's accomplishment of the postulated phase-specific tasks to outcome, measured independently one year later*. (See III, 2.[b][ii] in diagram.) In the present paper only the tasks specified for the engagement period are presented as illustrative of our methods in this exploratory study.

The tasks that confront engaged persons have been divided into two major groups—intrapersonal and interpersonal. It should be noted that different people accomplish the tasks at different times; some only begin working on them during the engagement period, while others have accomplished many of them by the time they get engaged. Our concern is with where individuals and couples stand with regard to task accomplishment by the *end* of the engagement period, i.e. by the time they actually get married, irrespective of when they began working on them.

With regard to the intrapersonal tasks, we are concerned with the way people make themselves *personally prepared* for marriage and how far they get by the time they actually do get married. This set of tasks is the most "individual," relating primarily to each person's intra-psychic factors as they interplay with the requirements of the inter-personal and sociological requirements of "getting married". This set of tasks implies some review on a conscious, preconscious or uncon-scious level of psychological maturity or readiness for marriage. The standards used for "readiness" will be affected both by the individual needs of a person and by his perceived subcultural norms.

THE THREE TASKS considered by us to be salient in this area of intra-personal preparation for marriage are: (I) making oneself ready to take over the role of husband/wife; (II) disengaging (or altering the form of engagement) of oneself from especially close relationships that *compete* or interfere with commitment to the new marital relation-ship; (III) accommodating patterns of gratifications of premarital life to patterns of the newly formed couple (marital) relationship.

For the first task our concern is with assessing each person's degree of *readiness to take over the new role of husband/wife* by the time of marriage. How ready is each, *as an individual*, to enter into the new status of married person and to perform adequately in the marital roles? In speaking of personal readiness we refer to a more general "set" of expectations for oneself and the other that cross-cuts subcultures. The detailed aspects of what we mean can be subsumed under the two large categories, emphasized by Freud and others, as the individual's capacity to love and to work, whether it be "woman's" or "man's" work.

For both man and woman, the love relationship involves the whole prospect of living in close physical relations with another person. While it is extremely difficult to gauge a person's readiness for entering into this new dimension of intimacy, it seems essential to make some assess-ment of it—based on the person's own expressed feeling of readiness and the interviewer's assessment of whether or not the individual has a realistic notion of what this will involve. We can already indicate some of the signs of readiness among individuals of the lower middle class range, from which most of our exploratory research couples come. Here it is expected that the male be prepared to take on the bread-winner role in the family. Signs that he is ready to do this are found in his work plans, his assessment of the financial requirements of the marriage, his activities toward providing for the fulfillment of these requirements and his readiness to accept the idea that others will be dependent on his stability and productivity.

Whatever the work situation, we are concerned with whether the particular individuals feel ready to enter into a situation in which they know what the potentialities and limitations are from an economic point of view, and in which they are able to work out an arrangement that deals both with keeping the household financially viable and with their own self-images as worker, breadwinner, supporter on the one hand, and homemaker, helper, enhancer on the other, such that the individual's sense of readiness is realistic in the context of the relationship that he is entering.

For the second task, we are concerned with assessing *how far people have disengaged themselves from relationships that interfere with commitment to the marital relationship.* Some people have dealt with this issue before they become engaged to marry; others deal with it focally during the engagement period. From our exploratory material, it seems that avoiding the issue altogether leads to difficulties later. These close relationships may be with a parent, sibling, some other relative, a friend, a peer group, a workmate, and so on. In order to assess the degree of accomplishment on this task, we will want to know whether each person had such relationships, with whom, and how they perceive that such ties relate to the proposed marital relationship. We are concerned with the fiancee's perceptions, what each person does with these relationships, and how conflicts are handled. We wish to know how much actual work of reconciliation has been done and how much still remains. Where the relationships have been gratifying, the work may be the loosening of a positive dependency tie. This then becomes involved in the third subtask of this area: giving up premarital gratifications. Where the negative aspect is uppermost, the work of the subtask relates to revising one's ideas about familial roles and attempting to make one's behavior fit this revision.

Accommodating the competing gratifications of premarital life to the new couple (marital) relationship is the third task in making oneself personally prepared for marriage. We are concerned here with whether individuals feel that getting married does involve relinquishing gratifications. Some can tell us the answer to this, others cannot and we shall have to infer from what they say what the psychological reality is for them. For instance, if someone thinks their premarital activities, such as going to frequent dances, will continue during marriage, and we find that the prospective spouse has no interest in this activity and does not intend to pursue it, we probably have a situation in which relinquishing this premarital gratification is not being dealt with. We want to know what individuals find particularly gratifying in their premarital life, whether these gratifications are likely to be possible in married life and if not, how far individuals give them up by the time they get married. It may be extremely difficult, for instance, for a woman to give up the gratifications of romantic courtship behavior. Outcome may be greatly affected, however, by how much recognition is given to this task and how far she is able to accomplish it. For men, this task seems in our exploratory couples to center more on the question of whether or not his "freedom" will be drastically curtailed. This involves no longer being able to think only of oneself in decisions and actions.

What we are primarily concerned with here, then, is estimating how far the *shift from self-orientation to mutuality* has been made by the end of the engagement period, for both men and women. This involves obtaining some data from the couple on how far they already have gone in the development of a couple identity. Again, the actual form of the couple identity will vary by subculture and should be rated accordingly. Agreeing to segregate activities may involve as much idea of such couple identity as agreeing to do things jointly.

THIS LEADS TO CONSIDERATION of the second major group of engagement tasks, namely those involved in the couple's *interpersonal* preparation for marriage. We are concerned with the work the couple has to do to develop an interpersonal adjustment or accommodation that will be satisfactory in the marital relationship. We are interested in many facets of this interpersonal work and want to relate how far the couple get in their interpersonal tasks by the time of marriage to various outcome measures a year after marriage.

The set of *interpersonal tasks* that we are concerned with here relates to and draws on intrapersonal phenomena and extrafamilial (or couple) relationships, but focuses on the phenomena in the premarital (engaged) couple's relationship. The concern throughout is on the work necessary to make this relationship a satisfactory and harmonious one. Our key organizing concept is that of *fit* (10). We wish to assess the couple's *fit* on a number of salient variables. A good fit may be arrived at in various ways. Partners need not be identical in the way they do things or in their personality configurations. Two partners may have a similar orientation to some aspect of life and the result may be conflict or unhappy competition in the relationship. Conversely, discrepant orientations do not necessarily indicate a poor fit. They may complement one another. The essential point is the effect of their "fitting together" efforts. A good fit is one that has the effect of harmonizing needs and values whether these are similar or dissimilar at the outset of the relationship. Conversely, a bad fit is one where there is disabling discord or conflict regardless of *a priori* resemblances or dissimilarities.

We are interested in how far the couple has accomplished the work involved for each of the tasks detailed below. This involves understanding where each person is on the dimension, and making a rating about the degree of accomplishment for the couple on the task. Thus, in considering a task such as "developing a mutually satisfactory friendship pattern for the couple," we need to know about each person's norms about friendship patterns, what they consider the pattern ought to be for an engaged couple, and what each feels he needs in his/her friendships. The rating, however, relates primarily to the accommodation made by the two persons to achieve a mutually satisfactory pattern, during the engagement phase.

The tasks we have specified in this area are:
1. establishing a couple identity;
2. developing a mutually satisfactory sexual adjustment for the engagement period;
3. developing a mutually satisfactory agreement regarding family planning;
4. establishing a mutually satisfactory system of communication between the pair;
5. establishing a mutually satisfactory pattern with regard to relatives;
6. developing a mutually satisfactory pattern with regard to friends;
7. developing a mutually satisfactory pattern with regard to work;
8. developing mutually satisfactory patterns of decision-making;
9. planning specifically for the wedding, honeymoon, and the early months of marriage that lie ahead.

Assessing Task Accomplishment

Each task has been broken down into a battery of items which are rated on a 7 point scale both for the individual and for the couple at the completion of our interviewing program. For example, the intrapersonal task of "making oneself ready to take over the new role of husband or wife" has a battery of 10 items as follows: degree to which the individual shows signs of readiness to be an exclusive sexual partner; shows signs of being able to enter freely into an intimate sexual relation with his/her fiance; shows signs of tenderness, affection, for the other; shows signs of interest in the other's emotional life and development; shows signs of sharing intimacies with the other; shows signs of merging his own plans with those of the other; degree to which the individual has a realistic appraisal of the personal characteristics of the prospective spouse; degree to which the individual has formed a realistic conception of the economic problems entailed in forming a marital pair; degree to which the individual has formulated a realistic picture of his own capacities to contribute to the economic needs of the new family unit; and degree to which the individual is ready to become a husband/ wife (global rating).

WE HAVE NOW STARTED to work with a second exploratory series of six young couples. Our major aim with this group is to work out more clearly what items seem useful to retain, to define them as operationally as possible, and to work out coding procedures so that we shall cease to be dependent on the ratings of expert clinical judges for our assessments.

In order to serve all these aims, we adopted the following procedures: A pair of interviewers, one male and one female, interview each couple. Four interviews are conducted during the engagement period, spaced so as to allow for one immediately before the wedding; a further interview is conducted as soon as possible after the honeymoon, one three months later and one a year later. The couples are interviewed jointly and separately. All interviews are taped. Each couple is then rated for all the items three separate times—once by the interviewers together with the supervisor of all the interviews, while second and third ratings are made by other interviewers who do not know the subject couple but have only listened to the recorded interviewing sessions. In these ratings by interviewers and supervisor, all of whom are trained clinicians and sociologically oriented, rationales for choosing one point in the scale rather than another have been elicited.

One further procedure we are attempting with this group of couples is to use an adaptation of what has been called a self-anchoring scale by Kilpatrick and Cantril (11). This enables each individual of the couple to indicate the content of the scale on the item in which we are interested. We have used this scale for two main areas—to get at individuals' own ideas of the characteristics of a man and a woman who is most ready for marriage and their own ideas about what constitutes a happy marriage one year after the wedding. After giving these notions, the interviewees are asked to rate themselves and each other on a scale anchored by the content they have given. We thus hope to get at their psychological realities about these factors and to relate them to outcome. This in itself might turn out to be a significant predictive device for types of outcome.

SUMMARY

This paper has emphasized some aspects of the conceptualizations and formulation of a research design to investigate a complex series of problems in the field of community psychiatry. The phenomena that have been discussed operate on many different levels, and it can be seen that personality dynamics is only one set of contributing forces in explaining them. It will be a long time before we are able to understand the weight and combinations of different kinds of factors in explaining the total variance of the phenomena with which we are concerned. However, we do know that it is important in understanding how people cope with various critical situations to take systematic account of significant elements of the family structures from which they come; the network of family and other relationships that is available to them when they enter the "newly married" state, and their own expectations of the way familial roles should be performed. Both the personal and social resources a couple bring to their marriage will affect its outcome, as will new aspects that later develop autonomously from their daily living together.

This paper has not concentrated on results as these are not yet systematically available. It has, rather, elaborated on the development of ideas and methods in an intensive exploratory study which should hopefully form the basis for a more decisive formulation and testing of hypotheses.

REFERENCES

1. CAPLAN, G., "Patterns of Parental Response to the Crisis of Premature Birth: A Preliminary Approach to Modifying the Mental Health Outcome," *Psychiatry*, 23, 365–374, 1960.
2. LINDEMANN, E., "Symptomatology and Management of Acute Grief," *Amer. J. Psychiat.*, 101, 141–148, 1944.

3. TYHURST, J., "Individual Reactions to Community Disaster," *Amer. J. Psychiat.*, 107, 764–769, 1951.
4. ERIKSON, E., "Identity and the Life Cycle: Selected Papers," *Psy. Issues*, 1, 1–171, 1959.
5. BIBRING, G., et al., "A Study of the Psychological Processes in Pregnancy and of the Earliest Mother-Child Relationship," *Psychoan. Study of the Child, Vol. 16*, New York, Int. Univ. Press, 1961. pp. 9–27.
6. JANIS, I., *Psychological Stress*, New York, Wiley, 1958.
7. KAPLAN, D., and MASON, E., "Maternal Reactions to Premature Birth Viewed as an Acute Emotional Disorder," *Amer. J. Ortho.*, 30, 539–552, 1960.
8. BALINT, M., *Primary Love and Psychoanalytic Technique*, London, Hogarth Press, 1952.
9. RAINWATER, L. and WEINSTEIN, K., *And the Poor Get Children*, Chicago, Quadrangle Books, 1960.
10. RAPOPORT, R., "The Family and Psychiatric Treatment," *Psychiatry*, 23, 53–62, 1960.
11. KILPATRICK, F. P., and CANTRIL, H. "Self-Anchoring Scaling, A Measure of Individuals' Unique Reality Worlds," *J. Ind. Psy.*, 16, 158–173. 1960.

21

Experimental Assessment of Modes of Conflict Resolution

D. WELLS GOODRICH, M.D.
DONALD S. BOOMER, PH.D.

THIS PAPER DESCRIBES a brief experimental technique for studying the coping behavior of husband and wife when they attempt to resolve a marital conflict. The specific conflict to be resolved is standardized, consisting of an apparent difference in perception of a set of colors. The interpersonal difference arises because the stimuli presented to husband and wife, while apparently identical, actually differ in a manner which is not readily discernible.

On the basis of experience with 50 marital pairs, we wish to report that this technique evokes meaningful differences in styles of interpersonal conflict resolution. While quantitative aspects of the behavior profiles obtained will not be reported here, certain qualitative dimensions will be described. This method of assessing interpersonal conflict we refer to as *the color matching technique*.

The technique was devised for a longitudinal pilot study of the initial stages of family formation (3, 4). It is used in conjunction with joint interviews with husband and wife, individual interviews with each spouse, questionnaires, home observations, role-playing and experimental observations. A major focus of the study is the nature of the initial marital bond in couples married for the first time. The subjects are a group of middle class paid volunteers aged 18 to 27 years. The project follows changes in this marital bond from the fourth month after the date of marriage, through the first pregnancy to the three month period immediately following the birth of the first infant. The research explores patterns of husband-wife behavior which are relevant to the mastery of these developmental stages. A major interest is the formulation of a meaningful typology of coping behavior patterns. The stability of these patterns from the newlywed stage to the first neonatal stage is of particular interest to us. Our hope is that stable coping patterns—if they can be identified—may serve as a basis in future research for predictions of marital adjustment from the time of marriage to the first neonatal phase.

Differences in perception and evaluation tend to occur naturally when any two people are faced with a new or strange situation; the first pregnancy or the first-born infant present a number of such new and ambiguous situations. The style of coping observed in an experimental situation may be characteristic and hence may have predictive power for the couple's adequacy or inadequacy when confronted with other puzzling or ambiguous natural situations. Thus by means of such techniques it may become feasible to predict a couple's ability to cope with ambiguous situations which occur naturally with developmental changes.

The task[1] belongs to a class of experimental problem-solving situations which have been investigated by those interested in cognitive processes, personality, and group problem-solving. In many such situations the task is deliberately left unstructured in order to evoke the subject's characteristic mode of resolving ambiguity. There is evidence from these studies that individuals often have rather stable and somewhat predictable tendencies in their manner of evaluating ambiguous stimuli and of approaching a solution.

An important characteristic of the color matching technique is that it taps dimensions of dyadic relationships; it is not designed for studying individuals or small groups. In this situation any bit of behavior by a single person is considered as one step in an interactive sequence of communication and decision-making. Thus in reporting on various styles of conflict resolution shown by various couples, we do not refer to individual capacities or inadequacies but rather to the adequacies or incapacities of the two persons working together. The adequacy of the

---

[1] The color matching technique evolved from discussion with Jack Block, Ph.D. about his unpublished explorations with Don D. Jackson, M.D. of family coping behavior evoked by skeins of colored yarn.

marital relationship itself is considered a better predictor of stability or change in family interaction patterns than would be an assessment of the husband or wife separately.

METHOD

The procedure takes 10 to 20 minutes and is presented at the outset of the second full evening that husband and wife spend as subjects. They are seated opposite one another with a large two-sided easel between them. Neither subject can see the other, but both can see the experimenter who stands beside the easel. Each subject has, on his side of the easel, a numbered display of small colored paper squares, arranged in 5 vertical columns of 6 squares each. The 6 squares in each column are varying shades of one basic color.

The task is ostensibly a test of the subjects' ability to discriminate slight gradations of color. Before presenting the instructions the experimenter administers the Ishihara test for color blindness and records the results. Actually, the presence of color blindness makes little apparent alteration in the experimental situation since the conflict items all involve differences of shading rather than color, and since all the color columns are labeled at the top of each column, "red," "yellow," etc.

The following explanation and instructions are given by the experimenter:

This is an experiment about color appreciation. When you were a child, each of you learned to identify the primary colors: red, blue and yellow. As you have grown older, you have increased in the ability to recognize finer and finer differences between colors. Adults differ from one another in this respect. Some see fine differences best with one color and other people see fine differences best with another color.

The colors on the board in front of you are standards against which you will match special color samples which I will show you. The procedure will be simple. I will show you a color sample card, hung from this nail—like this—and each of you will compare it very carefully with the colors on the board in front of you. *Take plenty of time deciding on the closest match.* When you have decided, say, *"Okay,"* nothing else. Then I will put the color sample card away.

At this point the most difficult part of the experiment begins. It is necessary for you to arrive at an agreement with each card as to the best possible match. *Only your agreements count toward your score in the experiment.*

Take time to discuss the colors and matches, as long as you wish, in order to discover the best possible match. While some of the matches are difficult, in all cases there is one best match. The more times you both can discover and agree upon the best color match the higher your score.

One other thing: it is often thought that women have a better eye for color than men. Many men may find this a convenient excuse to get out of being consulted on colors for draperies and slip covers and the like. We have already established that both of you have normal color vision so that neither of you has any real handicap in this regard. (With a color blind subject, substitute, "We have taken care of the problem of your color blindness by labelling all of the principal colors used in the test.") Are there any questions?

Remember that your score depends upon the agreement you both come to about the best match. All right—let's begin.

The experimenter then presents the first color; the couple is reminded not to start the discussion until after each has made the choice silently, said *"Okay,"* and had the standard removed from view by the experimenter. Thus the discussion is carried on in terms of their recollection of the color and in the absence of the real stimulus.

The first few rounds go smoothly, the two subjects agreeing each time as to the proper match for the test color. On the fourth round, however, a disagreement arises. The husband announces that number 12 is the best match, but the wife differs. She says that 12 is quite close to the test patch, but that 19 is an identical match. Husband then compares their two choices carefully and finally answers that she has it backwards—19 is almost right, but 12 is precisely right.

This disagreement has been built into the procedure by the fact that their boards have been "rigged." The arrays of colored squares have been so arranged that certain pairs of corresponding colors on the two boards have different numbers. In the above instance, for example, his number 12 was exactly the same shade as her number 19.

A discussion of varying length ensues, and the disagreement is resolved in one of several ways, which will be discussed later. The next round goes smoothly again with instant agreement, but the following match results in another disagreement. The agreements and disagreements occur irregularly throughout the task. Of a total of 20 matches, 10 have contradictions built into them and the other 10 permit immediate agreement without discussion of any kind. The entire proceeding is tape-recorded, which eliminates the necessity of taking notes or maintaining protocols during the experimental session.

After the task is completed, certain couples are somewhat shaken in their confidence in their own color vision or are upset at the intensity of the mysterious disagreement that has just occurred. Others simply are desirous of having their correct diagnosis confirmed. To forestall any lingering hostilities or anxieties, the experimenter says:

Thank you both for your cooperation in this difficult situation. We want you to know before you leave that neither of you has shown any handicap with regard to color vision, and that the test has certain built-in difficulties which all couples encounter who take the test. We would prefer not to state what these difficulties are at this point, but we want you to know that you have both performed quite adequately.

Behavioral Differences between Couples

Experience with 50 couples has shown meaningful differences in the behavior of marital pairs in coping with the 10 conflict matches. These differences can be reliably coded or scored. A profile of conflict resolution behavior can be expressed for each couple in terms of such dimensions as activity level, involvement in discussion of color, effectiveness of communication, perspective on the situation, capacity to reach agreement, dominance-submission and maintenance of esteem. The categories will not be described here, but we will discuss some relations between these dyadic behaviors and the structure of, and rationale for, the situation.

The behavioral differences are best examined in the light of the nature of the problem. Our color matching technique has the virtues and limitations of a situation which is relatively simple, which involves judgments about physical reality rather than social reality, and which contains only one ambiguity, namely the source of the difference in the two participants' matches. In simplest terms, each individual is required to do three things: perceive accurately, verbalize the perception clearly, and agree with the other person on some solution. Of these, only the agreement presents a problem. The simplicity of the problem narrows the range of behaviors elicited and assists us in the search for independent quantitative variables.

The actual pattern of coping with this experimental interpersonal conflict reflects the couple's own style of involvement of energy and affect in problem situations as well as their style of exploring alternative solutions to marital disagreements. In our initial experience with the color matching technique it was surprising to us, considering the trivial nature of the task, that nearly all of our couples became motivated to work at this task, often intensely motivated. With our volunteer subjects, this technique is presented after the initial relaionship to our interviewer has been established and the couple has had the opportunity, usually with a good deal of satisfaction, to share with the interviewer the recent courtship and early marriage experiences. Thus they approach the color matching technique with trust and with a desire to cooperate with the experimenter as well as with some sense of being on trial. The fact that the first three color items are easily agreed upon reinforces the plausibility of the instructions which imply that agreements are possible on all items. As indices of the couple's level of motivational and affective involvement we have explored activity level (in terms of amount of verbal behavior) and certain affective expressions.

When the couple is confronted with their first disagreement on the fourth color item, the major behavioral differences begin to emerge as they explore alternatives and search for solutions. Couples range from those who can tolerate the situation of disagreement only for a brief time and thus can accomplish very little of this exploration of alternatives and must rapidly seek a decision, to those couples who tolerate uncertainty well and explore together a resourceful diversity of alternatives. We have observed that it is rather easy to distinguish (a) couples who consider only those alternatives implied by our instructions to discuss color differences from (b) couples who show ability to gain perspective and consider alternatives of their own, such as what there might be in the structure of the test that is leading them into a disagreement.

Couples vary in their readiness to risk committing themselves to a solution, and also in the type of solution decided upon. The solutions used to cope with the sequence of ten conflicts seem to depend on two general factors—the type of alternatives they consider and the degree to which the situation stirs up anxiety, confusion or other forms of inadequate coping behavior. Whether or not coping inadequacies appear, the couple may recover their integration at any point in the process and in the end be able to agree. It is important to note that we also regard as adequately coping couples those who perceive the impossibility of the task and agree to disagree. What interests us is the coping style and whether or not *some* mutually agreed upon solution can eventually be achieved.

Adequate coping can take place only in relation to color conflicts in which both husband and wife remain sufficiently non-anxious that they continue to perceive and to discuss the color matches accurately. When anxiety appears in the discussion it may take the form of perceptual confusion, displacement of perceived conflict to a non-conflict item, or denial of a clearly perceived conflict. Coping adequacy can be assessed in relation to cognitive, affective, and decision making behaviors, as well as in relation to these perceptual functions. When a couple first begins to consider alternatives to explain their disagreement, the commonest behavior is *discussion of color*. This may include attempts to find words to describe particular shades or hues; with more imaginative couples recourse will be made to comparisons with referent colors elsewhere in the experimental room or in their own home. Frequently there will be discussion of lighting conditions in the room, highlights, and so on. All of this falls within the direction for discussion implied in our instructions to them. After some period of this serious searching for alternatives in terms of colors, the couple may figuratively step back and "take a second look" at this puzzling situation and begin to consider other hidden elements embedded in the test situation to explain their persistent disagreements. This behavior we refer to as *achieving perspective on the situation*. Couples vary considerably too in their *maintenance of esteem* for self and for spouse throughout the discussion of each conflict. In the absence of a sense of mutual esteem and trust couples have much greater difficulty in committing themselves to an agreement and may become anxiously deadlocked or show other uncollaborative behaviors.

To summarize, the joint tasks confronting the couple are to become mutually involved, to perceive accurately, to examine alternatives which might provide a basis for agreement, and to commit themselves to a solution. The behavior profiles differ from couple to couple as they cope with these tasks; these differences appear to provide a meaningful basis for certain evaluations of coping effectiveness.

DISCUSSION

Two aspects of coping style have particularly interested us on theoretical grounds: the achievement of perspective on the situation and the maintenance of self esteem. Both of these aspects of behavior, which are quantifiable, would seem related to adequacy of coping with the developmental issue of intimacy.

In a substantial subgroup of couples there occurs a sense of help-lessness and discouragement which then is expressed in disparaging comments about the self or about the spouse. The spouse may be ac-cused of being color blind or of not being sufficiently careful or sys-tematic in the matching judgment. Observation[2] of a small number of couples in psychiatric treatment has supported our clinical impression that this failure to maintain trust in each other's perceptions and the emergence of hostile or disparaging comments represent an inability to cope with stressful natural situations. Frequently when this hap-pens, the discussion changes from rational exploration of alternatives to a power struggle, the aim being to defend the self and prove that the other is wrong. Again whether the task is met with at least a veil of good humor, or whether a bitter attack supervenes, would seem indicative of the general level of mutual esteem shared by the marital pair.

Such a shift from a position of valid negotiation to a position of rather frantic search for some basis for resolution may be taken as evidence for a state of less open communication between the husband and wife. The inability to engage in controversy and useful combat is one of the criteria Erikson uses to describe failure to achieve in-timacy (2). Indeed the ability clearly and comfortably to repudiate is part of his definition of the achievement of intimacy.

Perspective on the situation is manifested by discussion of hidden factors other than color and lighting in the test which might account for their disagreement; it frequently is followed by the couple using their own purely arbitrary basis for agreement. The possibility of hidden factors is more commonly suggested by the husband than the wife; usually he guesses that the numbers which label the colors may have been switched by the experimenter or that actually there is no cor-rect match for one or both subjects. When a couple takes this position it is based upon trust in each other's perception and judgment and on a greater willingness to consider that the difficulty lies in the situation rather than in themselves; therefore we consider it a sign of mutual confidence, and usually a sign of coping adequacy. This mutual achievement reminds us of the psychological position fostered in psy-chotherapy sometimes called "the constructive splitting of the ego." It characterizes couples who are able to maintain their involvement with each other without defensive withdrawal and who are able, at

---

[2] We are indebted to Dr. Lyman Wynne, Chief, Adult Psychiatry Branch, NIMH for his collaboration in gathering these data.

the same time, to monitor their feelings and thoughts and to evaluate their involvement objectively. Couples who are able thus to extricate themselves from a fruitless discussion of color often go on to suggest arbitrary solutions such as taking turns, or "you take the reds and I'll take the greens." In a few instances, such perceptive, self-confident couples have simply refused to follow the instructions and have agreed to disagree.

Interestingly enough we can observe episodes in the course of the discussion when a couple vacillates between gaining this perspective on the situation, which enables them to find a non-anxious decision, and again being caught up in an anxious power struggle with each other. The precise sequence of mutual influences, the "give and take" between husband and wife during these crucial moments of shifting coping style, suggests much about the sources of coping adequacy or coping inadequacy in each spouse.

It will be noted that we have defined coping adequacy in a rather global manner. We have not suggested analysis of coping adequacy in terms of the classical defense mechanisms. This is partly because the majority of our subjects are too flexibly integrated to be usefully described in terms of defenses and partly because we are not interested in studying symptoms, psychopathology, or disorders based upon failure to resolve the early phases of psychosexual development.

Our theoretical substructure follows more directly from Erikson's conceptualization of ego development (2). From this point of view, our newly married couples are engaged in mastery of the stage of *intimacy*. From our assessment at this point we wish to predict the likelihood of their successfully managing the transition to *generativity* when children are born to them. We believe, with Erikson, that psychosocial development, though parallel to and influenced by psychosexual development, is not irrevocably determined by pre-oedipal and oedipal events. There is clinical information to suggest that two people who individually struggle against certain neurotic or even psychotic tendencies in themselves may together cope reasonably adequately with certain aspects of later psychosocial development under supportive environmental conditions.

In much past clinical theorizing insufficient credit has been given to the conflict-free sphere of the ego described by Heinz Hartmann (5), and to the question of identifying individuals who have achieved what he referred to as the "average expectable developmental state." We do not believe it is useful to consider that the average expectable developmental state of marital relationship ever remains stable or non-anxious for very long. Rather we conceive of marriages and families as periodically having to cope with new, ambiguous and stressful situations. The price of less adequate forms of coping with these normal life situations may not be psychiatric disorder. The price may rather be a failure to develop and change in as positive a fashion as other married couples. The toll of such "pre-pathological" coping inadequacies may be expressed in terms of later psychiatric disorder in an offspring of the marriage.

By observing systematically the interpersonal processes of communication and decision making when the couple attempts to cope with the experimental interpersonal disagreement described above, we hope to assess some dimensions of their styles of coping with other natural situations.[3] The problem of what types of test situations are most likely to yield stable profiles has been discussed in the course of a review of small group research by Bales (1). He believes that past studies indicate that stable behavior dimensions are more likely to emerge (a) when the participants can check their assertions about the task by reference to the physical environment, rather than by reference to social values, (b) when the emotional commitment of the participants to the task and to each other is high and (c) when the task is specific and urgent. Perhaps it is because the color matching technique fulfills these criteria that it now appears to be yielding meaningful behavioral profiles.

REFERENCES

1. BALES, R. F., "Small Group Theory and Research," in *Sociology Today*, Basic Books, Inc., New York, 1959. Chapter 13.
2. ERIKSON, E. H., "Identity and the Life Cycle," *Psychological Issues*, 1: 1, 1959.
3. GOODRICH, D. W., "Recent Research in Early Family Development, and Child Personality," in *Proc. of Third Institute on Preventive Psychiatry*, State University of Iowa, Iowa City, Iowa, 1961. Chapter 3.
4. GOODRICH, D. W., "Possibilities for Preventive Intervention During Initial Personality Formation," in *Prevention of Mental Disorders in Childhood*, Basic Books, Inc., New York, New York, 1960. Chapter 11.
5. HARTMANN, H., *Ego Psychology and the Problem of Adaptation*, International University Press, New York, 1958.

---

[3] The research interviews have been designed to assess coping with natural life situations. Comparison of the color matching data with these interview data will be reported subsequently.

22

Decision-Making in Normal and Abnormal Two-Child Families

ANTONIO J. FERREIRA, M.D.
WILLIAM D. WINTER, Ph.D.

T HE INVESTIGATION of the process of decision-making in families (2, 7) has disclosed a number of variables of considerable interest to the understanding of family interaction and the nature of psychopathology. Of particular note have been the variables called Spontaneous Agreement, Decision-Time, and Choice-Fulfillment, on the basis of which important differences were found between groups of "normal" and "abnormal" families. Since measurements along these variables were shown to have an unusually high degree of stability (8) it seemed worthwhile to pursue this line of investigation and to attempt to generalize the findings to larger family groups. Two questions arose: so far, research had been confined to family triads, i.e., father, mother, and child—would the findings hold for family tetrads, i.e., father, mother, and two children? Previous investigations had defined "abnormal" families as those where the child in the tested triad had been identified as a patient—now, would the findings hold for a much looser definition of family abnormality, for families where simply emotional problems were acknowledged, whether attributed to any individual member (identified as "patient") or to the family group (e.g., marital problems)?

METHOD

The Families As used in this project, the families were tetrads of father, mother, and two children who met the following criteria of acceptance: they had all been living together as a family for at least the last two uninterrupted years; the children in the test were at least 9½ years of age; they were all Caucasians and at least second-generation Americans; they were all free from any known physical illness or handicap; and they contained no psychiatrist, psychologist, social worker or other sort of psychiatrically sophisticated family member.

The Classified Groups Once they met the criteria of acceptance, the families were classified in one or the other of two groups. The *normal group* (Nor) was composed of families in which: there was no known emotional or criminal problem for any of its members for a period of at least five years prior to the testing; no family member or members had received, or been recommended to receive, any form of psychotherapy for at least the past five years; and the overall behavior of the family had not been considered abnormal by the referring source. The *abnormal group* (Abn) was composed of all families that met the criteria of acceptance in the study but did not meet the criteria of normality outlined above; accordingly all of these *Abn* families were known to have some emotional or criminal problem in at least one of its members (the father, the mother, or one of the children) who might be or might have been in some form of psychotherapy in the five years period prior to the testing.

A total of 85 families were tested in this project, 36 *Nor,* and 49 *Abn.* The families were obtained through, and tested at, the facilities of the Mental Research Institute, in Palo Alto, California. The *Nor* families were invited to participate in the project on a voluntary basis from available rosters of local schools; the *Abn* families were referred by therapists in the area. The general characteristics of these families (educational level and age of the parents and children tested, number of children per family, duration of marriage, sex of the children, and distance in age between the children tested) are summarized in Table 1. Chi-square analyses showed that in the characteristics considered, there were no major differences between the groups, except for the age and education of the mothers which turned out to be significantly

TABLE 1

General Characteristics of the Families

Variable	Diagnostic Groups	
	Nor	Abn
Age of F.	46.0	45.6
Age of M.	44.2	41.7
Age of C_1.	16.0	17.3
Age of C_2.	13.7	12.8
Age difference (C_1-C_2).	2.6	2.6
Education of F.	16.1	15.6
Education of M.	15.2	13.4
Education of C_1.	10.4	10.4
Education of C_2.	7.9	8.1
Duration of Marriage.	20.2	19.5
No. Children in Family.	3.5	3.9

F—father, M—mother, C_1—older child, C_2—younger child. All variables are expressed in median values.

higher (Median test) for *Nor* than *Abn* families. As indicated above, the *Abn* group was quite heterogeneous as to the identified patient and the diagnosis involved; any member might have been identified as a patient (Table 2), and the diagnostic labels ranged from schizophrenia or delinquency to scholastic underachievement, alcoholism, or simply marital problems.

Testing Procedure In every respect, the testing procedure duplicated that used in the previous investigation of family triads (7). The family members were instructed to fill out a questionnaire referring to a number of "situations." For every situation in the questionnaire the family members were to indicate the three choices they liked the most, and the three choices they liked the least or not at all, among ten given

TABLE 2

Frequency of Abn Families' Members Identified as Patients

Identified Patient	No. Families
Father.	2
Mother.	6
Child, older (C_1).	8
Child, younger (C_2).	9
Child, other.	4
Several or none.	17
Unstated.	3

alternatives. To fill out copies of the questionnaire family members were placed in separate rooms that completely isolated them from each other. Upon completion of these individual tasks, the four family members were brought together. They were then instructed to fill out the same questionnaire again but this time *as a family*, that is to say, with the understanding that their choices were meant to represent a family decision and as such to apply to all four of them. They were, therefore, to discuss among themselves the matter of their choices and fill out the questionnaire indicating again for every "situation" the three alternatives they, as a family, liked the most, and the three alternatives they liked the least or not at all. With these instructions, the family was then left alone in the testing room, with the door closed, until the questionnaire had been completely filled out. With their full knowledge, the ensuing verbal interchange among family members was recorded on tape.

The Questionnaire The questionnaire was also the same as the one used in the previous investigation (7). It contained seven "situations" with ten alternatives or choices each. The situations were intended to be as neutral as possible and applicable to all family members in the test regardless of sex or age, whether considered as individuals or as a family. The alternatives given for each situation were quite comparable in their assumed cultural or social desirability. The seven make-believe situations referred to: (a) famous people they might want to meet if they were "going to a party this weekend"; (b) foods they might want to eat if they were "going out for dinner tomorrow night"; (c) films they might want to see if they were "going to a movie this weekend"; (d) countries they might want to go "to live for a year"; (e) sport events they might desire to attend; (f) magazines they might wish to subscribe to; and (g) two-tone colors they might prefer for their next car.

VARIABLES

This investigation focused upon three measurable dimensions, or variables, defined as follows:

1. *Spontaneous Agreement (SA)* This indicated the number of agreements, i.e., similar choices, among family members. It refers to agreements that were found to exist "spontaneously," that is to say, prior to any family discussion. The SA score was obtained by comparing the

individually filled out questionnaires and counting units of "spontaneous agreement"; these units were defined as instances where a family member's positive choice (i.e., an alternative marked as "liked") coincided with another family member's positive choice, and similarly, where a negative choice (i.e., an alternative marked as "disliked") matched a negative choice of another. This SA score (agreement of positive and negative choices) had a theoretical range of 0 to 42 for any dyad, and of 28 to 252 for the tetrad. The score for the tetrad was obtained by summing the scores for all six dyads.

2. *Decision-Time* (*DT*) This was defined as the time in minutes spent by the family to complete the joint questionnaire. It was regarded as a measure of the efficiency of the family functioning inasmuch as, other things being equal, the more time a family required to reach a decision, the less efficient it could be said to be.

3. *Choice-Fulfillment* (*CF*) This reflected the extent to which the family choices fulfilled the individuals' choices. It was defined as the number of instances where the individual's choices (as expressed in the individual's questionnaire) became the family's choices (as expressed in the family's questionnaire). In this manner the CF score represented the sum of two scores: the PP score (*P*ositive individual choices that became *P*ositive in the family) and the NN score (*N*egative individual choices that became *N*egative family choices). The sum of the individual family members' CF score constituted the family's CF score. This family CF score was regarded also as a measure of family efficiency in decision making, since it represented the degree to which the family met the wishes of its members.

HYPOTHESES

In regard to the differences between *Nor* and *Abn* families, this investigation was concerned primarily with the following hypotheses:

H_1. *The SA score would be greater for Nor than Abn families.*

H_2. *The DT would be longer in Abn than in Nor families.*

H_3. *The CF score would be greater in Nor than in Abn families.*

These main hypotheses, and other secondary ones to be mentioned in the next section, represented most of all an attempt to replicate with two-child families the results previously observed with one-child families (7), thus broadening the scope of conclusions to larger family groups and to a more holistic criterion of family abnormality.

RESULTS

All three main hypotheses were corroborated. The findings were as follows:

H_1. Accepted. *The mean Spontaneous Agreement score for tetrads was 107.33 for Nor, and 102.20 for Abn families,* a statistically significant difference (analysis of variance, $F = 4.25$, df 1/83, $P < 0.05$). However, it may be even more important to note that, as Table 3 shows, these differences in spontaneous agreement were to be observed in all six dyads, where with unexpected consistency, the SA scores were higher in *Nor* than *Abn* families.

As in the previous study, a *positive correlation between the age of the child in the test and his spontaneous agreement with the parents was found.* The correlation was significant for both *Nor* (Pearson's r = 0.326, $P < 0.005$), and *Abn* families (r = 0.245, $P < 0.01$). Accordingly, spontaneous agreement with the parents was found to be greater for the older than for the younger child tested.

In *Abn* families, to investigate possible differences in spontaneous agreement with parents between the child identified as "patient" and the child assumed "well," two subgroups of ten *Abn* families each, randomly selected, were compared. In one of these subgroups the older child was the identified "patient," the younger child was said to be "well"; in the other subgroup the labels were reversed. A two-way analysis of variance revealed that the differences between the "well" and the "patient" child in the same family were statistically significant: *The "well" child had a greater spontaneous agreement with the parents than the child identified as "patient"* ($F = 5.70$, df 1/36, $P < 0.05$).

Also as hypothesized, it was found that there was a tendency for the

TABLE 3

Mean Spontaneous Agreement in Dyads and Tetrads

	Spontaneous Agreement						
	In Dyads						In Tetrads
	FM	FC_1	FC_2	MC_1	MC_2	C_1C_2	FMC_1C_2
Nor	20.19	18.50	16.47	18.31	17.11	16.75	107.33
Abn	19.18	17.51	15.43	17.73	15.85	16.49	102.20

F—father, M—mother, C_1—older child, C_2—younger child.

child to have a *greater spontaneous agreement with the same sex than with the opposite sex parent*, ($\chi^2 = 32.85$, df 2, $P < 0.001$). This tendency appeared to be unrelated to the age of the child, the position of the child in family tetrad (the older, or the younger), or the diagnostic category (Nor *vs.* Abn) of the family.

A hypothesized correlation between the duration of the marriage and the spontaneous agreement in the dyad father-mother was not corroborated.

H_2. Accepted. *The mean Decision-Time, in minutes, was 19.75 for Nor, and 25.02 for Abn families*, a statistically significant difference (analysis of variance, $F = 7.15$, df 1/83, $P < 0.01$). When adjusted for the expected negative correlation with SA ($r = -0.176$), these means became 20.03 for *Nor*, and 24.81 for *Abn* families. The difference between *Nor* and *Abn* families remained significant (analysis of covariance, $F = 5.60$, df 1/82, $P < 0.025$).

Here, it was of particular interest to compare the DT of tetrads in this study with the DT of triads in a previous study (7). It had been predicted that a two-child family would probably necessitate more time to reach a family decision than a one-child family. The results, however, did not bear out this assumption. As Table 4 shows, there were no statistically significant differences between the triads and tetrads as to the mean DT required to fill out the questionnaire as a family.

H_3. Accepted. Measured in terms of the family PP, the *choice-fulfillment was 50.56 for Nor, and 47.10 for Abn family tetrads*, a statistically significant difference (analysis of variance, $F = 7.90$, df 1/83, $P < 0.001$). When adjusted for the predicted positive correlation with SA ($r = 0.418$), the means became 49.50 for *Nor*, and 47.72 for *Abn* families. This difference, although in the direction predicted, did not

TABLE 4

Mean Decision-Time (in minutes) for Nor and Abn One-child (Previous Study) (7) and Two-child Families

Families	Decision-Time Diagnostic Groups	
	Nor	Abn
Triads (7) (one child)...............	18.96	24.44
Tetrads (two child).................	19.75	25.02

TABLE 5
Mean Choice-Fulfillment (raw PP scores) for Members of Nor and Abn One-Child (Previous Study) (7), and Two-child Families

Family Member	Triads (7)		Tetrads	
	Nor	Abn	Nor	Abn
Father..........................	13.6	12.3	13.2	12.3
Mother..........................	13.5	12.1	13.1	12.3
Child...........................	13.0	12.0		
Child older (C_1).................			12.8	11.8
Child younger (C_2)..............			11.5	10.7

reach the desired statistical significance (analysis of covariance, $F = 3.50$, df $1/82, P < 0.10$). However, when the computation utilized the sum of both PP and NN scores as perhaps a more adequate measure of overall CF, significant differences were seen to exist between *Nor* and *Abn* families (analysis of covariance, $F = 4.61$, df $1/79, P < 0.05$).

Of added interest was the comparison of choice-fulfillment among individual family members, as well as between the scores obtained in this study of tetrads and the previous study of triads (7). In this respect, with focus on monads, it was found that in both studies *every individual member of Nor families derived a greater choice-fulfillment (PP scores) from the family decision than did individual members of Abn families* (Table 5).

A comparison between the *choice-fulfillment of the older with the younger child in the test disclosed no significant differences, in Nor families.* However, *in Abn families it was found that the younger child had significantly less choice-fulfillment than the older one* (analysis of covariance, $F = 8.16$, df $1/37, P < 0.001$). A similar inquiry into the CF of the "well" versus the "patient" child in *Abn* families revealed that although the "well" child seemed to derive a greater CF than the "patient" choice-fulfillment child, the difference was not significant when the correlation with SA was taken into consideration (analysis of covariance, $F = 2.62$, df $1/37$, n.s.).

On an Index of Normality based upon the linear combination of the scores on the three main variables (SA + 2 PP − 4/3 DT), the mean value was 181.4 for the *Nor* and 162.6 for the *Abn* groups of family tetrads. The correlation between the index and the "normality" of the families was expressed in a biserial $r = 0.452$, highly significant ($P < 0.0001$).

COMMENTS

In every respect, the results of this investigation with family tetrads have corroborated the formulated hypotheses and replicated the findings of previous work (2, 7). Thus, the main observations made about family triads have now been enlarged to tetrads using a broader definition of family abnormality. We are led to conclude then, that in the variables of spontaneous agreement, decision-time, and choice-fulfillment we have not only sensitive measures of family functioning but, further, meaningful and easily definable concepts with which to build towards a theory of family dynamics and family (group) pathology.

Once again, normal and abnormal families were shown to be different in spontaneous agreement. Reproducing the findings of two previous research projects with family triads, this study demonstrated that the hypothesis holds well also for tetrads. Worthy of note is the observation that the decreased *spontaneous agreement found in abnormal families is present in all dyads.* Although there may be a tendency for the "patient" child to have less spontaneous agreement with his parents than some other "well" sibling in the family, this decrease in spontaneous agreement seems to be a phenomenon that engulfs the whole family and is not a function of any single individual or pair of individuals.

As we have stated before (7), we speculate that spontaneous agreement reflects a somewhat static property of the family ensemble. The degree to which they "spontaneously" agree with each other in their likes and dislikes is probably a good indication of how intensely and how close they have lived together, that is to say, of how much they have tended to communicate and impart their feelings to each other. It is reasonable to suppose that when people live together, day after day, night after night, for years on end, their likes and dislikes will tend to converge and overlap. Their views of the world will become more similar as time goes by, and they will face situations (such as those suggested by the questionnaire in the test) with choices that will tend to agree. This convergence of tastes does not signify, of course, that they will become identical, but simply that in the broadest spectrum of what people may like the most or the least, *family members will tend to become more alike* to each other. The point seems trivial, for instance, when we consider that in the language they speak, the vocabulary they use, the social manners they adopt, etc., family members are easily seen to have much greater resemblances among themselves than an otherwise comparable random group of strangers. Obviously, the chances are that if collected at random from the whole world population the strangers would not "spontaneously" agree even in what language they would speak. Compared to a family, the group of strangers' decreased spontaneous agreement would be obviously predicated upon their lack of shared experiences or intensive living with each other. They had had no communication such as that which goes willy nilly with living together, in an atmosphere of interdependency.

So, to return to the question of decreased spontaneous agreement in abnormal families, we conclude that such a decrease is an indication (relative to normal families) of a dearth of shared emotional experiences, less intensive (noncommital) participation, and decreased exchange of self-revealing information. It is often stated that in abnormal families there is "no communication." From all appearances, their decrease in spontaneous agreement reflects their lack of communication, or better, their insufficient communication of the self-revealing sort. Clinical experience has indicated that in members of abnormal families (or, more traditionally, in individual patients) there is a marked tendency to hold back self-revealing statements, to remain silent and noncommittal (9). So this decrease in spontaneous agreement which our research has consistently shown to be a distinguishing feature of abnormal families could be regarded as a likely consequence of the lack of exchanged information among family members. This interpretation would be in line with the commonly stated clinical impression that in abnormal families there is a breakdown of communication, whereby family members tend not to talk to each other, to hide their true feelings, to prefer equivocal to explicit interchanges, to remain noncommittal, and to inform each other less about their own true likes and dislikes. It stands to reason that the long range effect of such barriers between people must be a greater strangeness to each other's ways, a greater ignorance of the true extent to which they may agree or disagree on a given issue, a greater avoidance of stating or learning about conflicting views, and, therefore, a greater incapacity to attune their wants.

However, we must further consider that this decrease in spontaneous agreement observed in abnormal families has also, *per se,* important consequences to family functioning. As evidenced by the correlations between SA and CF, and SA and DT, a decrease in spontaneous agreement causes the family to necessitate a longer time to reach decisions. Furthermore, it lessens the individual member's chances at choice fulfillment, since they start with a greater potential conflict (more "spontaneous" disagreement) of likes and dislikes than would be found in the average normal family. As a result, we can postulate that, even other things being equal, decision-making in abnormal families must be considerably more frustrating and less rewarding than in normal families. Thus, unhappiness, dissatisfaction with, and anger towards each other, must occur in larger amounts in abnormal families than in normal ones (3, 11, 12)—feelings which in turn are likely to lead to even greater difficulties in intra-family communication. It seems then that we may be seeing in the concept of spontaneous agreement, and its measurement as SA, an important element of a fundamental cycle of family pathology: *Spontaneous agreement both as cause and as effect of decreased intra-family communication.*

In the light of these considerations about spontaneous agreement, it may be worth emphasizing that the spontaneous agreement in the child-parent dyad was seen to grow with the age of the child. Also, in normal families and some subgroups of abnormal families, to which delinquency, and schizophrenia-producing families may be exceptions (7), SA is greater with the same-sex parent than with the opposite-sex parent. These findings are, of course, very important to an over-all understanding of family dynamics, or individual psychodynamics, since they substantiate popular clinical impressions and give solidity to some psychoanalytical speculations about the phenomenon of identification.

In all likelihood, spontaneous agreement increases with the duration of the relationship. Since spontaneous agreement probably reflects the long range effect of all of those collective actions which may bring family members closer together—explicit information exchanged, clear imparting of values, emulation of loved ones, history of efficient decision-making, etc.—it would be reasonable to suppose that in a family the SA would increase as the years go by, not only in the dyad, child-parent, as our study demonstrated, but also in the dyad, father-mother. So, we have predicted that spontaneous agreement between spouses would increase from wedding day onwards, with the duration of the marriage, and we anticipated that, in this respect, there might be some important differences between normal and abnormal families. However, the data did not corroborate the hypothesis. Yet, it must be stated that this negative finding may not be the final word on the hypothesis. The number of years that our families had been married fell within too narrow a range to test the hypothesis adequately. Due to the criteria for selecting the sample (children, living at home and older than 9½ years) the great bulk of our families had been married approximately from 16 to 24 years, and the comparison of the spontaneous agreement in the first with the later years in the relationship was, therefore, not possible.

Abnormal families required longer time to reach family decisions than normal families. The fact that this decision time is longer in abnormal families seems to be the consequence, as our findings indicate, of two factors. One factor is a lesser spontaneous agreement, which implies more conflict among family members and, therefore, a more difficult and more time-consuming task (thus the negative correlation between SA and DT). The other factor seems to be in the family group itself, in its dynamic incapacity to deal with decisions as economically, time-wise, as normal families do. For both triads and tetrads, our studies have demonstrated that even when statistically equalized for SA, the abnormal families required a significantly longer time than normal families to reach family decisions. This, of course, points to an inefficiency of the system, which seemingly compounds the difficulties inherent in the decrease in spontaneous agreement. We speculate here that such an inefficiency must have damaging results to the family group; it must consume more of the "energies" of its members and make the task more distasteful and less satisfying. Besides, since time is a fixed commodity, unacquirable and unstretchable, this inefficiency represents a waste of this precious element which must cut deeply into the possibility of its being used for other purposes, perhaps for other family decisions that may lie awaiting and unattended in the wings.

Of possible great interest here was the realization that family tetrads took practically the same amount of decision-time as family triads had done in the previous investigation (7). In this respect, normal and abnormal families preserved their distances as if both groups had been completely unaffected by the increased size of the families involved. This observation went against prediction. A priori, we had assumed that it would be more difficult, and therefore it would take longer, for four family members to reach a group decision than for three. But, seemingly, we had not fully realized that there may be a necessity for families and other structured groups to function with parsimony, in accordance with rules which may impose rigid limits as to the time apportionable for a given task. Perhaps we are dealing, here, with some basic aspect of human relationships which future research may attempt to elucidate. At any rate, investigators in this field will likely have to contend first with the questions indirectly raised above: Will the sameness of decision-time observed between family triads and tetrads hold true for pentads, hexads, or even much larger sized family groups? Will a similar phenomenon be observed in other internally organized groups, such as gangs, close friends, fellow workers, comrades-in-arms, etc.? And will it be present in the performance of that aggregate of total or quasi-total strangers studied in "small group" research?

Abnormal families derived less choice fulfillment from their decisions than normal families did even when taking into consideration their initial differences in spontaneous agreement. As it appeared, their decision-making process is in some way faulty. As a result, members of abnormal families must derive less satisfaction from their family decisions than do members of normal families. In this sense, abnormal families are definitely inefficient in their functioning, exhibiting a decrease in performance which must eventually lead to their heightened feelings of frustration, unhappiness, and anger. Probably, we are dealing here with another pathologic cycle of self-reinforcing difficulties. The experience of unsatisfying family decisions is likely to bring about a paucity of information exchanged among family members with further hindrance of the family decision-making process and, circularly, even less choice-fulfillment.

To return now to the results of this investigation with tetrads, we wonder as to the meaning of the finding that, in abnormal families (in contrast to normal families), of the two children in the test, the younger child had significantly less choice-fulfillment than the older one. But, we have not encountered a sufficiently convincing interpretation of the finding, and we are inclined to suspend judgment until some future opportunity to test its presence again. In this regard, we saw with interest that in abnormal families there seemed to be no measurable difference in choice-fulfillment between the "well" and the identified "patient" child: the difference that was first elicited was shown to be the consequence of differences in spontaneous agreement and in no way indicated that the "patient" was in that respect any more handicapped into choice-fulfillment than his "well" sibling. This observation, we felt, speaks loudly in favor of the general assumption underlying most family work, that the labelling of some one individual in a family as a patient (and by implication the labelling of other family members as non-patients) may be only a family myth (4, 6), that is to say, an expression of the covert rules of the relationship (5). At least, in terms of this project, we found no reason to assume that in a family with someone labelled a "mental patient" there would be a distinguishable functional difference between the "patient" and his "well" family associates.

The research technique used in these investigations was introduced by Ferreira (2) in a first investigation of the process of decision-making in normal and abnormal families. By analogy to Strodtbeck's (10) technique of revealed differences, this approach to the investigation of family (or group) decision-making could well be referred to as the technique of *unrevealed* differences. The crucial aspect of this approach is that when the family members are brought together for the expressed purpose of reaching a family decision, no family member knows for a fact what the other family members liked or disliked most among the given alternatives to the questionnaire "situations". As in real life, the extent to which they may be in agreement or disagreement is not revealed to them by an outsider; instead, family members have to face the task of family decisions with only those elements of information which they make available to themselves. Conceivably, this exchange of information about their likes and dislikes takes place along those channels of communication and patterns of interaction which are typical of their relationship. Parenthetically, it must be noted that here lies a fundamental difference between this type of family research and small group research: In the family a relationship exists which predetermines the combined behavior of all family members, whereas in the so-called small group there is no pre-established relationship among its members. The family is a blend of interdependent individuals who naturally belong together; they have a history of continuous interaction. The small group, on the other hand, is an aggregate of individuals artificially brought together for a purpose that is not meant to go beyond the immediate research task at hand. This basic difference makes these two kinds of data hardly comparable. But at the same time the realization of this difference opens up a new research area, as it may stimulate investigative efforts towards a clarification of relationships and the essential elements involved in the difference between families and unrelated groups of subjects.

A comment should now be made about the questionnaire used in this and previous studies. First of all, it must be clarified that there was nothing final about this questionnaire. It has not been copyrighted. As a matter of fact, its most salient characteristic is that not only it could, but that it *should* be modified to meet the exigencies of time and population to be sampled. As mentioned before, its "situations" and alternatives were chosen for their assumed neutrality, applicability, and meaningfulness to all family members regardless of age, sex, or position in the family. By design, it was a harmless questionnaire, that contained nothing that could be regarded by any one as right or wrong, good or bad, socially desirable or undesirable, normal or abnormal. Its sole purpose was to obtain the individuals' commitments as to relative likes and dislikes on some very obviously unimportant, trivial, and made up situations,—commitments which were assumed to become easy matters for any family, and any family member, to talk about and discuss without too great fear of possible reprisals. Apparently, the questionnaire fulfilled the *desideratum*. On the average, individual family members required only about five to fifteen minutes to answer the questionnaire. No one displayed the slightest reticence in complying with the instructions, and it often appeared that the tester's assurances of confidentiality sounded, if not believable, at least totally unnecessary.

Still, despite the assumed unimportance of the issues introduced in the questionnaire, the task of family decision-making as witnessed in this project always seemed to elicit emotionally laden and at times outright conflicting responses among family members. Apparently, *in a family there are no such things as neutral issues*. From these observations, we have been led to conclude that to a family even the most trivial subject can and often does stir up the members in the relationship, evoking feelings, and so revealing areas of friction as they may exist among family members. There would have been no need, therefore, to load the questionnaire with supposedly emotionally charged subjects, such as sex or aggression. As a matter of fact, it is conceivable that the presence of such items in the questionnaire might have tended to inhibit the family discussion and bring forth taboos whose varying effect from family to family would make the whole family performance rather difficult to evaluate. Certainly, the recent observations of Epstein (1) on the effect of highly structured stimulus material in projective techniques speak in this direction. Thus, we have come to regard this type of questionnaire as fundamental to the investigation of family decision-making processes. For, only with a questionnaire in which all items appear, as much as possible, neutral, comparable in emotional and cultural value, and equally meaningful to all family members, can we reasonably expect maximum freedom of expression among family members and an interaction relatively unhindered by cultural stereotypy.

In our investigation of families, we have assumed that, on account of the existing relationship among family members, the task of decision-making *under unrevealed conditions* was in most respects characteristic of, and perhaps unique to, the particular family. We have assumed that in the test the families use the same bargaining style, ploys and counter-ploys, threats and bribes, revelations and distortions that characterize their transactions in their ordinary and less artificial occasions of family decision-making. The opportunity to test many of these families in one-way vision rooms has permitted a number of direct observations which, in fact, robustly substantiate this research assumption.

The observation of a number of families involved in discussion over the choices on the questionnaire disclosed that these families seemed to take their task with the utmost seriousness. In fact the realism of their actions invariably astonished the observers behind the one-way vision mirrors. Apparently, under the testing conditions, the family could not help but behave like itself. There seemed to be very little elbow room for faking performance. Contrary to individual tests (e.g., Rorschach, MMPI, Szondi, etc.) where the opportunity does exist to control the results, it was the consensus among observers that this family test so immediately promoted the family members' involvement with each other as to supersede whatever intentions they might have had to control their responses or to disguise their picture of themselves.

As much as it could be ascertained, the behavior of the families in the testing room duplicated closely what we knew about their ordinary behavior. An example may be found in the following observation of a family:

Family A, a triad. The son, age 14, said to have a very poor scholastic record and to be given to temper tantrums. The father had been hospitalized twice for schizophrenic breaks and suicidal attempts. The mother, volunteering a description of herself as "very bossy and domineering," talked all the time and was a showy contrast with the aloof, cool, and silent attitude of her husband. Throughout the test they behaved very much the way their therapist of several months, hidden behind the one-way vision mirror, expected: The mother seemed to make every decision. Although occasionally she would seem to consult with the son, she was forever ignoring her husband, who sat on the distant side of the table, almost motionless, beholding the spirals of smoke that from his almost immutable cigarette slowly rose to the ceiling. Apparently, the mother dominated all. As previous knowledge of this family had made us anticipate, she spoke incessantly about the decisions to be made, gave opinions and took direction. Often she evoked the absent children to justify her choices which, in the name of the whole family, she would then proceed to mark on the questionnaire. The husband was only rarely heard to say something, and even then his was an almost inaudible mumble that did not seem to carry any weight. The son seemed to be physically and emotionally very close to mother, whom he joined in her continuous display of vivacity and ebullient assertions which set off even more the contrastingly quiet behavior of the father.

In every respect, then, this family behaved in the testing room in very much the same way they used to behave in the therapy room. Their behavior was representative. But there was more to be learned from the test observation. From their total behavior, it seemed very apt indeed to describe the mother as a very dominating creature and the father as an almost absent figure. Taking advantage of the characteristics of the test, we saw the immediate possibility of measuring just how dominating that mother, and how passive the father, had been. Since we knew (from the individually administered questionnaires) what each family member liked and disliked the most, it was an easy proposition to look upon the relative choice-fulfillment of the family members as an objective representation of their relative dominance. At once, we scored the CF, that is, the number of times when the family decision had in fact coincided with the choices made by the individuals. Now their inquiry had a most surprising result: The "dominating" mother had scored only 11 (PP), the child had scored 12—both very average scores—whereas the "submissive" father had scored 17, one of the highest scores ever attained by any family member! Obviously, our ideas about dominance and submissiveness in a relationship as inferred from clinical impressions could not be substantiated. In fact, this observation led us to conclude that these notions, if to be retained, cannot rest on what the people involved (patient and therapists) report and must seek some objective determinants instead.

Another good example of the similarities of behavior observed in testing and therapy situations occurred as follows:

Family B, a tetrad in which the father and older daughter, age 20, were known to be always at odds. In the course of the test they made a rather successful attempt to be affable and to tolerate with a smile their mutual differences in likes and dislikes. But when they began choosing a country to visit for a year they broke into a loud squabble. The father wanted the family to go to Russia, the daughter preferred Spain. But, somehow, (on suggestion from mother?), they started speaking of Egypt. The father became indignant: "but you know I've always wanted to go to Russia—why do you insist on Egypt?... Besides you know I can't take the heat..." The daughter picked up the argument as if in favor of that very choice: "...but there is so much interesting in Egypt, I mean Cairo... and it is not as hot as you think..." The argument went on, fast and fiery between the two for quite sometime while mother and sister waited in silence. Finally, father and daughter both gave in almost at the same time and agreed not to go to Egypt. They even marked it as not wanted by the family.

Again, the behavior of this family in the testing room was very similar to, and typical of what the therapist had seen many times take place in conjoint therapy sessions. But what the therapist could not know in therapy was that in this particular instance neither the father *nor* the daughter had chosen Egypt as a desirable place to go. In fact, they both had scratched it out indicating their dislike of the place among the alternatives available in the questionnaire. Still, to the therapist and other observers behind the one-way mirror, it seemed unquestionable that the daughter was putting pressure on the father to go to Egypt! If they could have seen each other's individual answers to the questionnaire, they would have known they were in absolute agreement about not going to Egypt. Then there would not have been much to argue about. As it was, their heated discussion proceeded unabated, and provided a very enlightening (to the family therapist) example of the kinds of interactional difficulties this particular family was facing.

A similar, and equally illuminating example was the following:

Family C, a triad in which the son, age 19, had been known as schizophrenic for some years. During the family decision, he was the one who became the "secretary" for the family, i.e., the one who did write down on the questionnaire the decisions the family had reached. However, his behavior was rather surprising to observers with advance knowledge of his answers on the individual questionnaire. He was writing himself off! Holding a pencil in hand he would question his parents about their wishes on the questionnaire. Meanwhile, he would look at his parents and shake his head sideways in a most negative fashion saying, for instance, "You would not want to go to a movie with Kim Novak, would you?" When the parents, reacting slowly to his approach, would essay a feeble "no", as if to please their boy, he would invariably echo their statements with a decisive "No, of course..." and, thereupon, scratch out the item in question. But the astonishing thing was that in this manner he was scratching himself out, that is, he was inciting the parents to say "no" to every one of the alternatives he had chosen for himself on the individually administered questionnaire!

Obviously, these are only tidbits of an enormous number of observations made in the course of this and previous projects. In reporting them we can hardly go beyond the anecdote and the impression, for they do not constitute wholly analyzable data. However, they exemplify some instances of enlightening, and, at times, amusing family interaction, and demonstrate the seriousness with which these families, normal or abnormal, undertook the testing situation.

To conclude, however, let us make clear that, in its present form, the testing instrument devised for this project does not seem sensitive enough to warrant diagnostic conclusions about any one particular family. Its utilization in the evaluation of a family will undoubtedly provide much data of possible usefulness to the diagnostician and to the therapist. On the objective side, the test will reveal the family measurements on the variables of spontaneous agreement, decision-time, choice-fulfillment, and others which will permit placement of the family in the spectrum of normal vs. abnormal scores already available through the findings of this and previous works; and on the subjective side, the testing will provide a batch of impressions through the observation of the family's overall deportment while attempting to reach family decisions. However, the application of this test to any single family could be of no lasting interest. This technique was devised as an investigative instrument and it is, therefore, in the area of research that it should prove its greatest usefulness. Hence, it could now be used, for instance, to investigate certain groups of families (such as families with cases of asthma, gastro-duodenal ulcer, ulcerative colitis, enuresis, functional speech, alcoholism, etc.) whose abnormality, as a family, has remained questionable; or to assess our diverse therapeutic abilities to ameliorate interactional pathology. We are beginning to feel some confidence in the solidity of these research findings. Despite enormous gaps in our knowledge, it seems that we have come across a number of tangible concepts about family decision-making and their correlation with a normal-abnormal classification. Still, we face a Daedalus. But we dare to hope that pursuit of the threads of Ariadne provided by these projects will guide us towards a greater understanding of the basic issues in family relationships, family interaction, family decision-making, and, ultimately, family normality and abnormality.

REFERENCES

1. EPSTEIN, S., "Some Theoretical Considerations on the Nature of Ambiguity and the Use of Stimulus Dimensions in Projective Techniques," *J. Cons. Psychol.*, 30, 183–192, 1966.
2. FERREIRA, A. J., "Decision-Making in Normal and Pathologic Families," *Arch. Gen. Psychiat.*, 8, 68–73, 1963.
3. FERREIRA, A. J., Rejection and Expectancy of Rejection in Families," *Fam. Proc.*, 2, 235–244, 1963.
4. FERREIRA, A. J., "Family Myth and Homeostasis," *Arch. Gen. Psychiat.*, 9, 457–463, 1963.
5. FERREIRA, A. J., "Family Myths: The Covert Rules of the Relationship," *Confin. Psychiat.*, 8, 15–20, 1965.
6. FERREIRA, A. J., "Family Myths," *Psychiat. Res. Rep. 20, Amer. Psychiat. Assn.*, 85–90, 1966.
7. FERREIRA, A. J. AND WINTER, W. D., "Family Interaction and Decision-Making," *Arch. Gen. Psychiat.*, 13, 214–223, 1965.
8. FERREIRA, A. J. and WINTER, W. D., "Stability of Interactional Variables in Family Decision-Making," *Arch. Gen. Psychiat.*, 14, 352–355, 1966.
9. FERREIRA, A. J., WINTER, W. D. and POINDEXTER, E. J., "Some Interactional Variables in Normal and Abnormal Families," *Fam. Proc.*, 5, 60–75, 1966.
10. STRODTBECK, F. L., "Husband-Wife Interaction over Revealed Differences," *Amer. Sociol. Rev.*, 16, 468–473, 1951.
11. WINTER, W. D., FERREIRA, A. J. and OLSON, J. L., "Story Sequence Analysis of Family TATs," *J. Proj. Techn.*, 29, 392–397, 1965.
12. WINTER, W. D., FERREIRA, A. J. and OLSON, J. L., "Hostility Themes in the Family TAT," *J. Proj. Techn.*, 30, 270–274, 1966.

23

Audience Reactions and Careers of Psychiatric Patients

STEPHEN P. SPITZER, Ph.D.
ROBERT M. SWANSON, M.A.
ROBERT K. LEHR, M.A.

THE TERM "career" encompasses at least two notions. It refers to the sequence of movements from a position in any particular network of social relations to another position in the same or in a different social network, and to the individual adjustments accompanying the movement. The concept of career has received a wide variety of applications. Hughes (16) has applied it to the analysis of organizational adjustment, Hall (14) to medical education, and Becker (2) to marijuana users and jazz musicians.

Recently, the concept of career has been extended to the area of mental illness. According to Goffman (11), the career has three distinct phases: a prepatient phase, which describes the person in the community prior to hospitalization; an inpatient phase, which describes the person in the psychiatric treatment center; and a postpatient phase, which describes the person as he is back in the community after hospitalization. In describing the patient career, Goffman focuses on the consequences of being regarded as psychiatrically deviant, accommodating to institutional life, and forming alignments with persons in similar circumstances and hospital personnel. The purpose of this paper is to describe the careers of psychiatric patients as they are influenced, perhaps determined, by family reactions. Specifically, this paper identifies two dimensions of family reactions to deviancy and the relationship of each to the patient career.

Considerable research has been directed toward the identification of predisposing factors in the development of mental illness, particularly schizophrenia (21, 23, 34). As a consequence, it is commonly recognized that the family plays an important part in the development of behavior pathology. Given the importance of the family in the etiology of mental illness, it seems reasonable to assume that the family has consequences more far reaching than that of the initial development of illness.

The family plays a major role in the identification of psychiatric deviance (4, 22, 30), determines the course of action to be taken once psychiatric deviance has been recognized (4, 25, 39), contributes to the stabilization of deviance (19, 29, 31), and influences case outcome both in terms of recidivism and interpersonal adjustment (8, 18, 32). The family also provides socialization into the sick role (27, 35), contributes to feelings of alienation and stigma (1, 5, 10, 38), intervenes in order to alter the course of hospitalization (6), and may also detract from the effectiveness of psychotherapeutic procedures (28, 33).

This is not to imply that the family is the only audience involved in mental illness. The part played by outside agencies, physicians, friends, and even the self as a definer has been repeatedly documented (4, 13, 15). However, because of its position of control and influence, the nuclear family is usually the most significant grouping intervening between the deviant act and the career path. Consequently, scrutiny of family reactions should enable us to make predictions concerning the particular directions in which the psychiatric career evolves.

In the course of conducting an investigation concerned with changes in self-identities, attitudes, and interpersonal relations, it became evident that different types of career patterns developed among psychiatric patients (7, 36, 37). Some persons entered the hospital, were discharged, and then returned to the hospital at a later date. Others had been discharged for a two year period with no indication that they would eventually return. Some persons entered treatment shortly after mental illness was "detected" but it took others many years to begin treatment. In interviewing family members of the patients, we were led to conclude that case outcome was closely tied in with the structure and attitudes prevailing in the patient's family. Inspection of the data led to the isolation of two "sensitizing concepts" or characteristics of the families that were associated with several career paths. One we call *Expected Level of Performance;* the other *Propensity for Action.* Each of these "sensitizing concepts" reflects a constellation of characteristics of particular families. They are largely summary predictors of attitudes toward the sick role, toward psychiatry, toward interpretation of deviance as symptomatic of mental illness.

Level of expected performance refers to what the family requires on various dimensions: economic, interpersonal, community relations, conformity, etc. In short, *what does the family expect for participation and membership?* Performance levels were explored in detail by Freeman and Simmons (8, 9). The family set up certain expectations for the "deviant" in terms of stability of employment and associative patterns. Performance level expectations were higher among middle class families and conjugal families and accounted for the higher recidivism rates in these families. Performance level expectations were found to be associated with the deviant's family position, with higher performance levels set for persons having a key role in the family (18). Although most research concerned with performance levels is confined to the postpatient phase, investigations in other phases also seem to bear on this concept. Gordon's (12) study of the sick role disclosed marked variations in expectations regarding the rights and obligations to be assumed once this role has been ascribed.

The second dimension is propensity for action. Because of several considerations, some families move persons into treatment rapidly and some move them slowly if at all.

Families differ in their readiness to ascribe the psychiatric label: What is regarded as psychiatric deviancy in one family is not necessarily recognized as such in another. Moreover, the ascription of psychiatric deviancy takes longer in some families than others when other things are equal such as the frequency, intensity and visibility of deviant behavior. Variations in the timing of events may be deduced from investigations concerned with discerning psychiatric problems (4, 15, 22, 30). In the families reported upon in this paper, marked variations were found, ranging from the immediate ascription of a psychiatric label, to as long as 20 years between recognition of deviance and awareness that a psychiatric problem had developed.

Families differ in how much deviation from expectations they are willing to accept: In some families the merest deviation from normative patterns is a source of immediate concern, regardless of the expected level of performance. Permissiveness was found to be considerably greater in lower than middle class families (25); Clausen and Yarrow (4) also report large differences in the degree to which family members are willing to support and tolerate deviance among the husbands in 33 families; Mechanic (22) has indicated that nonconformity is tolerated depending upon how serious the consequences of the deviation are for the group.

Even within a given family, tolerance limits established for different family members vary. Gurin, Veroff, and Feld (13) found that if the problem were one involving intrafamilial relationships and involved the spouse (rather than some other family member), there was a lower likelihood that the deviant would arrive at a professional help source. According to these authors this came about because problems involving the spouse were more difficult to identify, although we would tend to favor a differential tolerance limits interpretation. There was no indication that problems involving the spouse were any less severe than problems involving others, e.g., siblings, offspring, etc.

Families differ in their ability to tolerate or withstand stress: As Parsons and Fox (27) have indicated, the the American family is prone to reject deviant members, since deviance disturbs family equilibrium. Some families have such a lack of integration that the slightest deviance on the part of one member threatens the family with dissolution, or disturbs relationships so greatly that harmonious family relations are impossible. On the other hand, in some families the deviant serves an integrative function. According to Vogel and Bell (40), the schizophrenic child enables the family to maintain its unity by providing a convenient outlet for the personality difficulties of the parents. Lidz et al. (20) have noted that a schizophrenic child may serve to maintain the parents' marriage, resolving parental conflicts and the needs of both. Similarly, Bursten and D'Esopo (3) contend that families sometimes require that an individual maintain a sick role for the benefit of the family rather than the patient. Thus when the family is dependent upon the deviant and the deviant helps to maintain stability by fulfilling a needed role, the family is able to withstand considerable stress before initiating plans for treatment. (There may be another dimension involved which can be called: Degree of Adherence to the Medical Model of Illness. As a rule the American family has been socialized to believe that mental illness, like physical illness, is an abnormality that cannot safely be ignored. Concomitant with this is the belief that mental illness, like physical illness, can be remedied. If professional help is not sought, the illness will progress and the patient may deteriorate to a point where professional help would no longer be beneficial. Because the goal of some families is to protect the deviant from his illness, an obligation is felt to move the deviant into treatment as rapidly as possible. Allusions to this can be found in Nunnally (26), Parsons and Fox (27), Mechanic (22), and Korles (17).)

METHODS

The patterns described in the results section are the by-product of examining the histories of 79 first admission patients with functional disorders from a university teaching and research hospital. (The term patient is used in this paper regardless of phase.) Each patient and his primary significant other was interviewed prior to hospitalization. The primary significant other, i.e., that person whose opinion of him the patient regarded as most important, was almost invariably a nuclear family member.

In order to reconstruct the events and timing of events prior to hospitalization, the prepatient phase was broken down into three subphases: Definition and Appraisal of Deviance, Decision to Utilize Psychiatric Help, Implementation of Psychiatric Care. For each, respondents were queried in regard to *what* it was that was recognized and responded to, *when* this occurred, and *who* was involved. Information was also collected in regard to the influence of the various audience members and their particular reactions.

Case records compiled by the hospital were used to follow the patients through the inpatient phase and back into the community. In addition to the usual reports submitted by psychiatric and nursing staff, the records contained one or more evaluations by social workers. We could determine not only how each patient accommodated to institutional life and therapy, but also how the family responded to the situation. After discharge several of the patients were maintained on an outpatient basis at the hospital or at other treatment centers and some were eventually rehospitalized. If rehospitalized elsewhere this information was contained in the patient's files. In addition, we had the results from a postpatient follow-up conducted by the hospital one year after discharge of each patient. The follow-up records were particularly informative regarding attitudes that developed and events that occurred following the patient's hospitalization.

(Several considerations entered into selecting prepatients. Persons in the inpatient and postpatient phases could less accurately account for prior events, particularly in respect to the timing of family reactions. Thus although the design has retrospective elements, biases associated with errors of recall are less pronounced than if the starting point for investigation were a following phase. One disadvantage of focusing on a cohort of prepatients and their families is the time lag necessary to determine case outcome. None of the prepatients had been discharged for over two and one half years. It would be worthwhile to follow these patients over a more extended period, although it can be argued that the case would not be complete until death.)

RESULTS

By thinking of any given family as either high or low on the dimensions of Performance Level and Propensity for Action, four basic possibilities in respect to career paths are observed. These are shown in Figure 1. Sometimes more than one career path is entered in each cell of the 2 x 2 table. This is partly because the two major dimensions have been dichotomized rather than placed on a continuum, and because of the effects of several other variables, particularly attitudes toward psychiatry held by the patient and his family.

Seventy-six of the 79 cases could be classified according to the

		Expected Performance Level	
		High	Low
Propensity for Action	Low	Stoics Poltroons	Pacifists Stumblers Do-nothings
	High	Shape-up or Ship-out Altercasters	Dutch Uncles

FIG. 1. Career patterns based on family reactions

taxonomy in Figure 1. In the three remaining cases the patient either had no family or he separated from the family before the onset of deviant behavior. This does not mean that all cases fit perfectly into the taxonomy, but all could be classified with substantial agreement.

Psychiatric Career Paths Based on Various Family Reactions

Stoics: This kind of family is characterized by a "philosophical" outlook, taking life as it comes. As a consequence, their propensity for action is low when deviation of a family member is observed. They have a high tolerance level for deviant behavior, as well as a marked ability to tolerate or withstand stress. However, they do not adhere rigidly to the medical model of illness, believing that painful experiences can be endured and that illness does not necessarily lead to progressive deterioration. Their expectations for performance are high, but their demands on the deviant are minimal. They are silent and uncomplaining.

Stoics do not play a major part in moving their deviant family members into psychiatric treatment. The deviant behavior often comes to the attention of outsiders who then play a more active role. In such instances family tolerance limits are finally exceeded and treatment plans are initiated. During the inpatient phase they visit frequently, but they do not attempt to influence the inpatients' attitudes and behavior in any appreciable way. They accept the psychiatric definition of illness. During the postpatient phase they revert to their old behavior patterns. The demands on the patient are low and while they may be disappointed that he does not perform at a higher level, rarely is action initiated for rehospitalization. Rehospitalization may come about, however, at the urging of outsiders.

> Robert, age 17, had a long history of interpersonal difficulties and mediocre grades. At six years of age, family friends commented on Robert's awkwardness and inability to perform at the level of his age mates. Robert's mother suggested seeking professional help when the boy began stuttering at eight years of age. However, the father reasoned that his son would outgrow his difficulties if left alone.
>
> Both Robert and his family had made extensive plans for him to attend a large midwestern university. Three weeks prior to admission to the hospital, Robert was notified that his application had been rejected. The family became somewhat despondent because of this news, but urged Robert to apply to other colleges.

Because of suspected brain damage, interpersonal difficulties, and the obvious discrepancy between family aspirations and the boy's abilities, a high school counselor suggested that Robert reassess his career plans. Robert and the parents rejected this advice and were then referred to the local vocational rehabilitation office, which in turn, referred them to a psychiatric hospital.

Upon release from the hospital, Robert entered a local community college. At the end of his first year his grades were such that he was urged to "...make a more suitable career choice." Robert is now attending a small southern college and experiencing a great deal of difficulty. His parents maintain that they are confident that he will graduate if he works a little harder.

Poltroons: This family feels the necessity for removing the deviant from the family, but is hesitant to pay the interpersonal price of a direct confrontation with him. Because they do not want to hurt the deviant's feelings or to strain their relationship with him, their ability to tolerate stress is rather high. Similarly, they are willing to tolerate an excessive amount of deviant behavior. Often the feeling that stigma is associated with mental illness adds to their reluctance to take direct action. The course taken is to operate behind the patient's back. They may send their deviant to the family doctor on false pretenses (routine checkup, just to have him look you over) while the family doctor has been fully informed as to the real circumstances for the visit. The doctor has been urged to recommend psychiatric hospitalization. If the family doctor does not fulfill their expectation, an uninvolved peripheral family member such as an uncle or nephew plays the role of "complainant." As a consequence the deviant member is removed from the family and any animosity he may have is directed toward an incorrect source. The family plays a supportive role for the patient and laments his unfortunate circumstances, although they raise the possibility that hospitalization might be the best thing for him.

Once the prepatient has been hospitalized, they realign themselves with the hospital. If called upon, they cooperate fully with the hospital staff. They also exert pressures upon the patient to cooperate with the hospital staff. They are hopeful for full compliance. Once the patient is discharged, and the necessity for readmission arises, action on the part of the family is direct. They communicate to the postpatient their obligation to the hospital and play this obligation to the hilt. The postpatient in this kind of family is a potential readmission, for during this stage the expectations for performance are still high, but the ability to tolerate deviance is low. Therefore, the family can initiate rehospitalization without guilt.

Mr. Z. is a 49 year old farmer with a long history of paranoia. He is a high school graduate while his wife is a college graduate. His wife, a very domineering woman, owns by inheritance most of the family farm. She totally runs the household and makes all major decisions. This has made Mr. Z. feel that he is not needed and has helped support his feeling that his wife and others are plotting against him.

Mr. Z. apparently has had several attacks of depression, notably in Spring 1962 and 1965. The most recent one (1966) has been complicated by a prostate problem and other somatic complaints. During this same period he had become increasingly suspicious and jealous of his wife, accusing her of having an affair with the local feed salesman. His wife and daughters consistently tried to dissuade him of his allegations. Eventually he sought an attorney to keep the salesman off the farm. During this visit he developed shortness of breath and a numbness in his arm due to what he thought to be a heart attack. He was admitted to a general hospital, where his suspiciousness was noted. The family in collaboration with the attending physician, arranged to have Mr. Z. committed to a psychiatric hospital.

When an ambulance arrived to transport Mr. Z. to the psychiatric hospital, he thought that he was going back to the general hospital. Surreptitiously the family drove to the psychiatric hospital after him to provide information for a social worker. There was no direct confrontation between Mr. Z. and his family and he assumed that the physician was responsible for his commitment.

During his 10 days in the hospital, he was not visited by his family and continued to assume that they were not responsible for his commitment. He complained that he was being held against his will. His diagnosis was Paranoid Reaction.

At the time of discharge, his wife volunteered to report any future paranoid behavior and Mr. Z. was to appear at the hospital on an outpatient basis. In this respect, partial responsibility for rehospitalization rested indirectly with the wife. He has remained out of the hospital and although still jealous of his wife, agreed that in the future instead of accusing his wife, he would first talk to the psychiatrist about his feelings.

Shape-up or ship-out: The members of this kind of family stand on their own two feet. They are neither reluctant to inform the deviant that he might be mentally ill nor that his behavior is disruptive to the family. Their behavior is motivated by a number of considerations. They expect the patient to perform at a high level. Their value orientations are such that they will not tolerate deviance on the basis of principle. In other instances, family integration is so low that disruptions threaten to dissolve the family. Moreover, the family members may feel that illness must be treated as soon as possible for the patient's welfare. A valiant attempt may be made to evoke conformity through interpersonal pressures and family discussion. Once it becomes evident that the goal of conformity or apparent mental health cannot be attained through family mechanations, arrangements are made by the family for psychiatric treatment.

During the prepatient phase the family is not overly concerned with the prepatient's attitudes toward them, even if he has strong feelings of having been betrayed. After all, the prepatient had been repeatedly warned that hospitalization might be necessary, and they can stand on the moral justification that they have done the best thing for the prepatient as well as for the family group. They fervently hope that psychiatric treatment will be beneficial and that the patient will be thoroughly cured. But they know what they will do if problems crop up after discharge. If the postpatient deviates he is returned to the hospital.

> For as long as Richard could remember, he had been punished by rejection. His father, who had overcome a serious physical handicap to become a successful attorney, was repeatedly held up to him as a model to be emulated.
>
> When a child, Richard was sent to his grandmother's home in another city. His parents feared that his boyish misdeeds might cast a shadow upon the family's community reputation. At age 11 he was sent to a camp for problem children. Prior to his senior year of high he was sent to a military academy.
>
> Since his return from military school he entered a local college but encountered academic difficulties. Although he lived at home, he declined to take part in the family's active social life. Consequently his parents decided that psychiatric treatment should be sought. He was admitted to a psychiatric hospital during his twentieth year as a chronic undifferentiated schizophrenic.
>
> Richard adjusted very poorly while in the hospital. His behavior was described as hostile toward the staff as well as other patients. His parents notified both Richard and the hospital staff that he would not be allowed to return home until his behavior became more "respectable."
>
> After four months in the hospital it was decided that the subject should be discharged in order to seek employment since this would force him into

interpersonal relationships. He was to continue treatment on an out-patient basis. This decision was ratified by the parents. However, after a month's time, during which the subject made no apparent effort to find a job, his parents decided that he was incapable of managing his own affairs and committed him to a psychiatric institution which offered long term custodial care.

Altercasters: In many respects this type of family has many of the characteristics of the "Poltroons" and the "Shape-up or ship-outers." They desire to avoid any direct confrontation with the psychiatric deviant and go to great lengths to conceal from the deviant that they are responsible for his removal from the family. However, unlike the "Poltroons," they are more subtle. Rather than forming an active coalition with the family physician or psychiatrist, they present the help source with the deviant, casting him into the position of making some sort of a treatment decision. Now, no one can say that they are directly responsible. They may also be indirectly responsible in another way, by altercasting the patient. This may take the form of communicating to the patient that his symptoms correspond to psychiatric deviance to a point that the patient eventually internalizes this definition. If this takes place, the patient seeks psychiatric help and the family accomplishes the same purpose as if they had taken the patient to the help source themselves. Often what appears to be a self-made decision to implement psychiatric treatment is actually an outcome of the altercasting process.

During the prepatient phase the punitive and threatening attitudes of the "Shape-up or ship-outers" is absent. These attitudes are also absent during the inpatient and postpatient phases of the psychiatric patient career. Like the "Shape-up or ship-outs," the expectations for performance are high, and the propensity to initiate action is also high. But if the family has been particularly successful, further actions on their part are unnecessary, since the patient will automatically carry out what the family wishes him to do. In such instances, rehospitalization may be self-perpetuating.

Upon his election to the local school board, Mr. S. began to manifest symptoms of depression and suspiciousness. He felt that he couldn't handle the work on his farm and that he had taken on more responsibility than he could handle. He expressed thoughts that people were talking about him and accusing him of trying to gain prestige by running for school board member. He became insomniac and vacillated between periods of despondency and agitation.

Mr. S. was taken by his wife and brother to a local physician who prescribed medication. The family then tried another physician who immediately recommended psychiatric hospitalization and promised to arrange papers for commitment.

The family informed Mr. S. that the second physician recommended hospitalization, had already made out commitment papers, and that there was no turning back. Mr. S. was taken to the hospital where it was discovered that the papers had not been received. This made it necessary to persuade Mr. S. to enter. By stressing their obligation to carry out the physician's orders, the family eventually persuaded Mr. S. to enter voluntarily. The diagnosis given was Manic Depressive Psychosis—Depressed Type.

Mr. S. made a fairly good adjustment in the hospital and was allowed to return home on extended leave (a very unusual practice for this hospital) a week after admission. While his paranoia dissipated, his depression reappeared, but he was able to harvest his crop during the following month. He returned to inpatient status, was discharged two weeks later, and was then seen on an occasional outpatient basis.

The other pattern is one in which the family convinces the patient that he is ill, creating a moral obligation to seek help. Often the patient is unaware that the family has influenced his self-attitudes or determined his decision to seek psychiatric help. On the surface this pattern appears to be a self-referral.

For two years prior to hospitalization, Miss T.'s behavior was a source of embarrassment to her family. She is described by her mother as a rebellious girl who fails to live up to her family responsibilities. The subject is reported to show a great deal of disrespect for her mother's wishes. Most of her time is spent day dreaming or writing poetry. Her college grades have suffered causing her parents further consternation.

For some time Miss T.'s mother had suspected psychiatric problems and while almost daily urging her daughter to see a psychiatrist neither offered to make any arrangements nor suggested any paths to treatment. Her father remained passive during most of these "scenes," but when forced to voice an opinion, sided with his wife.

Miss T. appeared at the hospital alone and without a prior appointment. When asked why she had come, she stated that she was mentally ill and should have herself hospitalized.

The subject was subsequently hospitalized and diagnosed as Adjustment Reaction to Adolescence. During the course of hospitalization, marked improvement was noted with the exception of sporadic relapses which corresponded to her parents' visits. After two months, Miss T. was released as much improved with an excellent prognosis. She returned home where she remained for approximately one year before reappearing at the hospital. Her explanation was: "They think I'm crazy."

Pacifists: This family tends to accommodate itself to the deviant member. As a consequence, they have lowered their expectations for performance and their propensity for initiating any action to remove the patient from the family. At one time they tried to evoke conformity by a variety of mechanisms: begging, nagging, threatening, withdrawal of rewards, pointing out the deleterious effect of the problem on the family. All of these techniques have proved to be relatively ineffective and the family has come to the realization that they cannot make the problem disappear and that the prepatient is unable to help himself. As a result the family accommodates itself to the patient. He receives greater latitude for deviation and very little is expected of him. While this may create additional problems, the degree of family integration is such that accommodation is the lesser of the two evils. The family considers the necessity for professional psychiatric help, but is slow to initiate action. The problems in the family are not so severe that rejection of the deviant is an absolute necessity. They may be very concerned that the patient's "illness" may grow progressively worse, but again no action is immediately necessary. More than the "Stoics" and the "Poltroons," they subscribe to the belief that the deviation may be "outgrown" or that spontaneous recovery might occur.

Richard was referred from Neurology for a diagnostic evaluation because neurological examination failed to show any evidence of organic injury in a car accident. At about the age of 14 his grades began to drop in school. From the time his father entered the hospital for a serious back operation when Richard was 16, he became very rebellious toward the parents. Since that time he precipitated numerous incidents involving poor judgment and damage to property. Within a short time he abused two of his automobiles beyond repair. Against his father's warning, he took a tractor into a muddy field and got it stuck. In spite of the expense and inconvenience of extricating the equipment, the entire performance was repeated several days later. Later the patient knowingly drove a pickup truck without brakes, missed a curve, and overturned. Although the oil from the truck had drained out, he drove the truck home. During the following month he made obscene sexual comments to a neighbor lady and was found in the family living room masturbating and hitting his penis against the wall.

The mother tolerated all of the boy's deviations. Although she once had a level of expectation consonant with the patient's age, she came to respond to him more as a seven year old, i.e., bribing him incessantly and washing his face. The father was extremely disappointed. While he became able to tolerate misdeeds, he couldn't accept the boy's poor judgment and constantly compared the patient unfavorably to his siblings.

In the accident to the truck the patient received a hard blow on the head. The parents reported that during the month after the accident, the patient ate very little and was very sleepy, seemed not to hear, and did not follow orders. His personal appearance deteriorated, and he had little interest in anything, spent much time singing and mumbling to himself.

The extent to which the parents either used the accident as a pretext to seek medical treatment or simply began to notice an already existing pattern of behavior is not entirely clear. However, there is evidence that the patient underwent some personality change after the accident.

Richard disappeared from the hospital during his intake interview but was returned four days later. During the week and a half he spent in the psychiatric hospital, his mother visited daily. The ward personnel thought she was very overprotective and seductive with the patient. One evening the boy confided to his mother how homesick he was and on the next day again eloped from the hospital. He was returned the following morning and discharged. Diagnosis at discharge was Schizoid Personality. The patient was kept on drugs while at home and reported back to the psychiatrist periodically. His home adjustment was regarded as satisfactory by the mother, in spite of several "incidents."

Stumblers: The "Stumblers" recognize deviancy from a healthy state among family members and are ready to seek clarification of the problem. Invariably, whatever the problem happens to be, it is interpreted as a medical problem and the family facilitates contact with a medical practitioner, particularly the family doctor. The family doctor may recognize the problem as a psychiatric one and communicate this to the family. As these are generally passive and uninformed persons, the professional judgment is accepted and acted upon. Sometimes they do not have a chance to participate in the decision making, particularly when the physician makes the arrangements for hospitalization without consulting the family. For this kind of family, things are often taken from their control.

Since psychiatric treatment was hardly what the family had in mind, the entire experience is very disturbing. The inpatient is urged by the family to do whatever the treatment authorities deem necessary, but no attempt is made to induce the patient to accept the attitudes and orientations of professionals. Sometimes the activities of the family are directed solely to facilitate the deviant's release from the hospital.

It is difficult to predict the evolution of the patient career in this type of family, although two courses of development are prevalent. One course of action results from an uncritical acceptance of the professional definition. Although the family members do not really understand the concept of psychological motivation, any further deviation on the part of the subject is cause to seek out the old authority for clarification and advice. Another is to avoid rehospitalization. Quite by accident the family has stumbled into a path of treatment and they will not make the same mistake again.

Mrs. E. was admitted to a university general hospital with the complaint of inflammation of the lower extremities. After a course of treatment to remedy the inflammation, she was transferred to a university psychiatric hospital to explore techniques to reduce what was seen as an anxiety reaction resulting in a condition of obesity. At the time of admission, the patient weighed 380 pounds. After clinical evaluation Mrs. E. was diagnosed as Personality Trait Disturbance, mild anxiety resulting in extreme impairment (obesity). This 46 year old mother of five children and her husband were seen in a staff conference at which time the consulting psychiatrist recommended a three month stay for relief of the symptoms of anxiety and implementation of a medically controlled diet. Neither the husband nor the patient agreed with these recommendations. Mr. E. refused to see the wife's obesity as a problem. Furthermore, he did not identify his wife's anxiety response as a problem in his relationship with her or as interfering with her functions as mother or housewife. At the end of the week the patient was released at her husband's insistence with the agreement that she be placed on a diet and given medication to relieve her anxiety. This was acceptable to the patient and husband on the grounds that this form of treatment was directed toward a physical problem.

Do-nothings: This kind of family is characterized by a "do-nothing" attitude. Psychiatric deviancy may or may not be recognized. In some instances the deviation may be classified under some other term (trouble-maker, criminal, idiosyncratic) or hardly noticed. If the deviation is recognized as mental illness, the question of utilizing psychiatric treatment is not considered as a possible remedial action. The family may be opposed to psychiatric care but indifference is the predominant pattern. Accordingly, the expected level of performance is extremely low. As far as the fulfilling of family role obligations is concerned, only minimal performance is required, perhaps no more than contributing sporadically to the economic needs of the family, carrying out some simple household tasks, or in some cases merely refraining from interfering with the operation of the family.

Rarely do "Do-nothings" attempt to move the prepatient out of the home. The patient career begins because of the intervention of some outside agency or person. Since social control within the family is absent, the deviant may act in an increasingly aberrant fashion. As frequency and intensity of the deviation increases, it becomes more and more salient to the outside community. If a recommendation for psychiatric treatment is made to the family, they do little or nothing to facilitate treatment. They may endorse the decision to utilize psychiatric care, but acquiescence is the rule. Actual opposition is rare.

As the patient enters the hospital the family remains uninvolved. Neither the patient nor the family has received any presocialization for the events that occur. Although the family may be reticent to accept the definition of psychiatric deviancy, they eventually come to accept a professional definition, albeit passively and minimally. Once the inpatient returns home, however, the psychiatric definition quickly fades into the background. The likelihood that the family will become involved in rehospitalization is small, although the possibility of outside interference remains.

Mr. G. had a 20 year history of alcoholism. His wife was not particularly disturbed by his drinking behavior even though it resulted in intermittent employment. Following the birth of a child eight years ago, he became highly irritable and began to suffer from a variety of somatic complaints. His wife had earlier exerted pressure on him to stop drinking, but had ceased to make any such demands. Although he had threatened her and the child at gun point, the wife's major compaint was that when intoxicated he wished to have sexual intercourse. For this reason she once asked him to move out, which he failed to do. Several months later, however, she left him. Mr. G. continued to drink and experienced further complications with his health, showed depressive symptoms and a marked weight loss. His somatic complaints led him to see a local physician who recommended psychiatric treatment and advised Mr. G.'s adult daughter to this effect. The sheriff picked up Mr. G. for loitering in a nearby town. His family was notified and the daughter contacted the outpatient clinic of a nearby psychiatric hospital to inquire about assistance, although not admission. On his own initiative the sheriff brought the patient to he outpatient clinic of the same psychiatric hospital. After discharge Mr. G.

showed up inebriated at the home of his first wife with whom he is now staying. However, his second wife plans to "get together" again with her husband. His depression lifted moderately and his drinking tapered off as he was treated for several months in the outpatient clinic. The final diagnosis was Passive Dependent Personality, depressive reaction, chronic alcoholism.

A case in which the family was totally apathetic is as follows:

Ray, a 17 year old, was referred to the psychiatric hospital by the court for evaluation after having attempted to induce a young woman into a car. When she refused he threatened her with a knife. Although this resulted in his referral, the patient had been involved in numerous antisocial incidents since the age of seven at which time he began stealing. Other difficulties involved truancy, poor grades, absenteeism from school, superficially wounding another student with a knife, breaking and entering, and making a girl pregnant. The diagnosis at admission was Sociopathic Personality Disturbance, antisocial type.

Contact with the parents disclosed a mother who had never set up high performance expectations for the patient. In regard to the patient's antisocial behavior, the mother withheld information from the father. On several occasions the father attempted to discipline the boy, but the mother interfered and the boy was rarely punished. Although the mother had been hospitalized for psychiatric disorder, there was no indication that either she or the father regarded his behavior as deviant in a psychiatric sense. There are suggestions that the mother derives vicarious pleasure from the boy's behavior, as well as using the boy as a husband substitute.

After discharge and upon the hospital's recommendation, the charge of assault was held in abeyance. The court stipulated that Ray continue to receive outpatient treatment, but Ray missed half of his appointments. He was returned to the outpatient clinic by the probation officer of the juvenile court who reported that his adjustment at school and his relationship with his mother were satisfactory. He worked part time in a store and considered entering military service upon graduation from high school. He hoped to specialize in underwater demolitions.

Dutch Uncles: The expectations of this family for its deviant member are very low, but even the slightest degree of deviation is intolerable. In some ways they are a special case of the "Shape-up or ship-outs." But while the "Shape-up or ship-outs" have set down a lengthy list of expected performances, the Dutch Uncles present the deviant with only a few requirements. On those occasional instances when a whole series of expectations are enumerated, they actually anticipate superficial performance on the specified dimensions. In regard to their propensity for action, they adhere rigidly to the medical model of illness. In some instances hospitalization functions less to preserve the integration of the family than it does to punish the deviant member. But this takes place only when the family is willing to pay the price of conflict with the deviant. Occasionally they will use the same techniques to dispose of the deviant as the "Altercasters" or the "Poltroons." If an outside agency enters into the situation, they will refrain from interfering with efforts to remove the deviant from the home.

A person is moved into treatment most rapidly with this type of family. Moreover, rehospitalization is most highly probable here.

Carolyn, age 16, was referred to the hospital for evaluation by the county welfare agency in connection with child abuse charges pending against her parents. At the time of admission, 892 lacerations were found on the girl's back and lower extremities. The girl's condition was first reported by school authorities when she arrived at school, her blouse stained with blood. She claimed that she had fallen on barb wire. Since the authorities were suspicious of her story, she was referred to the hospital in order "to separate fact from fiction." Upon extensive questioning, Carolyn admitted that her mother had on at least two occasions beat her with a nail-studded paddle. It was learned that the parents showed very little concern with their childrens' activities. They demand only two things—refraining from smoking and drinking. The beatings occurred when the mother discovered Carolyn smoking prior to leaving for school. On both occasions the mother insisted that Carolyn see a doctor before going to school, but Carolyn went directly to school.

The parents are characterized as rigid, compulsive types who neither admit or deny administering these beatings. Family therapy was offered but rejected by the parents.

After a ten day period in the hospital, the subject was released to a foster home. During hospitalization it was determined that Carolyn had neurotic tendencies which would probably worsen in an unstable home situation. No specific diagnosis was given.

Because Carolyn was unable to adjust to her foster parents, she was returned to her parental home with the understanding that she would give up smoking. However, when once again she was caught smoking the family consulted the family doctor and urged that Carolyn be readmitted to the hospital.

DISCUSSION

The extent to which the career paths delineated can be generalized to those emerging in other kinds of institutions or among other kinds of psychiatric populations was explored by examining the case histories of patients and their families in two large state psychiatric institutions. Although some differences among hospitals were discernible, these referred more to the frequencies with which patterns occurred rather than to discrepancies in types of career patterns. This was particularly the case with long term as compared to short term patients, since the short term patients were more comparable to those at the university hospital. However, it is plausible that the career paths develop somewhat differently in private psychiatric hospitals or in V.A. installations. Variations in career paths could be attributed to the effects of hospital social structure, although it is more likely that potential differences are attributable to the characteristics of patients typically recruited by different hospitals. This is partly because age and sex characteristics indirectly determine the kinds of primary group audiences available.

No doubt the characteristics of the psychiatric populations under scrutiny determine the frequency with which family reactions are observed. In populations made up of relatively aged unmarried men, for example, one would expect family reactions to be less prevalent than reactions by other kinds of audiences. Notwithstanding differences in population characteristics the frequency with which family reactions are observed and reported is partly a function of research methodology. Wood, Rakusin, and Morse (39) reported that of 48 patients studied, families initiated hospitalization in 13 (27%) of the cases. However, what we call the "Do-nothings" and "Stumblers" have probably not entered into their calculations. What is often unappreciated is that lack of family involvement is a particular type of audience reaction, and that the consequences of noninvolvement may be equally as important for shaping the career as direct intervention. Unless this is understood, it may appear that previous studies have grossly underestimated the frequency of family reactions, or conversely, that we have made an equally inappropriate overestimate.

This is not to imply, however, that procedures as outlined in this paper and samples from similar types of psychiatric hospitals will reveal a frequency of reactions of family involvement comparable to our findings. There is evidence that mention of a relative sometimes influences a hospital's decision to accept a patient for admission (24). Samples of patients selected from hospitals adhering to such a policy would show an inordinately high percentage of family involvement. In the university hospital from which our cases were selected, it was the policy to request that persons seeking admission be accompanied by a relative when appearing for an intake evaluation. Persons not complying with this request were not necessarily denied admission, but a situation was produced which almost automatically implicated a family member. (An accompanying relative was not necessary at the two state hospitals and probably accounts for finding a lower degree of family involvement.) While this influenced the frequency with which family involvement was observed, the effects may be more far reaching. It is reasonable to suppose that commitments or ties are more pronounced among family members who have had contact with hospital treatment personnel than among family members with no such experiences. If so, this may be important not only for the attitudes directed toward the patient, but also for the decisions made by the family regarding the prepatient's security and welfare before, during, and after his admission to the hospital.

SUMMARY

In the process of acquiring information from psychiatric patients and their families in a larger investigation, it became apparent that in several respects the psychiatric patient career evolved and terminated according to family reactions. More specifically, the ways in which family members responded (or failed to respond as the case might be) to intrafamilial deviance was related to how patients arrived at the treatment settings. Family reactions were also seemingly related to the patient's acceptance or rejection of the sick role, adjustment to the hospital, attitudes toward the treatment staff, and finally the probability of readmission.

Review of the histories of 79 psychiatric patients selected from a university teaching and research hospital resulted in the isolation of two "sensitizing concepts" or dimensions based on family reactions to deviance. These were called "the level of expected performance" and "propensity for action." Using these dimensions, eight career patterns were described. The typology allowed for the classification of 95 percent of the cases reviewed.

It is hoped that even in the present state of refinement, this typology is useful for the understanding of the psychiatric patient career. Treatment agencies may also find the dimensions on which the typology is based helpful for planning patient care, prediction of readmission, and for decision-making in situations confronting patients and their families before hospitalization and after release from the hospital. A greater understanding of the dimensions along which family reactions to deviance vary may also provide additional clues as to how these reactions may be modified so as to better implement the goals of the therapeutic setting. These possibilities are the topic of another investigation in this series on the psychiatric patient career (41).

REFERENCES

1. ALIVISATOS, G. and LYKETSOS, G., "A Preliminary Report of a Research Concerning the Attitude of the Families of Hospitalized Mental Patients," *Internat. J. Soc. Psychiat.* 10, 37–44, 1964.
2. BECKER, H. S., *Outsiders*, New York, Free Press of Glencoe, 1963.
3. BURSTEN, B. and D'ESOPO, R., "The Obligation to Remain Sick," in Scheff, T. J., *Mental Illness and Social Processes*, New York, Harper and Row, 1967, 206–218.
4. CLAUSEN, J. and YARROW, M. (issue editors) Entire issue, "The Impact of Mental Illness on the Family," *J. Soc. Issues*, 11, 6–11, 1955.
5. CUMMING, J. and CUMMING, E., "On the Stigma of Mental Illness," *Community Mental Health Journal*, 1, 135–143, 1965.
6. DEASY, L. and WESTBROOKE QUINN, O., "The Wife of the Mental Patient and the Hospital Psychiatrist," *J. Soc. Issues*, 11, 49–60, 1955.
7. DENZIN, N., "The Self-Fulfilling Prophecy and Patient Therapist Interaction," in Spitzer, S. and Denzin, N., (eds.) *The Mental Patient: Studies in the Sociology of Deviance*, New York, McGraw-Hill, 1968.
8. FREEMAN, H. and SIMMONS, O., "Mental Patients in the Community: Family Settings and Performance Levels," *Am. Soc. Rev.*, 23, 147–154, 1958.
9. FREEMAN, H. and SIMMONS, O., "Social Class and Post-hospital Performance Levels," *Am. Soc. Rev.*, 24, 345–351, 1959.
10. FREEMAN, H. and SIMMONS, O., "Feelings of Stigma Among Relatives of Former Mental Patients," *Soc. Problems*, 8, 312–321, 1961.
11. GOFFMAN, E., *Asylums*, Garden City, New York, Doubleday, 1961.
12. GORDON, G., *Role Theory and Illness*, New Haven, Connecticut, College and University Press, 1966.

13. GURIN, G., VEROFF, J. and FELD, S., *Americans View Their Mental Health*, New York, Basic Books, 117–142, 1960.
14. HALL, O., "The Stages of a Medical Career," *Am. J. Soc.*, 53, 327–336, 1948.
15. HOLLINGSHEAD, A. and REDLICH, F., *Social Class and Mental Illness*, New York, Wiley, 1958.
16. HUGES· E., "Institutional Office and the Person," *Am. J. Soc.*, 43, 404–413, 1937.
17. KORLES, L., "The Impact of the Mentally Ill Children upon Their Parents," unpublished Ph.D. Dissertation, 1959; see *Dissertation Abstracts*, 339, June, 1959.
18. LEFTON, M., ANGRIST, S., DINITZ, S. and PASAMANICK, B., "Social Class, Expectations, and Performance of Mental Patients," *Am. J. Soc.*, 68, 79–87, 1962.
19. LEMERT, E., *Social Pathology*, New York, McGraw-Hill, 1951.
20. LIDZ, T. *et al.*, "Schizophrenic Patients and Their Siblings," *Psychiatry*, 26, 1–18, 1963.
21. LIDZ, T., FLECK, S. and CORNELISON, A., *Schizophrenia and The Family*, New York, International Universities Press, 1965.
22. MECHANIC, D., "Some Factors in Identifying and Defining Mental Illness," *Ment. Hygiene*, 46, 66–74, 1962.
23. MISHLER, E. and WAXLER, N., "Family Interaction Processes and Schizophrenia: A Review of Current Theories," *Internat. J. Psychiat.* 2, 375–430, 1966.
24. MISHLER, E. and WAXLER, N., "Decision Processes in Psychiatric Hospitalization: Patients Referred, Accepted, and Admitted to a Psychiatric Hospital," *Am. Soc. Rev.*, 28, 576–587, 1963.
25. MYERS, J. and ROBERTS, B., *Family and Class Dynamics in Mental Illness*, New York, Wiley, 1959.
26. NUNNALLY, J., *Popular Conceptions of Mental Health, New York, Holt*, Rinehart, and Winston, 1961.
27. PARSONS, T. and FOX, R., "Illness, Therapy, and the Modern American Family," *J. Soc. Issues*, 13, 31–44, 1952.
28. PAUL N., and GROSSER, G., "Family Resistance to Change in Schizophrenia," *Fam. Proc.*, 3, 377–401, 1964.
29. RAY, M., "The Cycle of Abstinence and Relapse Among Heroin Addicts," in Becker, H., *The Other Side*, New York, Free Press, 1964, 163–177.
30. SAMPSON, H., MESSINGER, S. and TOWNE, R., *Schizophrenic Women*, New York, Atherton Press, 1964.
31. SCHEFF, T. J., "The Role of the Mentally Ill and the Dynamics of Mental Disorder: A Research Framework," *Sociometry*, 26, 436–453, 1963.

32. SIMMONS, O., DAVIS, J. and SPENCER, K., "Interpersonal Strains in Release from a Mental Hospital," *Soc. Problems*, 4, 21–28, 1956.

33. SPECK, R. V., *et al.*, "The Absent Member Maneuver as a Resistance in Family Therapy of Schizophrenia," *Fam. Proc.*, 1, 44–62, 1962.

34. SPIEGEL, J. and BELL N., "The Family of the Psychiatric Patient," in Arieti, S., *American Handbook of Psychiatry*, New York, Basic Books, 1959, 114–119.

35. SPITZER, S., DENZIN, N. and BEALKA, R., "Family Influence on Psychiatric Patient Performance," paper presented at the annual meetings of the Midwest Sociological Society, April, Madison, Wisconsin, 1966.

36. SPITZER, S. and DENZIN, N., "The Career of the Psychiatric Patient in Two Types of Hospital Settings, Progress Report," Psychopathic Hospital, Iowa City, Iowa, June, 1967.

37. SWANSON R. and SPITZER, S., "Social Attitudes Among the Mentally Ill and Their Significant Others: A Study in Social Distance," paper presented at the annual meetings of the Midwest Sociological Society, April 1968. Omaha, Nebraska.

38. WHATLEY, C., "Social Attitudes toward Discharged Mental Patients," *Soc. Problems*, 6, 313–320, 1959.

39. WOOD, E., RAKUSIN, J. and MORSE, E., "Interpersonal Aspects of Psychiatric Hospitalization: I. The Admission," *Arch. Gen. Psychiat.*, 3, 632–641, 1960.

40. VOGEL, E. and BELL, N., "The Emotionally Disturbed Child as the Family Scapegoat," in Bell, N. and Vogel, E., *A Modern Introduction to the Family*, Glencoe, Illinois, Free Press, 1960, 382–397.

41. SPITZER, S., MORGAN, P. and SWANSON, R., "Determinants of the Psychiatric Patient Career: Family Reaction Patterns and Social Work Intervention," *Soc. Serv. Rev.*

24

The "Schizophrenogenic Mother" in Word and Deed

FRANCES E. CHEEK, PH.D.

SINCE 1948, when Frieda Fromm-Reichmann first pinioned her with a phrase (9), the "schizophrenogenic mother" has taken her place in the folklore of invidious womanhood. In Fromm-Reichmann's formulation, certain malevolent characteristics of the mother were, in many cases, associated with the etiology of the schizophrenic disorder. Thus, her coldness and rejection of the schizophrenic set in motion a fatal emotional and behavioral withdrawal culminating in the psychotic break. Schizophrenia as a defect of "mothering" made sense to many clinicians in terms of their formulations of family dynamics, while a variety of related findings such as the etiology of the disorder of "morasmas" supported the hypothesis.

In the years that followed much clinical and research attention was focussed upon the mothers of schizophrenics. The early studies consisted mainly of reports of clinical findings or examinations of case record material often without any attempt at controlled comparison. Later investigators, particularly psychologists and sociologists, introduced more rigorous techniques of investigation, while the entry of sociologists into the field in the 50's was associated with an enrichment of the conceptual tools for the handling of the problem with the introduction of concepts of social class (13) and the social system concepts of the Parsonian school (8).

However, despite a proliferation of studies in the area it proved to be quite difficult to arrive at a clear and unequivocal delineation of the characteristics of the mother of the schizophrenic. Quite contradictory findings emerged. In many studies the classical picture of the cold, rejecting, aloof mother appeared (1, 11, 24), but in others she was found to be overly protective, intrusive or symbiotic in her relations with the patient (2, 15, 20) while in some studies she showed none of these invidious characteristics (14, 17).

The variability in findings has been attributed to various causes, particularly to problems of the methodology used in the investigations. For instance, it has been suggested that the case record studies invariably reflect overprotection because the overprotective mother is most likely to contribute information in an anamnesis (21). Certainly a significant problem in all these investigations has been the fact that information about the characteristics of the mothers has been subject to coloration through the eyes of the clinician or through his informant, whether the schizophrenic, the father or the mother herself who may have quite biased ideas about her own characteristics.

In the present study an attempt was made to view the mother of the schizophrenic in a way that would circumvent the problem of subjective coloration. Thus, the characteristics of the mothers were studied by direct observation of their behavior in interaction with their spouses and schizophrenic offspring. (Verbal reports were also studied for a purpose and in a way that will be described later.) The Bales Interaction Process Analysis technique (3) which had been used to study the functioning of small groups, family groups in a few cases (22, 23), and the roles played in interaction by the group members was selected for the observational study.

Thus, in a highly standardized setting, the three family members were asked to discuss together certain problems and these discussions were recorded. By coding the recorded discussions with a set of categories designed to encompass the significant activities, both task and social-emotional, of the group in their performance of the joint task it was possible to derive profiles of the roles played in interaction by the various group members. By comparing the interaction of the families with schizophrenic young adults with that of comparable families (in terms of social class, ethnicity and religion, of the family and age and sex of the young adult) having a non-psychotic young adult, the interaction being obtained under similar conditions, it was possible to see whether in fact the "schizophrenogenic mother" emerged in the interaction as more cold, dominating, anxious and rejecting, or alternatively overprotective, than the mother of the normal young adult.

It is of importance of course to consider the representativeness of these samples of family interaction. Both evidence in the literature (4, 16) and certain findings already reported from the present study (6) indicate stabilities in interaction characteristics that would encourage us to regard these samples as typical.

The Bales code contains twelve categories which were expanded to twenty in the revision which was used to code the family interaction in the present study. What might we expect in terms of our categories if in fact the "schizophrenogenic mother" of the literature had been captured by our tape recordings?

Her cold and rejecting nature would probably be evidenced in low scores on positive social-emotional behaviors, possibly in high scores on negative social-emotional behaviors, as opposed to the mother of the normal. If her dominance is overt there would be high scores on procedural suggestions and total interaction though if, as some have suggested, the dominance is covert, these scores may be similar to those of the mother of the normal or perhaps lower. Her anxiety would be reflected in high tension scores; probably her tension release would be low.

However, in our study of the interaction profiles, we decided also to investigate a new and intriguing hypothesis. In a recent study of parent-child relationships in schizophrenia Fleck, Lidz and Cornelison (7) have suggested that the contradictions in findings regarding the mothers of schizophrenics may be related to the fact that in families of female schizophrenics the family configuration differs from that where there are male schizophrenics. Thus, in the family of the female the mother is apt to be aloof and cold, the father narcissistic and paranoid, while in the family of the male the mother tends to be disturbed and engulfing, the father passive and ineffectual. In their own sample of seventeen families Fleck and his associates noted such tendencies while this finding was also reported in the case of the mothers in an earlier study by Alanen (2) who noted that the mother of the schizophrenic son tended to be closer to him than to her other children and was "possessively protective" of him while the mothers of schizophrenic daughters were apt to be aloof and "inimically protective".

In our interaction profiles of the mothers we might therefore look for differences in terms of the sex of the young adult as well as the illness dimension. Specifically, we might expect especially low social-emotional behaviors in the mothers of schizophrenic females ("aloof" and "cold"). In the mothers of the schizophrenic males we would look for greater anxiety, perhaps more positive and negative emotional behavior, more procedural suggestions and more activity than in the mothers of females ("disturbed" and "engulfing").

Thus, the primary focus of the present study of the characteristics of the mothers of schizophrenics has been direct observation of family interaction, using small group discussion methods. However, the use of a questionnaire was occasioned by the necessity for developing a standardized technique for presenting problems for the family to discuss and thus leading into and structuring the discussion sessions. This presented an opportunity to derive additional information about the mothers from the questionnaire and to examine the correspondence between the questionnaire information and observational data.

In the observational study the mother, father and young adult were observed as they attempted to work out in a discussion the solution to four of the questionnaire problems. In the questionnaire study each member was asked to describe how the three family members ought to behave (normative expectation) and probably would behave (actual perceptions) in attempting to solve twenty problems of the sort that might arise when a young person lived with his or her parents.

Ten of the problems concerned the behaviors of the young adult towards the parents and three alternative solutions to each problem were offered which were based upon Parsons' types of deviant behavior (18). Thus the behaviors of the young adult towards the parents might be characterized by "active rebellion", "passive rebellion" or "conformity." The other ten problems concerned the behaviors of the parents towards the young adult. The solutions were based upon Parsons' mechanisms of social control (18). The behaviors of the parents towards the young adult might be characterized by "support-permissiveness", "role enforcement" or "withdrawal, ignoring."

The mothers of schizophrenics have been described as overprotective. In responding to the questionnaire we would expect them to be high on support-permissive responses. However, in view of the coldness and aloofness also reported we might expect them to be higher on withdrawal responses than the mothers of the normals and this withdrawal might be specially characteristic of mothers of female schizophrenics ("inimically protective").

Thus, we have approached the problem of studying the characteristics of the mothers of schizophrenics by two different methods. The first is the direct observation of the mothers in solving problems with the family group. The second is a verbal report of how the mothers feel these problems ought to be solved by each family member and how in fact they perceive each family member's behaviors in solving the problems. It is important to note that we have deliberately set our investigation both in the observational and questionnaire study within a theoretical framework (that of Talcott Parsons) which will allow us to interpret our findings regarding the family environment of the schizophrenic in social system terms.

From a sociological point of view this environment may be conceived as a social system containing a deviant member. Hence we may examine the family situation along a number of relevant parameters. How would the deviancy be manifested in the system and what types of social control would be associated with it? What characteristics of the system as a whole, normative consensus, coalition patterns, etc. would reflect the presence of the deviant?

In the present paper, which focuses upon the findings regarding the mothers of schizophrenics, discussion of the systematic aspects of the familial relationships is necessarily limited, but after we have described in separate papers the findings regarding the mothers, fathers and young adults, we will present a complete picture of the family as a group in which these systematic parameters will be fully explored and interpreted within the Parsonian framework.

Before presenting our findings regarding the mothers we must first briefly describe the somewhat complex and lengthy procedures which we undertook in order to obtain them.[1]

A DESCRIPTION OF THE STUDY

As we have said, the major purpose of the study was to obtain objective information on the roles of mothers (and fathers) of schizophrenics in their interaction with the patients and to compare this with the roles of mothers and fathers of non-psychotics in their interaction. The study was conducted at the Bureau of Research in Neurology and Psychiatry located at the New Jersey Neuro-Psychiatric Institute at Princeton. It was begun in July, 1958 with a grant from the Russell Sage Foundation.

---

[1] For a more complete account of the procedures, instruments, nature of the samples, methods of data analysis, etc. the reader is referred to Family Interaction with Schizophrenics, a Ph.D. dissertation at Columbia University (6).

It was decided to work with young adult convalescent schizophrenic patients both male and female, between the ages of fifteen and twenty-six, unmarried and living at home with their natural fathers and mothers, all three being literate and English-speaking. The schizophrenics must also have been released from a mental hospital with a diagnosis of schizophrenia (without organic complications) after September, 1957. In order to locate a large enough sample, and also to eliminate a possible bias by the selection of patients from any one hospital, the release records of all sixteen state, county and private mental hospitals in the state of New Jersey were scanned for suitable patients. One hundred and fifty-seven were located in this way.

Over a period of ten months, letters were sent out to each patient requesting that he or she come with his or her father and mother to the hospital where the patient had been hospitalized in order to take part in a study of the sorts of problems that might arise in families where a patient was convalescing from a mental illness. As an incentive, each family was offered travel money at seven cents per mile to cover the expense of the trip.

At the hospital, father, mother and schizophrenic son or daughter each filled in privately the twenty-question questionnaire described earlier. The three family members were asked to check which of the twenty problems had, in fact, come up in their own situation, which of the solutions offered for each problem seemed best to them in the case where a young adult had been hospitalized for a mental illness and had now returned to his or her family (normative expectations), and also which solution best described what would probably happen in their own family if such a problem arose (actual perceptions).

The filling out of the questionnaire was followed by two recorded discussions of fifteen minutes each by the three family members on two questionnaire problems on which they had covertly disagreed. The interviewer was not present during these discussions. After the discussions, in an interview with the mother, the convalescent adjustment of the patient was evaluated by means of a forty-item four-point rating scale. Information was obtained regarding such matters as patient performance of household routines, work and peer group adjustment, remaining symptomatology, etc. One week later, in the home of the patient, two more fifteen minute discussions between the three family members were recorded. Detailed instructions were prepared for the interviewers in order to ensure rigor in the conduct of the sessions and systematic notes on the progress of the interview were made at both hospital and home interviews on a prepared schedule. Later, information was abstracted from the hospital case records on a prepared schedule regarding the early background of the patient, course of illness and hospitalization, treatment, etc.

Of the one hundred and fifty-seven families which had been located and contacted, fifty-seven took part. In order to augment the sample the investigators returned to two of the state hospitals and located an additional thirty suitable patients. The original procedures were repeated and ten of this thirty were added to the sample to make a total of sixty-seven. Forty of the final sample were male and twenty-seven were female. It had been hoped that it would be possible to complete a design for the sample which would include five male and five female patients in each of Hollingshead's five social classes (12). However, the sample which arose as a result of the selection procedure used was heavily weighted towards the two lower classes.

In order to compare the results obtained from the schizophrenics and their families with other families where there had been no hospitalization of the young adult for a mental disorder it was now necessary to locate and study a comparable group of 'normal' young adults in the same way. The normal young adults must be aged 15 to 26, unmarried and living at home with their natural fathers and mothers. There must be no history of mental disorder in the young adult or his siblings. It was decided to attempt to make the normal sample comparable to the schizophrenic one in terms of social class, religion and ethnicity of the family and age and sex of the young adult.

Suitable normal families were located in factories, university groups, the New Jersey 4-H Club, by private referrals, etc. Originally, each family was offered $5.00 for taking part; however, in order to locate special categories of family towards the end of the study, this amount was increased to $15.00. The families were told that the investigators were interested in getting the opinions and attitudes of typical American families towards the sorts of problems which might come up in a family where a young adult was living with his or her parents.

Each family was asked to come to some neutral place such as a school, factory, etc. for the first interview and the same procedure as before was carried out with the questionnaires and recorded discussions. In the home one week later, two more discussions were recorded and at that time the interviewer questioned the mother regarding the same material which had been obtained from the case records on the birth history and early development of the schizophrenics. The

mother was also questioned regarding the forty items on the convalescent adjustment schedule which had been used to rate the behavior of the schizophrenics.

Fifty-six normal families, thirty-one with male young adults and
twenty-five with female young adults, were studied in this way. It
proved to be very difficult to draw lower class families into the sample.
They were not joiners and thus available through clubs, like the
middle class. Also, they proved to be suspicious of the study and less
interested in the financial reward than the middle class families. Thus
it was not possible to match the groups perfectly on social class,
religion and ethnicity of the family and age of the young adult. Statistical controls by partial correlation were therefore necessary in
the data analysis.

One year after the original interivews each mother of a schizophrenic was contacted by telephone and an interview with her in
the home requested. At this interview the investigator once again
questioned the mother regarding the convalescent adjustment of the
patient using the forty-item rating scale. The case record data on
early development of the patients having proved to be sketchy, the
interviewer also questioned the mother regarding all the information
previously sought in the case records and also obtained with the
normals.

PROCESSING AND ANALYSIS OF THE DATA

The data obtained was processed in the following fashion. All the
questionnaire, rating scale, interview note, developmental and illness
history had been gathered with instruments constructed for easy
transfer of information to I.B.M. cards and this was done. The hour
of interaction data available for each schizophrenic and normal family
was coded from the tape with a variation of the twelve Bales interaction categories developed by Edgar F. Borgatta (5). The variation
included twenty categories which were capable of collapse into the
original twelve. These are shown in Chart I.

CHART I

Revised Scoring Categories

1. Social acknowledgment
      (common friendly gestures)

2. Showing solidarity through raising status of others
    (offers of assistance, working together, alleviation of conflict of joking directed toward amusement of group, praise)
3. Shows tension release, laughs
4. Acknowledges, understands, recognizes
5. Showing agreement, concurrence, compliance
6. Gives a procedural suggestion
    (actions that are directed toward organization for attaining a given goal)
7. Suggests solution
    (statements attempting to resolve a problem, following a discussion)
8. Gives opinion, evaluation, analysis, expresses feeling or wish
9. Self-analysis and self-questioning behavior
    (relatively objective self-evaluation)
10. Reference to the external situation as redirected aggression
    (paranoid blame, etc.)
11. Gives orientation, information, passes communication
12. Draws attention, repeats, clarifies
13. Asks for orientation, information, clarification
14. Asks for opinion, evaluation, analysis, expression of feeling
15. Asks for suggestion, direction, possible ways of acting
16. Disagrees, maintains a contrary position
    (disagreement with contents of statement or position of another)
17. Shows tension, asks for help by virtue of personal inadequacy
    (general characteristics of nervousness including broken phrases and hesitancy in expression, direct indications of social and psychological inadequacy including guilt and shame)
18. Shows tension increase
    (tenseness that grows out of impasses or bankruptcy of conversation, awkward pauses for group as a whole, also tension in heated discussions)
19. Shows antagonism, hostility, is demanding
    (actions directed to be either socially or psychologically destructive of the other, aggressive personal attack even by ignoring, also hostile humor)
20. Egodefensiveness
    ("It wasn't my fault.")

Certain items were elaborated by the Borgatta system; for instance, agreement (category 5, Bales) became both acknowledgment (category 4, Borgatta) and agreement (category 5, Borgatta). The coder, who had approximately 200 hours coding experience, had previously established reliability with another coder trained in a very similar system. The coded interaction data was also transferred to I.B.M.

The hour of interaction was reduced to 48 minutes to eliminate certain time problems, and profiles of the activity of each family, father, mother, subject and total group, in each of the twenty categories, as well as a total interaction category, were now derived by I.B.M.

The data was analysed in the following fashion. One hundred and fifty-eight variables including questionnaire, interaction, interview note, developmental, demographic and adjustment variables characterizing each schizophrenic and normal family were selected for analysis. For the schizophrenics, an additional seven variables concerned with chronicity, length of hospitalization, the follow-up adjustment measure, etc. were added.

It was desired to study the interrelationships amongst those variables for the schizophrenic group separately, the normal group separately and for the two groups combined. Hence, three product-moment correlation matrices were now prepared. Also, as we have indicated earlier, we decided to investigate separately the significance of the variables relating to the illness status and sex of the young adult. The statistical technique selected to study these differences was the two-way analysis of variance (10) providing information regarding the significance of schizophrenic vs. normal young adult, male vs. female young adult, and their mutual influence on the one hundred and fifty-eight variables. With this sort of analysis we were in a position to study whether, on any particular variable, families with schizophrenics differed from families with normal young adults (schizophrenic vs. normal); whether families with female young adults differed from families with male young adults (male vs. female), and whether families with schizophrenic females differed from families with normal females in the same or in a different way than families with schizophrenic males differed from families with normal males (interaction between illness and sex variables).

RESULTS

With a variety of methodological approaches we have investigated the characteristics of the mothers in sixty-seven families with schizophrenic young adults, forty male, twenty-seven female, and fifty-six families with normal young adults, thirty-one male, twenty-five female. We shall first present some findings obtained with the questionnaire which introduced the interaction. Let us look at the patterns of agreement of the family members concerning the solutions to the twenty questionnaire problems.

Symbiosis and Consensuality between Mother and Schizophrenic

As we have said, the three family members were asked to indicate which of the three solutions offered for each of the twenty problems seemed to them the best solution (normative expectation) and what would most likely happen in their own family (actual perception). The similarity of responses provided a means of studying consensuality of opinions among the various pairs, mother-father, mother-subject and father-subject. In Table I these agreements are shown.

When we examine mother-subject, father-subject and mother-father agreement in the schizophrenic and normal families on normative expectations and actual perceptions we find the normal families showing higher mother-subject, father-subject and mother-father agreement. However, only the father-subject and mother-father differences are significant. This suggests that the father of the schizophrenic differs significantly from the father of the normal in his agreement with the mother and subject and this difference in attitudes would suggest that he occupies a peripheral position in the family. A mother-schizophrenic symbiotic relation is thus a possibility though it is of interest that the mother-schizophrenic agreement is in general lower than that of the normal and his or her mother, suggesting a closeness by default. Not, perhaps, that the mothers are so close but that the fathers are so far.

Further, in families with schizophrenics, mother-subject agreement is higher than father-subject or mother-father agreement. In normal families mother-father agreement is highest. This suggests again a stronger mother-subject coalition than father-subject or mother-father in the schizophrenic families and in the normal family a stronger

TABLE I

Agreement on Normative Expectation	Families with Female Subjects		Families with Male Subjects	
	Schizophrenic	Normal	Schizophrenic	Normal
Mother-Subject	11.89	12.56	11.73	12.10
Father-Subject	10.93	13.04	11.03	11.97
Mother-Father	11.67	13.68	11.45	12.84
Agreement on Actual Perceptions				
Mother-Subject	10.59	11.72	11.18	10.61
Father-Subject	9.59	11.84	10.28	11.23
Mother-Father	9.93	12.80	10.03	11.29

F-Ratios	M.S.		F.S.		M.F.	
	N.E.	A.P.	N.E.*	A.P.*	N.E.*	A.P.*
Schizophrenic-Normal	—	—	8.71	8.35	11.96	12.99
Male-Female	—	—	—	—	—	—
Interaction	—	—	—	—	—	—

* significant above the .01 level.

Means and F-Ratios for Mother-Subject (M.S.), Father-Subject (F.S.) and Mother-Father (M.F.) Agreement on Normative Expectations (N.E.) and Actual Perceptions (A.P.) for Families with Female and Male, Schizophrenic and Normal, Subjects.

mother-father coalition. These differences hold for both families with male and female schizophrenics.

Overprotectiveness and Maternal Expectations and Perceptions of Support-Permissive Behavior

We have now found indications of a closeness in the relationship of mother and schizophrenic, though as we have said, the closeness is not greater than in the normal family, rather it appears that the fathers of the schizophrenics are more distant. We will now look at some findings which may clarify the mother-schizophrenic relationship.

Behaviors of the parent towards the young adult investigated by the questionnaire were "support-permissiveness", "role enforcement" and "withdrawal, ignoring." Mothers of schizophrenics have been described as overprotective; would this overprotectiveness appear in high support-permissive responses? In Table II the questionnaire responses of the mothers are shown.

The mothers of the schizophrenics are evidently very much higher

TABLE II

Normative Expectations	Mothers of Female Subjects		Mothers of Male Subjects	
	Schizophrenic	Normal	Schizophrenic	Normal
Support-Permissive	4.96	2.96	4.75	3.29
Role-Enforcement	4.18	6.56	5.53	5.65
Withdrawal	.85	.48	.63	1.00
Actual Perceptions				
Support-Permissive	4.70	3.00	4.98	3.58
Role Enforcement	4.18	6.28	3.83	5.70
Withdrawal	1.11	.72	.80	1.00

F-Ratios	N.E.			A.P.		
	S.P.†	R.E.†	W.	S.P.†	R.E.†	W.*
Schizophrenic-Normal	25.31	25.00	—	21.36	29.03	3.88
Male-Female	—	—	—	—	—	—
Interaction	—	—	—	—	—	—

* significant above the 5% level.
† significant above the 1% level.
Means and F-Ratios of Questionnaire Responses for Mothers of Female and Male Subjects in Schizophrenic and Normal Family Groups.

on normative expectations and actual perceptions of parental support-permissive behaviors. The mothers of female schizophrenics are much higher than mothers of female normals on both normative expectations and actual perceptions of withdrawal. This suggests the "inimically protective" picture of the mother of the female schizophrenic reported by Alanen. On the other hand, the mothers of male schizophrenics are much lower than mothers of male normals on withdrawal which may suggest Alanen's "possessively protective" mother of the male schizophrenic.

The Interaction Profiles

To this point we have found some rather equivocal suggestions of symbiosis and overprotectiveness in the mother-schizophrenic relation. We now turn to the interaction profile of the "schizophrenogenic mothers." As we have indicated earlier we have in our analysis studied separately the profiles of mothers of male and female schizophrenics. In Table III are shown the profiles of the mothers, while

TABLE III

Interaction Profiles (Means of Scores) of Mothers of Female and Male,
Schizophrenic and Normal, Young Adults

	Mothers of Female Subjects		Mothers of Male Subjects	
	Schiz.	Nor.	Schiz.	Nor.
Positive Social-Emotional				
Social Facilitative (2)	3.4	4.1	3.8	3.8
Acknowledgment (4)	19.3	18.5	20.5	23.2
Agreement (5)	7.5	10.4	7.0	8.7
Negative Social-Emotional				
Projected Hostility (10)	.6	1.4	1.1	.4
Disagreement (16)	3.3	6.6	3.5	4.3
Overt Hostility (19)	3.8	6.3	5.4	4.6
Egodefensiveness (20)	.5	.8	.6	1.2
Tension Behaviors				
Signs of Tension (17)	19.6	23.3	26.3	20.8
Tension Release (3)	12.1	6.7	4.4	11.1
Task Behaviors				
Procedural Suggestion (6)	11.4	11.9	10.0	11.9
Suggests Solution (7)	.1	.1	.1	.1
Gives Opinion (8)	62.5	78.3	57.0	64.0
Self Evaluation (9)	.1	.2	.1	.2
Gives Information (11)	16.4	15.4	13.7	18.0
Explains, clarifies (12)	105.0	125.0	103.2	106.7
Asks for Information (13)	3.4	4.3	4.0	5.1
Asks for Opinion (14)	4.9	6.9	6.5	6.9
Asks for Suggestion (15)	1.1	.6	.6	1.0
Total Interaction (21)	274.8	321.0	269.9	292.4

in Table IV appear the F-ratios from the two-way analysis of variance (sex and illness status of the young adults).

Total Interaction: Probably our most striking finding is with regard to the total rates of activity (category 21) of the mothers. The mothers of the schizophrenics present a markedly withdrawn and underactive picture as compared with the mothers of the normals. This underactivity which characterizes both mothers of females and males could relate to the reported aloofness of the mother of the schizophrenic.

Positive Social-Emotional Behaviors: Mothers of both female and male schizophrenics show low total rates of positive social-emotional behaviors (categories 4 and 5) thus reflecting probably the coldness which has been reported.

Negative Social-Emotional Behaviors: Mothers of male schizophrenics show somewhat more projected and overt hostility than

TABLE IV

*F-Ratios Derived from Two-Way Analysis of Variance of Interaction Scores of
Mothers of Female and Male, Schizophrenic and Normal Subjects*

	Mothers of Schizophrenic vs. Normal	Mothers of Male vs. Female	Interaction
Positive Social-Emotional			
Social Facilitative (2)			
Acknowledgment (4)			
Agreement (5)	3.12		
Negative Social-Emotional			
Projected Hostility (10)			
Disagreement (16)	6.17*		3.87*
Open Hostility (19)			2.06
Egodefensiveness (20)	3.81*		
Tension Behaviors			
Signs of Tension (17)			
Tension Release (3)			8.62†
Task Behaviors			
Procedural Suggestion (6)			
Suggests Solution (7)			
Gives Opinion (8)	4.60*	3.33	
Self Evaluation (9)	2.61		
Gives Information (11)			
Explains, Clarifies (12)			
Asks for Information (13)			
Asks for Opinion (14)			
Asks for Suggestion (15)			5.46*
Total Interaction (21)	11.74†	2.79	

* significant above the 5% level.
† significant above the 1% level.

mothers of male normals. Perhaps we have here a reflection of the "disturbed" mother reported by Alanen. Mothers of female schizophrenics show somewhat less of both than the mothers of female normals. On the other hand, disagreement is much higher in the families of both male and female normals as is ego defensiveness.

Tension Behaviors: It is of interest that the mother of the female schizophrenic is low in tension and high in tension release as compared with the mother of the female normal while the mother of the male schizophrenic is high on tension and very low on tension release. This finding may again relate to Alanen's description of the mother of the male schizophrenic as "disturbed."

Task Behaviors: The mothers of the schizophrenics do not appear to be overtly dominating. They are lower than the mothers of the normals, though not significantly, on procedural suggestions. In general, their participation in the task behaviors is lower than that of the mothers of the normals.

In summary, our interaction profiles have shown us probable reflections of aloofness, coldness and withdrawal in mothers of both female and male schizophrenics. In the mothers of the males, signs of disturbance in terms of high projected and overt hostility and high tension and low tension release have appeared. However, it is apparent that the most marked differences lie in the schizophrenic vs. normal dimension. The sex of the schizophrenic appears to have some significance in relation to the characteristics of the mother but the differences, while in the direction suggested by Fleck and Alanen, are certainly not dramatic.

Word and Deed

We can hardly fail here to be struck by the marked disparity between the picture of the mothers of the schizophrenics obtained in the interaction and in the questionnaire data. In the interaction they are low on supportive behaviors (categories 4 and 5) but we find them in the questionnaire to be very high on support-permissive responses. It is of course possible that these mothers are not really supportive but rather permissive. The fact that they are low on disagreement (category 16) in their interaction would tend to support this hypothesis. Thus support-permissiveness would mean not high support but rather low disagreement. This hypothesis we can very readily test by means of our correlation matrices relating the interaction and questionnaire data.

In Table V we examine the correlation between the interaction of mothers of schizophrenics and normals on categories 4 and 5 (acknowledgment, agreement—support) and 16 (disagreement—permissiveness) in relation to mothers' normative expectations and actual perceptions of support-permissiveness and role enforcement in the schizophrenic and normal families.

The findings in Table V tend to support our hypothesis. In the case of the mothers of schizophrenics high support-permissive questionnaire responses are not highly related to actual interaction scores of support; however they are related to low disagreement. Also, high role enforcement questionnaire responses in the mothers of schizophrenics are not related to support but are related positively to disagreement. In the normal families the pattern is quite different. If the

TABLE V

Correlations Between Questionnaire Responses and Interaction Data for
Mothers of Schizophrenics and Normals*

	Mothers of Schizophrenics			Mothers of Normals		
	Positive Sanctions		Negative Sanctions	Positive Sanctions		Negative Sanctions
	04	05	16	04	05	16
Normative Expectations						
Support-Permissiveness	−.06	.01	−.18	.30	.10	.00
Role Enforcement	−.02	.04	.22	−.27	−.03	−.07
Actual Perceptions						
Support-Permissiveness	.14	.20	−.00	.29	.13	−.11
Role Enforcement	−.05	.02	.23	−.36	−.12	−.02

04 Acknowledgment
05 Agreement
16 Disagreement
* Normals, .30 significant at 5%; Schizophrenics, .24 significant at 5%.

mother is high on support-permissive questionnaire responses, the interaction data shows her to be high on support though little relation to disagreement appears; if the mother of the normal is high on role enforcement questionnaire responses, the interaction data shows her to be low on support though again little relation to disagreement appears.

Thus, in the schizophrenic families the mothers' high support-permissiveness turns out to be tolerance or permissiveness rather than active support.

DISCUSSION

What may we conclude regarding the "schizophrenogenic mother" and the contradictions and perplexities surrounding her? In general, our findings have supported Frieda Fromm-Reichmann's original insight for in our interaction profiles we have indeed found evidences of coldness and aloofness. However, by means of our many-faceted approach, we have also managed to clarify some of the confusion in the situation. Thus, we have found in relation to the sex of the schizophrenic certain differences in the characteristics of the mothers in the direction suggested by Alanen and also by Fleck and his associates. In the questionnaire data we find in the high withdrawal responses of the mothers of female schizophrenics suggestions of the "inimically protective" mother described by Alanen and in the low withdrawal responses of the mothers of male schizophrenics suggestions of Alanen's "possessively protective" mother. In the interaction profiles of the mothers of the male schizophrenics we find traces of Alanen's "disturbed mother" in the high rates of tension, low rates of tension release and high rates of negative social-emotional behavior.

However, we have located a probably more cogent source of confusion regarding the characteristics of the mothers than the sex of the schizophrenic. If we looked only at questionnaire responses we would think the mothers of schizophrenics to be highly support-permissive; if we looked only at the interaction profiles we would find them cold and withdrawn. However, when we examine the correlations between questionnaire and interaction data we find that in fact support-permissive responses of the mothers of schizophrenics are not related to support behaviors in the interaction but rather to low disagreement. On the other hand, support-permissive responses of the mothers of normals are related to high support behaviors in the interaction but not to disagreement. Clearly, unless we pay attention to the behavioral meaning of the verbal report we can not assess its true significance. The mothers of the schizophrenics are characterized not by active support but by tolerance or permissiveness.

This finding suggests problems of communication for the investigator or therapist who seeks to work with the mother of the schizophrenic. Evidently, what is said can not be taken to mean behaviorally what is meant in the normal situation. In the case of the researcher confusion regarding findings could result, but in the case of the therapist a more invidious situation could eventuate. The therapist who wished to elicit more active support from the mother toward the patient might only succeed, with verbalizations lacking in communality, in increasing her tolerance or permissiveness towards the patient which might be quite damaging. Thus, for either researcher or therapist it would be extremely important to move between verbal report and actual observation of interpersonal behaviors in order to clarify the relation of the two.

This presentation of the characteristics of the mothers of schizophrenics suffers, as we have said, from an obvious defect. While the study was oriented in terms of both theoretical framework and methodology towards an examination of the family environment as a total social system, we have in this paper described only the characteristics of the mothers. When we have also reported the characteristics of the young adults and the fathers we shall deal with the characteristics

of the family group. For this reason it is difficult at this point to discuss the significance of the characteristics of the mother; however, it
is possible for us to make some preliminary suggestions.

We have noted that in the families of schizophrenics the mother-
subject coalition appears to be strongest, while in the family of the
normal the mother-father coalition is strongest. It is of interest that
this finding contradicts that of Lyman Wynne and his associates (25)
who found a close mother-father relationship in the family of the
schizophrenic which invidiously excluded the schizophrenic. With
regard to the patterns of coalition in schizophrenic and normal families
we may consider a comment from Talcott Parsons with regard to
coalition patterns and stability of the small group. He states:

> the stability of a small group is dependent on the differentiation of in-
> strumental and expressive roles and a coalition of the instrumental and
> expressive leaders (19).

The father in the American family is characteristically the instrumental leader, the mother the expressive leader. In the normal family
we now find evidence of a coalition between these leaders, whereas in
the family of the schizophrenic another type of coalition, perhaps
invidious, predominates the mother-schizophrenic relationships.

The reasons for the necessity of coalition of the mother and father
rather than either parent and the child are obvious. Unless the two
socializing agents can agree, the child is torn between their contrasting sets of values and attitudes and exposed to contradictory reinforcements for his behavior which confuse him and lead him to
seek refuge in a coalition with one parent which operates to widen
the breach between them. In the case of the schizophrenic this coalition appears to be primarily with the mother. In a later paper on the
characteristics of the father we will discuss further why this resolution
is adopted.

But let us now consider the results of this situation. The cold and
aloof mother of the schizophrenic is a very poor choice as a socializing
agent. To quote Parsons again:

> It is very difficult for one person to produce desired and lasting change
> in the behavior of others, or even in himself, without a positive mutual
> emotional attachment (19, p. 304).

The mother of the schizophrenic tends to be low on the expression of
positive sanctions which as Parsons has remarked are basic to the
operation of the socialization process:

the most direct and immediate rewards which are possible for conformity are the attitudes of the significant persons...that is, their
approval and esteem. This is of particularly crucial significance to
the problem of social control since approval and esteem....may be
regarded as the first-line stabilizing or control mechanisms of the social
system, that is, the most immediate mechanisms of motivation to conformity with normative patterns (18, p. 264).

Further, the mother of the schizophrenic is low on negative sanctions of disagreement which Parsons has suggested are essential in the
actual control of deviance in everyday interaction:

When we turn to the consideration of normal social interaction within
such an institutionalized framework as a process of mutually influenced
and contingent action we see that a process of social control is continually going on. Actors are continually doing and saying things which
are more or less 'out of line,' such as by insinuation impugning someone's
motives or presuming too much. Careful observation will show that
others in the situation often without being aware of it, tend to react
to these minor deviances in such a way as to bring the deviant 'back
into line,' by tactfully disagreeing with him, by a silence which under-
lines the fact that what he said was not acceptable, or very often by
humor as a tension-release, as a result of which he comes to see himself
more nearly as others see him. These minor control mechanisms are,
it may be maintained, the way in which the institutionalized values are
implemented in behavior. They are, on a certain level, the most fundamental mechanisms of all, and only when they break down does it become necessary for more elaborate and specialized mechanisms to come
into play (18, p. 303).

Recent psychological theories have been concerned with behavioral
manipulation in terms of positive and negative reinforcements. Our
"schizophrenogenic mothers" are inadequate emittors of positive and
negative reinforcements or sanctions to control the behaviors of the
schizophrenic. In a later paper concerned with the characteristics of
the family of the schizophrenic as a social system containing a deviant
member we will go more fully into this problem of deficiencies in the
sanctioning system and how the total family situation conduces towards the deviancy.

We must, however, point out that in fact we do not know whether
the behaviors of the mother have caused the behaviors of the schizophrenic or whether the schizophrenic has elicited this set of behaviors from his mother as a result of his own behavior. This question

we can not resolve at this moment though it is our hope that by further investigating the data gathered in this study we may come up with findings bearing upon this important problem. We can only say now that with a mother who behaved in such a fashion a deviancy such as schizophrenia could readily result.

In future studies it will be of great importance to investigate such problems as the characteristics of family interaction with both the schizophrenic and a non-schizophrenic sibling to find whether the mothers present the same inadequate behaviors in both cases. Also it will be of interest to examine the interaction of mothers in families with other types of illnesses in the young adult such as tuberculosis, or other deviancies such as alcoholism, drug addiction, etc.

SUMMARY

This study has attempted to throw light upon the characteristics of the mother of the schizophrenic, a much investigated but confused and contradictory area. A variety of methodological techniques, including actual observation of the interaction of mother, father and young adult and also a questionnaire concerned with family interpersonal behaviors have been used to study sixty-seven families with schizophrenic young adults, forty male and twenty-seven female and fifty-six families with non-psychotic young adults, thirty-one male and twenty-five female.

In general, Frieda Fromm-Reichmann's original insight has been supported, for the mothers of the schizophrenics have emerged in the interaction as cold and withdrawn. Also, differences in the characteristics of mothers of male and female schizophrenics in the directions suggested by other studies have appeared. However, a probably more significant source of confusion has been located. In the questionnaire study the mothers of the schizophrenics were high on support-permissive responses, though in the observational study they appeared to be cold and withdrawn. When the relation between questionnaire responses and actual interaction was examined it turned out that high support-permissive responses of the mothers of the normals were associated with high support behaviors in the interaction, whereas high support-permissive responses of the mothers of the schizophrenics were not related to high support in the interaction but to low disagreement. Thus, for the mother of the schizophrenic support-permissiveness meant tolerance rather than active support.

Characteristically, the mothers of the scizophrenics were low in both positive and negative sanctions in their interaction. Such a maternal pattern of reinforcement could have occasioned a deviancy such as schizophrenia though it is possible that the schizophrenic may himself have elicited these behaviors from the mother.

REFERENCES

1. ABRAHAMS, J. and VARON, E. J., *Maternal Dependency and Schizophrenia: Mothers and Daughters in a Therapeutic Group*, New York, Internat. Univ. Press, 1953.
2. ALANEN, Y. O., "The Mothers of Schizophrenic Patients," *Acta Psychiat. Scand.*, Suppl. 124, 1–361, 1958.
3. BALES, R. F., *Interaction Process Analysis*, Cambridge, Addison-Wesley, 1950.
4. BORGATTA, E. F. and BALES, R. F., "Interaction of Individuals in Reconstituted Groups" in A. P. Hare (ed.), *Small Groups*, New York, Knopf, 1955.
5. BORGATTA, E. F., "A Systematic Study of Interaction Process Scores, Peer and Self-assessments, Personality and Other Variables," *Genet. Psychol. Monogr.*, 65, 219–291, 1962.
6. CHEEK, F., *Family Interaction with Schizophrenics*, Ph. D. Dissertation, Columbia Univ., 1962.
7. FLECK, S., LIDZ, T. and CORNELISON, A., "Comparison of Parent-Child Relationships of Male and Female Schizophrenic Patients," *Arch. Gen. Psychiat.*, 8, 1–7, 1963.
8. FREEMAN, N. E. and SIMMONS, O. G., "Mental Patients in the Community: Family Settings and Performance Levels," *Amer. Soc. Rev.*, 23, 147–154, 1958.
9. FROMM-REICHMANN, F., "Notes on the Development of Treatment of Schizophrenics by Psychoanalytic Psychotherapy," *Psychiatry*, 11, 263–273, 1948.
10. GUILFORD, J. P., *Fundamental Statistics in Psychology and Education*, New York, McGraw-Hill, 1950. p. 157.
11. HILL, L. B., *Psychotherapeutic Intervention in Schizophrenia*, Chicago, Univ. Chicago Press, 1955.
12. HOLLINGSHEAD, A. DEB. and REDLICH, F. C., *Social Class and Mental Illness*, New York, Wiley, 1958.
13. HOLLINGSHEAD, A. B., *Two Factor Index of Social Position*, New Haven, 1957.
14. HOTCHKISS, G. D., CARMEN, L., OGILBY, A. and WIESSENFELD, S., "Mothers of Young Male Single Schizophrenic Patients as Visitors in a Mental Hospital," *J. Nerv. Ment. Diseases*, 121, 452–462, 1955.

15. MARK, J. C., "The Attitudes of the Mothers of Male Schizophrenics Toward Child Behavior," *J. Abnorm. Soc. Psychol.*, 48, 185–189, 1953.

16. MATARAZZO, J. D., SASLOW, G. and GUZE, S. B., "Stability of Interaction Patterns During Interviews: A Replication," *J. Consult. Psychol.*, 20, 267–274, 1956.

17. OLTMAN, J. E., McGARRY, J. J. and FRIEDMAN, S., "Parental Deprivation and the 'Broken Home' in Dementia Praecox and Other Mental Disorders," *Amer. J. Psychiat.*, 108, 685–694, 1952.

18. PARSONS, T., *The Social System*, Glencoe, Illinois, The Free Press, 1951.

19. PARSONS, T. and BALES, R. F., *Family Socialization and Interaction Process*, Glencoe, Illinois, The Free Press, 1954. p. 96.

20. PROUT, C. T. and WHITE, M. A., "A Controlled Study of Personality Relationships in Mothers of Schizophrenic Male Patients," *Amer. J. Psychiat.*, 107, 251–256, 1950.

21. SANUA, V. D., "Family Environment and Schizophrenia," *Psychiatry*, 24, 246–265, 1961.

22. STRODTBECK, F. L., "The Family as a Three-Person Group," *Amer. Soc. Rev.*, 19, 23–29, 1954.

23. STRODTBECK, F. L., "Husband-Wife Interaction over Revealed Differences," *Amer. Soc. Rev.*, 16, 468–473, 1951.

24. TIETZE, T., "A Study of Mothers of Schizophrenic Patients," *Psychiatry*, 12, 55–65, 1949.

25. WYNNE, L. C., RYCKOFF, I. M., DAY, J. and HIRSCH, S. I., "Pseudo-Mutuality in the Family Relations of Schizophrenics," *Psychiatry*, 21, 205–220, 1958.

SOURCES

The chapters in this volume were previously published in the journal *Family Process*, as follows:

CHAPTER

1	Volume I, No. 1, March 1962
2	Volume II, No. 1, March 1963
3	Volume I, No. 1, March 1962
4	Volume VII, No. 2, September 1968
5	Volume IV, No. 2, September 1965
6	Volume I, No. 2, September 1962
7	Volume VIII, No. 2, September 1968
8	Volume I, No. 1, March 1962
9	Volume IV, No. 1, March 1965
10	Volume III, No. 1, March 1964
11	Volume V, No. 2, September 1966
12	Volume III, No. 2, September 1964
13	Volume I, No. 2, September 1962
14	Volume VII, No. 2, September 1968
15	Volume VII, No. 2, September 1968
16	Volume IV, No. 1, March 1965
17	Volume IX, No. 1, March 1970
18	Volume III, No. 1, March 1964
19	Volume IV, No. 1, March 1965
20	Volume II, No. 1, March 1963
21	Volume II, No. 1, March 1963
22	Volume VII, No. 1, March 1968
23	Volume VIII, No. 2, September 1969
24	Volume III, No. 1, March 1964